Character

About the Author

Dr. Ryan M. Niemiec, is Education Director of the VIA Institute on Character, a nonprofit organization in Cincinnati, Ohio that is viewed as the global leader in advancing the science and practice of character strengths. Ryan is author of several books, including *Mindfulness and Character Strengths: A Practical Guide to Flourishing*, and coauthor of *Positive Psychology at the Movies* and *Movies and Mental Illness*. Ryan is an award-winning psychologist, certified coach, international workshop leader, and is adjunct professor at Xavier University, University of Pennsylvania, and a visiting lecturer at several other institutions.

Ryan develops (or codevelops) VIA's courses, reports, and programs and applies strengths as the centerpiece of Character Strengths Coaching. At VIA, he helps professionals in counseling, coaching, business, disability, and education around the world apply character strengths, personally and professionally in their work. He has published over 60 peer-reviewed or invited articles/chapters on character strengths, mindfulness, and related topics. He has been an associate editor or consulting editor for four scholarly journals, including the APA journal *PsycCRITIQUES* since its inception in 2004. He is especially interested in the intersection of character strengths with mindfulness, savoring, resilience, intellectual/developmental disability, and health promotion.

In 2014, Ryan reached a feat of delivering over 100 presentations on character strengths within 1 year. In 2015, he presented a national workshop tour across Australia, at universities in Iceland and Spain, and gave the Rex J. Lipman Fellow address at St. Peter's College in Adelaide, Australia. He's been an invited presenter or keynote at five leading positive psychology conferences. He was awarded Fellow of the International Positive Psychology Association in 2017.

Over the last 15 years, Ryan has been a leader in the mindfulness community, leading hundreds of mindfulness groups for various audiences and has delivered keynotes, retreats, and workshops on character strengths and mindfulness. He's the creator of the evidence-based mindfulness-based strengths practice (MBSP) program, the first structured program for building character strengths. Ryan adapted MBSP as a track on the web/app-based platform Happify, called "Awaken Your Potential."

On a personal level, Ryan's signature strengths are hope, love, curiosity, fairness, honesty, perspective, and appreciation of beauty. He enjoys spending quality time with his wife and three children, traveling, playing basketball, watching positive psychology movies (and *The Walking Dead*), following Michigan State University athletics, playing online chess, and collecting Pez dispensers and komodo dragon and stingray figures.

Follow Ryan through social media:
- Ryan's blog on Psychology Today is called "What Matters Most?"
- LinkedIn: ryanVIA
- Twitter: @ryanVIA
- TEDx talk: Search "Ryan Niemiec" and "TEDx"

Character Strengths Interventions

A Field Guide for Practitioners

Ryan M. Niemiec

 hogrefe

Library of Congress Cataloging in Publication information for the print version of this book is available via the Library of Congress Marc Database under the Library of Congress Control Number 2017941142

Library and Archives Canada Cataloguing in Publication
Niemiec, Ryan M., author
    Character strengths interventions : a field guide for practitioners
/ Ryan M. Niemiec.
Includes bibliographical references and index.
Issued in print and electronic formats.
ISBN 978-0-88937-492-8 (softcover).--ISBN 978-1-61676-492-0 (pdf).--
ISBN 978-1-61334-492-7 (epub)

    1. Positive psychology. 2. Character. I. Title.
BF204.6.N54 2017   150.19'88   C2017-901547-8
                                                                 C2017-901548-6

© 2018 by Hogrefe Publishing
http://www.hogrefe.com

PUBLISHING OFFICES
USA: Hogrefe Publishing Corporation, 7 Bulfinch Place, Suite 202, Boston, MA 02114
                  Phone (866) 823–4726, Fax (617) 354–6875; E-mail customerservice@hogrefe.com
EUROPE: Hogrefe Publishing GmbH, Merkelstr. 3, 37085 Göttingen, Germany
                  Phone +49 551 99950–0, Fax +49 551 99950–111; E-mail publishing@hogrefe.com

SALES & DISTRIBUTION
USA: Hogrefe Publishing, Customer Services Department,
                  30 Amberwood Parkway, Ashland, OH 44805
                  Phone (800) 228–3749, Fax (419) 281–6883; E-mail customerservice@hogrefe.com
UK: Hogrefe Publishing, c/o Marston Book Services Ltd., 160 Eastern Ave., Milton Park,
                  Abingdon, OX14 4SB, UK
                  Phone +44 1235 465577, Fax +44 1235 465556; E-mail direct.orders@marston.co.uk
EUROPE: Hogrefe Publishing, Merkelstr. 3, 37085 Göttingen, Germany
                  Phone +49 551 99950–0, Fax +49 551 99950–111; E-mail publishing@hogrefe.com

OTHER OFFICES
CANADA: Hogrefe Publishing, 660 Eglinton Ave. East, Suite 119–514, Toronto, Ontario,
                  M4G 2K2
SWITZERLAND: Hogrefe Publishing, Länggass-Strasse 76, CH-3000 Bern 9

Hogrefe Publishing
Incorporated and registered in the Commonwealth of Massachusetts, USA, and in Göttingen, Lower Saxony, Germany

Printed and bound in the Czech Republic

ISBN 978-0-88937-492-8 (print) • ISBN 978-1-61676-492-0 (PDF) • ISBN 978-1-61334-492-7 (EPUB)
http://doi.org/10.1027/00492-000

Praise for the Book

The GO-TO book for building character.

Martin E. P. Seligman, PhD, Zellerbach Family Professor of Psychology, and Director of Positive Psychology Center at University of Pennsylvania, Philadelphia, PA

As inspiring as it is practical. The practical applications of this holistic approach to human behavior are dizzying. This guide to positive psychology is tailor-made for leaders, and is a must-have book that will inspire any leader!

Marshall Goldsmith, PhD, The Thinkers 50 #1 Leadership Thinker in the World, and international bestselling author and editor of 35 books including What Got You Here Won't Get You There *and* Triggers.

Ryan Niemiec takes one of the most important scientific tools in modern psychology for improving our well-being and makes that research come to life in a practical way for practitioners, parents, and coaches. In challenging times, we each desperately need to know, hone, and utilize our unique strengths to tip this world toward hope, health and happiness.

Shawn Achor, PhD, New York Times *bestselling author of* The Happiness Advantage

Dr. Niemiec – the world authority on character strengths – has masterfully married science with practice in this book which provides practitioners with a comprehensive field guide of character strengths interventions. This book guides practitioners in the importance of understanding context to ensure the right intervention is used for the right reason with the right person. It is thought-provoking and hope-promoting. The raft of character strength interventions are clearly explained and the handouts are a particularly useful resource. This is a must-have book for anyone doing work with character strengths!

Lea Waters, PhD, President of International Positive Psychology Association; Gerry Higgins Chair at Centre for Positive Psychology, Melbourne Graduate School of Education, University of Melbourne, Australia

I'm so glad you wrote this book! Very important work. This book provides an invaluable guide for teachers and parents, consultants and managers – in fact, for anyone passionate about human flourishing.

Tal Ben-Shahar, PhD, Bestselling author of Happier *and founder of Happier.TV*

For the reader who seeks to understand why Harvard's Howard Gardner once said that *the science of human character strengths* is the most important development in psychology over the past half century my advice is: Begin with this book. Ryan Niemiec's brilliantly conceived "strengths interventions" brings it to life and helped me see the vast vistas ahead with character strengths psychology—for revolutionizing everything from early childhood education to leadership development in business, government, and civil society.

David L. Cooperrider, PhD, Distinguished University Professor at Case Western Reserve University, Cleveland, OH

The gap between theory and practice of strengths has now been officially closed – all you need to do is read this book and you could easily apply strengths interventions and exercises for yourself, clients, or research. With the inspiring Dr. Ryan Niemiec navigating this boat of applied strengths you simply can't go wrong – read the book and unleash the super-powers of Strengths.

Itai Ivtzan, PhD, Director of Masters in Applied Positive Psychology (MAPP) at University of East London, UK

Sufficient scientific research has accumulated such that it cannot be denied, recognizing, appreciating, and harnessing strengths in yourself and other people, is one of the most efficient and effective paths to a life of success and fulfillment. What has been missing is a manifesto on HOW to do this. In your hands is the most comprehensive account to date.

Todd Kashdan, PhD, Professor of Psychology and Senior Scientist at the Center for the Advancement of Well-Being, George Mason University, Fairfax, VA; Author of The Upside of Your Dark Side

This book is a wonderful resource for clinicians or coaches who want to incorporate a strengths-based approach into their work in a variety of settings. Built around the strengths and virtues of the VIA Classification, this book is comprehensive, based on evidence when available, and remarkably practical. I think it will be essential reading for anyone interested in a strengths-based approach to intervention.

Robert McGrath, PhD, Professor at School of Psychology, Fairleigh Dickinson University, Teaneck, NJ; Senior Scientist at VIA Institute.

Ryan Niemiec's new book is an all in one place resource for those interested in theory, research, and application of character strengths. Research on character strengths and signature strengths have matured and we know that their use in interventions is effective. Therefore, it is time to disseminate the research-informed, best practices in applied areas. Being the first of its kind and written by the Education Director of the global leader in the science and practice of character, this book will have a long shelf life.

Willibald Ruch, PhD, Professor of Psychology at University of Zurich, Switzerland; Founder and President of Swiss Positive Psychology Association; Senior Scientist at VIA Institute.

I just finished reading Ryan Niemiec's *Character Strengths Interventions: A Field Guide for Practitioners* and I had to stop for few minutes to take in and savor the feat he has accomplished. His book truly is a field guide. As someone who deeply knows and clearly loves the exciting territory of character strengths, Ryan expertly guides us so we can see the wonders that can be found there, shares its history, warns us about possible pitfalls, and invites us to explore and enjoy its riches. And we can even take them home with us, thanks to Ryan's generosity in sharing so many resources that he has created and compiled.

He sees strength practitioners as gardeners who can't – and shouldn't try to – "mold" their clients, but rather, can create optimal conditions for growth and development. I believe that Ryan's own strengths of love, hope, perspective and appreciation of beauty may have created the conditions for the flowering of this wonderful work, and I am grateful for it.

Margarita Tarragona, PhD, Director of PositivaMente; Honorary Fellow of the Centre for Positive Psychology at the University of Melbourne, Australia

Contents

Dedication IX

Foreword XI

Preface XIII

Acknowledgements. XVII

Chapter 1   Foundations of Strengths-Based Practice: Seven Core Concepts of the Science of Character 1

Chapter 2   Signature Strengths: Research and Practice 22

Chapter 3   Practice Essentials: Six Integration Strategies for a Strengths-Based Practice 46

Chapter 4   Behavioral Traps, Misconceptions, and Strategies 76

Chapter 5   Advanced Issues in Applying Character Strengths 94

Chapter 6   Character Strength Spotlights: 24 Practitioner-Friendly Handouts. 119

Chapter 7   How to Apply Character Strengths Interventions 146

Chapter 8   Research-Based Interventions for Character Strengths. 156

Chapter 9   Afterword 242

References 244

Appendix A Background on the VIA Classification of Character Strengths and the VIA Survey 274

Appendix B Checklist for Strengths-Based Practitioners 279

Appendix C A Sampling of Strengths-Based Models. 280

Appendix D Frequently Asked Questions About Character Strengths 281

Appendix E Comparison of VIA Survey with StrengthsFinder (Gallup) and Myers-Briggs Type Indicator (MBTI). 287

Appendix F Flagship Papers on Character Strengths 288

Appendix G 10 Character Strengths Concepts and Applications in Specific Movies . . . 290

Appendix H About the VIA Institute on Character 292

Index 293

Dedication

For

R⁴ x M

Rachelle

Rhys

Ryland

Maya

I treasure the uniqueness of each of you which has an exponential effect
on me and our family synergy.

Foreword

Let's go straight to the bottom line: Dr. Ryan Niemiec is the world's foremost authority on the science, practice, and teaching of character strengths, and, with this book, he summarizes in clear and practical terms what practitioners need to know to put this new knowledge to work for themselves and their clients. In my opinion, this book brings to practitioners the most important insights into actualizing positive human potential since the insights of cognitive psychology! Character strength science is the backbone of a "new" psychology – one focused on the array of beautiful psychological characteristics with which all human beings have been imbued – characteristics that can be used to help each and every one of us live our lives most fully, both individually and collectively.

In 1999, Dr. Martin E. P. Seligman, then 1 year post-President of the American Psychological Association, began writing about the need for the science of psychology to augment its efforts to understand and remediate psychological suffering with developing scientific knowledge about "the plus side" of the human experience – how we can construct lives with positive emotions, relationships, and achievements along with high degrees of engagement and meaning. In other words, he made a call to the profession of psychology to learn about the processes that lead to human flourishing. He envisioned efforts to understand positive emotions, positive psychological characteristics, and positive organizations, with positive characteristics being "the backbone" of this new "positive psychology." As a clinical psychologist and president of a philanthropic foundation, I responded to his call to the field. To make a long story short, Dr. Seligman and I worked together to conceive of a 3-year project to create the two basic tools any new scientific effort requires – an intellectual framework and language of what we want to understand, and tools of measurement. When asked to identify the most qualified person in the world to colead this effort, Dr. Seligman identified, without hesitation, Dr. Christopher Peterson of the University of Michigan. We fortunately were able to recruit Dr. Peterson for a full, 3-year hiatus from his university responsibilities to focus 100% on this project.

As it is said, the rest is history! Drs. Seligman and Peterson, with input from 55 noted scholars and positive youth development practitioners, embarked on the most comprehensive and robust effort ever to understand what's best about human beings and how we build full and flourishing lives for ourselves and others. The work was presented in a groundbreaking publication in 2004 entitled *Character Strengths and Virtues: A Handbook and Classification*. That book describes the intellectual foundation for the VIA Classification – a classification of 24 universal psychological characteristics – along with introducing the strategies for measuring these characteristics in adults and youth. At the same time, the VIA Institute on Character made the VIA Surveys available for free on its website, and, without any marketing promotions, after about a year over 1 million people from around the world had found and taken a VIA Survey! During the period of the next few years, people continued flocking to the site to discover their character strengths, positive psychology journals and associations took form, and it became apparent that the new subdiscipline of positive psychology had taken root and was here to stay. Fast-forward to today and over 5 million people from every country in the world have taken a VIA Survey which is currently translated into 37 languages, and there are over 300 scientific publications relating to the Survey in professional journals.

Dr. Niemiec was the one of the first psychologists to jump into this work with both feet. He coauthored a book on movies and character strengths in 2008 with Danny Wedding, and then became the first employee of the VIA Institute after the hiring of an executive director. When I first interviewed Dr. Niemiec, he was moving to Cincinnati, Ohio where the VIA Institute resides, and was looking for employment. VIA did not yet have the capacity to hire him. When I asked how long he could wait for a position to open I recall his answer: "Working for VIA would be a dream job, and for that, I would wait forever!" Unbelievably, his enthusiasm for the work has only grown and he has been *the* major teacher of this work across the globe. Additionally, he has continued to merge his personal interests with the science, having published *Mindfulness and Character Strengths* in 2014, and creating the related mindfulness-based strengths practice (MBSP) program. As a central figure with the VIA Institute, Dr. Niemiec has been deeply involved with the Institute's ever evolving thinking about the potential of this important work for helping to tip humanity towards its better nature. With this book, he shares the most current thinking and research-to-date on such topics as signature strengths, situational (phasic) strengths, dynamics between strengths, overuse and underuse, and strengths blindness, among others.

So, what's the big deal about character strengths? As a psychotherapist who has spent thousands of hours across 15+ years sitting with people trying to help them move their lives forward, I can say that I wish I had the advantage of this knowledge when I was doing that work. Practitioners are always needing tools. When Skinner uncovered the processes by which contingency schedules of reinforcement affect human behavior, it provided tools for practitioners wanting to help clients change behaviors. When Ellis, Beck, and Seligman – the giants of cognitive psychology – uncovered processes by which different thought forms affect emotions and behavior, it provided practitioners with strategies for modifying thinking in order to modify unwanted feelings and associated maladaptive behaviors. In this vein, the uncovering of the corner of the human psyche where the 24 strengths of character reside provides practitioners with levers that can be pulled to activate achievement, enhance well-being, and elevate others towards becoming their best.

Let me be more specific. If a couple presents at a practice with relationship problems, now a therapist can ask them to take the VIA Survey, discuss their use of strengths with each other, and structure a relationship enhancing process for recognizing and appreciating the strengths in their partner on a regular basis. If a person wants to improve their engagement and satisfaction at work, now a manager or counselor can create a program by which they have the client deliberately apply their top strengths of character in their jobs on an ongoing basis and to select roles at work that match best with who they are. Now, when a parent or teacher wants to help a child flourish, they can focus on recognizing the character strengths in their child as they are revealed, nurture those strengths, and help the child develop their self-concept – their personal narrative - around their strengths of character. Now, psychotherapists can build their relationships with clients from the point of assessing what's strong vs what's wrong. The emerging applications of character strengths seems to be nearly endless, and it is only a very young field!

In this book, Dr. Niemiec organizes and describes dozens of specific applications that have various amounts of supporting evidence. Unlike any other book of its kind, this book distinguishes itself by clarifying vs. obfuscating what kind of evidence actually exists at the time of publication for each of the specified applications. While some applications have replicated evidence from double-blind, placebo-controlled studies, others have more anecdotal evidence. Practitioners can select applications with full knowledge of what the level of evidentiary support is and, of course, what seems relevant to their client. And, as with any field of practice, it is part-art and part-science. So, astute practitioners can use the content of the book to stimulate their own adaptations to tailor interventions as they see fit.

This book opens up the practice field of character strength psychology. The genius of the VIA work of Peterson and Seligman is not so much that it is a listing of important psychological characteristics, but more so that it uncovers a psychological *system* that has dynamics that are only beginning to become understood. Dr. Niemiec brings us up to date on what we know about that system, and I am confident that he will remain our leading guide into the future as more and more becomes discovered about how we all can actualize our highest potentials together through the application of our character strengths!

Neal H. Mayerson, PhD
Chairman of VIA Institute on Character

Preface

In 2004, something groundbreaking took place in the field of social sciences. For the first time in history, a cross-cultural, common language describing the best qualities in human beings was born – the VIA classification of strengths and virtues. A new science of human character had arrived. Along with it, a measure (test) of positive traits was being dispersed freely around the globe. The practical ramifications of this emerging work have been substantial. It has been regarded as the most or one of the most wide-reaching efforts in positive psychology, and, by Harvard scientist and multiple intelligences theorist Howard Gardner, as one of the most important initiatives in psychology in the last century.

Meanwhile, in 2004, I was busy practicing as a clinical psychologist in St. Louis, working every day in clinical pain management, a psychology and religion program, and a general outpatient clinic, assisting people in relieving their suffering and trying to help them find mental, physical, social, and spiritual health along the way. I came across this VIA classification by Peterson and Seligman. I was lured in, enamored by its holistic nature. After a short courtship, I was in love. I began planning my future. This was to begin by using the classification to study movies with a positive lens (Niemiec & Wedding, 2014) as my colleague and I had already done this from a psychopathology lens (see Wedding & Niemiec, 2014). My study led me to practice with the VIA classification with my clients – to experiment, to question, to wonder, to appreciate. A couple short years later my wife and I decided to move to Cincinnati, which would be closer to our families of origin. As we engaged in the process, I came to realize that the VIA Institute on Character (formerly referred to as Values in Action Institute), the nonprofit that championed the entire project that culminated in this common language and measurement tool, had its headquarters in the city I was moving to. Do you believe in synchronicity?

A Unique Role

Neal Mayerson recalls that when I met with him and Donna Mayerson over breakfast discussing a potential job at the VIA Institute, he asked me how long I was willing to wait for a position at VIA. Even though my wife and I were already in the process of moving to Cincinnati and crunched for work, I spoke from the heart, "For that job, I'd be willing to wait forever."

Fortunately, I did not have to wait that long and I formally started as Education Director at the VIA Institute in March 2009. My task, according to Neal, was simple: aggregate and disseminate. He and the VIA Institute wanted me to: (a) gather all the latest research and best practices on character strengths or relating to character strengths – connect with scientists and pioneering practitioners in positive psychology/character strengths across disciplines to further gather knowledge; (b) give it all back to the positive psychology community – find channels and create outlets to share the research and practice of character strengths to coaches, counselors, managers, educators, and consumers. And so, that has been my work the last 8 years. One could argue that that's when the writing of this book started.

I would describe my work in accordance with what positive psychology researchers refer to as a "calling," which means the work is an extension of who you are, a meaningful purpose. And, how could it not be a calling for me? I study and teach on those core qualities that help us understand the human condition – that make us more humane, help us improve ourselves, build up and support others, and contribute to goodness. What could be a better focal point than the focal point that lies deep within us? I've gotten spoiled with my work because I talk with others who are either barely getting by in their work, focusing solely on retirement down the road, or are, at best, content with what they do. I leave such conversations surprised by the lack of meaning people find in their work, but also grateful for the work I am honored to do each day.

Many times I'm asked (by established professionals and by students), "How do I get a job like yours?" I tell them "I have no idea." There's no job like it and few points of comparison. I'm not solely a practitioner or a pure academic. Rather, I'm part-practitioner, part-researcher, part-educator, part-consultant, part-scholar, part-blogger, part-innovator. I tell people I'm an educator-writer-networker-practitioner and, first and foremost, a core VIA staff member on a team of five that takes action each week that is global in scope.

I've had my ear to the ground for over a decade in the field of positive psychology, working closely with thought leaders, researchers, and practitioners. I listen to stories of suffering and stories of success. I am privileged to hear the challenges coaches, psychologists, teachers, and managers face when working without character strengths. In discussing how this science of character strengths might be integrated, a mutual learning effect and virtuous circle unfold that helps me, and hopefully them.

The Science–Practice Gap

Science is slow moving, whereas practice is rapidly moving. This creates a large gap, and the field of positive psychology is particularly vulnerable to this. Graduate and certificate programs in positive psychology are collectively churning out thousands of students in the world each year. Most of these students are practitioners of some kind and therefore want the best practices to offer clients, students, and employees ... and to offer those practices right now! It is striking to contrast this with the pace of science: a typical researcher could be faced with the following scenario:

- In September 2017, a researcher attends a conference and a new idea is catalyzed for an intervention they would like to conduct to boost well-being.
- He/she reflects on this idea for 1 month, and examines the resources they have, resources they need and 6 months later determines the project is feasible.
- He/she proposes the idea to their institution, supervisors, a granting agency, or other decision-makers. 6 months later, he/she gets the green light to pursue the project.
- Luckily, the timing is right and they can begin recruiting subjects in 2 months.
- He/she recruits participants for the study over a 2-month period.
- He/she randomizes the participants into groups and runs a 6-month intervention study and completes it.
- He/she takes 1 month to analyze the data.
- Upon having encouraging and interesting results, he/she takes 6 months to collaboratively write up the data into a paper that could be publishable.
- He/she submits the paper to a journal, following the steps and requirements of the journal being pursued (1 month).
- One month later, the journal's editor sends the paper out to peer reviewers instructing them to review the paper and offer feedback within 4 months.
- The editor receives the feedback at that deadline and takes 1 month to review the paper and this feedback. He/she sends all this feedback to the researcher. It is a rejection with encouragement to resubmit.
- The researcher discusses this feedback with colleagues and they decide to make the changes and resubmit the paper. They do this within 3 months.
- A month later, the editor sends the revised paper back out to the peer-reviewers.

- These reviewers send feedback back to the editor within 3 months and 1 month later the editor sends this information back to the researcher. It is an acceptance, with revision.
- The research team happily makes the final, additional changes and get the again-revised manuscript back to the editor within 1 month. Two months later it is accepted.
- The paper is now officially in-press and it is placed in the journal's queue. It will be published in 12 months.
- The journal releases the paper (electronically) on schedule. The recipients of the journal can now read the paper. It has come out 60 months following the original idea. The date is now September 2022.
- Sadly, the paper has no support from the press or the researcher's institution in terms of marketing, and only a small percentage of people actually read the article, despite the positive results for this new intervention. It is, however, archived in several online databases.

Five years! These numbers vary – more or less – based on the individual researcher, the institution, their home country, and the journal submitted to. Many additional obstacles and steps will be at play for some researchers such as a lack of good results, a lack or loss of funding, flaws in the design that cause the study to cease, continued rejection from journals, etc.

As a point of comparison, here's the typical scenario for the everyday practitioner:
- In September 2017, a practitioner takes a new workshop on character strengths.
- The next day, they look at their schedule and see that eight clients, all of whom are suffering in life, need their help. With the first client they see, they weave a character strengths intervention into their existing approach to help them.

The contrast here – 5 years versus 1 day – is stark. The numbers may shift on either side – for example, some journals have a much quicker turnaround process especially those that are online, and some practitioners will discern, reflect, read, and discuss new ideas for a considerable amount of time before applying. But the contrast remains.

Considering this gap, a bridge is needed in the field of character science. This book intends to contribute to that bridge – true to VIA's namesake – as a bridge to support and inform both the science and practice.

Why Now?

Too many times I would offer a practical workshop or lecture on character strengths and people came up to me afterward and said – this was great, how do I apply it? I would look at the individual dumbfounded as if either: a.) they walked in at the last 5 minutes of the workshop; b.) I was an awful workshop leader; or c.) they could not make the leap from practical exercises for themselves to helping their clients/students. This, along with the encouragement of many, strengthened my interest in writing this book as a "field-guide" for practitioners.

The *Character Strengths and Virtues* text (Peterson & Seligman, 2004) on the VIA classification is 13 years old. That is also when practitioners began applying this work. In the field of positive psychology, there has been no book for practitioners that squarely targets the richness of concepts surrounding the VIA character strengths and lays out what is known about best practices with character strengths. This book for you, the helper, has been a long-time coming.

Positive psychology's backbone has exploded in this time amounting to hundreds of scientific and scholarly publications. While there is much to learn about the application of character strengths, core concepts and strong practices are emerging. When applied, character strengths have strong potential to boost well-being, foster resilience, improve relationships, and create strong, supportive "cultures" in families, classrooms, and organizations. To this end, character strengths lubricate and catalyze the good life while managing hardships and life challenges.

But, are character strengths best taught through words on a page? Probably not. Nothing replaces the experience and connection that flows from receiving genuine love from another or expressing profound curiosity to another. However, words on a page set the stage, offer depth, provoke new ideas, and reflect examples and exercises – all to then be put into action by the reader, for themselves or for others.

Throughout the book, I frequently use these two words:

- Practitioner: I am referring to any helping professional, such as a psychologist, counselor, social worker, mentor, coach, manager, teacher, physician, nurse, health technician, mediator, or professor. In many cases, the word might be stretched to a parent helping a child, a spouse helping a spouse, or a consumer acting as the practitioner for themselves. My approach here is no doubt most strongly reflective of my work as a psychologist/coach/ educator, therefore, those in a similar professional will likely find the most alignment with the suggestions and exercises throughout the book.
- Client: I am referring to any person being helped or supported, such as a patient, counseling client, coachee, student, employee, or even oneself.

It is assumed that any practitioner picking up this book at least values a strength-based approach to working with clients. This book is purposefully written with that reality in mind. Any manager, counselor, coach, or teacher can pick up the book and learn the core concepts of character strengths and signature strengths (Chapters 1 and 2), the most crucial applied considerations (Chapter 3), ways to troubleshoot and fine-tune an approach to character strengths (Chapter 4), and advanced topics relating to character such as overuse, strengths collisions, morality, and the integration with savoring, flow, and mindfulness (Chapter 5). Practitioners and clients can then review detailed information on each of the 24 strengths in one-page handouts (Chapter 6), and work with user-friendly, research-based practices (Chapters 7 and 8) and a number of additional resources (Appendices).

There Is No Algorithm for Life

In his text on virtues, Fowers (2005) offers this adage which is also true for character strengths. Despite the hundreds of studies referenced in this book, over 100 research-based character strengths activities, and numerous core concepts involved in applying this work, there remains, and perhaps always will remain, a subjectivity, a demand for understanding the myriad of individual and context-based factors. Hence, there is no algorithm for completely understanding and applying character strengths. Therefore, this book is not "a 10-week program" or "6-steps to apply the science of strengths" approach. Not that such programs shouldn't be done – because they should, and are. But, such programs are always an extension of the individual practitioner who is creating and leading it. There is not one way.

May something in this book help you clearly see the wisdom that lies beneath, express the goodness that is you, and help others find their way.

Ryan Niemiec
May 2017
Cincinnati, Ohio

Acknowledgements

The part of my books that I reread the most are the acknowledgements sections. I enjoy relishing in gratitude and humility about all the people that have had an impact on me and/or offered support and wisdom.

My full-fledged gratitude to the core VIA Institute team, where there are five of us: VIA Chairman, Neal Mayerson, one of the unsung founding fathers of positive psychology, who displays an almost inhuman level of creativity, judgment/critical thinking, and perspective, meaning that he comes up with ideas and pathways on the smallest of scales and the largest of scales, both hammering through the nuances and visioning the long-term future, sometimes in the same sentence. Neal occasionally talks about VIA's 50th anniversary and where it will be in that year of 2050; he says he won't be there for it, but, considering his perseverance, I think he might. In either case, he will surely be honored for this unparalleled organization and the many great decisions, made by him and others, that got VIA to where it is today.

In every good team, there is a relationship-oriented person – someone to offer support, handle conflicts, and express emotion clearly and directly in a tone of everyday conversation … someone to do the little things that after a while are taken for granted … someone who goes out of their way to help just to help (and thereby proving altruism can indeed be unselfish) … someone who is brilliant but would never say it, magnanimous but focuses more on walking the talk. I am, of course, speaking of the inimitable Donna Mayerson, VIA Practice Director.

And there is Breta Cooper, VIA Business Director, who is remembered by each person she meets. She is remembered because she is impressive. She uses her razor-sharp mind to wield a planful "what's-next" prudence, an always-appropriate social intelligence, and a politely challenging judgment/critical thinking. It can take people by surprise as she surveys the situation, gathers where people are coming from, slices and dices ideas/thoughts/responses in her mind, and then shares. No doubt this combination of strengths brings her to successfully lead our VIA team meetings and so many happenings at VIA in so many ways, I won't even dare to count.

Finally, Kelly Aluise, VIA Communications Specialist, e-mails and talks with hundreds of people each month, helping them with a research code to study the VIA Survey, navigating the terrain of their inquiry and proposal, and a myriad of other tasks that help professionals and consumers use their own strengths or help others to do so. In what amounts to thousands upon thousands of people, I would be willing to bet there are zero or almost zero who have had a negative experience with Kelly. The exact opposite of a negative response is actually the norm. Kelly is an exemplar for teamwork; she could be interviewed and studied around how she brings forth this strength so strongly and for the benefit of others, especially the VIA team.

All in all, the VIA team is a collaborative one. There's isn't a day that goes by that it doesn't build a bridge and offer support/advice/hope for another. That's the kind of nonprofit organization I want to be part of. It's a team that pushes and challenges, and, especially, it leads. On a bad day, this team is on fire with ideas and critical thinking. Imagine what it's like on a good day.

Others at work whom I frequently speak with about character strengths include the always-ready-to-fill-in, quick-to-accomplish-a-task Chris Jenkins and the Mayerson art gallery guru and grant manager, Jeff Seibert. While I appreciate many things about Chris and Jeff, perhaps most appreciated is our conversations about *The Walking Dead*, which help me manage my sanity, work through theories, and relish in postapocalyptic fantasy. I could fill the remaining pages describing the talent and graciousness of Clare Blankemeyer, who champions the innovative Mayerson Service Learning Program. On our company volunteer day, Clare was the one on top of a tall ladder, with a drill, various screws, and other tools, while balancing on one leg to put up a trellis in a low-income neighborhood, while everyone else safely watched from below (I was good at holding the ladder!). I think that I'm busy and accomplish a lot, then I see Clare and I'm brought back down to Earth – thanks Clare! The kind-hearted, good natured and character strengths-based conversations and stories that emerge when I speak with Rachel Gray and Maureen Heckmuller are also always deeply appreciated.

With appreciation for VIA's senior scientists, Bob McGrath and Willi Ruch, both of whom function at an extraordinarily high level of sophistication, integrity, and perspective. They are lighting the path of character science with their innovative research, their nurturing of research disciples, and the deep foundation of knowledge they have laid for the decades to come. With additional appreciation to VIA consultants and my friends, including Michelle McQuaid, Jillian Darwish, Tayyab Rashid, and Fatima Doman.

There are some people in positive psychology whose enthusiasm soars and simultaneously moves me to new heights. Some might say it's something intangible within the person; I would say it's a certain way that they express their strengths that speaks to me. When I hear these individual's names, I can't help but to smile and appreciate their gifts and my connection with them. These people include Itai Ivtzan (whom I refer to as "the Roberto Benigni of positive psychology"), Dan Tomasulo, Shannon Polly, Margarita Tarragona, Tayyab Rashid, and Roger Bretherton. Each is brilliant in their work and an authentic exemplar of what it means to be in this field.

In the same way, I can't say enough positive things about the talents, enthusiasm, and collaborative nature of my friends and colleagues, David Giwerc, James Pawelski, Scott Bautch, Lea Waters, Maria Sirois, Lucy Hone, Meriden Peters, Rene Oehlenschlaeger, Claudia Morales Cueto, Aaron Jarden, Bob Bradley, Ruth Pearce, Christina Madrid, Darren Coppin, Kristin Truempy, Eileen Henry, Ebbe Lavendt, Lotta Wallin, Katie Curran, Megan McDonough, Jane Anderson, and Mads Bab.

And a deep bow of gratitude to a few of my collaborators, associates, and/or supporters: Hadassah Littman-Ovadia, Suzy Green, Sven Roovers, Karrie Shogren, Mike Wehmeyer, Dan Lerner, Seph Fontane Pennock, Fred Bryant, Mathew White, Judy Lissing, Dave Shearon, Kate MacKinnon, Mark Linkins, Linda Rufer, Cypress Walker, Hugo Alberts, Tim Lomas, Nirb Singh, Veronika Huta, Carol Kauffman, Kelly Michael, Mary Gregerson, Mike Steger, Lisa Sansom, Greg Pejda, Paul Wong, Charles Walker, Caroline Adams Miller, Cooper Woodard, Keith Oatley, and Tal Ben-Shahar.

With appreciation for those who have gone out of their way to support my presentations, university connections, touring, and/or writing: Karl Stuckenberg, Tim Bryant at the Center for Ethical Leadership Development at Mount St. Joseph University, Jim Hudson, Mike Sontag, Leanne Hides, Tash Dean, Jan Walburg, Juan Humberto Young, Dora Gudsmundsdottir, Sajel Bellon, Jennifer Cory, Todd Finnerty, Deb Easley, Mike Holman, Jane Wundersitz, Margarita Tarragona, James Pawelski, Judith Saltzberg, Hans Henrik-Knoop, Marlena Kossakowska, Sandra Scheinbaum, Dianne Vella-Brodrick, Aaron Jarden, Kathryn Britton, Nancy Snow, Senia Maymin, and Ohio State University's Todd Gibbs, Amy Barnes, Vicki Pitstick, and James Larcus (as a rabid Michigan State University fan/graduate, I might not root for your school but I certainly root for your character strengths integration work).

With gratefulness for VIA Institute partners, including Ofer, Tomer, and Tiffany at Happify; David Covey and Stephan Mardyks at SMCOV; the brilliant Rabbi Irwin Kula and Rabbi Rebecca Sirbu at CLAL; Megan McDonough and colleagues at the WholeBeing Institute; Craig Case and colleagues at Q Works; Paula Felps, Deb Heisz, and the staff from Live Happy magazine; the gifted Tom Lottman and Sarah Zawaly from Children Inc., a national leader in early child development and teacher training. And, of course, VIA's innovative, central partner in the field of education, bringing character strengths to teachers and youth in a substantive way – the Mayerson Academy. This nonprofit organization that trains the public-school teachers throughout the Cincinnati region is spearheaded with thoughtful strategy and compassionate heart by Jillian Darwish along with the supreme talents of many, including: Lynn Ochs, Karen Graves, and Lisa Scheerer. Special thanks to all those researchers who send me updates on what they are working on and forward their articles ahead of publication to keep me (and the VIA community) informed, including but not limited to Hadassah Littman-Ovadia, Willibald Ruch, Marianne van Woerkom, Bob McGrath, Todd Kashdan, Shiri Lavy, Claudia Harzer, Rene Proyer, Thomas McGovern, Marco Weber, and Kim Sperber.

On behalf of the world, I'm happy to share thankfulness to the emergence of the VIA classification, specifically the *Character Strengths and Virtues* text authors, directors, and advisors, which include positive psychology founder Marty Seligman, the inimitable genius that is the late Chris Peterson, along with 53 distinguished scientists. I often have Chris in mind while writing books on character strengths, hoping that he is somehow beaming with pride and feeling like justice is being done for his path-blazing work.

Locally in Cincinnati there is a movement called Strong Cincinnati, which is working to make the city of Cincinnati to be *the* global leader in character strengths applications in the community (see http://www.strongcincinnati.org). Indeed, if you look up the following incredible organizations, each at different levels of character strengths integration, and each with character strengths pioneers, you'll know what I mean: Children Inc., Talbert House, Mayerson Academy, Beech Acres Parenting Center, Down Syndrome Association of Greater Cincinnati, Lindner Center of Hope, Starfire, Public Allies, Interact for Health, Living Arrangements for the Developmentally Disabled (LADD), Mount St. Joseph University, Northern Kentucky University, Reel Abilities Film Festival, Cincinnati Children's Hospital Medical Center, and Xavier University.

Also in Cincinnati, with appreciation for my friends/colleagues: Teri Caudill, Tara and Brad Proano-Raps, Bob Pautke, Lou Flaspohler, Jim Mason, Tim Vogt, Susan Brownknight, Molly Lyons, Steph Weber, Dave Brewer, Jami Cabrera, Neil Tilow, Robin Arthur, Nickol Mora, Jason Harris, Jennifer Sharp, Rick Reckman (my positive psychology teaching partner at Xavier University), and the one and only, Deb Pinger.

For those in St. Louis that sent me on my way to VIA in Cincinnati, only wanting the best for me: With a lifelong appreciation to my writing partner Danny Wedding, my friend and former boss, Ron Margolis, and my dear friend Marilyn Wussler, as well as my buddies Bob and Renae Achter, Helen Friedman, and Rob Furey.

In an age where other publishers are decidedly uncourageous or stuck in their ways, it is Hogrefe that has stepped up as one of the leading publishers in the positive psychology movement. Their outstanding collaborative team and the incredible people that make up the team are what make this publisher outstanding to work with. For this book, I am speaking of Rob Dimbleby, who leads and juggles projects with strong social intelligence, perspective, and critical thinking, and Lisa Bennett, whose blend of mind and heart while editing helped to make my words shine. Anyone who appreciates this book should send a thank-you note to Rob and Lisa.

It might sound cliché to say that I have learned from thousands of people, but in this case, it is true. Since I joined the VIA Institute on Character, I have taught thousands of people, e-mailed thousands of people, and had hundreds of personal conversations – formal and informal – with people about this character strengths work. The people have ranged from Oprah Winfrey to a 5-year-old child; CEOs to janitors; distinguished positive psychology luminaries to young students; from disgruntled to enthusiastic VIA Survey takers; stalking naysayers to cheerleading zealots. How could I not learn from all of you? Each interaction, whether face-to-face, phone, Skype, or e-mail has played a role in informing, challenging, and supporting my understanding of this beautifully complex, universally enlightening, constantly-evolving area of character strengths. My gratitude to all of you, named and unnamed!

To my family at a distance: First off, thank you to my Mom and Dad, both of whom most strongly influenced who I have become today. And, Lisa, Joey, Bob, Gloria, Monica, J. P., Zara-zen, Danny P., Ellen, Betty, Alex, Danielle, Marley, Kelly, Jade, Hedy, Chris, Scott, Erin, Benjamin, Stacey, Austin, Alayna, Aunt Jeanne, Uncle Jerry, Julie, Danny, Kelly, Steve, Dave, Daniela, Dominic, Charlotte, Uncle JJ, Aunt Laurie, Morgan, Jacob, Aunt Gwen, Uncle Don, and the whole Juszczyk family – I'm grateful to have you in my life.

And to my family at home – Maya, Ryland, Rhys, Rachelle – it has now become common-place for me to say "it won't take long for me to write that book." And then it does. Truth be told, a few months of evening and weekend writing is not a long time but any bit is too long if it takes me away from you. Thank you for your patience in allowing me to follow my passion. Thank you for teaching me work–home balance. Thank you for being R^4 x M.

Chapter 1

Foundations of Strengths-Based Practice

Seven Core Concepts of the Science of Character

Introduction

It was 2009. I had written a book on character strengths the previous year and was one of only a couple of people who had devoted themselves to such an effort on this topic. Yet, I realized I knew very little about character strengths. I had thoroughly studied the 24 strengths, the research, the existing applications, and the extensive background on the VIA classification, but a true depth around the nature of character and versatility of the practice was not there. It would have been easy for me to think I already knew it all as I arrived at the VIA Institute, but that would have been a fixed mindset, expert-minded, fateful error. With appreciation for my strengths of curiosity and hope, I set forth on a course of being open to new ideas and views. It was not until I had conversations with Neal Mayerson (Chairman of the VIA Institute) that I expanded my thinking of what is really meant by character. With these dialogues, in addition to being challenged by the critical thinking and creative thinking of the VIA Institute team, day after day – along with solitary reflection – I began to truly understand the depths of this work. It is clear that those who work with character strengths are engaged in the work of a lifetime. These strengths are the catalysts of positive speech and action that we can use in any situation for the rest of our life.

By reading this chapter you will build a foundation of character strengths knowledge on which the practices and character strengths interventions (CSIs) offered in later chapters will rest. I outline seven core concepts that underlie the character strengths: a common language, dimensionality and context, plurality, all character strengths matter, different types of strengths, character strengths can be developed, and being and doing. While the concepts discussed are not exhaustive, they serve as a springboard for readers, and especially for practitioners working with individuals from a strength-based approach. To this end, "strengths-based practitioner tips" are offered to assist the practitioner in moving the idea into action.

As a supplement to this chapter, I recommend your reading Appendix A which offers a background on the VIA classification of character strengths and virtues and the VIA Survey measurement tool. Many practitioners will find it helpful to explain these concepts to their clients. Snapshot 1.1. lists a number of definitions of character strengths from the character strengths literature.

Character strengths are positive traits/capacities that are personally fulfilling, do not diminish others, ubiquitous and valued across cultures, and aligned with numerous positive outcomes for oneself and others.

Snapshot 1.1. What Are Character Strengths?

- The wellsprings or mansions of the good life – a life well-lived (Seligman, 2002).
- Psychological ingredients – processes or mechanisms – that define the great virtues (e.g., wisdom, justice, temperance) … distinguishable routes to virtues (Peterson & Seligman, 2004).
- Capacities for thinking, feeling, and behaving (Park, Peterson, & Seligman, 2004).
- Positive traits that are core to our being/identity and our doing/behavior (Niemiec, 2014a).
- Basic building blocks of a flourishing life; character strengths are the pathways to well-being, described as PERMA – Positive emotions, Engagement, positive Relationships, Meaning, and Accomplishment (Seligman, 2011).
- The inner determinants of the full life – a life of pleasure, engagement, and meaning (Peterson, Park, & Seligman, 2005).
- A family of positive traits reflected in thoughts, feelings, and behaviors (Park & Peterson, 2010).
- Aspects of personality that are morally valued…the foundation of optimal life-long development and thriving (Park & Peterson, 2009).
- A power to act well, a force that has or can have an effect, the will to act in a human way ("virtue" described in Comte-Sponville, 2001).
- In summing up what these and other researchers across cultures are saying about the character strengths, the VIA Institute on Character explains that the VIA classification is a "common language" of personality traits that:
  1. Reflect our personal identity;
  2. Produce positive outcomes for ourselves and others (e.g., well-being, positive relationships, achievement); and
  3. Contribute to the collective good.
  These are also referred to as the three refractions of the VIA classification.

Common Language

The 24 character strengths, as a group, are a common language that describe what is best in human beings. This is an innovative discovery as, historically, there has never been a language of character that crosses cultures. The realities of this principle are everywhere: Coaches and counselors use this "common language" with their clients to help them identify their best qualities. Managers use the "language" to help their employees become more productive and happy at work, and teachers use it to help their students entrench themselves more deeply in learning. Families use it to create a positive culture at home and individuals use it in their self-development. Having a language readily understood by all permits each person to be "on the same page" with others when approaching a challenge, engaging in conversations, and supporting one another.

It is important to understand that this language is not a random assembly of positive words. Quite the contrary, as it was the result of a 3-year project and collaboration among scientists. Under the auspices of the VIA Institute on Character (see Appendix H), a global nonprofit organization, scientists/scholars Chris Peterson and Martin Seligman led a team of 55 well-known scientists on this multiyear project that involved an extensive historical review and analysis of the best thinking on the topic of character in philosophy, virtue ethics, moral education, psychology, and theology over the past 2,500+ years. The result was a classification of six virtues (wisdom, courage, humanity, justice, temperance, and transcendence) found universally in human beings across religions, cultures, nations, and belief systems. After applying various strengths criteria, 24 character strengths emerged, strongly representing pathways to each of the six virtues. This research, analysis, and review is discussed at length in the text, *Character Strengths and Virtues: A Handbook and Classification* (Peterson & Seligman, 2004). See Snapshot 1.2. for an overview of the VIA classification of character strengths and virtues. Measurement tools were also developed and went through several iterations over the years until they were finalized with good psychometrics. Two assessments were created - the VIA Inventory of Strengths (VIA-IS; colloquially referred to as the VIA Survey) for adults and the VIA Youth Survey for youth between 10- and 17-years-old. Snapshot 1.3. offers talking points for practitioners on the VIA Survey.

Strengths-Based Practitioner Tip

Memorize the dimensions listed next to each character strength to expand your knowledge of the VIA language. You'll find this can also enhance the range of strengths you will notice in yourself and in your conversations with others.

A common language means communication doors open. It means practitioners have a template for thinking about and working with clients. It means clients have a new way of viewing themselves; the language serves as a guide for understanding the core of who they are. From this mutual understanding, interventions and strategies can sprout, and conversations in which client and practitioner mutually spot strengths emerge.

Snapshot 1.2. VIA Classification

- Prior to the early 2000s, there did not exist a consensual nomenclature, or common language, for understanding, studying, and discussing what is best about human beings.
- As a common language, the character strength words are readily understood by persons as young as 4-years-old (Fox Eades, 2008), and there is often an immediate resonance with these inherently good concepts.
- It is descriptive, not prescriptive. The emphasis is on classifying psychological ingredients of goodness in human beings rather than saying anything about what one "should" do.
  - It is not a taxonomy of strengths as taxonomies require an underlying deep theory explaining multiple relationships between constructs.
- It is holistic in its conceptual framework. The structure suggests cognitive strengths (wisdom), emotional strengths (courage), social & community strengths (humanity & justice), protective strengths (temperance), and spiritual strengths (transcendence).
- The classification is imperfect. Arguments can be made for strengths to be included or excluded and for virtue categories to be collapsed. Ongoing research is being conducted and it is possible that, as compelling science emerges, changes will be made.
- Within the VIA classification there is a hierarchy from the broadest construct to the narrowest (Peterson & Seligman, 2004).
  - *Virtues*: Characteristics valued by philosophers throughout time.
  - *Character strengths*: Pathways to the virtues.
  - *Situational themes*: Specific habits that lead people to manifest character strengths in given situations. These are highly variable to the person and .

Note. The distinction is made here between virtues and character strengths, that virtues are the higher order (over-arching) category within which the character strengths nest. There have been well-over 10 published factor analytic studies showing the clustering of character strengths under higher order factors, although the quantity of those factors is not consistent in the literature (see McGrath, 2014, for the largest factor analysis to date). As there is not a substantial, *practical* difference guiding us in the research literature on character strengths versus virtues, I will therefore give most attention in this book to using the term "'character strengths," which have been studied empirically in positive psychology far more than virtues.

Snapshot 1.3. VIA Survey

- The only free, psychometrically valid, online test measuring the 24 character strengths. Available at https://www.viacharacter.org
- User receives immediate rank-order results.
- The survey offers relative comparisons (comparison within oneself) rather than absolute comparisons (comparisons with others).
- Over 5 million users have taken the survey, with increasing numbers each year, and reaching every country across the globe.
- The survey is repeatable over time (good reliability) and it accurately measures what it is supposed to measure (good validity).
- About 37 translations of the VIA Survey.
- A new suite of VIA assessments (an outgrowth of the unfolding character strengths research) have been developed to substantially improve the measurement of character strengths. These include a significant revision of the VIA Inventory of Strengths (revisions to all 24 scales), two short forms, the Signature Strengths Survey, the Virtues Survey, and a handful of other measures of character strengths (McGrath, 2017). Users will use the same link to access the free VIA Survey. As studies emerge and continued analyses are conducted, the VIA Institute responds accordingly striving to offer the best measure of character strengths from a scientific perspective.

Strength-Based Practitioner Tip

Be careful to not become too rigid in limiting your thoughts about individuals to one strength or a handful of strengths (e.g., "here comes the creative person"). Practitioners can take lessons from certain medical and psychological professionals who rely so heavily on diagnosing others that they only see "the label" in front of them and lose sight of the actual person. This insight applies to those in character science too. In first learning the VIA language, individuals will quickly identify with one strength or a handful of strengths and may even overidentify with a particular strength. I am high in curiosity and individuals can describe me as a curious person but there is much more to who I am than this one construct. What strengths do you most readily identify with? Least identify with?

As mentioned earlier, the original model of conceptualization from *Character Strengths and Virtues* (Peterson & Seligman, 2004) explained the highest level of the hierarchy as virtues, followed by the 24 character strengths that make up each virtue, which are followed by situational themes that character strengths are expressed in (see Figure 1.1). As research has emerged from various studies around the world, additional levels can be considered, at least for practitioners to reflect on. Figure 1.2 offers some useful distinctions that are relevant for practitioners. Note that this is not a scientific model, but a conceptual one. The relationships between each of the elements in the figure have not been deeply explored. One of the two additions is context, i.e., is the character strength expressed at work, school, home, community, or another context in general? There are many studies that are context specific, such as the myriad of studies of character strengths in the workplace context (e.g., Harzer & Ruch, 2012) and the school setting (e.g., Weber, Wagner, & Ruch, 2016). These studies offer the practitioner and client wisdom as to what outcomes might occur at work or school or home or community, in general, should character strengths be deployed. This is distinct from the more nuanced level of situational themes, which has not been explored as deeply. For example, in the work context, how might signature strengths be expressed differently in a situation with one's customers or clients, a situation in which work projects and stress are piling up, a situation of interacting with one's boss during an employee review, or the situation of the employee feeling sick but knowing he or she has to get a project done? The quantity of potential situational themes are myriad and appear endless in each context. Nevertheless, that is the work of exploration within the practitioner–client dialogue in regard to strengths use.

The other addition in Figure 1.2 is the three virtues – caring, inquisitiveness, and self-control. McGrath (2015c) studied over one million individuals across four samples and multiple measures of character strengths and found support for the 24 character strengths splitting into 3 factors. This was found to be consistent with philosophical accounts of virtues as well as with the experience of leaders in the fields of moral character and character education. While it could be argued that these three virtues might replace the six original virtues in this practical conceptualization,

Figure 1.1.   VIA Classification hierarchy in *Character Strengths and Virtues* (2004).

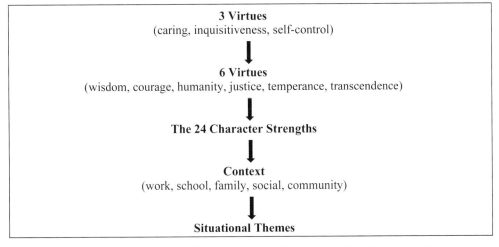

Figure 1.2.   A practitioner-friendly expansion of the VIA Classification hierarchy, hypothesized from emerging research.

this possibility has not reached a scientific consensus to do so, thus, I have retained the original to provide more nuance and dialogue for practitioners. Might there be one "master strength" at an even higher level? Some researchers, practitioners, and theorists argue for this, most commonly noting perspective/social intelligence (i.e., practical wisdom), self-regulation, humility, and gratitude, however, there is not much consistency across scientists in these arguments.

The focus in this book is, of course, the character strengths level; however, readers will find interventions for the higher levels and much discussion throughout the book on the application of strengths in different contexts and specific situations therein.

Dimensionality and Context

An honest man who works hard. A woman of integrity who makes good moral decisions. A business-person with a poor reputation. In today's world, each of these people would likely be described as having good or bad character. Such conceptions represent traditional, limited views of character, popularized over the decades. They have the unfortunate consequence of reflecting all-or-none perceptions of character. The labeling of people's character as good/bad, high/low, positive/negative is pervasive across many cultures and is quickly witnessed, absorbed, and displayed in societal views of presidents, leaders, movie stars, and professional athletes.

In reality, character is more complex than this. The character of a person, whether that be Tiger Woods or J. K. Rowling, is multidimensional. Dimensionality means that character is viewed in degrees; in other words, how much of the character strength of fairness are you displaying? This is in contrast to a categorical approach used in diagnosing psychological disorders and medical disorders in which an individual either meets the criteria for bulimia, panic disorder, or Type II diabetes, or does not meet the criteria. The person either has the disorder or does not have the disorder.

The VIA classification and VIA Survey reflect this dimensional approach as character strengths are expressed in degrees – we have degrees of creativity, honesty, zest, and so on. This is aligned with the concept of "continuous traits," in that any character strength can show up across a wide continuum of more and less (Miller, 2013). Explained another way, using the example of other personality traits:

> Introversion and extraversion are typically conceived and measured as dimensions (as are VIA character strengths) so asking how many introverts there are is like asking how many tall people there are. The answer depends on where we choose to make the cut along the dimension of interest. That said, psychological assessment is dimensional, and although we love the shorthand that allows us to speak about introverts or optimists or geniuses, the fact remains that there are precious few "types" in psychology, just extreme cases (Chris Peterson, personal communication, January 5, 2010).

Research using the VIA Survey shows that this view of dimensionality best describes character strengths (McGrath, Rashid, Park, & Peterson, 2010), but this does not fully exclude a categorical approach in which a person has or does not have a character strength in a particular situation, similar to Peterson and Seligman's (2004) criterion of "selective absence" in establishing the VIA classification. For example, a child ruthlessly beating another child on the playground may have an absence of kindness in that situation but that same child may go home and express genuine kindness to his mother (hence kindness is not completely absent from him). The same could, in general, not be said about a person with the "categorical label" of alcohol dependence; their alcoholism is present categorically within them whether they are at work, home, or with friends. Thus, while all-or-none categorical distinctions such as "you either have creativity or you do not" are less accurate globally about a person, they may be useful in particular situations. Some moral character scholars have argued that there is a minimal threshold or certain standards by which a character trait must first qualify (i.e., categorical trait) before it can be defined as a continuous trait (Miller, 2013).

Taken further, there is a multidimensionality to each character strength; for example, kindness involves dimensions of compassion, generosity, care, nurturance, altruism, and niceness, each offering a different flavor or dimension of this strength called kindness.

"There is no algorithm for life" explains Fowers (2005, p. 13) in his text on virtue practice; in other words, there will always be subjectivity, unique individual factors, and especially context-based nuances. The degree of character strengths expression is based on the context one is in. Context is crucial in understanding and ultimately using character strengths with a practical wisdom (Fowers, 2005, 2008; Schwartz & Sharpe, 2006). Individuals will likely express their character strengths in different ways and to a greater or lesser extent based on the circumstance they are in. For example, the level or amount of kindness expressed to an individual's relationship partner (e.g., offering to cook dinner) differs in scope from that expressed to a homeless person on the street (e.g., giving the person $5). Also, the individual might find it very easy to express kindness to fellow employees yet very difficult in another work situation, such as while consulting to a client or communicating with his or her supervisor.

Strengths-Based Practitioner Tip

Context is king. Most of life lies in the middle, and is not black or white, all or none, good or bad. Take your highest character strength. Write about the impact of context on the character strength. To do this, write about one situation in which you expressed the strength strongly; be sure to reflect on the situation and how it had an impact. Then, write about a different context in which you expressed the same strength to a much lesser degree. What about the situation – the environment, the people, the type of discussion – had the biggest impact on your expression of the strength to a lesser degree?

Character strengths don't operate in isolation from settings, rather they are shaped by the context we are in. One individual might call forth his or her kindness and curiosity when with friends, use self-regulation and gratitude when eating, draw on leadership and creativity at work, and show love and teamwork with family. The degree of character strength the person expresses with family may differ depending on the context – who they are with, where they are, what they are doing, what the expectations or demands of the situation are, past experiences in the situation, the family's culture, and so on. For example, one person's strength of love may be expressed to a different degree with a restrained mother versus a jovial father, and it will also vary based on the location with those people – is everyone at a crowded restaurant, a loud sporting event, or a movie theater? And, are there situational demands that encourage or discourage certain strengths (e.g., less humor at a funeral home, more zest when at an outdoor park)? Is there a family history of being in that situation or are there embedded expectations to behave a certain way?

Consider the expression of character strength(s) in response to each question as the context is detailed out and nuance and complexity increase:

- How much character strength do you express?
- How much curiosity do you express?
- How much curiosity do you express at work?
- How much curiosity do you express at work when you are with your boss?
- How much curiosity do you express at work when you are with your boss talking about personal matters?
- How much curiosity do you express at work when you are with your boss talking about personal matters and your boss is in a positive mood?

- How much curiosity do you express at work when you are with your boss talking about personal matters and your boss in a positive mood but you are running late for a special event?

Culture: A Special Kind of Context

The VIA character strengths are frequently described as universal, or ubiquitous, across human beings regardless of nation, culture, or religious affiliation. The cultural context in which a given character strength is expressed will often offer a unique appearance of the strength. Many times, the character strength will manifest itself in a different way for a different purpose, varying according to the culture; and cultural norms and rituals will frequently reinforce strengths which help the individual to keep family and community together (Rashid, 2012). In other words, there are culture-specific nuances in how character strengths are displayed.

At VIA, I am frequently approached by individuals from different cultures who say something similar to the following: "In my culture, we have _____ , and I think that's a strength too. Why isn't that in the VIA classification?" This important question needs proper exploration of the culture and exploration of the meaning of the word being queried. Generally speaking, there are several possible explanations for this, and although empirical evidence is needed around the nuances, the following points might serve as initial guidance and provide insight:

- The strength mentioned is a cultural expression of an existing VIA character strength. For example, the trait of *hospitality* common in Middle Eastern cultures might be noted. This is likely to be, in most instances, a variation of the character strength of kindness. In other words, kindness can be presented in a meaningfully unique way as hospitality (however, it is still kindness being expressed).
- The strength mentioned is a compound strength. It is a combination of existing VIA character strengths. For example, *tolerance* is hypothesized as the combination of fairness, kindness, and judgment/critical thinking (Peterson, 2006b; Peterson & Seligman, 2004). The strength of responsibility can be viewed as a blend of perseverance and teamwork (Peterson, 2006b). The strength of *patience*, on the other hand, is viewed as a combination of perseverance, self-regulation, and judgment/critical thinking (Peterson & Seligman, 2004), while others have emphasized fairness and forgiveness from their analyses (Schnitker & Emmons, 2007).
- The strength mentioned is a "culture-bound strength" linked to a particular culture and not ubiquitous – An important attribute of the VIA classification is the proclamation to not include any "culture bound strengths" (Peterson & Seligman, 2004). The example of *ambition* might apply here as a major Western trait that certainly exists in other cultures like certain parts of Africa, but perhaps with less priority and value.
- The strength mentioned is a more intense form of an existing VIA character strength. In the Finnish culture there is *sisu*, a special strength of determination and resolve to overcome major adversity. Sisu is cherished in Finland and one way to think about this is as an intense form of perseverance, and as that perseverance is deployed other character strengths naturally flow in sisu, including bravery.

I'm not suggesting one or more of the reasons above fully explain and capture all the cultural nuances (i.e., fairness, kindness, and judgment won't explain 100% of tolerance), but perhaps these explanations offer some substantial takeoff points for understanding cultural strengths and their contextual expression. In the end, the character strengths-based practitioner will ask questions and explore the nuances of the individual's culture, rather than offering an authoritarian or ethnocentric viewpoint.

There are seemingly countless examples of important qualities that arise when the nuances of an individual's culture are examined. Lomas (2016) conducted a quasisystematic search for "untranslatable" words relating to well-being, and "character" was one of three overarching categories in his framework which he further subdivided into resources and spirituality. Examples of resources include *sumud* and *baraka*, Arabic terms translating to steadfastness and a gift of spiritual energy transferred from one person to another, respectively. Also included were the Japanese terms *ikigai* and *sunao*, translating respectively to reason for being and a positive connotation of meekness exemplifying the respect a student gives a teacher. In Lomas' subcategory of spirituality, he offers a variety of untranslatable words such as *smriti*, the Buddhist concept for present-moment awareness. Rashid (2012) suggests additional words that are specific to particular cultures such as abidance, amiability, duty, piety, and savoir-faire.

Plurality

When Chris Peterson, lead scientist of the development of the VIA classification and former science director of the VIA Institute, was once asked to share his most important finding from the myriad of findings and advancements in character strengths science, he responded simply and distinctly: "Character is plural" (Peterson, personal communication, 2010). What Peterson meant is that people are not simply kind or humble, brave or hopeful, or honest. Rather, people have many character strengths, and these strengths are expressed in combinations, with each person having a unique profile of character strengths. This variation, multiplicity, and uniqueness informs the rich tapestry of an individual's character.

There is a structure to our character – this is best described as a unique profile of strengths with varying highs and lows (i.e., individuals have higher strengths, middle strengths, and lower strengths). There are over 5.1 million possible Top 5 combinations of character strengths an individual might have, and across the full rank order of character strengths from 1 to 24, the number of potential character strengths profiles is exponentially greater than the number of people living on the planet. While this seems virtually infinite, when one considers that each person's expression of character strengths is unique (e.g., no two people with creativity as a top strength will express the strength in an identical way), the expression of character strengths (i.e., frequency, duration, and intensity) for any individual is truly "one-of-a-kind." In this way, character is necessarily individualized and idiosyncratic.

Character strengths are not expressed in isolation but in combinations or constellations with one another (Biswas-Diener, Kashdan, & Minhas, 2011; Niemiec, 2013; Peterson, 2006a). It is unlikely that an individual expresses one strength alone. For example, as I sit here typing these sentences, I'm hopefully expressing some creativity and judgment/critical thinking but there are also degrees of hope, perspective, leadership, zest, and so on. When we express one character strength deliberately, many others automatically and fluidly come along for the ride. I have repeatedly observed that as situations become increasingly complex and challenging, the number of character strengths being expressed increases. For example, a parent coping with a new medical diagnosis for one of their children is in the position to act strongly with a panoply of character strengths, whereas the parent watching a movie with their child is not likely to express as many character strengths in terms of quantity or intensity.

This leads to the relational concept that character strengths are interdependent – they "inter-are" (Niemiec, 2012), to build from the Buddhist concept of interbeing (Nhat Hanh, 1993). There are dynamics that occur as the strengths interact with one another, cause increases in one another, or hinder the expression of one another. It is difficult to be creative without some level of curiosity. Can you express kindness in a strong way without expressing humility and perhaps a small dose of bravery? This concept of virtue interdependence has been observed by the great philosophers, including Plato, who observed that the four virtues of justice, wisdom, temperance, and courage are interdependent –if one virtue is missing, and especially if justice is missing, then the other three cannot be fully achieved. For the ancient Athenians, social contribution and personal flourishing were both wrapped up in the concept of virtue. A fundamental principle of their beliefs was that virtues represented a seamless whole. To be virtuous required excellence in all the virtues, not just one, an idea that has been called the reciprocity of the virtues. As the moral philosopher Susan Wolf has framed it (although not without philosophical rebuttals) – to have one virtue is to have them all (2007). And, when scientists have examined the correlations of the 24 character strengths with one another (i.e., creating an intercorrelation matrix), they have found that all the strengths have a relationship with one another to some degree. Some strengths relate very highly to one another (e.g., zest and hope), while others relate minimally to one another (e.g., humility and love of learning).

Strength-Based Practitioner Tip

Bring together the concepts of dimensionality, context, and plurality of character. Picture the character strengths as 24 stocks side-by-side on the New York Stock Exchange with jagged lines rising and falling throughout the day. These increasing and decreasing frequency waves represent your character strength expression. In any situation, you are expressing high, low, and medium levels of each of the 24 strengths. Choose an activity that you engage in that has a high level of meaning to you (e.g., giving a 2-hour presentation, leading an important work meeting, having dinner with a friend while conversing about life problems). Rate each of the 24 strengths from 1–10 in terms of the degree to which you are expressing them at the beginning, middle, and end of the activity. The plurality of strengths expression, the nuances of degree, and the importance of context should become immediately clear to you.

All 24 Character Strengths Matter

When people take the VIA Survey and look at their results, they are sometimes pleased and proud and other times they are disappointed. Much of this relates to the level of meaning and importance they place on certain strengths and where they expected or wanted those strengths to be in their rank-order profile. In reality, it doesn't matter if the individual is high in self-regulation or kindness or curiosity. Each of the 24 character strengths is positive and can be used for the good. Each is associated with different positive outcomes in character science. Each is a capacity that can be enhanced. Therefore, each of the 24 character strengths is important.

Some character strengths have more direct links with happiness; others enable opportunities in achievement and reaching goals; and others appear more connected to better physical health. Table 1.1 maps out a handful of the positive associations for each of the 24 character strengths as originally offered in Peterson and Seligman (2004). Some updates can be found in other sources (e.g., Niemiec, 2013; 2014a; Niemiec & Wedding, 2014).

Character strengths have important consequences. These consequences or outcomes differ according to the particular strength. For example, zest and hope are the character strengths found repeatedly to be the most strongly linked with happiness (Park, Peterson, & Seligman, 2004; Peterson; Ruch, Beermann, Park, & Seligman, 2007; Proctor, Maltby, & Linley, 2009; Shimai, Otake, Park, Peterson, & Seligman, 2006), and there is some evidence that character strengths can "cause" happiness (Proyer, Ruch, & Buschor, 2013). Perseverance is a character strength especially associated with academic achievement (Lounsbury, Fisher, Levy, & Welsh,

2009; Park & Peterson, 2009). The character strength of gratitude has been linked with high positive emotion, optimism, life satisfaction, vitality, religiousness and spirituality, and less depression and envy than less grateful individuals (Emmons & McCullough, 2003). These studies show that some character strengths matter more for specific outcomes. Likewise, some character strengths might matter more at particular periods in life. For example, in a representative sample of adults in Switzerland, strengths that promote affiliation and commitment were among those most aligned with well-being for adults in their late 20s and early 30s; strengths that support maintenance of family and work for those in their late 30s through mid-40s; and strengths that facilitate a vital involvement with the environment for those in their late 40s through late 50s (Martinez-Marti & Ruch, 2014).

Table 1.1. Character Strengths Associations Noted in Peterson and Seligman (2004)

Character Strength	Positive Correlates
Creativity	Openness to new experiences; cognitive flexibility
Curiosity	Positive affect; willingness to challenge stereotypes; creativity; desire for challenge in work and play; goal perseverance; adept at making complex decisions; excitement/enjoyment/attentiveness; engagement and achievement in academic settings; sense of subjective well-being
Judgment	Adept at problem solving; increased cognitive ability; more resistant to suggestion and manipulation; more effective in dealing with stress
Love of learning	More adept at navigating obstacles/challenges; autonomy; resourcefulness; increased sense of possibility; self-efficacy; healthy, productive aging; more likely to seek/accept challenges; decreased levels of stress
Perspective	Successful aging; life satisfaction; maturity; open-mindedness; even-temperedness; sociability; social intelligence
Bravery	Prosocial orientation; internal locus of control; self-efficacy; ability to delay gratification; tolerance for ambiguity/uncertainty; capacity to assess risk; capacity for reflection; involvement in socially worthy aims; capacity to create and sustain high quality connections with others
Perseverance	Achievement/goal completion; resourcefulness; self-efficacy
Honesty	Positive mood; life satisfaction; openness to new experiences; empathy; conscientiousness; capacity for self-actualization; agreeableness; emotional stability; effort/goal attainment
Zest	Autonomy; connection with others; goal attainment
Love	Positive relationships with others; healthy balance between dependency and autonomy; positive social functioning; higher self-esteem; less susceptibility to depression; capacity to cope with stress
Kindness	Overall mental and physical health; longevity
Social intelligence	Smooth social functioning; life judgment; lower levels of aggression; lower incidence of substance abuse
Teamwork (framed as citizenship)	Social trust; positive view of human nature
Fairness	Perspective; self-reflection; cooperation; leadership; altruism; prosocial behavior
Leadership	Cognitive skills/intelligence; flexibility/adaptability; emotional stability; internal locus of control; integrity; interpersonal skills; creativity/resourcefulness
Forgiveness	Prosocial behaviors; agreeableness; emotional stability; lower levels of anger, anxiety, depression, and hostility
Humility	Perspective; forgiveness; self-regulation; capacity to attain self-improvement goals

Table 1.1. Continued

Character Strength	Positive Correlates
Prudence	Cooperativeness; interpersonal warmth; sociability; assertiveness; positive emotion; imaginativeness; curiosity; insightfulness; physical health; longevity; optimism, internal locus of control; high achievement/performance; lower levels of anger expression
Self-regulation	High levels of academic achievement; self-esteem; self-acceptance; capacity to control anger; secure interpersonal attachments; high levels of satisfaction with social relationships; lower levels of anxiety and depression; perceived by others as more likable/trustworthy
Appreciation of beauty & excellence	Openness to experience; altruism; devotion to others/larger community; capacity for change/self-improvement
Gratitude	Positive emotion; life satisfaction; optimism; prosocial behavior; increased cardiovascular and immune functioning; longevity; lower levels of anxiety and depression; openness to experience; agreeableness; conscientiousness; less neuroticism
Hope	Achievement; positive social relationships; physical well-being; active problem-solving; lower levels of anxiety and depression; conscientiousness; diligence; ability to delay gratification
Humor	Positive mood; capacity to manage stress; creativity; intelligence; less neuroticism
Spirituality	Self-regulation; lower levels of substance abuse; positive social relationships; marital stability; forgiveness; kindness; compassion; altruism; volunteerism; philanthropy; happiness; sense of purpose; life satisfaction; capacity to cope with illness and stress

Reproduced with permission from Niemiec, R. M. (2014a). *Mindfulness and character strengths: A practical guide to flourishing.* Boston, MA: Hogrefe Publishing.

From what scholars, researchers, and practitioners are observing, each of the 24 character strengths appear to be present, in varying degrees, in human beings. It is easy to overlook or take for granted the smaller degrees of strengths use. In fact, you have probably used all 24 character strengths in the last couple days. For example, this morning did you brush your teeth, wash your body, get dressed, and eat breakfast? If you did any of these, you were using some level of self-regulation and prudence. These are "little" uses of two strengths that happen to consistently be two of the least endorsed character strengths across the globe (McGrath, 2015b; Park, Peterson, & Seligman, 2006). Researchers have long been interested in drawing distinctions between "big" and "small" uses of character strengths; for example, "big C" creativity (Simonton, 2000) can be seen in Mozart's 9th Symphony, Jean Pierre-Jeunet's film *Amelie* (2001), and Van Gogh's "Starry Night" painting, while "little c" creativity can be seen in a flash of insight we have about a personal struggle and in a new idea to arrange the flowers on our kitchen table. Elsewhere, I have shared several examples of "big" and "little" character strengths use found in the research literature and other sources (Niemiec, 2014a). To highlight the subtle, often unconscious uses of these character strengths, Table 1.2 offers examples of how each of the 24 strengths may appear in "little" doses. Of course, the word "little" should not be taken literally in terms of its importance as small doses of character strengths not only are the ingredients of "big" uses of character strengths but can potentially serve as important sources of meaning and positive impact in and of themselves.

Table 1.2. Examples of "Little" Character Strengths Use

Character Strength	"Little" Example of Everyday Use
Creativity	Thinking up a new story to tell your child.
Curiosity	Asking a neighbor a couple of questions.
Judgment/Critical thinking	Reading two very different news columns to get different views.
Love of learning	Reading three online articles about the same topic.
Perspective	Offering a one-liner of advice to a clerk who seems to be having a bad day.
Bravery	Driving downtown when one is afraid of heavy traffic.
Perseverance	Deciding to respond to 10 emails in a row and completing the task.
Honesty	Admitting a mistake when one recalls a situation inaccurately.
Zest	Taking a brisk 10-minute walk on a break.
Love	Listening carefully to a colleague who had a rough day.
Kindness	Holding the elevator for someone.
Social intelligence	Asking a family member how they are feeling when they show a distressed facial expression.
Teamwork	Asking a team member for feedback on a work project.
Fairness	When giving candy to neighborhood children, making sure every child gets the same quantity.
Leadership	Organizing a gathering of friends for lunch at a restaurant.
Forgiveness	Letting go of the tension created when someone cuts you off in traffic.
Humility	Holding off on sharing positive news so the other person can share their story.
Prudence	Planning a quick breakfast for two.
Self-regulation	Brushing and flossing one's teeth in the morning.
Appreciation of beauty & excellence	Marveling at the skill and grace of an Olympic downhill skier.
Gratitude	Offering a personal thanks to the universe upon waking up in the morning.
Hope	Feeling optimistic about an upcoming work meeting.
Humor	Smiling to a stranger on public transportation.
Spirituality	Feeling a sense of meaning during a mindfulness practice.

Strengths-Based Practitioner Tip

"Little" character strengths use is so commonplace and so often taken for granted that it easily occurs without our awareness. Consider each of the 24 character strengths. Jot down one way you used several of your character strengths this week that was at least moderately useful to you. Make note of the outcome that each strength led to or contributed to. For example, your conscientious planning in being on time for a meeting (prudence) led to extra time for productive group discussion; your good eating habits at breakfast (self-regulation) contributed to your feeling more vital and healthy throughout your morning; your favor for a colleague (kindness) led them to smile and experience a moment of joy thus contributing to your positive relationship with them. Note that there are often a multitude of factors that can contribute to such outcomes so your noting of the outcomes will often be speculation; however, this exercise can still be useful for drawing potential links between character strengths and benefits/valued outcomes.

One of the dominant theories in positive psychology is the well-being theory articulated by Seligman (2011) and framed in the acronym PERMA (see Snapshot 1.1), in which each letter stands for an independent, measurable pathway to a flourishing life – a full life of substantial well-being. Seligman describes the integral relationship the 24 character strengths have with flourishing as follows: "In well-being theory, these twenty-four strengths underpin all five elements, not just engagement: deploying your highest strengths leads to more positive emotion, to more meaning, to more accomplishment, and to better relationships" (p. 24).

Table 1.3 shows a handful of the empirical connections between these five areas of flourishing (i.e., PERMA) and character strengths. In practical terms, this means that an individual can deliberately use their character strengths to engage more fully in their work, to find more meaning in life, to experience positive emotions, to improve relationships, and to accomplish goals. One study (Peterson et al., 2007) looked specifically at the relationship between the character strengths and three PERMA elements (the pleasure/positive emotions, engagement, and meaning components of authentic happiness theory) and identified those strengths that most highly correlated with those elements.

Table 1.3. The Interconnection of PERMA and Character Strengths Research

Flourishing Element	Research Studies	Comment	Specific Correlates Found in Peterson et al. (2007)
Positive emotion	Güsewell & Ruch (2012); Lavy & Littman-Ovadia (2016); Quinlan, Swain, Cameron, & Vella-Brodrick (2014)	Study populations range from employees to students and people in the community	Humor, zest, hope, social intelligence, love
Engagement	Brdar & Kashdan, (2010); Madden, Green, & Grant, (2011); Peterson et al. (2005)	An abundance of studies link engagement, character strengths, and well-being	Zest, curiosity, hope, perseverance, perspective
Relationships (positive)	Kashdan, McKnight, Fincham, & Rose (2011); Veldorale-Brogan, Bradford, & Vail (2010); Weber & Ruch (2012a)	A critical factor here is the relational intimacy that is created by character strengths use	N/A
Meaning	Berthold & Ruch (2014); Littman-Ovadia & Steger (2010); Vella-Brodrick, Park, & Peterson (2009)	An abundance of studies link meaning, character strengths, and well-being	Spirituality, gratitude, hope, zest, curiosity
Accomplishment	Peterson & Park (2009); Shoshani & Slone (2012); Wagner & Ruch (2015)	Studies range from achievements in the military, classroom, and workplace	N/A

To drive home this concept that all 24 character strengths matter, consider the strength that typically turns up last in my character strengths profile – humor. I highly value humor and playfulness and use the strength regularly. I use it to connect with new people in conversation, to be socially appropriate, and sometimes consciously bring it forth to deal with life stress. I particularly love using playfulness with my young children. This is where my lower strength really shines. All that said, humor does deserve to be toward the bottom of my profile because I don't turn to humor as the first-line way to connect with others in social situations, telling jokes and funny stories that entice new connections or captivate audiences. I feel awkward when it seems that a situation calls for something funny in the moment and I don't have a witty remark to offer. As I reflect on my use of this strength, one of the key differences between me and someone who has humor as a signature strength is that I express it more *reactively* than *proactively*. With the exception of playing with my children, where I am very proactive with playfulness, I will typically be reactive with smiles and laughter in response to others' humor rather than initiating the jokes. Using humor and playfulness is important to help me be well-rounded, more versatile, and in some situations, happier. Could I train my humor strength and become a comedian? Sure, and there is research showing humor is malleable and can be built up with training (McGhee, 1999; Proyer, Gander, Wellenzohn, & Ruch, 2014a; Wellenzohn, Proyer, & Ruch, 2016a). But, in reality, the value for me personally to elevate this strength up to the ceiling is low. I'll leave my humor where it is, appreciated and valued, but in the basement.

Different Types of Strengths

An important pathway towards understanding character strengths is to understand what they are not. One way to explore this insight is to understand the other types of "strengths" that human beings have; namely, talents, skills, interests, resources, and values. Appendix E lists the differences between the VIA Survey and two other tests: the Gallup StrengthsFinder 2.0 and Myers-Briggs Type Indicator, which are two popular tests for strengths such as these. And, we can place a microscope on character strengths and examine its many subsets, such as signature strengths, phasic strengths, and lower strengths. What immediately follows are other general strengths categories and their connections with character strengths.

Talents (What We Do Naturally Well)

The study of expertise has found that developing a talent takes thousands of hours of practice, actually 10,000 hours of deliberate practice over at least 10 years (Ericsson & Ward, 2007). How could the world-class pianist, the superstar home-run hitter, or the champion chess player possibly develop their talent without intense use of the character strengths of perseverance and self-regulation? Several other strengths need to be used, such as zest where the individual exerts significant energy, passion, and enthusiasm, throwing themselves into their practice each day. The leading work in talents/abilities is the theory of multiple intelligence from Howard Gardner (1983), a Harvard psychologist, who proposed humans have not one intelligence but at least 7 core intelligences or talents: Intrapersonal, interpersonal, logical-mathematical, spatial, bodily-kinesthetic, linguistic, and musical. This theory has stood strong for over three decades. The Olympic athlete actualizes his or her bodily-kinesthetic intelligence/talent, in large part, because of extensive self-regulation, perseverance, prudence, hope, and many other character strengths, whereas the person who is naturally gifted at communicating with others (i.e., an interpersonal intelligence/talent) is probably using perspective, social intelligence, fairness, and creativity. Consider the young man who used his curiosity and interest in the world to build his spatial intelligence. He asked questions about his environment, explored new neighborhoods where he lived, and soon he had mentally mapped out the city he lived in; he had used his curiosity to make the most of his talent for spatial reasoning.

Skills (What We Train Ourselves to Do)

As individuals build up a proficiency, such as learning on-the-job tasks and trades, it is likely they are being driven by the character strength of hope in that there is a wider purpose or reason that they are learning the skill. For example, the person may be trying to gain promotion in their place of employment by learning a new computer program or attaining a certification in some skill which will help them improve their job performance. In some cases, the strength of love of learning might be a driver. Conceivably, any of the 24 character strengths can drive the building of a skill. Youth are often trained in certain skills that schools, parents, coaches, and other professions perceive the child or adolescent is lacking, such as anger management skills or communication skills. In these instances, it is often the strength of the parent or professional that is driving the interest in skill-building, such as the character strength of love to want the best for the child or hope for the child to have a better life.

Interests (Our Passions)

Research is showing an important link between our signature strengths and our interests; namely our natural, harmonious passions in life (Forest et al., 2012). Our highest character strengths – and not only love of learning and curiosity – are intrinsically linked with our interests and life passions. We might choose hobbies and other interest areas in order to express particular character strengths. I play one-on-one sports because I can express my perseverance and zest, team sports because I can bring forth teamwork and social intelligence, and online chess so I can exercise my judgment/critical thinking and perspective strengths together. No doubt my passion for collecting Pez dispensers allows me to tap into my playfulness/humor strength. In my work, I have a strong interest in educating others about universal phenomena in human beings such as character strengths, mindfulness, savoring, and spirituality. When my interests and passions are ignited, so are my character strengths. As I teach, my zest and enthusiasm elevate, and my hope and love strengths enliven as I see the immediate impact these teachings have on people's lives and the many ways these could be used in their future and my future. The connection between my strengths of character and my strengths of interest seems inseparable. It is a synergy – a swirl of fervor and excitement.

Resources (Our External Supports)

The only category of strengths that is external to us is resources. Resources are those important supports to us such as living in a safe neighborhood, having several close friends, being part of a good learning community, and having family to rely on. Building up and maintaining our social and spiritual resources takes character, such as those strengths that help us in relationships (e.g., fairness, kindness, forgiveness) and those that help us connect outside of ourselves (e.g., spirituality, gratitude, hope).

Values (What We Internally Hold Dear)

Values live in our heads and thus exist in our thoughts and emotions; values do not tell us about our actions or behaviors. An individual can have a value for family but that resides in their thoughts and emotions; to spent time with family and show love, kindness, and fairness to one's family takes "character" and is essentially putting one's values into action. Thus, character is not only about cognition and emotion, it is also about bringing what's in our head into our behaviors in the world. It's interesting to note that the name of the nonprofit organization behind the work of the VIA classification and VIA Survey was originally "Values in Action Institute." The name was later changed to appropriately represent what is central to this work – character – hence the name for well over a decade has been VIA Institute on Character.

The Driving Force

Character strengths cut across each of the strength categories as a *driving force*, catalyzing or intimately connecting with the other strength domains. There's a moving story of a young man named Benny, a talented and influential presenter to businesses and youth education programs. Benny was married, had two children, a strong spiritual community, and many friends. He was a charismatic man with many talents, resources, and interests. Unfortunately, job stress, financial struggles, and peer temptation began to impact Benny and he turned to selling drugs to supplement his income. Benny noticed his resources began to dwindle as he prioritized the wrong crowd and avoided his childhood friends. His situation worsened as he sunk deep into this dangerous lifestyle. One day, when walking to his car in broad daylight, he was shot several times in the stomach and arms. Benny underwent 17 surgeries and meanwhile lost all his financial savings, could no longer hold down his job, his wife left him, and he became estranged from his children and church community. These circumstances were accompanied by deep feelings of depression which almost always means anhedonia – a loss of interest in what he was previously interested in. As the young man recounted his story to me he also shared a stirring insight that came to him one day while lying in a hospital bed staring at the ceiling: "I had lost everything, the people in my life, my money, my job, and even use of parts of my body, but one thing I did not lose was my core strengths. These could not be taken away from me." He was speaking about his bravery, honesty, creativity, social intelligence, and hopefulness.

In summary, talents can be squandered, resources can be quickly lost, interests wane and change, skills diminish over time, but when all seems completely lost, we still have our character strengths. When focused on, our character strengths crystallize and evolve and can integrate with these other positive qualities to contribute to the greater good.

Strengths-Based Practitioner Tip

Neal Mayerson has offered the concept of the "power zone" to refer to the successful alignment of talents, character strengths, resources, and interests. Many people are deployed at work in areas within their competence (talent) but the work does not connect with them as human beings (character). Mayerson (2015) describes these people as "succeeding without fulfillment." However, if our strengths can be aligned with what we are good at and what we are interested in, then we can succeed with fulfillment and meaning. For example, an accountant who is talented and passionate about working with numbers and configuring information on computers can find ways to apply their highest character strengths at work (e.g., perhaps they regularly use judgment/critical thinking to solve computer problems or they use their zest/energy in their work interactions on breaks and at team meetings). They are then said to be in the power zone. This would be viewed as an area of optimal functioning or flourishing. However, future research is needed to bear out the various benefits of integrating and aligning these different types of strengths.

Think of a time when you were working and in the power zone. Describe your experience in terms of your expression of each of the types of strengths. How might you create more power zone experiences in your future? What strengths would you need to get involved?

Character Strengths Subsets

Most of these concepts are explored in greater depth in later chapters and therefore the following explanations will be short. These are listed below in order from most to least researched.

Signature Strengths

Those character strengths that are most central to who the person is and that best capture their uniqueness or essence. They also are likely to be more energizing to use and more natural to express than the other strengths in the person's profile.

Happiness Strengths

Across several studies in different cultures, a handful of character strengths repeatedly emerge as most correlated with life satisfaction, a type of happiness. Those strengths, starting from (typically) the strongest correlation are zest, hope, love, gratitude, and curiosity (see, for example, Buschor, Proyer, & Ruch, 2013; Park et al., 2004).

Lower Strengths

Sometimes called lesser strengths or bottom strengths, these character strengths emerge in the Bottom 4–7 of an individual's profile. These are not viewed as weaknesses, rather as strengths that are either undeveloped, unrealized, not as valued as other strengths, or, at the least, less used compared to other strengths in the profile.

Phasic Strengths

The "rise to the occasion" strengths, meaning that when a given situation demands use of a particular strength that is not the person's signature strength, the individual can not only call the strength forward but do so strongly and adaptively.

Middle Strengths

Character strengths that likely support or readily enhance the display of an individual's signature strengths. Sometimes called "supportive strengths," these round out the middle of a person's character strengths profile.

Lost Strengths

These character strengths have gone dormant for a period or eroded from the individual's consciousness and use. A character strength might have been suppressed by an authority figure (e.g., parent, teacher, manager, sport coach, sibling, friend) or discouraged due to cultural or social constraints. A lost strength can conceivably be any character strength in the individual's profile.

Character Strengths Can Be Developed

I recall a middle-aged woman approaching me prior to a workshop I was about to deliver in Sydney, Australia. She approached me with excitement, eager to share her news. She told me she had taken the VIA Survey 6 years prior and discovered her character strength of self-regulation to be number 24 in her rank order. She had been unhappy about this and so worked hard to deliberately improve her self-regulation over the years, discovering it was fairly easy for her to do so. When she took the VIA Survey a week prior to the workshop, she found it to be number 2. She shared several explanations for how she elevated her strength. While there can be many reasons for this shift in rank-order and what precisely accounted for her change in self-regulation, there is reason to believe she directly impacted one of her character strengths.

A commonly held traditional belief over the last century is that our character – much like an engraved mark etched in stone – is immutable and unchanging. New research in personality psychology shows that personality is more changeable than originally thought (Blackie, Roepke, Forgeard, Jayawickreme, & Fleeson, 2014; Harris, Brett, Johnson, & Deary, 2016; Hudson & Fraley, 2015; Roberts et al., 2017), and that the change is not necessarily slow and gradual, occurring across many years, which was another previously held assumption. In addition, the new science of character strengths ushered in by the VIA classification has shed light on this error. First, it's important to appreciate the stability of character strengths. Data from 11,635 repeat VIA Survey takers, separated by at least 6 months, found that less than 1% of repeat takers have no overlap among their Top 5 strengths from Time 1 to Time 2, and 76% of repeat takers have 3–5 strengths in common in their Top 5 from Time 1 to Time 2 (Niemiec, 2009). In addition, longitudinal research examining the virtues of the VIA classification in children between the ages of 12 and 14 found character virtue stability over 3 years; these researchers noted that in addition to girls scoring higher than boys across the six virtues, there was only a slight increase in the virtues of humanity and justice over three assessment periods (Ferragut, Blanca, & Ortiz-Tallo, 2014).

We are learning that character strengths can be developed. Research in personality has found that personality traits can shift for a number of reasons, including normative changes based on our genetics and predictable changes in social role (e.g., getting married, having a child) as well as nonnormative changes. Nonnormative changes include less common but deliberately chosen changes in one's social role (e.g., joining the military) and atypical life events (e.g., going through a trauma) (Borghans, Duckworth, Heckman, & ter Weel, 2008). In a study of the latter, gratitude, hope, kindness, leadership, love, spirituality, and teamwork all increased in a US sample (but not a European sample) 2 months after the September 11th (2001) attack on the World Trade Center in New York City (Peterson & Seligman, 2003). Ten months later these character strengths were still elevated but to a lesser degree.

Another factor that has been shown to impact personality change is deliberate interventions focused on improving a trait. The latter is particularly exciting and applicable to the themes in this book as strength-based practitioners are especially interested in impacting changes in one part of our personality – our character strengths. Intervention studies are showing that our traits are malleable and that intentional changes can have a positive impact (Hudson & Fraley, 2015; Roberts et al., 2017; Yeager, Johnson et al., 2014). Personality theorist Will Fleeson (2001) has written widely about this with his "density distribution model" of traits, which offers a promising resolution to the decades-old, person-situation debate: Is personality mostly the result of individual trait differences or changes in context/situational cues? According to Fleeson's model, traits are stable in that there is reliable between-person variation (people are consistently distinct from one another), and are changeable in that there is significant within-person variation (people display a variety of qualities) based on the situation (Blackie et al., 2014; Fleeson, 2001, 2004; Fleeson, Malanos, & Achille, 2002). This model suggests there is a wide range of possibility for people to develop their traits, especially strengths of character. In discussing virtue theory, Bright (2016), echoing numerous philosophers over the centuries, explains that virtues are traits that are second-nature to the person, developable, and acquired through intention and effort.

In a study of thousands of employees across 65 countries, Michelle McQuaid and the VIA Institute on Character (2015) tested a brief strengths intervention involving three steps of habit change – cue, routine, reward – based on McQuaid's work connecting character strengths and positive habits (McQuaid & Lawn, 2014) and research on habit theory (Duhigg, 2012). They found that strengths (not specified as character strengths per se) were malleable to the degree that there were the following results among this large sample of employees:

- 41% improved their ability to name their own strengths.
- 60% became better at setting weekly strength-based goals.
- 41% improved their feeling of having the opportunity to do what they did best each day.
- 39% improved the likelihood of having a meaningful strengths conversation with their supervisor.
- 32% felt their organization was more committed to developing their strengths.
- Additional benefits included: greater flourishing, engagement, and feeling valued, energized, and like they were making a difference.

The development of character is not a new topic, and neither is the argument that intentional or deliberate interventions can be deployed to improve a character strength. Many centuries ago, Aristotle (4 BCE/2000) and Saint Thomas Aquinas (1265–1273/1989) emphasized that virtue could be acquired through practice. One of the founding fathers of the US, Benjamin Franklin (1962), set up a personal system in which he placed his attention on improving one virtue per week while leaving the other virtues to "their ordinary chance." Franklin tracked his progress and journaled about his experiences. In his autobiography, he described this approach as contributing greatly to his happiness and life successes. People can learn to be more curious, more grateful, more fair, or better critical thinkers. The key is to create new habits through practice and effort over time, which allows us to break free from routines. Many others have recently echoed the importance of building character strengths through practice and habit creation (see Franklin, 2009; Linley, 2008; McQuaid & Lawn, 2014; Niemiec, 2014a; Peterson, 2006a).

> **Strengths-Based Practitioner Tip**
>
> Remember what Aristotle observed and Chris Peterson echoed: "We are what we repeatedly do." We can make a practice out of virtue and out of strengths use. Making the practice a routine is one route of strengths development. Using this observation as a personal motto (for yourself and your clients) can serve to awaken your potential.

Being *and* Doing

The mindfulness literature has offered an important distinction between being and doing (Kabat-Zinn, 1990; Niemiec, 2014a; Segal, Williams, & Teasdale, 2013). We can go about our day as "human doers" running around from task to task, multitasking, thinking only about what's next to do, and not present and aware for most of it. Or, we can infuse a sense of being present to our day – connecting with the food we are eating, noticing the greens of the trees as we drive down the expressway, seeing the smile on our loved one's face, and so on. Mindfulness practice, in many ways, is about developing "our mode of being."

The concepts of being and doing are also relevant to this character strengths work, but in a different way. The work of character strengths is clear: it is being and doing. It is "being" because character strengths work is about our identity, understanding who we are, and helping us to "be ourselves." It is also about "doing" because character strengths are about expressing these 24 strengths into the world, taking action, and doing the good that needs to be done. It's about putting our values into action.

There is support for both approaches in the literature: Research on signature strengths reflects our "being" – our identity – those strengths most core to us (for example, Seligman, Steen, Park, & Peterson, 2005). As researcher Rhett Diessner observed: "Traits are ontologically closer to the core of human being than is thinking or reasoning" (Diessner, Davis, & Toney, 2009, p. 255); existence and being before thinking. At the same time, there is plenty of research linking character strengths and different types of performance – which can be viewed as our "doing" – putting our best qualities into action (for example, Lounsbury et al., 2009; Wagner & Ruch, 2015).

During psychology graduate school, I spent a lot of my free time writing poetry, drinking scotch, and reading philosophy books. I'm not sure how much I retained from the latter but one thing was clear – there was a heated debate around the nature of humans as people who are essentially "being" or "becoming." Loosely speaking, "being" refers to wholeness and completeness in the moment, while "becoming" refers to the constantly changing and evolving nature of life. In extrapolating from the complexities and depth of the philosophy, I'll offer a simplistic vision. The character strengths describe our essential nature – who we are in the world (i.e., our being-ness). For example, someone might say "I define myself as a person who is kind, loving, humble, and curious." At the same time, the expression of our character strengths reflects what we are "becoming" – not only our actions and how we connect but our changing nature (i.e., our doing-ness). For example, expressing love to a spouse, gratefulness to a coworker, and leadership to a staff.

In the words of the virtue scholar Andre Comte-Sponville (2001):

> Virtue is a way of being, Aristotle explained, but an acquired and lasting way of being: it is what we are (and therefore what we can do), and what we are is what we have become…it is our way of being and acting humanly … our power to act *well*. (p. 3)

We can view ourselves through the lens of our character strengths and see our true nature is both being strong at being ourselves (i.e., authenticity) and doing well by bringing that strength to benefit others (i.e., expressing goodness).

Chapter Summary

- The character strengths provide a common language to describe what is best in human beings.
- An optimal approach to character is a dimensional view rather than a categorical one, and, taken a step further, the character strengths themselves are multidimensional. We have more or less of a particular strength, therefore strengths are expressed in degrees, which vary by the context.
- Character strengths are plural in that each person has a unique profile of character strengths and they are expressed in combinations rather than in isolation.
- All 24 of the character strengths are within each person and associated with different positive outcomes, therefore all 24 character strengths matter.
- There are many kinds of strengths human beings have, such as talents and interests, and there are many subtypes of character strengths, such as phasic strengths and happiness strengths.
- Character strengths are somewhat stable, context-dependent characteristics; they can be developed with practice.
- Character strengths are both "being" and "doing" – they are essential for both understanding who we are and for behavioral expression/performance.

Chapter 2

Signature Strengths

Research and Practice

Introduction

In the *Character Strengths and Virtues* publication (Peterson & Seligman, 2004) that articulated the criteria, development, and framework for the VIA classification, there were over 2,000 scholarly references and 800 pages of discussion of these 24 character strengths yet not more than a few sentences addressed the topic of "signature strengths." Nevertheless, those few words were enough as numerous studies on signature strengths have emerged since 2004, articulating the benefits and value of signature strengths. Studies have examined correlation, causation, mediators, moderators, populations, assessment, and interventions in attempting to understand this robust topic. This chapter reviews those research findings and offers practical strategies for working with signature strengths.

Why Are Signature Strengths Important?

The case can quickly be made for the significance of signature strengths from not only the science that has emerged over the last couple decades but also from the perspective of the problem of chronic disengagement across organizations, relationships, and individuals. Here's a snapshot of both.

- *Disengagement of individuals – A lack of flourishing.* Research has found that less than 25% of the US population is flourishing (Keyes, 2003), and similar results are found in other countries such as New Zealand, (Hone, Jarden, Duncan, & Schofield, 2015). This means that people are not functioning with a high level of well-being, socially and psychologically.
  - *Support for strengths.* One study found that those people who use their strengths a lot are 18 times more likely to be flourishing than those who do not use their strengths (Hone et al., 2015). Each of the core elements of flourishing – positive emotions, engagement, meaning, positive relationships, and achievement (Seligman, 2011) – are significantly linked with character strengths (see Table 1.1 in Chapter 1).
- *Disengagement of individuals – A general unawareness of strengths.* Survey research has shown that two-thirds of people are unaware of their strengths (Linley, 2008). Thus, if people don't know who they are and what they're capable of, how can they be expected to perform well on the job or in life?
  - *Support for strengths.* A representative sample of New Zealand workers found that those who were highly aware of their strengths were nine times more likely to be flourishing than those who were unaware (Hone et al., 2015). Character strengths have been connected with engagement in a number of studies (e.g., Peterson et al., 2007).

- *Disengagement of couples.* Relationships are suffering, with high divorce rates for *new* marriages.
  - *Support for strengths.* Research is mounting not only for the value of appreciation but, in particular, for strengths appreciation. In studies of couples, those who report that their partner both recognizes and appreciates their signature strengths have higher relationship satisfaction, are more committed to the relationship, and report their basic needs are getting met (Kashdan et al., 2017). Several studies draw connections between character strengths and relationship health (e.g., Lavy, Littman-Ovadia, & Bareli, 2014a, 2014b).
- *Disengagement of employees.* Worker disengagement rates are above 70% according to the Gallup Organization, and there is a misalignment between character strengths required of individuals and character strengths that come naturally to them (Money, Hillenbrand, & Camara, 2008).
  - *Support for strengths.* Signature strengths use is connected with work engagement, productivity, work satisfaction, and work-as-a-calling (e.g., Harzer & Ruch, 2015, 2016; Lavy & Littman-Ovadia, 2016; Littman-Ovadia & Davidovitch, 2010). A 3-year analysis of employee engagement found that signature strengths were one of the most crucial drivers (Crabb, 2011). The Gallup Organization has found that employees who have the opportunity to use their strengths are six times more likely to be engaged in their work (Sorenson, 2014).

Disengagement appears to be remarkably high across the many domains of our life. This calls for new action. Signature strengths are emerging across domains as not only an important source of engagement but also as a central pathway.

Strengths-Based Practitioner Tip

Examine the main domains of your life: work, school, social and intimate relationships, family relationships, community, spirituality. In which domain are you most engaged, i.e., highly connected, interested, and in flow with what you are doing? Which domain are you least engaged in? How might you learn from your domain of high engagement? What does your high engagement domain have to teach you about your disengaged domain? What character strengths, especially signature strengths, might you bring forth to become more engaged across domains?

Core Concepts

Signature strengths are one of the most researched and practiced concepts in positive psychology. Working with signature strengths has many of the hallmarks of success:
- It's very easy to do: Practitioners don't have to change their style or approach.
- Clients find immediate benefit.
- It has scientific support.
- It is novel and unique for clients who are accustomed to focusing on what is wrong within themselves.

Signature strengths have been discussed in academic and consumer forums. The original publication on the VIA classification, *Character Strengths and Virtues*, discusses signature strengths as those positive, personal traits that an individual owns, celebrates, and frequently exercises

(Peterson & Seligman, 2004). Thus, signature strengths are linked with the person's identity and conception of who they are, and they cannot be considered apart from context.

Seligman (2002) offered several ways to think about signature strengths, suggesting that a signature strength would meet most, if not all, of these criteria:

- A sense of ownership and authenticity ("This is the real me").
- A feeling of excitement while displaying it.
- A rapid learning curve as the strength is first practiced.
- A sense of yearning to find new ways to use it.
- A feeling of inevitability in using the strength ("Try and stop me").
- Invigoration rather than exhaustion after using the strength.
- Creation and pursuit of personal projects that revolve around it.
- Joy, zest, enthusiasm, even ecstasy while using it.

The convention among positive psychology researchers has been to target the individual's Top 5 strengths in their profile as their signature strengths. Initial research suggests that individuals have between three and seven signature strengths (Peterson & Seligman, 2004). The VIA Institute on Character investigated the construct further and conducted four studies examining the initial concept as discussed in the two preceding texts, attempting to understand the quantity of signature strengths within individuals (Mayerson, 2013). Different tactics were deployed along with varying levels of strictness in the criteria used to determine a signature strength. Signature strengths were found to have significantly higher VIA scores than nonsignature strengths, hence highlighting signature strengths as a distinct category of strengths. A few years later, Robert McGrath conducted three studies to develop and validate the Signature Strengths Survey (SSS). The first study examined mean differences between strengths on VIA Survey data from nearly a half-million people, and the second study involved administering a preliminary SSS and then interviewing subjects on their patterns of responding. When asked to provide justification for their signature strength choices, the most common response was that the strength is "part of who I am." These studies informed a final iteration of the SSS which was administered (third study) to 4,131 people and led to the identification of 5.5 strengths as signature, on average (more details on these studies can be found in the technical manual by McGrath, 2017). These results support the construct of signature strengths and indicate that the average number of signature strengths that people think of themselves as having is consistent with what positive psychology researchers originally proposed, although the criteria are more stringent than originally hypothesized. The criterion for determining a signature strength that seems to matter most, which has been corroborated by other research, is whether or not the strength is viewed as core or essential to who the person is.

Strength-Based Practitioner Tip

If you are trying to determine whether or not a client's strength is "signature" and you only have time to ask one question, make it: "Is this strength essential to who you are?" Or, more broadly, "Which of these highest strengths is most core to who you are and defines you as a person?" In other words, if you want to get to the heart of the matter, ask about identity.

Another tactic to thinking about signature strengths that drives home their central importance in our life is to engage in a mental subtraction exercise. Consider what life would be like if you did not have one of your signature strengths. Can you imagine how your life would be if you could not express your strength of creativity? What if the strength of curiosity was just plucked out of you? In leading this as an experiential exercise for thousands of people, I've found that many respond to it with an "ah-ha" reaction, and it's not uncommon for me to hear gasps of shock and horror at the thought of their not having their core strength. Here are a few typical responses:

- "It would be as if I was suffocating without my creativity. Like I was gasping for breath."
- "Prudence and caution are who I am. It's what I do. How could you take that from me?"
- "To not have my curiosity in life would be like I'm barely alive."
- "Without my social intelligence, I don't know how I'd interact with people."

Strengths are portrayed and exhibited all around us, especially in the media. My colleague, Danny Wedding, and I wrote about over 1,500 movie examples that exhibit each of the character strengths of the VIA classification (Niemiec & Wedding, 2014). In Appendix G, there is a short list of character strengths concepts and corresponding movie articles of a scholarly nature. In movies, we learn about the signature strengths of each character, and often we see our own signature strengths reflected back to us. One can also turn to books, television shows, websites, blogs, and social networking outlets and notice the signature strengths of the individual(s) being depicted or doing the creating.

When reading a book, ask yourself: What are the signature strengths of the narrator and of the supporting characters? What are the signature strengths of the celebrity on television? The leaders in government or business? Wherever we look, we can spot strengths and name the signature strengths of individuals or characters. This kind of approach has received increasing attention in schools (e.g., White & Waters, 2014). Consider an Academy Award winner for Best Motion Picture, *The King's Speech* (2010). This film provides the perfect metaphor for what signature strengths are really about – being authentic and expressing our true selves. In the film, King George VI of Great Britain (Colin Firth) suffers from a severe stuttering disorder and is unable to speak clearly to help inform and assuage a panicked public at the brink of World War II. The king begins to work with a speech coach, Lionel (Geoffrey Rush), who uses a large degree of creativity, curiosity, kindness, and perspective to help the king find his voice. The "finding of one's voice" is a metaphor for the expression of our signature strengths. Lionel encourages the king to "have faith in your own voice," and one poignant interaction in which the king moves beyond stuttering and expresses himself clearly goes as follows:

King: Listen to me!

Lionel: Listen to you? By what right?

King: By divine right if you must, I am your king.

Lionel: No you're not, you told me so yourself. You didn't want it. Why should I waste my time listening?

King: Because I have a right to be heard. I have a voice! …[pause]

Lionel: Yes, you do … You have such perseverance, Bertie, you're the bravest man I know.

It is in this conversation when the king finds his voice (his core, authentic self); it is clear, forceful, and genuine. Lionel uses a variety of approaches in the role of "coach" – paradoxical intervention, confrontation, resistance, advisor, and supporter – helping the king realize his true self matters and that he can express it. In the preceding interaction, the viewer is also made aware of Lionel's perceptiveness in spotting and valuing two of the king's signature strengths – bravery and perseverance.

We can notice the signature strengths of individuals in virtually any situation. Consider the following obituary:

> Sadly, Mary herself suffered much tragedy throughout her own life, outwardly as well as inwardly. Her character strengths were determination and the will to surpass adversity. Most often her compassion for others outweighed her own illness. (Pocono Record, 2012).

These three sentences from this obituary inform us that Mary was a woman with signature strengths of perseverance and kindness – she was someone who overcame internal and external obstacles and kept going as well as emanated a sense of care for others along the way.

Snapshot 2.1. offers a summary of important points to remember regarding our signature strengths.

Snapshot 2.1. Signature Strengths

- Usually the highest strengths in a character strengths profile.
- An important part of identity, especially when the expression is authentic and natural.
- Part of the human psyche in that signature strengths are expressed through thoughts, emotions, volition, and behavior.
- Naturally emerge in communications, verbally, nonverbally, and written.
- Exhibited across media such as in books, movies, websites, blogs, social networking venues.
- Expressed across each of the domains of life.

Signature Strengths Research

Signature Strengths in New Ways

In what is currently the most cited intervention study in positive psychology, Seligman et al. (2005) conducted a double-blind, random assignment, placebo-controlled study – a gold standard study in terms of good research. The study consisted of 577 adults who were randomly assigned to one of five intervention groups or a placebo group. Here are the groups and the main intervention task for each:

- *Gratitude visit.* Write and deliver a letter of gratitude in person to someone who has been especially kind to you but who you have not properly thanked.
- *Three good things.* Write down 3 things that went well and the causal explanation each night.
- *You at your best.* Write about a time when you were at your best and reflect on the strengths displayed in the story; review this story and the strengths once per day.
- *Using signature strengths in a new way.* Take the VIA Survey, review the Top 5 strengths, and use one of these Top 5 strengths in a new and different way each day.
- *Identifying strengths.* Take the VIA Survey, review the Top 5 strengths, and use them more during the week.
- *Placebo.* Write about an early memory each night.

While there were initial benefits for each intervention group, the lasting benefits were found in two groups: the "three good things" group (also referred to as "counting blessings" or "practicing gratitude") and the "using signature strengths in a new way" group. These two groups had significant increases in happiness and decreases in depression for effects lasting up to 6 months. Not only are the effects striking, but it is similarly impressive to note that the interventions were delivered online without the live counsel of a practitioner offering support or guidance. If these interventions were paintings, they would be considered "minimalists."

The interventions lasted only 1 week; however, Seligman and colleagues (2005) found that those with the stronger outcomes decided to continue the intervention on their own for a period of time. This speaks to how intrinsically rewarding working with signature strengths can be as well as the fact that it takes time and persistence to create new habits.

The intervention of using signature strengths in new ways compared to control groups and other interventions has been replicated or partially replicated in several settings, populations, and cultures. The long-term benefits (6 months) of signature strengths use was replicated in a European sample (Gander, Proyer, Ruch, & Wyss, 2013), and benefits have been found in other countries, including Canada (Mongrain & Anselmo-Matthews, 2012), Australia (Mitchell, Stanimirovic, Klein, & Vella-Brodrick, 2009), the UK (Linley, Nielsen, Gillett, & Biswas-Diener, 2010), and China (Duan & Bu, 2017; Duan, Ho, Tang, Li, & Zhang, 2013). Another study found three interventions and placebo to have positive effects (e.g., significant elevations in happiness) with the signature strengths intervention improving the most by a substantial margin and the placebo group understandably improving the least after 6 months. The study, however, suffered from a high dropout rate in which less than a quarter of the subjects that started the study completed it (Woodworth, O'Brien-Malone, Diamond, & Schüz, 2017).

Populations ranging from youth to older adults have targeted signature strengths with success. For example, youth who worked on their signature strengths along with meaningful goal-setting experienced increases in engagement and hope (Madden et al., 2011). In a population of older adults (aged 50–79 years), the group assigned to work on using a signature strength in a new way was the most effective intervention overall as it led to *both* increases in happiness and decreases in depression. Other interventions were partially effective relative to placebo; for example, conducting a gratitude visit and recounting three good things benefited happiness levels while recounting three funny things reduced depression levels (Proyer, Gander, et al., 2014a).

Another randomly controlled study assigned individuals to (1) a group instructed to use two signature strengths, (2) a group instructed to use one signature strength and one bottom strength, or (3) a control group. Results revealed significant gains in satisfaction with life for both treatment groups compared to the control group, but there were no differences between the two treatment groups (Rust, Diessner, & Reade, 2009). Both treatment groups wrote about an event or occurrence in the past when they successfully used their character strength. Each week, they also wrote about a plan or situation for the coming week in which they could apply the strength. Similarly, in a nonrandomized study, Rashid (2004) found groups of students who worked on signature strengths or nonsignature strengths to experience significant increases in well-being compared to a control group. A study with law students found that the use of one's top strengths led to a decreased likelihood of depression and stress and an increase in satisfaction in the students (Peterson & Peterson, 2008). Another randomized trial found that an intervention group that received strengths work, gratitude, kindness, and other exercises had improved balance of positive to negative affect over time compared with a control group (Drozd, Mork, Nielsen, Raeder, & Bjørkli, 2014). In a longitudinal study, strengths use in general (not VIA character strengths) was found to be an important predictor of well-being and led to less stress and increased positive affect, vitality, and self-esteem at 3-month and 6-month follow-up (Wood, Linley, Maltby, Kashdan, & Hurling, 2011).

Strength-Based Practitioner Tip

After your client takes the VIA Survey, talk with your client about their signature strengths. Be sure to have them "confirm" the signature strengths they choose to focus on. While the VIA Survey does well at identifying top strengths in individuals, it should not be considered the "final answer" for clients. Rather, it is the client who offers the confirmation as to whether their highest strengths are indeed essential and authentic to who they are, energizing and natural to use, and expressed widely across settings. A popular practitioner suggestion is to

> remind clients that "the results don't trump life" – a client who perceives they are living a
> life of deep kindness and perseverance should have those observations given special atten-
> tion even if they do not show up high on the VIA Survey.

Signature Strengths Across Contexts

Signature strengths interventions have been successfully applied in a variety of psychological settings with positive effects; for example, an inpatient unit for people with depression/suici-dality (Huffman et al., 2014), a neuropsychology unit for people with traumatic brain injury (Andrewes, Walker, & O'Neill, 2014), an outpatient setting for adults with psychosis (Riches, Schrank, Rashid, & Slade, 2016), a Veterans Administration rehabilitation, where veterans car-ried around a prompt to remind them to use their signature strengths (Kobau et al., 2011), and in a career counseling context (Littman-Ovadia, Lazar-Butbul, & Benjamin, 2014). In the latter study, strengths-based career counseling was compared with conventional career counseling and both client groups had an increase in daily strengths use but only the former had enhanced self-esteem. At 3-month follow-up, the strengths-based career counseling group had a higher rate of employment (81%) than the conventional career counseling group (60%).

Positive psychotherapy is an approach to therapy that focuses on building positive emotions, strengths, and meaning in clients' lives in order to promote happiness. Preliminary trials have found it to be superior to treatment as usual for depression (Rashid & Anjum, 2008; Seligman, Rashid, & Parks, 2006). Tayyab Rashid has noted that well over 50% of positive psychotherapy revolves around character strengths use and practice (Rashid, personal communication, 2011). Sessions focus on general character strength interventions (e.g., two sessions on identifying and cultivating signature strengths; two sessions on "family tree of strengths" and "gift of time" to promote meaning), specific strengths (e.g., a session on forgiveness; a session on gratitude), and promoting a core positive psychology theme (e.g., love to cultivate engagement; hope to cultivate pleasure).

Successful outcomes associated with a focus on strengths (not character strengths) have also been found in Minhas (2010) and Cox (2006); the latter finding that a strength-based approach (when also endorsed and practiced by the therapist) led to a reduction in scores for various social and emotional problem behaviors.

Character strengths interventions are frequently integrated into broader programs that focus on building well-being, resilience, achievement, and other areas within the positive psychol-ogy field. Most often, the approach taken in these programs is to help participants identify their signature strengths and then take action in some way with these strengths. These pro-grams have spanned a number of settings including education, business, and the military. Al-though the results of these programmatic initiatives are very encouraging and, in some cases, groundbreaking and highly influential, researchers usually do not separate out the contribution made by signature strengths and other character strengths components from the other positive psychology interventions. Despite signature strengths often being described as the "core" of many of these programs, questions remain such as: What is the most crucial element in these comprehensive programs? How much value-add do the character strengths components bring to these programs?

What follows are common domains where character strengths work, especially signature strengths work, is being applied. Research findings are offered here and peppered throughout the book.

Business

The organizational/workplace context has been a particularly robust domain of study for the science of character (see Mayerson, 2015). Claudia Harzer and Willibald Ruch have conducted a number of studies in the workplace. They found that workers who used four or more of their signature strengths at work had more positive work experiences and work-as-a-calling than those who used less than four strengths (Harzer & Ruch, 2012) and that signature strengths are connected with positive work experiences, irrespective of which strengths are highest (Harzer & Ruch, 2013). In other studies, they found character strengths were connected with job performance (Harzer & Ruch, 2014) and with coping with stress (Harzer & Ruch, 2015). Finally, in an intervention study, they discovered that the alignment of employees' signature strengths with their job tasks led to increases in work-as-a-calling (Harzer & Ruch, 2016).

A study of supervisory support found that employees who received supervisor support (but not colleague support) increased their strengths use the following day (Lavy, Littman-Ovadia, & Boiman-Meshita, 2016). These same researchers published another study in the workplace finding that the use of all kinds of strengths (signature strengths, happiness strengths, lower strengths) were associated with positive outcomes. For example, signature strengths were the biggest contributor to work performance, organizational citizenship behavior, and lower counterproductive work behavior; happiness strengths were the biggest contributor to work meaningfulness, engagement, and job satisfaction (Littman-Ovadia, Lavy, & Boiman-Meshita, 2016). A qualitative study examined the use of character strengths by women in the workplace and found that in all cases strengths led to a virtuous circle in which the strengths use helped them overcome obstacles that had impeded strengths use (Elston & Boniwell, 2011). All subjects derived unique value from using character strengths at work. Another study of workers found that using signature strengths in new ways combined with a 10-minute structured debriefing was beneficial for increasing strengths use and the number of goals set compared to a group that only used signature strengths in new ways (Butina, 2016).

Organizations are recommended to find ways to help employees use their strengths more often at work as strengths use in general (not using the VIA Survey) has been linked with employee levels of self-efficacy and proactive behavior (van Woerkom, Oerlemans, & Bakker, 2016), positive affect and psychological capital (Meyers & van Woerkom, 2016), and reduced absenteeism (van Woerkom, Bakker, & Nishii, 2016). The climate of an organization can also support employees to use their strengths. In a study of 442 employees across 39 departments in eight organizations, a strengths-based psychological climate was linked with positive affect and work performance (van Woerkom & Meyers, 2014). The Gallup Organization has focused its research on strengths in the workplace and found that the two most important predictors of employee retention and satisfaction are: (1) reporting the use of top strengths at work and (2) reporting that an immediate supervisor recognizes one's top strengths. Sadly, Gallup has found that only about 20% of employees think their supervisors know their strengths and about a third of employees say they have an opportunity to do what they do best every day. When an organization's leadership does not focus on the individuals' strengths, the chances of an employee being engaged are 9%; however, when the leadership focuses on the employees' strengths, the odds increase to 73% (for examples and details, see Asplund et al., 2007; Clifton & Harter, 2003; Hodges & Clifton, 2004).

Education

Character strengths have not only been found to be an important source of well-being among students (Gillham et al., 2011), they have also been a major focus in positive education programs around the globe. In a seminal article arguing for character strengths integration in education, Linkins, Niemiec, Gillham, and Mayerson (2015) outline why traditional character education approaches in the US and other countries should shift from monolithic and one-size-fits-all approaches (the school authority chooses a handful of strengths for all students to build up) to individualized approaches that work with students' unique signature strengths.

While character strengths play an important role for creating positive well-being (Oppenheimer, Fialkov, Ecker, & Portnoy, 2014) and positive classroom outcomes (Weber & Ruch, 2012b; Weber et al., 2016), character strengths have been woven into entire schools, involving staff, teachers, students, and program leaders. Some programs deploy character strengths as the sole focus (see Fox Eades, 2008; Proctor & Fox Eades 2011), as well as a major focus (see Yeager, Fisher, & Shearon, 2011). Strengths Gym, created by Carmel Proctor and Jennifer Fox Eades, is an example of a character strengths-based positive psychology intervention program in which children and adolescents participate in numerous activities involving character strengths applied directly to the students and integrated into school curriculum. One study evaluated the impact of Strengths Gym on adolescents and found that adolescents who participated in the strengths exercises had significantly higher life satisfaction than those adolescents who did not participate (Proctor et al., 2011). In a Chinese educational context, a strengths training intervention (involving noticing when, where, and how top strengths are used and writing about this) was found to be effective in boosting life satisfaction in the short- and long-run. The researchers ruled out a placebo effect by having some participants informed of the purpose of the study and some not, and knowing/not knowing the purpose had no long-term effect on life satisfaction (Duan et al., 2013).

Positive education programs have also been found to increase academic scores, social skills, and students' enjoyment and engagement in school as well as improve character strengths such as curiosity, love of learning, and creativity (Seligman, Ernst, Gillham, Reivich, & Linkins, 2009). Preliminary results from a 3-year follow-up of a positive education program (Gillham, 2011) showed positive education had an impact on engagement and achievement, but not subjective well-being. Extensive positive education programs have been implemented at a number of schools, including Geelong Grammar School and St. Peter's College, both prestigious private schools in Australia, and have resulted in major volumes outlining the trainings, creative use of character strengths, and other methods of implementing positive psychology (see Norrish, 2015, and White & Murray, 2015, respectively). The work on character strengths is typically viewed as the backbone of this course-work, usually taught in the first session, and involves identifying signature strengths, writing narratives about times at one's best, interviewing family members about strengths, learning how to use strengths to overcome challenges, developing lower strengths, and identifying teachers and other leaders on campus whom students believe are paragons of particular strengths. Character strengths work is further embedded into the curriculum and activities throughout the school, from identifying strengths in classic literature (e.g., *Death of a Salesman*, *Macbeth*, and *Metamorphosis*) to infusing strengths in athletics. White and Waters (2014) describe the approach at St. Peter's College and detail examples of five initiatives in which character strengths were woven throughout the areas of sport, student leadership, counseling, and English curriculum.

Exciting work is on the horizon in the public-school domain as well. The VIA Institute has partnered with the Mayerson Academy, which has begun integrating character strengths programming into over 40 public schools (Bates-Krakoff, McGrath, Graves, & Ochs, 2016), in the Cincinnati, Ohio region, involving student and teacher trainings, gamified learning online through Happify, and teacher coaching. Evaluation of this programming, referred to as Thriving Learning Communities shows promising early results, such as increases in social-emotional learning (SEL) competencies, self-awareness around strengths, capacity to enjoy school, and lower absentee and disciplinary rates and higher GPAs (Jillian Darwish, personal conversation, September 26, 2016).

Military

Character strengths have been deliberately assessed and/or used in numerous military forces across the globe, including Norway, Sweden, Argentina, Australia, and India, to name a few (see Banth & Singh, 2011; Consentino & Castro, 2012; Gayton & Kehoe, 2015; Matthews, Eid, Kelly, Bailey, & Peterson, 2006). The US Army is an example of an organization that has systematically embedded character strengths as a core component of their positive psychology and resilience training, called the Comprehensive Soldier Fitness Program (Cornum, Matthews, & Seligman, 2011; Reivich, Seligman, & McBride, 2011). Character strengths are among the core areas assessed in the Global Assessment Tool implemented in this program (Peterson, Park, & Castro, 2011; Vie, Scheier, Lester, & Seligman, 2016). One of the core modules of the training program includes the identification of signature strengths, the practice of identifying strengths in others, and the practice of using both individual and team strengths to overcome a challenge or reach a goal. After taking the VIA Survey, the soldiers are asked to explore the following questions (Reivich et al., 2011):

- What did you learn about yourself?
- Which strengths have you developed through your service in the military?
- How do your strengths contribute to your completing a mission and reaching your goals?
- How are you using your strengths to build strong relationships?
- What are the shadow sides of your strengths, and how can you minimize these?

The soldiers then engage in individual and team exercises involving review of individual and team experiences with overcoming obstacles and reaching successes, review of case studies, writing "strength in challenges" stories, and completing a team mission requiring the use of team character strengths.

Military researchers have also written about the benefits of labeling character strengths such as courage (Hannah, Sweeney, & Lester, 2007) and about the importance of "Big-C" character in leadership (Hannah & Jennings, 2013).

Other Domains and Populations

Character strengths matter in a myriad of contexts and with a variety of populations. Character strengths/signature strengths are being studied and applied in assessing and/or treating youth and adults with various disabilities. Some of these include youth with intellectual/developmental disabilities (Biggs & Carter, 2015; Carter et al., 2015; Shogren, Wehmeyer, Lang, & Niemiec, 2017; Shogren, Wehmeyer, & Niemiec, 2017), vocational interests in adolescents (Proyer, Sidler, Weber, & Ruch, 2012), parents of children with disabilities (Fung et al., 2011; Woodard, 2009), adults with intellectual/developmental disabilities (Samson & Antonelli, 2013; Tomasulo, 2014), adults with physical disabilities (Chan, Chan, Ditchman, Phillips, & Chou, 2013), people with dyslexia (Kannangara, 2015; Kannangara, Griffiths, Carson, & Munasinghe, 2015), and adults with autism without an intellectual disability (Kirchner, Ruch, & Dziobek, 2016). The practical application of the research and practice of character strengths has been outlined with suggested adaptations for people with intellectual/developmental disabilities (Niemiec, Shogren, & Wehmeyer, 2017).

Character strengths have been applied in examining various dimensions of physical health, including healthy eating, physical fitness, personal hygiene, substance avoidance, and living an active way of life (Proyer, Gander, Wellenzohn, & Ruch, 2013). In randomized controlled trials involving thousands of girls in poverty in India, girls who received a curriculum which incorporated character strengths (identification and use of signature strengths and concrete examples of other strengths) exhibited significantly greater physical health and psychosocial health benefits in comparison to those girls who received a similar curriculum which did not include character strengths and girls who did not receive any curriculum at all (controls) (Leventhal et al., 2015, 2016). Qualitative analyses also revealed and explained how girls perceived that building character strengths helped them to improve their school engagement and to avoid child marriage, gender-based violence and harassment, and school dropout (DeMaria, Andrew, & Leventhal, 2016). A randomized-controlled trial with seriously ill children found that a "granting a wish" intervention reduced nausea and increased life satisfaction, positive emotions, and strengths, compared to a control group (Chaves, Vazquez, & Hervas, 2016). In another study, these researchers found that increases in character strengths (gratitude and love) and benefit-finding predicted life satisfaction over time in children with a life-threatening illness (Chaves, Hervas, García, & Vasquez, 2016).

In terms of other unique populations examined, there have been many studies examining signature strengths and/or character strengths dynamics, including faculty (McGovern & Miller, 2008), teachers (Chan, 2009; Gradisek, 2012), abuse survivors (Moore, 2011), homeless people (Tweed, Biswas-Diener, & Lehman, 2012), addictions (Krentzman, 2013; Logan, Kilmer, & Marlatt, 2010), clinical treatment with different populations (Smith & Barros-Gomes, 2015), very young children through parent's descriptions (Park & Peterson, 2006c), musicians (Güsewell & Ruch, 2015), call center employees (Moradi, Nima, Ricciardi, Archer, & Garcia, 2014), couples (Goddard, Olson, Galovan, Schramm, & Marshall, 2016; Guo, Wang, & Liu, 2015), leisure experiences (Coghlan & Filo, 2016), service leadership (Shek & Yu, 2015), adults who practice their religion (Berthold & Ruch, 2014), in relation to outcomes of a sport tournament (Proyer, Gander, Wellenzohn, & Ruch, 2014b), parents as related to children's school adjustment (Shoshani & Ilanit Aviv, 2012), the character strengths desired in adolescent romantic partners (Weber & Ruch, 2012a), and law students (Kern & Bowling, 2015), to name a couple handfuls.

Strength-Based Practitioner Tip

Make a signature strengths plan and test progress! Do the following for yourself first, then apply it with a client. Choose one of your signature strengths and use it in a new way each day for 1 week. Test your progress by giving yourself (and your clients) a pretest and posttest with a measure of happiness. With psychotherapy clients, I routinely give measures such as the Satisfaction with Life Scale (Diener, Emmons, Larsen, & Griffin, 1985), the Flourishing Scale (Diener et al., 2009), and the Beck Depression Inventory (Beck, Ward, & Mendelson, 1961) as a baseline and then following an intervention or a short time, I administered the same test again. Clients were always interested in learning if they had grown, declined, or stayed stable.

Amplify a Top Strength or Remediate a Weakness?

The field of psychology has spent over a century focusing on remediating deficits, targeting problems, and helping others to alleviate suffering. This approach of "fixing" what is wrong has pervaded many disciplines, including business, education, and healthcare. Therefore, asking a client, student, or employee to spend time thinking about their strengths is a substantial shift. It is a question that leaves the recipient double-checking: Are you sure? You don't want me to talk about my latest stressor or difficulty? Despite decades of research successes supporting the deficit-based approaches used in cognitive-behavior therapy (Beck, Rush, Shaw, & Emery, 1979), Cheavens and colleagues (2012) decided to put the notion of "deficits versus strengths" to the test. They randomly assigned adults with serious depression (major depressive disorder) to either trained therapists who targeted their unique "CBT strengths" or to trained therapists who targeted their unique "CBT weaknesses" (Top 2 strengths or Bottom 2 weaknesses, respectively). The areas of strength or weaknesses were assessed spanning four areas – behavioral skills, cognitive skills, interpersonal skills, and mindfulness skills – all important for depression management. The results showed that it was the strengths group that had faster changes in depression symptoms and maintained this improvement for the 16 weeks of treatment. Compared to the weakness group, the strengths group had greater and more lasting improvements. This study, although needing replication, challenges conventional wisdom around remediating problems and deficits. It challenges us to shift our approach: to target and enhance what is best in the client.

This approach of targeting a client's strengths is referred in the Cheavens study as "capitalization," in other words, capitalizing on what is already working. A study by researchers in the Netherlands also found benefit from the capitalization model, with subjects focusing on strengths development demonstrating stronger increases in personal growth than those focusing on deficiencies (Meyers, van Woerkom, de Reuver, Bakk, & Oberski, 2015). The strengths development group involved participants gathering feedback from five to seven people about their strengths (referred to as the reflected best self exercise; Spreitzer, Stephens, Sweetman, 2009) and reflected on their strengths and discussed these in a small group. In addition, they designed a poster highlighting how they use their strengths in their daily life, compared their strength profiles to job vacancy profiles, considered the fit between the strengths and the job function, and developed a 30-second elevator pitch emphasizing their strengths for an imagined job. In another study, employees' perceived organizational support for strengths use, and strengths use behavior were each significantly correlated with self-ratings and with manager ratings of job performance, while perceived organizational support for deficit correction and deficit correction behavior were unrelated to performance (van Woerkom, Mostert et al., 2016).

These studies relate to one of the most common questions posed by practitioners who are learning about character strengths: Should attention be given to signature strengths or to lower strengths? Although the lower strengths in clients' character strengths profiles are not viewed as weaknesses, the wisdom of these studies on capitalizing on one's best qualities can be heeded. This is not to say that there's no value working on lower strengths as research has offered some support for that as well (e.g., Rust et al., 2009). One study has taken a closer look at some of the differences among those who target top strengths versus bottom strengths. This randomized, controlled trial divided participants into three groups: adults who targeted their Top 5 strengths, adults who targeted their Bottom 5 strengths, and a placebo group. The two intervention groups showed benefits to happiness for up to 3 months and depression benefits as well. Those participants with initially higher strength levels tended to benefit more from working on lower strengths, while those initially lower in strengths levels tended to benefit more from working on higher strengths (Proyer, Gander, Wellenzohn, & Ruch, 2015).

Currently, it can be concluded from the research that working on any strength is beneficial as the individual is taking positive action to improve themselves. Although it has not been closely studied, it is reasonable to believe that working on signature strengths will be superior to working on lower strengths in the *long-run* as top strengths are more self-reinforcing and energizing and lead the individual to feel more authentic than attempting to build up a strength that might lead to energy depletion or might not be as internally motivating.

Why and How Do Signature Strengths Work?

A natural next question after determining the success of a practice is to attain a better understanding of the reasons why the practice was successful. In practical terms, it is probably obvious to most of us that if a person is unable to express their signature strengths they will soon feel a sense of emptiness (e.g., Escandón, Martinez, & Flaskerud, 2016), but it's important to understand this question from a scientific perspective as well. What are the mechanisms of action that help to explain the success of the intervention? Alex Linley and his team took on such an investigation and found initial evidence to support a number of reasons why using signature strengths is connected with well-being (Linley et al., 2010). They found that signature strengths use relates to progress on one's goals and with satisfying one's basic psychological needs for autonomy, relatedness, and competence, i.e., the core elements of self-determination theory (Deci & Ryan, 2000). This makes good, practical sense: Signature strengths come naturally to us; they are an expression of who we are. Therefore, when we allow that core part of ourselves to be expressed, we are meeting basic human needs that have to do with making connections in our relationships and accomplishing as much as we can in this life. Success with our goals naturally flows from this. As a result, we experience greater happiness. This explanation, however, is only one part of the explanation.

In another study, the use of signature strengths elevates individuals' "harmonious passion," which refers to individuals doing activities that are freely chosen without constraints, are highly important, and a part of the individual's identity. Harmonious passion then led to higher well-being (Forest et al., 2012). Self-esteem has been another mechanism that links strengths use and life satisfaction (Douglass & Duffy, 2015).

Quinlan, Swain, and Vella-Brodrick (2011) suggest a number of other mechanisms by which character strengths might influence well-being. They note the distinction of effects that are "between us" (i.e., social) and those that are "within us" (i.e., personal) and hypothesize the following mechanisms:

- Strengths increase our effort and perseverance thereby boosting well-being (Dweck, 1986).
- Strengths increase relationship satisfaction (Gable, Reis, Impett, & Asher, 2004).
- Strengths help individuals overcome hedonic adaptation (Diener, Lucas, & Scollon, 2006).

Self-concordance is another explanation or mechanism at play. Scientists have found there are many benefits to setting and pursuing goals and making progress toward goals (Miller & Frisch, 2009; Sheldon & Elliot, 1999; Sheldon & Houser-Marko, 2001). More specifically, when we set a goal that is aligned with our values and interests, this is called having goals that are self-concordant. Research shows we experience greater happiness when we reach a self-concordant goal rather than when we reach a goal that is not consistent with who we are (Sheldon & Kasser, 1998). We clearly value our signature strengths and feel energy and enjoyment when we can express them, therefore aligning goals and strengths is a way to be more successful in creating the life you want to live.

In another study that found significant benefits for the use of signature strengths in new ways over standard placebo, Mongrain and Anselmo-Matthews (2012) suggest that the individual's access of positive, self-relevant information might be the mechanism that explains the benefit of this intervention. Wellenzohn, Proyer, and Ruch (2016b) looked at the character strength of humor in an intervention study that showed a boost to happiness and a decrease in depression, and studied some different mechanisms: They found there was an attentional shift towards the positive for interventions geared toward the present or future and there was the savoring of positive emotions for interventions geared toward the past or present.

In the organizational context, positive affect was found as a mediator explaining the connection between signature strengths use and a variety of workplace outcomes such as work engagement, meaning, job satisfaction, job performance, organizational citizenship behavior, and counterproductive work behaviors (Littman-Ovadia et al., 2016). In another work study, positive affect was found to be a mediator for strengths use and work well-being (Meyers & van Woerkom, 2016). Similarly, in another study, positive emotions and engagement explained the connection between character strengths use at work and productivity, organizational citizenship behavior, and job satisfaction (Lavy & Littman-Ovadia, 2016). This mechanism of positive affect as well as other previously discussed mechanisms, such as access to internal positive qualities and goal-setting, have strong links with the broaden-and-build theory of Barbara Fredrickson (2001), as originally applied to positive emotions. This theory states that positive emotions broaden a repertoire of action potentials in the present and build resources for the individual in the future. This process creates an upward spiral of well-being (Fredrickson & Joiner, 2012). Perhaps character strengths, especially if viewed from the perspective of traits being density distributions of emotional states (Fleeson, 2001), can be viewed from the vantage point of this broaden-and-build theory. This would mean that strengths are connected to well-being because they broaden the possibilities for optimal action in the moment and simultaneously build up our personal resources for later action.

In a study examining the relationships (moderators) of signature strengths use, signature strengths level, life calling, and life satisfaction, individuals low in calling and high in signature strengths levels had the strongest connection between signature strengths use and life satisfaction (Allan & Duffy, 2013). A key finding in this study was that the use of signature strengths is particularly important for those low in meaning and purpose.

In what is the longest-running positive psychology intervention study, Proyer, Wellenzohn, et al. (2014) examined the connection between various positive interventions (e.g., signature strengths in new ways, three good things) and the type of intervention fit with the person in predicting happiness/depression. They wanted to examine under what conditions signature strengths and other positive interventions work best in the long run. Building on the person–activity fit concept of Lyubomirsky and Layous (2013), Proyer and colleagues found the following four elements to be particularly important as predictors of happiness and/or depression 3.5 years after the intervention:

- *Continued practice.* Voluntary continuation of practice above and beyond the designated time frame (as found serendipitously in Seligman et al., 2005). Continued practice helps to facilitate the development of a habit (Lyubomirksy, Sheldon, & Schkade, 2005).
- *Effort.* How people work with the intervention, such as completing more or less of the instructed time.
- *Preference.* Whether or not people like or perceive benefit from the intervention (an important variable as found in a study of preferences by Schueller, 2010).
- *Early reactivity.* How people react to the intervention. Do they show a quick response, such as an immediate increase in positive emotions?

They found that the combination of these four indicators was most successful in predicting happiness and depression in the long-run. They explained that "the way people *think* about positive psychology interventions, the way they *work* with them, and the way they *react* to them play a role in predicting well-being at a later point in time" (Proyer, Wellenzohn, et al., 2014, p. 14). It is these elements of the fit between the person and intervention that contribute to the long-term benefits.

As is probably clear, there are a number of factors that explain the link between character strengths and well-being. Each of these gives us further explanations why strengths use, especially signature strengths use, is a successful intervention. As the mechanisms become more clearly understood, it is likely the findings will be aligned with the natural tendency that human beings have to develop their core capacities, use their natural potentials, and become all they can be (Buckingham & Clifton, 2001; Linley & Harrington, 2006). Linley and Harrington (2006), in their arguments promoting strengths-based coaching, summarize the substantial historical base on which strengths-based approaches rest:

> And most fundamentally, a strengths-based approach is solidly grounded in established learning and psychological approaches that have a lineage back to Aristotle, through Carl Jung, Karen Horney, and Carl Rogers, to the modern coaching approaches of Whitmore and Gallwey, integrating finally with the definition of coaching psychology that now underpins the further development and direction of this new discipline (p. 42).

Key Issues in Working With Signature Strengths

This section delves into important topics practitioners should closely consider that relate to signature strengths expression, and begins to dip into the "how" of working with signature strengths. There are many ways to work with character strengths, as you will read about in each chapter of this book. This section highlights some core ideas to help you get started as you begin to explore your own signature strengths and those of your clients.

Types of Strengths Blindness

In order to deepen one's understanding and appreciation of signature strengths, it's important to first consider the concept and problem of strengths blindness. Snapshot 2.2. gives a summary of important reminders about character strengths blindness. Niemiec (2014a) has offered four categories of character strengths blindness. These are presented in order of the degree of unawareness, starting with what is most likely to represent the least aware.

1. General Unawareness of Strengths

This reflects a pervasive lack of self-awareness or disconnection with who one is (identity). Many people find it difficult to recognize their strengths (Linley & Harrington, 2006). It's not uncommon to encounter individuals who are stunned like a deer in the headlights when asked what their strengths are at a job interview or in the first session of a coaching or psychotherapy encounter. Some of these individuals are unreflective and lack psychological mindedness, while others have simply never given the topic of "their strengths" much thought. Personally, I continue to feel a wave a sadness when I ask a client what their strengths are and they say: "I don't know" or "I don't have any," and they look down at their shoes. Unfortunately, this has been a fairly common response.

2. Disconnect With Meaning

Survey research has found that only one third of people have a meaningful awareness of their strengths (Linley, 2008), although there is reason to believe this number is increasing in the context of work (McQuaid & VIA Institute on Character, 2015). Some individuals offer a light response to the general question of naming their best strengths, but their answer is not a substantive one. Responses are vague (e.g., "I have good qualities") or confuse character strengths with other strength domains such as interest (e.g., "I like listening to music") and talent/skill (e.g., "I'm good at baseball"). A person may say they perform better than the average person at recreational baseball, however, it's character that makes the connection with meaning and substance. In this example, it is the strengths of perseverance, teamwork, and self-regulation on the baseball field that start to tell us something about this individual's strengths.

3. Seeing Strengths as Ordinary Rather Than Extraordinary

Sometimes individuals minimize or downplay their strengths, or, at best, are matter-of-fact about their having strengths (Biswas-Diener et al., 2011). In these cases, the individual takes the VIA Survey and reacts with a response of "Yeah, I already knew that, no big deal." This kind of indifference is a red flag for strengths blindness. It might be true that the person would have guessed their highest strengths, but that's far from the point. It's likely the individual is not appreciating that they have engaged in something that has the potential to be a springboard for many positive outcomes, including meeting their own personal goals. Instead of taking a curious, growth mindset, they are approaching themselves with a fixed mindset. They are glossing over their core traits, not actively drawing connections with strengths and their experiences, not engaging in a strengths conversation in the moment, and not actively brainstorming ways to grow with strengths expression.

Strengths underuse is a phenomenon that likely underpins each of the three categories above. I believe that all people underuse their strengths from time to time. In other words, 100% of us have blind spots in regard to our character strengths self-knowledge. There are always new approaches, tweaks, uses, and perspectives that can be taken when it comes to strengths use, especially if one is embodying a growth mindset with one's signature strengths (Dweck, 2006). A given individual can be blind to the use of one of their strengths in a particular context or situation, blind to how a strength might be present but in disguise, or unaware of how their strength presents in daily routines, when stressors arise or when working toward a particular goal. In this vein, it's probably fair to say that most people could benefit from greater mindfulness when understanding and applying their character strengths.

4. Strengths Overuse

The overuse of character strengths is a fourth and special type of blindness. Strengths overuse occurs when an individual puts forth their strength(s) too strongly in a particular situation. A person might express so much curiosity that they become nosy or so much leadership that they appear controlling. Often, strengths overuse has an impact on relationships and the individual who is doing the overusing is unaware (i.e., blind) to this impact or at least the extent of the impact. At other times, the individual might be blind as to what to do about their heavy exertion of prudence at work or their overuse of humility that pushes their individuality to the side. Strengths underuse and overuse examples and strategies for management are discussed in greater detail in Chapter 4.

One way to work with each of the types of strengths blindness is to integrate mindfulness and character strengths. The cultivation of mindfulness to improve character strength use is referred to as "mindful strengths use" and the use of character strengths to bolster a mindfulness practice is referred to as "strong mindfulness" (Niemiec, 2012; Niemiec, Rashid, & Spinella, 2012). A manualized program called mindfulness-based strengths practice (MBSP) for integrating and enhancing both phenomena has shown promising results (Ivtzan, Niemiec, & Briscoe, 2016; Niemiec, 2014a; Niemiec & Lissing, 2016).

The takeaway from this section is that strengths blindness is pervasive. Here's a personal example: One of my children is having some developmental delays and was well-behind his peers in crawling and walking. He had gone to a variety of specialists and early intervention practitioners to assist him. I spent many hours speaking with these helpers, with family members, and others about what he should be doing and the strategies to getting there. I routinely expressed concern about the developmental delays and the potential impact on his brain development and social relationships. In one of my discussions with a daycare worker about my agenda for the staff to maintain a variety of strategies to try to get him to crawl, she made a comment: "He is scooting all over the place. He's getting to where he needs to go. Despite not crawling, he is scooting really well! He sees a toy or a group of kids on the other side of the room that he wants to get to, and so he scoots there." That's when it hit me. My son was already expressing several strengths and meeting developmental needs relating to exploring, curiosity, and cause-effect mobility going from point A to point B. I had been missing – or at least not appreciating – this fact, which was right under my nose! I was entrenched in a more deficit-minded approach, spending my time and resources focusing on what he wasn't doing or should be doing rather than studying and celebrating what he was doing (and doing quite well). His scooting – although far less traditional from what most kids do – was something to build upon. This conversation shifted me immediately to a mode of savoring. I savored his scooting, knowing that he would soon surpass this interesting and wonderful stage. I set up opportunities for him to practice scooting which filled me with joy (and my phone with videos). I did not ignore the problem-based aspects, instead I built upon them; rather than walls, the problems became stepping stones. This worker helped me break my strengths blindness in that situation.

Snapshot 2.2. Important Reminders About Strengths Blindness

- We need both a problem focus and a strengths focus, not one or the other. And it's instructive to see how problems can be stepping stones rather than walls.
- We are constantly popping back and forth between these two processes (especially those who are strengths-based).
- We will forget or neglect strengths countless more times in our life. Knowing this builds humility.
- A strengths-based approach is not static. It is not permanent. It is a process to engage in and return to when we forget.
- Strength blindness is complex, pervasive, and subtle.
- Mindfulness and savoring help break through the subtleties of strengths blindness.
- People who are strengths-based are collecting moments of mindfulness and strengths. As this "collection" builds, so does personal and relational meaning.
- Mindful awareness of strengths is temporary. There are other blind spots persistently operating, waiting for the light of mindfulness and strengths.
- We need honest feedback and support from others to help break through the varieties of strength blindness.
- We can create habits of virtue and build upon our strengths. And we are always moving toward this thing called a "strengths-based approach." If you think "I've got it!" or "I've figured it out," you are demonstrating, ironically, strengths blindness.

The Strengths Paradox

There exists an interesting paradox in strengths-based work. On the one hand, individuals tend to not be very tuned in to their best qualities much of the time. So strengths are easily unattended to, forgotten about, and treated as ordinary. On the other hand, when individuals are prompted to explore their best qualities, they readily find strengths in their stories and in conversations with others. In general, character strengths are easy to talk about and identify with and even the complexities around strengths (e.g., see Chapter 5) are readily understood, if individuals are given the opportunity. This was shown in early research exploring VIA character strengths with high school students (Steen, Kachorek, & Peterson, 2003). Even very young children can readily understand each of the 24 strengths when time is taken to teach them (Fox Eades, 2008). And, practitioners who lead strengths discussions with clients – even those very depressed or disengaged – find that clients are interested and engaged. It is as if a new door has opened allowing the client to see things in a new way.

I call this disconnect between unawareness of strengths and high potential for strengths use "the strengths paradox." Practitioners can learn to use the strengths paradox to their advantage. Our signature strengths seem to be largely preconscious (to steal a term from Freud over a century ago). It is as if our signature strengths and these strengths conversations are waiting to be tapped into from just below conscious awareness. This means that there is great potential for every client to break through their blind spots, move below the surface of their consciousness, and unleash a positive quality.

I've referred to signature strengths as a real "game changer," especially when working with clients (Niemiec, 2014a). Signature strengths help practitioners close the gap on the strengths paradox. In every sporting event, there is often a moment when the momentum shifts to one team's favor, rallying the energy, teamwork, and leadership, and propelling that team to victory. It might be a fiery shout by a player, a defensive steal, an energizing slam dunk, or a diving effort. Signature strengths can be that game changer with clients. Even the savviest of clients have blind spots. Then, when strengths are brought to their attention, there is often a reaction of "Oh yes, of course!"

Beyond Character Strengths Awareness

There is virtually no disagreement among any of the leaders in strengths psychology and strengths coaching that knowing one's top strengths is important and necessary for well-being (Biswas-Diener et al., 2011; Buckingham & Clifton, 2001; Cooperrider & Whitney, 2005; Dutro, 2003; Forster, 2009; Kauffman, Silberman, & Sharpley, 2008; Linley, 2008; Lopez, 2008; Madden et al., 2011; Niemiec, 2012; Peterson, 2006a; Proctor & Fox Eades, 2011; Rashid, 2009; Rath, 2007; Seligman et al., 2005). And, it is noteworthy that some have reported benefits from simply identifying one's character strengths with the VIA Survey as being beneficial in and of itself, across a range of populations (e.g., Kobau et al., 2011; Seligman et al., 2005; Sims, Barker, Price, & Fornells-Ambrojo, 2015). However, knowing one's strengths is probably necessary but not sufficient for particularly important outcomes, such as human flourishing. It is the expression of character strengths that appears to bring about substantive benefits. And, it is becoming clearer that character strengths can be deliberately developed (e.g., Biswas-Diener et al., 2011; Louis, 2011; Seligman et al., 2005).

Research has supported the important benefits of character strengths use as distinct from only awareness (Littman-Ovadia & Steger, 2010). This became clearer in a study I mentioned earlier – with a representative sample of New Zealand workers by Lucy Hone and colleagues (2015), who examined strengths awareness, strengths use, and flourishing levels. These researchers found that workers who were highly aware of their strengths were nine times more likely to flourish than those who were not aware of their strengths, but those who reported a high amount of strengths use were eighteen times more likely to flourish than those who reported a very low amount of strengths use. While these numbers do not mean strengths awareness or strengths use causes flourishing at these rates, it is compelling to see the distinctions between not only strengths awareness and strengths unawareness but also between strengths awareness and strengths use.

Many people who take the VIA Survey realize this as they look at their character strengths profile and in gathering some self-awareness of their strengths look to the practical utility and ask about strengths use, saying: "Okay, I took the VIA Survey, now what do I do?"

Many practitioners fall into the trap of a simplistic approach to strengths work and jump immediately from "identify" to "use" which is generally insufficient as an approach (Biswas-Diener et al., 2011). Niemiec (2013) has noted there is a basic but crucial step such practitioners miss that occurs after identifying strengths and prior to setting up a plan of action – helping the client explore their strengths. This Aware-Explore-Apply model is discussed in detail in Chapter 3.

While there are a number of relevant principles to keep in mind (see Chapter 1 and Chapter 3), two general concepts are crucial when working with character strengths: (a) prioritizing the signature strengths and (b) that all 24 strengths matter. Helping a client to focus on, fine-tune, and master their signature strengths in various settings is likely to give the client the most benefit and most amount of traction in reaching their goals. At the same time, clients need to be reminded that they have many strengths that can be developed and deployed. For a client new to the strengths world or new to putting on "strengths goggles," it can be intimidating – if not impossible – to attempt to focus or build up all 24. Therefore, it's typically best to start where they get energized and excited and can naturally express themselves (signature strengths) and then go from there. That said, many people throughout time have gone systematically through the major virtues or strengths attempting to build them up one-by-one. The 18th century American statesman Benjamin Franklin (1962) wrote about how he tracked, journaled, discussed, and attempted to improve various virtues, focusing on a different virtue each week.

People sometimes find it surprisingly challenging to come up with new ways to use one of their signature strengths. This is because we are not well-practiced at using our strengths, and when we do use them, we do it without much awareness. For example, have you paid much attention to your use of self-regulation as you put on your clothes? Your level of prudence or kindness while driving? Your humility while at a team meeting?

How to Use Signature Strengths in New Ways

As the research around using signature strengths in new ways is robust and continuing to expand, practitioners and clients are often eager to take action with it. Therefore, I offer here four strategies: simple behaviors, anchoring, context mapping, and holistic mapping.

These practical tips, some of which I mention in *Character Strengths Matter* (Polly & Britton, 2015), will help you and your clients expand upon signature strengths and will make this exercise more personal, easy to use, and even refreshing. Readers might also wish to return to Table 1.2 in Chapter 1 to review the examples of "little" everyday strengths use I offered for each of the 24.

Simple Behaviors

To get jump-started, many practitioners and clients find it helpful to start with a general list of signature strength behaviors. Table 2.1 includes two ideas for using each character strength in a new way.

Table 2.1. Using Signature Strengths in New Ways

Creativity	Think of one of your problems and two possible solutions. Present the solutions nonverbally as an act or mime to someone.
	Turn an inanimate object (e.g., like paperclips, toothpicks) into something meaningful.
Curiosity	Try a new food for the first time, preferably from a culture different than your own.
	Take a different route home and explore a new area or neighborhood.
Judgment (critical thinking)	Watch a political program from the opposite point of view of your own, and keep an open mind.
	Ask one or two clarifying questions of someone who has a different approach to life or different beliefs than you (e.g., a vegetarian).
Love of learning	Read some of the original works of Gandhi online.
	Consider your favorite subject matter. Do an Internet search and surprise yourself by discovering something new about the topic.
Perspective	For one of your interactions today: First, listen closely. Second, share your ideas and thoughts.
	Consider the wisest quotation you have come across. Think of one way you can live more true to that quote.
Bravery	Take on a new adventure or hobby that fits with one of your areas of interest.
	Consider one of your personal fears. Take one small, healthy action toward facing it right now.
Perseverance	Complete a small project that you have been putting off.
	Set a new goal today, list two potential obstacles that may come up, and ways that you will overcome them.
Honesty	Write a poem that expresses an inner truth.
	Contact a family member or friend whom you have told a "partial" truth and give them the complete details.
Zest	Exert your energy in a unique way – jump on a bed, run in place, practice yoga or body stretching, or chase around a child or pet.
	Express your energy through an outfit, pair of shoes, and/or accessories that are striking and colorful.
Love	Surprise somebody with a small gift that shows you care (e.g., flowers, a Starbucks coffee).
	Tell someone about a strength you saw them use and how much you value it. Words of affirmation are a powerful, verbal force for the expression of love.
Kindness	Put coins in someone's parking meter that has run out of money.
	Stop by a hospital or nursing home and offer to visit someone who is lonely.
Social intelligence	Start up a conversation with someone whom you normally would not say much more to than typical pleasantries. This person might be the woman at the checkout counter, a telemarketer, or a new employee.
	Express a feeling of frustration, disappointment, or nervousness in a healthy, direct way that someone can easily understand.

Table 2.1. Continued

Teamwork	Spot and express appreciation for the strengths shown by your team members.
	Savor a positive team interaction from the past by replaying it in your mind; share it at a team meeting.
Fairness	Look for beings (e.g., people, animals) that are cast aside or typically held in disgust and go out of your way to treat them right.
	Include someone in a conversation who is typically excluded from groups or is a newcomer.
Leadership	Discuss with someone who reports to you about how they can align their top character strength more in their work.
	Gather and lead a group to help support a cause you believe in.
Forgiveness	Let go of a minor irritant or a grudge.
	Give yourself permission to make a mistake.
Humility	Consider an interaction that typically involves you doing more talking/sharing and flip it to where the other person talks/shares more.
	Ask someone you trust to give you feedback on your struggles and growth areas.
Prudence	Before you make a decision that is typically very easy, take one full minute to think about it before you take action.
	Write down your plans for each hour of the remainder of the day, no matter how trivial.
Self-regulation	The next time you feel irritated or nervous today, pause and breathe with the experience for a count of 10 breathes.
	Monitor all the food and drinks you put in your body. Write it down on a tracking sheet.
Appreciation of beauty & excellence	Go outside and stand still in a beautiful environment for 20 minutes.
	Listen to a song or piece of music that is viewed as extraordinary; allow yourself to marvel at the talent that went into producing it.
Gratitude	Tell someone "thanks" who deserves it and is typically not recognized.
	Share your appreciation on a post-it note that you put on someone's desk as a surprise or send it in a spontaneous e-mail.
Hope	Consider a problem or struggle you are having. Write down two optimistic, realistic thoughts that bring comfort.
	Watch a movie that promotes a message of hope and think about how the message applies to your life.
Humor	Do something spontaneous and playful around another person (e.g., saying something silly, contorting your body in a weird way, or telling a funny story or joke).
	Watch a classic comedy show you haven't seen before and laugh as much as possible.
Spirituality	Read about a religion/spirituality different from your own and look for ways in which the core messages parallel one another.
	Contemplate the "sacredness" of this present moment. Allow yourself to find meaning in the moment.

Anchoring

Anchor the signature strength with a daily activity that you are already doing. What do you do each day that is part of your routine? Driving, making lunch, attending a meeting, creative writing, playing with your kids, relaxing with your spouse, e-mailing friends. Start by choosing one of these routine activities and commit to using one or more of your signature strengths during that activity. For example, if you anchor fairness with conversing with your spouse, you can consciously be sure to give your spouse an equal amount of time sharing about their day and choosing the relaxing activity for the two of you to do together. If you anchor kindness with driving, you might deliberately find one or two ways on each trip to be sensitive to the potential needs of others drivers and going out of your way to let them in, smile/wave to them, and drive with care.

Context Mapping

As you consider the major domains of your life – work, school, family, relationships, community – make note of the degree to which you comfortably and regularly express each of your signature strengths in each domain. Many people find there is a gap to the degree in which they express a strength in one or two domains relative to others. Generate some examples of your signature strengths expression by writing about how you use your top strengths in each domain. For which domains is your writing most fluid and rich? Which domains do you have trouble coming up with examples? Allow each domain to inform the others as you generate more and more ideas for using your signature strengths in new ways.

Holistic Mapping

Originally based on the two-factor model of Peterson (2006a), character strengths have been mapped successfully across two continua (VIA Institute, 2014): strengths that are from the heart (e.g., feeling, body, emotion, intuition) or head (e.g., logic, analysis, reasoning) and strengths that are more interpersonal (with others) or intrapersonal (when alone). Figure 2.1 depicts the revised circumplex graph of the VIA classification, referred to as the "two-factor balance graph" from data analyzed by Robert McGrath in 2014 (see also a sample report with the circumplex mapping at http://www.viacharacter.org/www/Portals/0/VIA%20Pro%20 Report.pdf).

Mapping out each of your signature strengths across the four facets is yet another way to expand your thoughts and actions around how you can use your signature strengths. This allows for a more complete, holistic view of oneself and can serve to ignite the potentiality of each character strength. See Figure 2.2 for an example using the strength of gratitude.

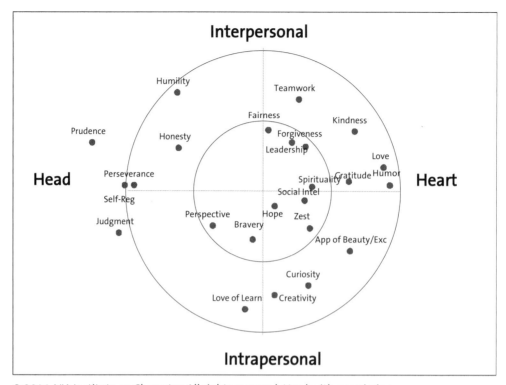

Figure 2.1.   Two Factor Balance Graph of the 24 Character Strengths.

Intrapersonal	Heart (feelings, body)
• I can express thanks to my body for its healing capacities. • I am grateful for my connectedness with the universe and want to give back to the environment.	• Warmth in the chest. • Relaxing heaviness in the shoulders. • Tingling in the fingers and hands. • Sense of opening up to others and the world.
Interpersonal	**Mind (thoughts and beliefs)**
• Verbally expressing thanks to a friend. • Showing appreciation by offering kindness in return.	• My family means the world to me. • I am appreciative of this person's gift. • I am connected to this person.

Figure 2.2.   Holistic mapping of the strength of gratitude.

Chapter Summary

- Signature strengths is a concept of such importance in character science and positive psychology that an entire chapter is devoted to flesh it out from both a research and practice perspective.
- Signature strengths are those strengths most core and essential to the individual, usually appearing in the top of the individual's character strengths profile.
- The intervention "Use a signature strength in a new way each day" has received good evidence for boosting happiness and lowering depression.
- The application of signature strengths has been applied widely across populations (e.g., children, elderly, people with traumatic head injuries) and in different contexts (including psychiatric, education, business, and military settings).
- There are several studies exploring why the use of signature strengths are connected with well-being, such as their contribution to goal progress, positive emotions, and the meeting of basic psychological needs.
- Strengths blindness is a pervasive human phenomenon with many types, but it can be improved with mindfulness and enhanced character strengths use.
- The application of signature strengths can be used in the form of various activities, such as simple behaviors, anchoring, context mapping, and holistic mapping.

Chapter 3

Practice Essentials

Six Integration Strategies for a Strengths-Based Practice

Introduction

A well-conceived, strengths-based approach is at best transformative and at worst well-intended. A central attribute of a strengths-based approach is that it either provides a necessarily complement to a deficit-based approach or it provides clients with a significant alternative that some will view as especially beneficial and refreshing. The practice-based themes offered in this chapter are intentionally broad. These are the essentials for integrating character strengths into practice, improving practitioners' character strengths fluency, and deepening the work of how a strengths-based practitioner helps clients. Readers might supplement this chapter with the strengths-based practitioner checklist in Appendix B and the "flagship papers" referenced in Appendix F.

The six integration strategies recommended for character strengths-based practitioners in this chapter are:

1. Recognize, label, and affirm strengths in yourself.
2. Character strengths are social, therefore never stop strengths-spotting in others.
3. Align character strengths with activities and tasks.
4. Use the strengths-based practice model.
5. Embed character strengths into your professional approach and theory.
6. Use your own strengths in sessions and meetings.

Strengths-Based Practitioner Tip

What is strengths-spotting? Strengths-spotting means to take notice – to label – character strengths. There are two levels to strengths-spotting: spotting strengths in oneself and spotting strengths in others. Strengths-spotting applies to each of the 24 strengths. It remains one of the easiest and best initial activities in strengths work. Not only is it a clear first-step for those new to character strengths work but it is a tool that intermediate and advanced strengths-based practitioners can use as they continue on the path of self-development and as they deepen client relationships, forging new connections with others.

---

1. Recognize, Label, and Affirm Strengths in Yourself

I learned my highest character strength is curiosity," said the university freshman. "I never would have referred to my tendencies to ask questions and explore things as a strength, but it is true. That is exactly how I am. It's part of everything – whether I'm with friends, family, classmates, or people in my neighborhood – I'm always looking for something new to do or something I can investigate further." Then, he began to laugh a bit: "Some people say I ask too many questions but that's just me. I'm curious. I want to know. I want to learn. It's how I connect with people and how I connect with what I'm learning. I'm also very curious about technology, social media, sports, the environment, religion, politics … pretty much everything! I even use curiosity when I'm overwhelmed with school. When I start asking myself questions about my stress and the situation, I get new ideas or feel less bothered by it all. And, I'm sure I could use my curiosity even more. Actually, I'm curious about my curiosity!

This young man recognized, labeled, and then affirmed his highest strength. He found that having a positive label to describe his identity made a real difference in his life. It was a catalyst – an opening for new discoveries and possibilities. He had never labeled himself as being curious so this was a surprise for him. Although he had been using curiosity most of his life, this part of his identity had previously been outside of his awareness.

As was true for this student, most of us are accustomed to recognizing and even labeling our mistakes, problems, stressors, and bad qualities, and far less accomplished at doing the same for our positive qualities. This is where the practice of strengths-spotting in oneself can make a big difference. Strengths-spotting requires us to be on the lookout for character strengths. When we recognize a strength, we can give it a clear label.

Strengths-Based Practitioner Tip

The labeling of problems can bring forth a lot of good. For example, proper diagnosis (label) can lead to treatment, recovery, and healing. Labeling can also motivate people to take action and make real change in their life. At the same time, I've seen many people get carried away with negative labeling. They rely so much on their label that they become it; the label becomes their identity. They don't know where the label ends and where they, the human being, begins. Positive labeling, on the other hand, is particularly motivating and energizing. It catalyzes mini and large shifts in how people perceive themselves. It sets people off on a new direction, empowered toward horizons of hope. Can we go overboard with positive labeling? I think so. Everything has its limits. The main caution is to not be blind to what's wrong, and to not avoid problems and negative labels. Quite the contrary, positive labels can help us face problems (e.g., using bravery) and notice what's wrong along with what's strong.

Know thyself. This mantra is the starting point for character strengths work. One way to build self-knowledge is by learning to name character strengths as they occur in the moment. This takes practice yet can be pursued by engaging in a variety of strengths-spotting exercises, such as those found in the following sections.

Self-Assessment and Self-Nomination

There are many ways to practice spotting strengths in oneself. The most common and obvious starting point is to take the VIA Survey to measure the 24 strengths. Looking at those character strengths toward the top of your results page is a way to begin generating greater awareness of strengths in yourself. If a person does not have access to the Internet, then the individual can examine a list of the 24 character strengths with definitions (such as the VIA classification list on the inside cover of this book or online at https://www.viacharacter.org/www/Character-Strengths/VIA-Classification). The person then writes down the 5–7 strengths that best describe who they are. This approach is called the self-nomination of strengths.

Self-Monitor for Strengths

Others prefer to take a more systematic approach than self-nomination and instead self-monitor. This means to closely observe yourself for a period of time, such as each morning for 1 week. With this approach individuals set an alarm on their smartphone to signal themselves every 30 minutes or so and each time the alarm goes off, they pause and ask themselves: "What character strengths was I just using?" They keep a running log or chart that tracks the time, location, activity they were engaging in, the strength(s) used, and how they were using the strengths. After a period of time, the tracking sheets can be examined for themes. In taking this approach, individuals notice a range of themes. Some common examples include noticing a wide range of character strengths used, the use of strengths in micromoments (e.g., hopeful thinking while in the shower, prudence while brushing teeth), alignment of strengths language with behaviors, an emphasis on two or three particular strengths used together, and a general lack of consciousness around strengths. Indeed, this practice of self-monitoring assists the individual in developing a more mindful strengths use.

> **Strengths-Based Practitioner Tip**
>
> Part of strengths understanding comes from examining your stories, the realities by which you have used your character strengths in the past. Another way to deepen knowledge and understanding is to not be afraid to frequently ask yourself several questions:
> • What do I believe about my character strengths, my signature strengths?
> • How well do I really know my highest strengths?
> • What do I most need to learn about my highest strengths?
> • Why are my signature strengths of value?
> • How are my other character strengths of value to me?

The Power of Narrative

And then there are stories. Daniel McAdams is a researcher who has spent decades studying stories and life narratives as they relate to our personalities. He concludes that we are multifaceted by nature and that there are three levels by which we might consider our personality traits. In addition to a global view of ourselves and a contextual view of ourselves, there is a third level called the integrative life story view that includes internal and evolving stories of ourselves that reflect how we understand ourselves, others, and the world around us (McAdams et al., 2004). These stories are ripe with potential for spotting character strengths.

The good news is our lives are filled with stories: big stories of our wedding day, the birth of a child, the death of a loved one; smaller stories such as sending a difficult e-mail, playing in a softball game, and watching our child play the piano; and microstories of our drive to work this morning, about paying the checkout clerk at the grocery story, and our bedtime routine. Then, there are not only these stories from the past that reside in our minds but also stories of the future – how we might propose to our significant other, how we might react upon receiving an award, or the story of who will be at our funeral. All of these stories are alive within us waiting to be said aloud or at least to be reminisced or fantasized about. Some of these are defining moments in our lives that catalyze a change or that significantly contribute to our identity. All of these types of stories have something in common – character strengths comprise part of the ingredients.

Character strengths are present in every story, and although they are not necessarily present in optimal doses, they are there for the spotting. This means that stories can be reflected upon for the strengths. We can ask ourselves and our clients to tell a story and then consider: What character strengths can you spot in the story? What character strengths were being used?

Consider the two stories below in which the exact same thing happens in each.

> I woke up this morning, had breakfast, and got dressed. As I drove to work, I encountered a lot of bad traffic and the drivers on the road seemed angry and aggressive, often cutting me off. I arrived late for a work meeting and therefore apologized to my boss.

> I woke up this morning with a feeling of zest, excited to start the day. For breakfast, I used prudence to be thoughtful and careful about my choices as I have high cholesterol, therefore I selected some fresh vegetables to go with my white-egg omelet. As I got dressed, I paused to marvel at the smoothness of the material and vibrancy of the colors of my clothes (appreciating the beauty and excellence), which my spouse had pressed for me the preceding day. I felt spurts of gratitude for my spouse. As I drove to work, I encountered a lot of bad traffic and the drivers on the road seemed angry and aggressive, often cutting me off. I practiced forgiveness, letting go of these minor irritants as they occurred, while being aided by perspective, seeing the possible bigger picture that perhaps some had emergencies to attend to and others were experiencing the affliction of anger and therefore in need of kindness and compassion. I arrived late for a work meeting and feeling a bit embarrassed, I mustered up the bravery to apologize to my boss. I was honest about the situation but was clear to self-regulate my urge to blame the traffic and instead took responsibility for not having planned ahead enough to account for the traffic.

Although the plot of each story is the same, a significant difference emerges in the details, the nuances. The first is mundane whereas the second adds the infusion of character strengths, which makes all the difference. Clearly, the second scenario offers insight into the person – how they approach life in general and specific situations therein. It is the nine character strengths mentioned directly (and others alluded to) that give color and intrigue to the story. This infusion of strengths leads to a deeper understanding of the person's psyche and their relationships. It allows the listener/reader to generate more questions.

When asked to spot strengths in their story, some people have the tendency to play the "humility card" and say that they feel too awkward to talk about themselves in a positive way. This will be addressed in greater depth in Chapter 4; however, it is important to note here that we should help our clients to get to know who they are, so that we can see that depth and color and intrigue first-hand. Strengths-spotting in oneself can be nonchalantly reflected in a statement such as: "That enthusiasm you are sensing from me around this topic is my character strength of *zest* coming alive." We have all performed "better than ordinary" at one time or many times in our lives. These are experiences to share and to build upon. Research has found that sharing them brings benefit to both you and the receiver (Gable et al., 2004; Reis et al., 2010). Why would we not want to foster that mutual benefit?

Strengths-Based Practitioner Tip
Consider your happiest moments. Replay one of these moments in your mind and be on the lookout for the character strengths that were present.

Who Sees You?

Another activity that facilitates spotting strengths in oneself is to consider a person in your life – a friend, a mentor, a spouse, a boss – who really "sees" you. They "get" you and understand what makes you tick. You have felt understood by this person. What is it that this person saw in you? What did they "get" about you? And, what character strengths were they seeing? What impact did this have on you? This exercise allows you to spot strengths in yourself, but through the eyes of another.

When I lived in St. Louis, I went to breakfast once a month with a wise friend who was a 70-year-old, zestful, liberal-thinking nun named Sr. Marilyn. We had wonderful conversations about spirituality, living life fully, and expressing meaning and purpose in life. In each conversation, it was clear that we "got" each other, we understood where the other was coming from and saw what was best in one another. Sr. Marilyn would find a way to comment on a positive quality I was expressing or that she had witnessed in me in the previous months. These comments always addressed one or more of my signature strengths. I was often quite surprised when she made these observations about my character, but they left me feeling understood, connected, and energized. In fact, I would insist on our having meetings in the morning because I knew that the enhanced energy I would gain would stay with me throughout the workday.

Affirming Strengths

After labeling and deepening understanding of one's top character strengths, an important next step is to affirm these strengths. This means to not only confirm that one strongly has the strength being focused on, but that one can also affirm, or see the value in the strength. Self-affirmation theory (Steele, 1999) explains that the affirmation of personal values expands one's view of oneself, facilitates perspective on what is most important, and can be protective against a variety of stressors. Studies have shown that participants who write about their values (i.e., character strengths and other values) can lead to significant positive changes in behavior, improving health and relationship outcomes (Cohen & Sherman 2014), lowering cortisol responses (Creswell et al., 2005), and increasing the likelihood of acknowledging the health risks of smoking (Crocker, Niiya, & Mischkowski, 2008). This research demonstrates that it is therefore of benefit to write about how we value any of the 24 character strengths.

2. Character Strengths Are Social

Although character strengths reside internally and can be expressed while we are alone, a critical feature of character strengths is their social nature. Character strengths are communal. We express our character strengths, consciously and unconsciously, in one-on-one situations and in groups; at home, work, and school; in public and private spaces; in peak moments and in dire situations. Our character strengths knowledge and practices can be seen as a communal, shared good we have to contribute to others (Fowers, 2005). The expression of one's character strengths is inextricably connected with other people. This warrants practical activities to accentuate an awareness of this connection. The practice of strengths-spotting in others aligns solidly with this and is the focus of this section.

I've asked thousands of people in character strengths workshops across the globe this question: Which do you think is easier: strengths-spotting in yourself or strengths-spotting in others? Overwhelming, people say it's easier to spot strengths in others. I would estimate that over 90% of the practitioners in these workshops (counselors, coaches, managers, teachers) report this.

No doubt this is because, in part, of the added value of interpersonal relating. Spotting strengths in others usually means there's an opportunity to connect with someone. And, seeing behaviors displayed outside of ourselves seems more real than the subjective feel of our intrapersonal evaluation (which is often habitual). Another reason is that the energy, enthusiasm, and excitement that typically accompanies character strengths use is palpable and engaging, hence easier to spot. This points to the idea that our relationships are a good place to start with our strengths work.

To operationalize this process, I offer three concrete steps that can be deployed when giving feedback on character strengths observed in others and can be used in teaching clients, students, and employees to engage in strengths-spotting.

1. *Labeling.* Name the strength you notice.
   – What do you observe?
2. *Explaining.* Give an explanation/rationale for the strength.
   – What is the evidence?
3. *Appreciating.* Express appreciation/affirmation.
   – How might you convey you value the person's strength expression?

Before sharing the rationale for these steps, it's important to realize there are a couple prerequisite steps in order to optimally engage in the process. First, the strengths spotter should be familiar with the "language" of character strengths. This provides a foundation of meaning and a systematic framework for knowing what to look for. It's useful to have a listing of the VIA classification on hand (see the inside cover of this book). Learning not only the virtue categories and strength definitions, but also the synonyms and dimensions of each character strength will help widen strengths fluency – a flexible repertoire for your strengths-spotting.

A second prerequisite to strengths-spotting is to consciously put on strengths glasses in which you have a mindset to look for and find character strengths in people. As our negativity bias and inclination toward what's wrong or bad is a dominant force within us, such an emphasis on walking into interactions with character strengths primes our mind for the good. This can be done by fine-tuning observation and listening skills. What do strengths look like in action (the nonverbal level)? What do they sound like in the midst of the words within stories (the verbal level)? On a nonverbal level, there will often be changes in energy such as a lightness coming over the face, more smiling or laughing, improved posture, increased use of hand gestures, and positive emotions such as joy, contentment, excitement, and hope. In workshops offering strengths-spotting activities, I debrief the experience and one of the most common responses, across cultures, is a report from the listener that when their partner was speaking to character strengths their eyes would "light up." On the verbal level, the person conveying their character strengths will often express a stronger, more assertive voice, improved vocabulary and clarity of speech, and use of strength words. There will be variation on the verbal level as some individuals will speak more quickly and even tangentially, reflecting on new ideas and showing excitement about the topic; while others will speak more slowly, directly, and methodically when a strength is present, signifying a thoughtful and calm confidence.

Why Labeling?

To give words to a behavior or cluster of behaviors is powerful. This is evident in labels of medical and psychological disorders, such as "diabetes, type II," "major depression," and "alcohol dependence." Although labels can lead people to overidentify with a condition or feel boxed in, there is much power to such labels; for example, informing about treatment approaches, giving words to complex phenomena, and empowering awareness and action. The labeling of character strengths is equally powerful and with less baggage. Researchers have pointed out the benefits of labeling strengths, for example, labeling the strength of courage is a way to enhance that strength (Hannah et al., 2007). A fairly common example can be seen in a helping professional who was tutoring a student with a learning disability and ADHD. The student was visibly struggling in the meeting, unable to tackle the learning task at hand. The professional (who had been trained in character strengths) then said the following which made an emotional impact in the moment and a behavior impact weeks later for the student's strengths use:

> Let's pause here for a moment so I can give you some feedback. I view you as an incredibly brave and courageous young woman. Each day you face adversity. You stand up for yourself when other students tease you. You see fear but you don't let it stop you. You go to each class every day knowing that it will be difficult and challenges will emerge. But, you face that adversity head on. Your courage is remarkable. Clearly, you have used it very strongly in many ways in your life.

Why Explaining?

Labeling character strengths offers people an opportunity to make shifts, giving them a surprising insight into their behavior in a given moment. But, sometimes, labeling alone (e.g., "I saw kindness in you yesterday" or "you are curious") can leave people with more questions. They may think: "That's nice, but I don't know what they're referring to." If only the label is given, there is the enhanced tendency to disregard the comment (e.g., "OK, thanks. So what's for dinner?"). Offering a rationale for what you labeled is a way to counteract these problems. The explanation is the behavioral evidence for what you noticed.

Why Appreciating?

To *express appreciation* is to express value for a person or their actions. It moves the strengths-spotting to a deeper level, allowing the recipient to see – and often to *feel* – that their character strengths matter. Science tells us that appreciation matters on many fronts. Those who express appreciation to their partner are more committed to them and more likely to stay in the relationship (Gordon, Impett, Kogan, Oveis, & Keltner, 2012), and those who appreciate their past or present have greater happiness than those who do not (Bryant, Smart, & King, 2005). The expression of appreciation toward one's partner has been associated with stronger relationships, higher marital satisfaction, and greater willingness to share concerns in the relationship (Algoe, Gable, & Maisel, 2010; Gordon, Arnette, & Smith, 2011; Lambert & Fincham, 2011; Schramm, Marshall, Harris, & Lee, 2005), while the expression of character strengths appreciation, in particular, is linked with higher commitment in relationships, higher relationship satisfaction, and higher sexual satisfaction (Kashdan et al., 2017). One study of a large sample of workers found that those who felt appreciated by others were 30 times more likely to be flourishing than those who do not feel appreciated (Hone et al., 2015).

At a recent workshop, a participant told me: "It feels awkward to spot strengths in a conversation and even *more* awkward to deliberately express appreciation." This can be true for many people. But isn't that a sad reality, that so many of us find it personally challenging to label a positive, core quality in another person and to tell them we appreciate them? Many people are not practiced in giving positive feedback around strengths, or in receiving it, therefore, working to diminish awkwardness can be helpful. This means practicing strengths-spotting and strengths appreciating. Appreciation is often vague and general, such as a mindless "thank you" or a passing comment like, "I appreciate your help." To transcend such mindlessness, strengths spotters are encouraged to be specific and to practice regularly in different settings to increase confidence and hence to minimize any awkwardness. Some practicing of strengths appreciation, along with some knowledge of the research, can go a long way in shifting this awkwardness, at home or at work.

For the very next movie or TV program you watch or the fiction/nonfiction book you are currently reading, label the character strengths you observe in the main characters. What is the evidence for each strength you are spotting? This exercise is typically welcomed with open arms as homework for clients and students as well!

Putting the Steps Together

In my coaching work, I set up a personal rule-of-thumb to spot strengths in every session with every client. Some meetings have character strengths activities and strengths-spotting as the focal point; in other meetings they are peppered throughout. Examples involving the three steps follow:

> Wow, Mary, you really dealt with that challenging personal situation with a high level of social intelligence. It is clear you tackled a sensitive social situation and offered your brother a number of different options for handling his crisis. And you did it with kindness, as you made it clear you were there to support him throughout the ordeal. This is a nice display of two of your signature strengths – social intelligence and kindness. I suspect your brother appreciated this, even if he didn't say so.

> Bill, I was impressed by how well you kept your cool during that heated discussion with our colleague David yesterday. That took a lot of self-control on your part! Thanks for demonstrating such strength as our whole office could have been negatively affected if you had approached it differently. Well-done.

> Piper, may I give you some feedback? I watched how you included everybody in the discussion during the team meeting earlier today. You displayed a great level of fairness by pulling in the typically quiet members. And you did so with humility because I know you could have spoken eloquently for hours on the topic but you prioritized everyone else's views instead. I want to let you know how much I appreciated seeing your character strengths in action. I have a meeting I'm running in a few hours and I'm going to remember your approach of fairness and humility and attempt to run the meeting in a similar way.

> Mom, you seem to always offer me warmth and kind words at just the right time. This is exactly what helps me feel cared for and supported. I want you to know how much I value your love.

Practitioners are encouraged to be creative in applying these character strengths-spotting steps. One educator, Mark Linkins, did just that when consulting to the Newark Boys Chorus School, helping them to embed strengths-spotting practices throughout the school. In what was called the Badge Project, each student wore a lanyard/badge around their neck each day that had the 24 character strengths written on separate cards. When they observed a classmate strongly displaying any strength, they took out that card in their badge and handed it to the student, explaining and appreciating the strength that was displayed. This was done among staff first and then among the students, across grade levels. This project is a creative example of operationalizing strengths-spotting throughout a classroom or system while boosting strengths fluency, connectedness in relationships, confidence, and well-being.

Strengths-Based Practitioner Tip

At your next work meeting or family gathering, enter the environment wearing "strengths goggles." This means walking in with a mindset to look for strengths as they occur. Use a cue to remind you to keep your goggles on throughout the event – you might place a sticker on your phone or wear a bracelet to remind you to see people and their interactions through the lens of character strengths. Spot your coworker asking lots of questions (curiosity) or discussing collaborations on a project (teamwork). Notice when your mother puts her arm around you when she speaks (love) or when your brother keeps the family entertained with a funny story (humor).

Train Yourself to Look for Strength Behaviors

Character strengths can be expressed in our thoughts, feelings, and behaviors. Thoughts and feelings are subjective and, of course, pose a challenge for observers to spot strengths. Behaviors, on the other hand, are observable expressions that come across in speech or action. In many instances, behaviors offer a clear display of character strengths that can be spotted. There are probably an infinite number of potential behavioral manifestations for the 24 character strengths – some "little," everyday behaviors as well as big, obvious strength expressions, as discussed in Chapter 1. Table 3.1 offers two examples of behaviors for each of the 24 character strengths. These behaviors are not necessarily true for everyone but they offer the practitioner general ideas about how the character strength might manifest. For some behaviors, there is an overlap in the strength that could be represented. Some examples might appear simplistic; however, people frequently do not draw a conscious connection between character strengths and behaviors, therefore they offer a good starting point for awareness building.

Table 3.1. Character Strength Behaviors

Creativity	• Shares new ideas at each team meeting. • Brainstorms easily, offering contributions quickly and often.
Curiosity	• Asks questions frequently, especially at every new conversation. • Comments on trinkets, paintings, etc. when walking into a new office.
Judgment/critical thinking	• Shares a new angle or vantage point each time a core issue or problem is brought up. • Disagrees about a premise or core theme a colleague is sharing and is able to cite evidence/rationale to the contrary.
Love of learning	• The individual carries a book around with them wherever they go (e.g., a physical book or a device with a collection of e-books). Reads books on breaks. • Registers for new classes or attend lectures (even though they already have an advanced degree).
Perspective	• Gives practical advice to people who share their problems with them. • Offers comments that reflect big-picture topics and issues important to humanity.
Bravery	• Challenges conventional ideas brought up by their boss. • Raises their hand and speaks up at public forums and large meetings.
Perseverance	• Finishes short-term and long-term projects within the expected time frame. • Receives special awards and commendations for accomplishments.
Honesty	• Shares vulnerabilities about oneself. • Gives constructive, sometimes unfavorable, comments when asked to give their feedback/opinions.

Table 3.1. Continued

Zest	• Regularly takes walks or other form of exercise/movement on breaks. • Spends money on experiences with people rather than on products for themselves.
Love	• Expresses warmth, genuineness, and attentive listening with good eye contact when in conversation with others. • Engages in physical touch with others (e.g., hugging, pats on the back).
Kindness	• Goes out of their way to check in on a colleague who had a rough week. • Brings a colleague a cup of coffee without being asked to do so.
Social intelligence	• Says the "right" thing at a meeting and most people in the group nod their head. • Gives empathy to a friend who is upset and stressed out.
Teamwork	• Inquires about the opinion of each team member on a project. • When given the choice, decides to work on a project involving discussion with others rather than by oneself.
Fairness	• Resolves a dispute among family members by looking for and pointing out the common ground. • On a break, they make the effort to include a coworker in a conversation in which that person appears to be on the periphery.
Leadership	• Organizes a get-together among friends for a weekend event. • Shares visions and ideas for others to follow and rally behind.
Forgiveness	• Gives a friend a second-chance saying "let's move on" after the friend offended them. • Practices a meditation focusing on "letting go" as a way of managing stress.
Humility	• Spends more time listening in a conversation than trying to add their own views. • After having accomplished something important, they emphasize the group effort and contributions of others.
Prudence	• Keeps various e-mail folders and subfolders and uses them. • Arrives on-time or early for meetings and appointments.
Self-regulation	• Goes for a jog or swim each day, which is part of their regular exercise routine. • Selects healthy choices such as fruits and vegetables when eating out for lunch.
Appreciation of beauty & excellence	• Often has tickets to attend the theater, opera, concerts, or other cultural events. • Surrounds oneself in office and home with paintings and other artwork.
Gratitude	• Frequently expresses "thanks" for favors and good things said/done for them. • Places sticky-notes of appreciation on the desks of colleagues.
Hope	• Speaks about personal and professional goals and what they are working toward. • Shifts the focus in a conversation, no matter how dire, toward the silver lining.
Humor	• Tells jokes, funny stories, and makes witty remarks in groups. • Teases or is playful with others in one-on-one situations.
Spirituality	• Displays religious symbols in their home, office, and on their person (e.g., a cross necklace). • Spends time during breaks in quiet reflection, meditation, or contemplation.

3. Align Character Strengths With Activities

If character strengths are natural energy resources within us and signature strengths are a core part of our identity, then why not bring them forth deliberately in all the domains of our daily life? The phrase "character-strengths alignment" captures this concept of bringing the best parts of who we are into the space of the present moment we find ourselves. People want to not only do things that they can do well but also do things that they care to do well (Mayerson, 2015, 2016).

A recent survey of US workers (McQuaid & VIA Institute on Character, 2015) shows that 64% of workers think their success at work depends on building on their strengths, whereas only 36% think success will improve by remediating weaknesses. Nevertheless, only about half of workers report getting to use their top strengths each day and 27% report getting no recognition at all of their strengths from their bosses. Opportunities for creating character strengths alignment are needed in the workplace.

Research is revealing the importance of character strengths alignment at work (Harzer & Ruch, 2016; Littman-Ovadia & Niemiec, 2017), and showing an important link between strengths over interests when it comes to job crafting (Kooij, van Woerkom, Wilkenloh, Dorenbosch, & Denissen, 2017). In one study, workers were randomly assigned to either a strengths alignment group or a control group (Harzer & Ruch, 2016). The workers in the strengths alignment group were asked to plan and use their Top 4 signature strengths more at work during their specific daily tasks and activities. These workers experienced significant increases in work-as-a-calling and global life satisfaction compared to workers in the control group, and these changes were sustained for 6 months. How might character strengths alignment play out in the workplace? Table 3.2 reveal two examples of a worker's signature strengths, three of their work tasks as a human resources manager, and the alignment between the two.

Table 3.2. Examples of Character Strengths Alignment Across Three Work Tasks

Top Work Tasks	Signature Strength	Potential Alignment Activity
E-mailing customers	Curiosity	Use language in messages that conveys interest, intrigue, novelty, newness, and curiosity.
	Kindness	Check in on and prioritize the customer's needs, being generous wherever possible.
Attending daily review meetings	Curiosity	Ask at least one question that explores possibilities at each meeting.
	Kindness	Be thoughtful by offering employees water/coffee; check in on how they are doing.
Troubleshooting work problems brought forth by staff	Curiosity	Emphasize an inquiry approach rather than an authoritarian approach; help staff explore solutions to each unique situation.
	Kindness	Be concrete with your compassion for the employee's struggle; listen attentively; let them know you support them.

An individual's character strengths profile can be used as a guide to facilitating alignment with work. Research has supported this, revealing a connection between character strength profiles and the workplace role or function that the individual finds most engaging and satisfying. Mayerson (2015) conceptualized the following seven categories or roles common to work teams and Ruch, Gander, Platt, and Hofmann (2016) found empirical support for these categories, in addition to devising the character strengths algorithm underlying each:

1. Creating ideas.
2. Gathering information.
3. Analyzing information for decision-making.
4. Implementing ideas/programs at work.
5. Influencing others, internally (e.g., key decision-makers) or externally to the organization (e.g., investors, consumers) as to the merits of the work.
6. Managing relationships of coworkers.
7. Energizing the work team and the work itself to carry it through times of challenge.

Ruch and colleagues found, for example, that people high in *creativity* and *perspective* tended to be engaged by creating ideas, whereas people high on *zest, hope*, and *bravery* matched best with the role of influencing others. Knowledge of each employee's unique profile of character strengths can be used to predict which roles an employee may find most energizing and fulfilling. Job assignments can then be made to align with the employee's roles considering their character strengths profile; this helps put each employee to their highest and best use and optimizes performance (Mayerson, 2015). This is certainly consistent with the robust research supporting "job crafting" for employees (Wrzesniewski, LoBuglio, Dutton, & Berg, 2013).

While the workplace is the most studied area for character strengths alignment activities, and thereby offering many opportunities for client application, other domains of life can benefit from alignment of one's top strengths as well, such as the domains of school, community, family, social, and spiritual. Table 3.3 offers examples of character strengths, family activities, and their alignment. It is conceivable that any of the 24 character strengths could be aligned with and enhance a myriad of family activities.

Table 3.3. Character Strengths Alignment With Family Activities

Family Activity	Your Signature Strengths	Alignment
Going outdoors	Leadership	Organize a family picnic – logistics, food, fun for the evening.
Bedtime rituals	Prudence	Be clear with children on when bedtime is and when the bedtime rituals (pajamas, brushing teeth, etc.) should begin. Follow through with the plan.
Cooking	Creativity	Make new twists (i.e., new spices, new combinations, new side dishes, new pairings) for familiar dishes.
Reading books together	Love of learning	Read together each night, review and discuss key lessons learned from each book.
Group dancing	Zest	Engage in a family dance party in which each member takes turns choosing a different song for the group to dance to.

Character strengths work is more about synthesis than analysis. This is particularly the case with alignment interventions. Psychology has spent decades picking apart problems and the issues that life brings. Strengths work, however, is largely about connecting aspects of life together – synthesizing qualities, memories, thoughts, feelings, and strengths to elicit a whole. Practitioners will ask individuals to recount times when they were at their best, to think of past successes, and to put together ideas that would make a promising future; each of these help the individual to draw connections and to merge experiences rather than to analyze and break them down. For example, a practitioner might ask a client, "What strength are you using right now?" and help them synthesize strength awareness and use with the present moment. In addition, a practitioner might specifically encourage a client to tap into their bravery in order to have a challenging conversation with their father or to admit one of their personal shortcomings. These are examples in which the practitioner is helping the client synthesize the strength with a memory or with a difficult situation.

4. Use the Strengths-Based Practice Model

Are you strengths-based? When I ask large audiences of practitioners this question, most hands shoot up. But, there is little consistency in what each person means by strengths-based. Is there even such a thing "to be strengths-based"? Most meanings of strengths-based have the connotation that this is the person's default mode or modus operandi – that they are always this way as a counselor, teacher, parent, or manager. That is a fallacy. With our heavy negativity bias and neurological wiring to find flaws and inconsistencies in our environment, it would be a tall order to overcome all of this and always look for the positive in situations or the good or strengths in everyone we encounter.

It's more likely that we are *situationally strengths-based* in that we are more strengths-based in certain workplace situations or at specific times when we interact with our friends. Even more to the point, we are *momentarily strengths-based*. We have fleeting moments where we are nice to a stranger, we ask a positive-oriented question, we reframe the negative into a positive, we empower another person with an encouraging remark, or we spot one of their character strengths. These are moments of being strengths-based. Most often, they are short-lived. Our hard-wiring quickly shifts us back to problem-based mindsets.

This is one reason why we need to use mindfulness with our strengths. Mindfulness serves as a process for us to notice those potential moments for strengths. It opens the door to further action we might take: Perhaps after a moment of strengths, we will practice cultivating more moments of strengths, attempt to elongate the positive emotion of a strength (called savoring), or stay on close lookout for the next opportunity to see a strength, which is only seconds away.

Despite calling myself a strengths-based practitioner, educator, writer, and researcher – hence occupying much of my day with strengths work – there are plenty of times when lapses of strengths pile up. To be honest (one of my signature strengths), I have far more lapses than uses of strengths. One way that I keep strengths in mind is when I am coaching a client online, I keep his or her character strengths profile on my computer screen, right next to their live image from Skype. Throughout the conversation I never lose sight (literally) of their strengths. Even this practical approach is subject to habituation. Thus, sometimes I need to deploy "cues for my cues"! When I have lost sight of the person's strengths entirely, I eventually see a unique expression on their face or a smile perk up, and these are my cues to return to their strengths.

Ideally those who call themselves strengths-based abide by the tenets, definitions, concepts, and research on strengths. It shouldn't be something that is said because it sounds good to clients, employers, or the public. Appendix B offers a checklist of some key questions for determining how much your work is based in strengths. There are many strengths-based models and approaches. Many of these are reviewed in Appendix C. The following section reviews the aware-explore-apply model because this is the model that was explicitly created for the VIA character strengths and it has been successfully used since the arrival of the VIA classification in 2004.

Background: Aware-Explore-Apply Model

After the VIA classification was published (Peterson & Seligman, 2004), I became immediately interested in applying this character strengths work to help others. At the time, I was working as a clinical psychologist for several client populations – chronic pain clients, clergy in religious life, clients with severe addictions, and clients with depression, anxiety, stress disorders, and a variety of medical conditions. With that range of suffering, I needed a general, wide-reaching, uncomplicated way of being strengths-based, and I wanted the approach to be stepwise and to not rely solely on the flow of interaction in the moment. I then did what a good investigative reporter would do (or I simply did what someone high in curiosity or love of learning would do): I spoke with strengths-based practitioners across disciplines (i.e., medicine, physical therapy, nutrition, psychology, social work, spiritual direction, clergy, psychiatry). I investigated, researched, observed, and asked questions, attempting to better understand what was known and unknown about strengths-based approaches up to that point. After reading books, watching videos, reviewing articles, and, most importantly, sitting in on sessions of talented, strengths-based practitioners from the various disciplines, I noticed a pattern. It became clear to me that these professionals were doing three processes in their strengths work: they helped clients become aware of something positive the client had been blind to, they coexplored that positive phenomenon through questions, activities, challenges, and reflections, and they took this information and helped the client make meaningful action of it, usually setting concrete goals and next steps. These three processes became the aware-explore-apply model (AEA). See Snapshot 3.1. for an overview of the model when applied to character strengths.

A study in the work context using the same three themes of AEA as an intervention to train workers on strengths found the intervention led to increased well-being and strengths use (Dubreuil et al., 2016). These researchers also found that subjects who had high increases in strengths use also had significant increases in work performance and harmonious passion.

The AEA model can structure a quick interaction or form part of a long-term process over weeks and months. For example, with regards to the former, imagine you are watching *Star Wars: The Force Awakens* (2015) and seeing the female protagonist, Rea, repeatedly displaying bravery. This triggers awareness for you about bravery and your own level of bravery (aware). You then ask yourself how much you display this strength in your daily life and what parts of your life could use more bravery (explore). You decide that you need to bring more bravery to a workplace scenario in which you'll need to confront a colleague who has been offending you with their political comments. You take action the next day, determined to rally your bravery to not only start the conversation but to stay strong throughout the conversation as well (apply).

Snapshot 3.1. Character Strengths-Based Aware-Explore-Apply Model

- Reflects and accentuates two central processes of strengths development: intrinsic motivation and mindfulness.
- Reflects the basic strengths-based approach that expert practitioners deploy in their work with clients.
- Occurs over short or long periods of time, such as unfolding in one particular interaction or situation, or as reflected in an ongoing interaction over time with a client, student, or employee.
- Is a cyclical process that is worked through and repeated. The three phases of AEA are a virtuous circle that build and reinforce one another in a positive way, from phase to phase.
- The simplicity of what the practitioner needs to memorize (i.e., 3 words) is intentional so that there is a simple model present within the complexity of strengths work.
- Helpful when practitioners feel "stuck," not knowing what to do next with a client. The practitioner asks themselves: Does this client need to generate more awareness of their strengths, explore them more deeply, or are they ready to set some goals?
- Offered as a tool for clients to work on strengths in between sessions.

In detailing this model, I offer a description of each phase, followed by questions and sample activities for clients to engage at each phase.

Using the Aware-Explore-Apply Model

Aware

Description

- The first step of understanding yourself or making any kind of change is to increase your self-awareness (i.e., to "know thyself"). Taking the VIA Survey is a great first step. This helps you to get in touch with a "common language" of strengths. Many people are surprised to realize that they have all 24 of these strengths within them. Others are happy to see the positive strengths that describe who they are at their core. Some individuals find themselves saying, "I already knew that about myself." If you find yourself saying this, challenge yourself to build a growth mindset mentality, where you attempt to see every experience as an opportunity to learn – to build further awareness of yourself.

Reflection Questions

- What is your gut reaction? What surprises you most about your VIA results?
- Do the highest strengths resonate for you as signature strengths?
- Do you feel the top strengths are the most core to who you are and most energizing and natural for you to use?

Sample Activities for Clients

- Take the VIA Survey or VIA Youth Survey at https://www.viacharacter.org
- Create a strengths introduction using the key concepts in Chapter 1 and parts of other chapters that are interesting to you. Include your rationale for using a strengths-based approach and link it to your client's problems or goals. Writing it out will help you become clear on what you've learned. This can be used to educate your client, build their strengths awareness, and contribute to "client buy-in" for your strengths-based approach.
- Help your client understand each of their signature strengths. Answer questions they have about the meaning of each signature strength, going through them one by one.
- Help your client confirm their signature strengths, assisting them in drawing connections between their words and their behaviors. Encourage them to affirm these character strengths in themselves by sharing your own appreciation for your client's expression of them.
- Engage in strengths-spotting by pointing out an example in which the client used a character strength in the immediate session. Be sure to include the rationale for what you observed.
- Understand your client's emotional reactions to the VIA Survey and the results. Validate their emotions, ask clarifying questions, offer education on the topic, and correct misconceptions.

Explore

Description

- This phase involves connecting character strengths, particularly those highest in your profile, with your past successes, your relationships, your achievements, times when you are happiest, and times when you've faced great challenge or difficulty. This phase helps you dig deeper into the connections between strengths and your past, present, and future; it helps you understand how character strengths have shaped you, and how they are part of what matters most to you. This phase may involve discussions with others about your strengths, solitary reflection and journaling, and taking a close observation of yourself and others in various situations.

Reflection Questions

- When you consider times when you were successful, what strengths were you using? How did each of your signature strengths come into play?
- How do you express each of your signature strengths every day?
- When you imagine a best possible future for yourself, what strengths will you need to bring forth to get there? What might you need to do differently?
- When you think of a time when you were anxious, depressed, or highly stressed, which strengths did you lean on to move forward?
- What strengths do you bring forth most strongly in your close relationships?
- What are the pluses and minuses of working on your character strengths?
- Consider your past or current mentors (or role models). What strengths did they embody? How did they express them? What strengths did they see in you?

Sample Activities for Clients

- You at your best, with strengths-spotting.
- Reflect on past strengths use.
- Explore ways to widen and extend strengths use.
- Explore a problem through a strengths lens.
- Review a VIA interpretative report (specifically, the VIA Pro Report or VIA Me Pathways Report), and exploring the content and graphs to view oneself from different perspectives.
- Best possible self exercise.
- Reflect on the overuse of character-strengths.

Apply

Description

- This phase involves action planning. This may take the form of concrete goals and objectives around strengths or it can simply be a reflection on the action one would like to take. This phase is about making strengths part of your life routine. It is the doing phase. After thinking about and discussing your strengths, it's time to impact your behavior!

Reflection Questions

- Consider the knowledge you have built up in the aware and explore phases, where do you go from here?
- Which strengths are you interested in applying in your daily life?
- How might you use your signature strengths in new ways each day?
- How might you use your strengths to reach your goals?
- What kind of improvement or positive change would you like to make in your life?
- How much energy/time do you have to make the change?
- Do you suspect that making this change will be worth it? Why or why not?

- What is your highest motivation in terms of your self-development?
- How do you want to "be" in this world and what do you want to "do" in this world?
- What do you want to do in the long-run in terms of your strengths expression?
- For what purpose are you intending to use your strengths? Is it linked with bringing more good into the world (e.g., being a "better person") or with being more true to yourself and acting more authentically (e.g., being a "better me")?

Sample Activities for Clients

- Attend to strengths: Set up a system (e.g., sticky notes or other cues) to remind yourself to pay attention to strengths … to not forget them! When you get caught up in the routines of your day, how will you shift your mindset back to a focus on strengths?
- Align strengths: Do you use your signature strengths regularly in your work and your relationships? Find ways to align your strengths with your tasks and in your conversations. For example, if you're high in curiosity, ask unique questions of your friends and family. If you're high in appreciation of beauty/excellence, be sure to set up your work environment where beauty is around you, take moments during the day to be out in nature, and bring forth high quality work in even mundane tasks.
- Acknowledge and appreciate the strengths of others: Be on the lookout for the strengths of others; you can probably spot them in any interaction you have. A first level response with strengths is to label (acknowledge) the strengths we witness in others (e.g., "John, you showed a lot of perseverance and bravery speaking up at that meeting this morning"). The next level is to show value for (appreciate) the strengths you observe (e.g., "Sue, I really appreciate your hopeful and grateful approach to life. I might not always say it, but it really gives me a lift to be around you.")
- Activate your behavior: What is one small action you might take to work on your strengths?
- Review the various character strengths interventions mentioned in this book (especially those detailed in Chapter 8): Choose one or two that you are most motivated to practice or to set up for your client.
- Set strength goals: Set up specific and concrete action steps, tell others about your intentions, and monitor your progress (see interventions in Chapter 8 on goal-setting).

Maintain

Description

- The AEA process is self-maintaining in that an individual continuously cycles through it, improving and digging deeper as they do the work. Nevertheless, a core part of any change is maintenance. Some practitioners will find it useful to emphasize this as a fourth phase.
- Making a change is easy; maintaining it is not.

Reflection Questions

- What will you do for the rest of your life with your strengths work?
- Where is your motivation highest around strengths work?
- How can you keep your strengths work fresh and interesting?
- How might you maintain a vision of yourself as constantly growing and evolving?
- How will you get support from others around your strengths work?

- Are there strengths activities you would like to do with people you care about? How might you set up a plan with someone in your life to work on strengths together?

Sample Activities for Clients

- Use character strengths as the mechanism for maintaining and revising goals (perseverance, hope, and prudence are core concepts for understanding goal-setting and maintaining goals, i.e., hope to envision the goal and its pathways, prudence to map it out in detail, and perseverance to carry it out).
- Build character strengths routines in daily life.
- Approach character strengths as if you are trying to establish a good habit.
- Use mindfulness exercises to keep up a strengths consciousness.
- Managers should deploy regular strengths-based performance reviews.

This character strengths-based approach helps to facilitate a personal paradigm shift for clients. Snapshot 3.2. offers a summary of these phases to facilitate that shift.

Snapshot 3.2. Summary of the Flow of AEA With Maintain

- Aware: From autopilot/blindness to awareness
- Explore: From general awareness to deeper insight
- Apply: From insight to positive action
- Maintain: From initial positive action to chronic positive action

5. Embed Character Strengths into your Professional Approach

There is substantial value in integrating positive psychology elements into clinical and counseling psychology approaches, as well as management, education, coaching, and related disciplines. In specifically considering effective psychotherapy, integrative approaches have strong empirical support; it is important for counseling approaches to use empirically based solutions and to integrate interventions that accommodate the individual and cultural characteristics of the clients (Norcross & Goldfried, 2005). The argument here is for the integration of character strengths into one's professional approach and theories around how clients change.

Positive characteristics have been shown to uniquely predict disorders, buffer the impact of negative life events, and have some role in preventing the development of disorders (Wood & Tarrier, 2010). In addition, they've been argued as a focal point for psychotherapists to use to cultivate clients' pleasure, engagement, and meaning to improve psychotherapy (Duckworth, Steen, & Seligman, 2005). It has been argued that character strengths, in particular, should be a core element for assessment and intervention in establishing a balanced clinical practice (Rashid, 2015; Rashid & Ostermann, 2009).

Clients seeking a practitioner, especially practitioners in the psychotherapy/counseling field, are looking for help with their problems. Their mindset reflects a desire to remediate their problem, and they are hoping that the practitioner can join their mindset and alleviate their suffering. Clients will expect to spend time recounting the details of their problems, attending to what is going wrong in their life, and feeling bad about their deficits and weaknesses (Rashid & Niemiec, 2013). As research has repeatedly shown that bad is stronger than good (Baumeister, Bratslavsky, Finkenaeuer, & Vohs, 2001), practitioners of all kinds are equally vulnerable to this negativity bias.

Seligman (2002) has often emphasized that psychotherapy should not settle by only offering a relief from suffering but to also emphasize boosting individuals to flourishing. When mental health and mental illness are viewed on two continua, revealing four quadrants, research has found that people who have strong mental and social health are likely to be flourishing but even a small percentage of people who are suffering from mental illness can simultaneously flourish (Keyes, 2002). Psychotherapy is thus about both – helping to alleviate suffering and helping people to maximize strengths and well-being.

Whatever your approach to psychotherapy, coaching, educating, or managing, you can weave character strengths into your approach. This means integrating, not replacing. Character strengths provide a seamless and substantive overlay to enhance approaches that help people change, whether that is a solution-focused or problem-focused orientation. This is also applicable to any setting and any population because all human beings have these strengths, and therefore there is always potential for working in a character strengths-based approach. As discussed in the previous section, the AEA model is one pathway in which character strengths can be used as an "overlay" to the practitioner's orientation.

If you're a psychotherapist, it is likely that you relate to one of the approaches outlined in the 10th edition of the classic graduate school text *Current Psychotherapies* (Wedding & Corsini, 2013), which features the most current and successful, evidence-based psychotherapy models/ orientations. Character strengths can be woven into any of these approaches, and I will exemplify several in this section. The newest therapy to be added is positive psychotherapy (PPT; Rashid & Seligman, 2013), which integrates the latest research and practice from the positive psychology field. In this 14-session model that has been shown to be more effective than treatment as usual for depression (Seligman et al., 2006) and effective in a number of pilot studies for a variety of clinical populations, including depression, schizophrenia, nicotine dependence, and borderline personality (Rashid, 2015), it is character strengths that are the most dominant positive psychology element, appearing as a key feature in most of the sessions. This includes a focus and practice on gratitude, kindness, and signature strengths.

Another positive psychology model, which builds on the research-based effectiveness of mindfulness-based cognitive therapy for depression (Segal et al., 2013), is mindfulness-based strengths practice (MBSP; Niemiec, 2014a). This is the first program to use mindfulness to explicitly target what is best in human beings (Baer, 2015). Early pilot research is promising (Ivtzan et al., 2016; Niemiec, 2014a), and has been used in a number of settings, such as the workplace (Niemiec & Lissing, 2016) and education (Lottman, Zawaly, & Niemiec, 2017; Sharp, Niemiec, & Lawrence, 2016).

At the present time, most therapists are not applying MBSP or PPT in their practice, therefore, I'll discuss some ways to integrate character strengths into some of the most popular theoretical orientations practitioners adhere to. Each subsection offers some integration examples but by no means is meant to be construed as exhaustive or comprehensive for any orientation (in fact, I'm confident entire books could be written on the integration of VIA character strengths with any of the following).

Psychodynamic Orientation

Psychodynamic approaches are known for helping individuals to examine their past experiences, including childhood, and helping the client look for patterns that are causing or perpetuating present-day struggles. With this angle of treatment, there is a unique opportunity to explore character strengths – the origins of character strengths, the character strengths of each parent/ caregiver, how strengths dynamics ensued in the family to create positive or negative experiences, how character strengths progressed over time (i.e., developmental trajectory), and how character strengths were nurtured, suppressed, ignored, discouraged, or championed by others. Exploring these robust areas can serve as a strong adjunct to therapists' existing psychodynamic approach.

In their chapter on integrating positive psychology into psychodynamic/psychoanalytic approaches for a textbook on positive psychiatry, Summers and Lord (2015) argue that traditional psychodynamic approaches emphasizing the therapeutic alliance, working through, and termination can be expanded and deepened by applying insights from positive psychology, including character strengths. Whereas traditional approaches emphasize how maladaptive and immature defenses can cause symptoms and problems, they argue that positive psychology approaches explain that client well-being is influenced by both positive and negative emotions and that character strengths can buffer against stress and loss. In their discussion of termination in the psychodynamic psychotherapy process, Summers and Lord offer the following question for therapists to ponder with each client: "To what extent has the patient achieved an ability to respond with resilience to future life stressors, and what is the nature and extent of the patient's character strengths?" (p. 185).

Character strengths serve an important role in relationship building, and the therapeutic relationship in psychodynamic work presents an opportunity ripe for strengths integration. Some character strengths are obvious, central qualities of good relationships (e.g., kindness, love, forgiveness, honesty), and other strengths are particularly user-friendly in terms of their application "toward the other" (e.g., curiosity, gratitude, teamwork). In addition to discussing that character strengths are part of a dynamic process within the relationship, therapists might take two important approaches: directly target a client's strengths and share their own character strengths as a self-disclosure strategy to positively influence clients.

Therapists may say, "Tell me about your problems," "What has been troubling you lately?," and "What are your greatest struggles or weaknesses?" Strengths-based, psychodynamic therapists may continue to ask those questions but also weave in "What are your signature strengths?," "How might you apply your character strengths to deal with that problem," and "What went well this last week and how did your character strengths contribute to that experience?"

Humanistic Orientation

Many of the theories of Maslow and Rogers are used as a foundation for contemporary theorizing on positive psychology practice in which concepts such as the client as their own best expert and the actualizing tendency in human nature, and the basic goodness in people are integral (Joseph & Linley, 2006). The strong alignment with and appreciation for humanistic approaches is clear in those therapists who help clients understand, explore, and use their strengths of character.

The foundation of person-centered or humanistic psychotherapy approaches includes the therapist embodying and conveying warmth, unconditional positive regard, and empathic listening to their client (Rogers, 1961). This involves bringing forth the humanity strengths of love, kindness, and social intelligence. In addition, to offering a genuine, unconditional positive regard, a therapist brings not only kindness but the wider view of perspective to accept and respect the person without judgment.

One of the key concepts in humanistic psychology is congruence. This refers to the therapist's having a match between their ideal self (who they wish they could be) and real self (who they actually are in their life). A therapist's level of congruence is considered integral to forming a strong therapeutic relationship and, ultimately, for fostering healing for the client.

The awareness of signature strengths and acting from signature strengths is a reflection of this concept. If a therapist is naturally curious or grateful or kind then they will find ways to appropriately express curiosity, gratitude, and kindness in therapy sessions.

Abraham Maslow's (1973) hierarchy of needs toward self-actualization is one of the most influential theories in all of psychology, and builds from the work of Rogers (1961) and Kurt Goldstein (1934/1995). Self-actualization refers to "becoming one's potentialities," having a "full realization of one's potential," and "expressing one's true self," all of which are common phrases used in character strengths work. As individuals come to know and express all their character strength capacities, especially their signature strengths, they are moving toward these elements of self-actualization. For Rogers, the "fully functioning person" was someone continuously working toward becoming self-actualized. Research has shown that the character strengths most highly correlated with the fully functioning person are zest, bravery, honesty, leadership, and spirituality, while humility and fairness were negatively correlated (Proctor, Tweed, & Morris, 2016). Humanistic therapists can use the key concepts and practices in character strengths to assist not only themselves but also their clients in finding growth.

Cognitive-Behavioral Orientations

Cognitive-behavioral approaches, whether that be traditional CBT, schema therapy, or rational-emotive behavior therapy, are rich in the provision of structured methodology and techniques for challenging distorted thinking patterns, irrational beliefs, vexing schemas, and maladaptive behaviors. CBT therapists will turn to many of their own character strengths in their work with clients, such as curiosity to gently explore patterns of thinking, judgment/critical thinking to examine what is rational/irrational and logical/illogical in what clients are saying, and perspective to help clients see the bigger picture, to name a few. In turn, therapists can train the clients to deploy the same character strengths throughout the therapy process.

In the various CBT approaches, character strengths can be integrated on the level of foundation or technique. For the former, a good example comes from the work of Christine Padesky, a prominent CBT scholar, who conceptualized "strengths-based cognitive-behavioral therapy" (Padesky & Mooney, 2012). Created as a model for building resilience, this four-step approach invites clients to search for strengths, construct a personal model of resilience, apply the model, and then practice resilience through behavioral experiments.

Also, character strengths can be woven into any technique in the CBT therapist's armamentarium. CBT therapists emphasizing the correction of faulty client schemas can draw an immediate connection to character strength schemas that might counteract, replace, or bring balance. In the construction of formal thought records, a staple in most CBT practices, clients are guided to examine a problematic situation from several perspectives: the emotions and intensity of these feelings, body sensations, unhelpful thoughts/images, facts that support the unhelpful thought, and facts that provide evidence against the unhelpful thought. Many thought records then encourage the generation of alternative/realistic/balanced thoughts, a process into which character strengths can be woven into. In addition to providing options around counterbalance and healing, character strengths can be explored from the perspective of being unhelpful and out of balance, in which the therapist examines the overuse of strengths as they contribute to the problem. Therapists can also deconstruct situations in which strengths use is the target instead of only deconstructing troublesome situations. This is referred to as a strengths-based functional analysis and assists clients in drawing connections between thoughts, feelings, behaviors, and strengths. Wallin (2013), who writes about the integration of CBT and character strengths (in Swedish), offers an example of a strengths-based functional analysis (see Table

Table 3.4. Strengths-Based Functional Analysis

Situation	Behavior	Thoughts, Feelings	Consequences	Strengths	Insights Gained/Learned
As you reflect on the last week, think about situations in which you used your character strengths. Think about situations that gave you energy the last week? Choose one situation. When did it occur? Where were you? Who were you with?	What did you do? What did you say? What was the interaction you had with others? Be specific.	What is going through your head? What are you thinking? What are you feeling (positive and negative emotions)? Rate the intensity of each feeling: 0–10	What does this lead to in the short-run? In the long-run?	What character strengths are you using in this situation? Give a rationale/explanation for each character strength you notice.	What do you take away from this analysis? What might you remind yourself of as you move forward?
Tuesday at 10:00 A.M.: Brainstorming in a meeting with my colleagues.	*I came up with and shared new ideas for the campaign. Most of the ideas were about how we can integrate social media.* *I gave positive feedback to my two colleagues about several of their ideas.*	*Thought: This is fun!* *Thought: I want to make sure I share as many ideas as possible.* *Thought: I want to help out with my time; I know we can make an impact.* *Excitement: 9* *Anxious: 2* *Joy: 7*	*Short-run: Positive emotions. I have a lot of energy. I feel connected with my colleagues.* *Long-run: Some of the ideas will lead to concrete actions for our company. I will likely be part of implementing one of the ideas in the months to come.*	*Creativity: I thought of many new ways of doing things.* *Zest: I expressed a high level of energy and enthusiasm, especially once the three of us got on a roll.* *Bravery: I shared each of my ideas; I did not hold back even when I thought that my teammates might consider one of my ideas to be silly.* *Teamwork: I did my part and worked hard for the group and for the success of the project. I reinforced the effort of others.*	*I feel strong and confident when I brainstorm new ideas on the marketing campaign with my team.* *I realize I have many character strengths I can draw upon.* *My strengths are a source of joy and excitement.* *I will remind myself how much energy it gives me to use my character strengths at work.*

Adapted and used with the permission of Lotta Wallin, http://www.styrkebaseratarbete.se

3.4) and strengths-based goal-setting (see Table 3.5). Both are strengths-based variations of classic CBT exercises.

Table 3.5. Strengths-Based Goal-Setting

Situation	Behavior	Character Strengths	Consequences	Tracking and Learning
In what situations or life domains do you want to practice developing this character strength? Where, when, with whom?	What specifically will you do or say to practice with this strength? For how long?	What strength(s) will you practice developing? How will you express the strength in a balanced way? How will you manage overuse?	What will this practice lead to in the short-run for you? In the long-run?	What will you learn from this practice? Who might support you in making progress? How will you track your progress?

Adapted and used with the permission of Lotta Wallin, http://www.styrkebaseratarbete.se

Family Therapy

Researchers Sheridan and Burt (2009) argue for a family-centered positive psychology that focuses on problem-prevention and is strengths-based, which they define as building on the family's existing competencies and promoting the family's motivation toward growth. This type of approach emphasizes "collaborating with" rather than "treating" families. The idea of working with strengths is not a new concept to most family therapists; however, working with a system of strengths and a validated assessment tool accompanied by structured, practical strategies provides a new dimension for practitioners.

Some application examples for family therapists to consider using with their clients, several of which come from Niemiec (2010a), are offered here:

- Each family member should be encouraged to take the VIA Survey or VIA Youth Survey to attain valid results. For family members under the age of 10, the family can discuss and come to a consensus as to the character strengths of other members (no family member should be excluded!)
- Top character strengths (e.g., Top 3–7) can then be posted in a prominent place in the house for all family members to see.
- Family members are encouraged to set up mutual validation systems by memorizing one another's strengths and weaving them into conversations, and using positive or negative situations as opportunities to offer mutual strengths-spotting and strengths appreciation. Some formal examples include, "I really appreciated your creativity in helping me on the science project, Mom," "You showed skillful leadership today, Bobby, you really got everyone involved in the game," and "Dad, I want to thank you for being so *forgiving* to me over the last few weeks while I've been so stressed out and angry about school."
- Family therapists can work to set up character strengths discussions around core themes. For example:
  - *Family strengths culture.* What are the most common character strengths themes or virtue themes across the family?
  - *Strength uniqueness.* Who is high in a character strength that no one else is high in? How can the family make the most of this person's unique strength to bring benefit to the family?
  - *Strength management.* What is a strength no one in the family is high in? Does the lack of a strength or virtue have a positive/negative impact? How might that be managed as a family?

- *Strength cueing.* What will be a reminder system for keeping up with these strength activities?
- Strengths genogram or "family tree of strengths" can be used to map out top character strengths in a structured format, for not only the nuclear family but over several generations. This provides stimulating and fascinating discussions around the origins of character strengths and enhances family bonding and interconnection.
- The family can practice strengths-spotting by setting up a ritual movie night to watch movies with a character-strengths lens. Each family member practices spotting the top strengths in the protagonist(s) and discusses how they used the strength, developed it, or struggled to use it. Looking to exemplars in movies, such as the character of Leigh Anne Tuohy in *The Blind Side* (2009), provides families with healthy role models of good communication, problem-solving, and growth, and engenders opportunities for families to talk about important life issues (Wedding & Niemiec, 2003). For a comprehensive list of positive psychology movies, including family-friendly films, see the authoritative text on the topic by Niemiec and Wedding (2014).

Solution-Focused Approaches

Focusing on solutions is an approach used by therapists (i.e., solution-focused therapy) and is a popular orientation for many coaches (e.g., life coaches). Solution-focused approaches are generally goal-oriented, collaborative, future-focused, and prioritize helping the client look for possibilities through structured questions. At the heart of solution-focused approaches rests the support for the client in understanding and using their strengths to generate solutions, new avenues, and make progress on their goals. Practitioners taking a solution-focused approach will enhance their work by helping their clients build upon their signature strengths, boost up lower strengths, and help them discover a wide, balanced use of character strengths across contexts. Tools and techniques in the armamentarium of solution-focused practitioners include naming previous solutions to the client's problem, looking for exceptions to the client's problem, validating what the client is doing well, and inviting clients to do more of what's working (Berg & Dolan, 2001). Character strengths can play several important roles: being integrated into questions, as attributes to be boosted and as mechanisms used by the therapist to enact the technique. Table 3.6 offers examples of character strengths integration pathways for solution-focused approaches. In the table, there is the quintessential solution-focused therapy technique referred to as "the miracle question" (Berg & Dolan, 2001), which is usually stated similar to the following:

> Imagine that you go to bed tonight and then wake up in the morning and a miracle has taken place during the night – your problem is solved! And as you slowly emerge from your sleep, what would be the first small sign that helps you see that a miracle did indeed take place and your problem is gone?

Equally important to this question are follow up strategies around scaling and coping, such as "On a scale of 1 to 10 where 10 is having the problem solved, please rate your current experience in regard to the problem"; "How do you know you are at a __ (number chosen)?"; and "How have you managed to move from a __ to a __ (number chosen)?"

Table 3.6. Solution-Focused Techniques and Examples of Character Strengths Integration

Classic, Solution-Focused Technique	Example of Character Strengths Integration
Name previous solutions to problems	What character strengths did you deploy back then to reach that solution?
Look for exceptions to problems	Practitioner uses critical thinking/judgment (and encourages the client to use this strength) to see the nuances, such as times when the problem resolved or lessened.
Validate what is going well	Practitioner uses strengths-spotting with client.
Acknowledge the difficulty of problems	Practitioner deploys empathy (social intelligence) and compassion/kindness to the client. Encourages the client to apply social intelligence and kindness inwardly (i.e., self-compassion).
Use present- and future-oriented questions	What strengths are you using right now, just being here with me, talking and working to develop solutions to your problem? What character strengths might you use to make further progress?
Take more action with what is working	Behavioral activation with character strengths.
Set and work toward a specific goal	How will one of your character strengths act as a concrete pathway to help you reach your goal?
Miracle question	What were the essential character strengths you used to make the miracle a reality (or to make progress toward the miracle)?
Scaling	How have you used your character strengths so far to be at this number? What is one small way you can use one of your strengths to move up one number on the scale?
Coping	What character strengths are involved with the prevention of your getting worse?

Coaching Approaches

There are many models, approaches, and types of coaching, but there are some common threads across the approaches of life coaches, health/wellness coaches, executive coaches, and parent coaches.

The International Coach Federation, the leading credentialing organization in coaching, says this about coaches on their webpage:

> Coaches are trained to listen, to observe and to customize their approach to individual client needs. They seek to elicit solutions and strategies from the client; they believe the client is naturally creative and resourceful. The coach's job is to provide support to enhance the skills, resources, and creativity that the client already has. (http://www.icfminnesota.org/about-coaching)

These natural, internal resources in clients are their character strengths, which can be accessed and deployed to support the coach or the client. As coaching involves a shift from observer to participant, from passive to active, from negative to positive, from teaching to experiencing, and from telling to listening (Rock & Page, 2009), character strengths support the coach with each shift. This is because character strengths are naturally energizing, easily made to be action-oriented, and are participative, leading to activities that are engaging and positive in the coaching sessions.

Few would disagree that the heart of coaching is the establishment of a good relationship, helping clients understand themselves, and helping clients set and work toward goals that will assist them in gaining greater well-being, engagement, and meaning, higher achievements, or better relationships. The VIA character strengths are at *the* core of each of these areas (Seligman, 2011). This is why character strengths are referred to as "the backbone of the science and practice of positive psychology."

Ultimately, the utilization of character strengths allows a coach to take a more rigorous approach to strengths assessment and intervention (i.e., awareness, exploration, and use). Three process are particularly useful to accomplish this in coaching (Niemiec, Rashid, Linkins, Green, & Mayerson, 2013): strengths knowledge, strengths use, and strengths-spotting. In addition, all coaches must be proficient in the science of goal-setting (Halvorson, 2011; Miller & Frisch, 2009). One important link between character strengths and goal-setting is that character strengths can pose as the means or the ends to the goal. In other words, character strengths might be the *goal itself* (e.g., "I want to build up my strength of self-regulation") or the *pathway* to reaching the goal (e.g., "I will use my curiosity strength to create a pathway of asking a friendly question to one new person each day, which will help me reach my goal of having more friends at work"). In terms of specific character strengths and the construction of personal and professional goals, a coachee probably uses hope to conceive of a goal, prudence to plan for it, and perseverance to carry it out.

Ultimately, coaches are helping coachees get better in touch with themselves and empowering them to use their best qualities to enhance well-being, manage problems, improve relationships, and find success.

There are many coaching programs and models that have integrated character strengths work, and each is unique to its own context (see Gibbs & Larcus, 2015, and Larcus, Gibbs, & Hackmann, 2016, for successful integration examples in wellness coaching). In terms of models, one of the most widely used models that provides a conversational structure to coaching is the GROW model, championed by Sir John Whitmore (1996). Each of the phases of the GROW model (goal, reality check, options, will/way forward) are associated with important questions to support a client in taking action (Stoltzfus, 2008). As with the phases and steps with any coaching model, character strengths can be seamlessly integrated to support the coachee at each phase. Table 3.7 maps out the description and sample questions for each phase of the GROW model, along with examples of potential pathways for character strengths integration.

Table 3.7. The GROW Model of Coaching and the Integration of Character Strengths

GROW Model	Description	Sample Questions	Character Strengths Integration
Goal	Co-construct the desired objective for the coaching experience.	What specifically do you want to accomplish in our work together? What outcome would make our conversation a success?	What character strengths will help you get there? What character strengths have you previously used to get you where you are today with that?
Reality check	Determine an objective starting point for change. Gather facts, not opinions.	What have you accomplished with this in the last week? How many times? When did this occur? Who was involved?	What character strengths did you use this week when this was occurring? What difference did using your strengths make?
Options/ obstacles	Develop several potential solutions by encouraging the thinking of things through.	What action did you take? What obstacles emerged? What are your options for overcoming this obstacle?	What character strengths have others used to manage a similar situation successfully?

Table 3.7. Continued

GROW Model	Description	Sample Questions	Character Strengths Integration
			Which of your strengths will be most helpful in facing/overcoming this barrier?
			What character strength might you use right now to brainstorm potential courses of action?
Will/way forward	Turn the preferred solution into concrete action steps.	What is one step you can take this week to move you toward your goal?	What character strengths will help you with this specific step?
		What option do you want to turn into action?	When obstacles arise, which character strengths will you turn to?
		On a scale of 1–10, how likely is it you will take this step this week?	

Any Therapeutic Orientation

Research on psychotherapy has abounded over recent decades due to the work of many scholars, not the least of whom is Bruce Wampold, whose studies of what accounts for change in psychotherapy has deeply impacted the field. To the surprise of many practitioners, the type of therapy used is not strongly associated with the amount of change that occurs in personality traits (Roberts et al., 2017). Quantitative research has supported a "general equivalence" across the main therapeutic orientations, meaning that there are similar positive results across the valid, structured psychotherapies and that most of change is accounted for by relational and contextual factors (Laska, Gurman, & Wampold, 2014). Client factors therein are estimated to be the biggest contributor to impactful change yet have been a much-neglected factor (Bohart & Tallman, 2010). Targeting a client perspective is congruent with the "client as self-healer" paradigm (Bohart, 2007). Therefore, a comprehensive qualitative analysis was conducted examining 109 studies, which revealed five core, client change clusters (some of which highlighted character strengths (Levitt, Pomerville, & Surace, 2016). Three of the five overarching clusters along with hypothesized character strengths are: (1) client change as occurring through structured curiosity and engagement in pattern identification and narrative reconstruction (e.g., curiosity, judgment/critical thinking, perspective); (2) the caring and acceptance of therapists to allow clients to internalize positive messages and enter the change process (e.g., kindness, social intelligence); and (3) therapy progresses as a collaborative effort with discussion of differences (e.g., teamwork, leadership).

An exploratory study of experienced psychotherapists examined their perceptions of how signature strengths enhance their work, and three themes emerged: signature strengths contributed to meaningful work, higher energy levels, and enabling work environment conditions (Atkinson, 2007). Therapists who take a strengths-based approach with clients are described as more likely to experience vicarious resilience in working with clients (Edelkott, Engstrom, Hernandez-Wolfe, & Gangsei, 2016).

The work of integrating character strengths into the myriad of forms of psychotherapy, coaching, and other helping professions is just beginning. Practitioners can turn to virtually any element of the practitioner–client relationship, the client themselves, or the change process and find benefit in applying character strengths.

6. Use Your Own Strengths in Sessions and in Meetings

In general, a character strengths-based approach is viewed as having the following descriptors:
- *Collaborative.* Involves a two-way street that is explorative and productive.
- *Honest.* Acknowledges problems, but doesn't get lost in them.
- *Positive.* Brings what's best (strengths) into the session and attempts to engender the same within the client – to build the positive but also to manage difficulties and conflicts.
- *Empowering.* Encourages and advances the individual.
- *Energizing.* Uplifts and fuels the person.
- *Insightful.* Adds to the person's knowledge of themselves and how they relate to others.
- *Connecting.* Brings the person closer to not only themselves but to others (including the coach), aiding in mutual connections.

These are qualities the practitioner expresses, directly or indirectly, to clients. These are not true all the time for every encounter. For example, at times clients will not walk away feeling "energized" (and neither will the practitioner). It is likely that those practitioners who embody their signature strengths (and a range of other character strengths) will be optimally embodying and thereby facilitating these elements.

Strengths-Based Practitioner Tip
As you help others explore their character strengths, consider how you might benefit from exploring your own character strengths in the context of a practitioner–client encounter (adapted from McQuaid, Niemiec, & Doman, in press). • How might I bring forth my signature strengths into the process as I interact with clients (or students or employees)? • How comfortable am I with how I will introduce character strengths, the rationale for strengths, VIA Survey instructions, and the debriefing of the results with my clients? Do I need to script some of this out to help me remember the key points? • What character strengths interventions do I need to personally practice before trying them out with my clients? • How will I integrate strengths interventions into my existing framework in order to be of maximum benefit for my client?

One of the challenges practitioners face is simply remembering to attend to their own strengths during sessions and meetings as it can be surprisingly common for practitioners to forget to turn to their own inner resources. Mindfulness approaches can serve as a direct path for practitioners to stay more carefully tuned into their own processes and to their character strengths which can be deployed in the session (Niemiec, 2014a). The use of mindfulness revolves around the use of two character strengths in particular – self-regulation and curiosity (Bishop et al., 2004) – and is an emerging adjunct for practitioners to use for self-development (Hall, 2013; Passmore & Marianetti, 2007; Pollak, Pedulla, & Siegel, 2014).

Practitioners who are mindful of their own strengths begin to realize that any of the 24 character strengths can be applied to assist themselves in engaging with the client, maintaining attention, and facilitating a positive interaction. For example, a practitioner high in curiosity may draw upon this strength to deeply explore a client's goals; creativity to facilitate the brainstorming of ideas; self-regulation to maintain focus on the topic at hand; prudence to manage time wisely; bravery to challenge a client at the right time; love to bring forth an approach that is warm and genuine; and teamwork to capitalize on the collaborative nature of the therapeutic or coaching relationship.

According to Harvard psychologist Carol Kauffman and colleagues, practitioners and clients directly benefit from use of the VIA Survey and a character strengths focus in at least three ways:
1. Develops a new language for labeling and accessing strengths;
2. Elevates the coach's self-efficacy, effectiveness, and enthusiasm during challenging times; and
3. Assists in creating an optimal practitioner–client relationship (Kauffman et al., 2008).

One of the most helpful insights a practitioner can remember during a therapy or coaching session is to deploy their own signature strengths during the experience. Why not bring forth your best, most authentic self into your work with clients? Of course, it makes perfect sense, but this idea typically sits preconsciously in the practitioner's mind, often untapped and underutilized.

A client of mine, "Chris R.," was beginning his own practice of coaching in the field of health and wellness. He shared with me his insecurities about coaching, how he felt uncertain about what he was doing, and how it seemed as if everyone else in his coaching training cohort knew how to coach others well. Everybody but him. Of course, he was describing the universal phenomenon known as the "imposter syndrome." In starting out new work – especially interactive work like coaching, psychotherapy, teaching, or managing – part of the experience involves feelings of uneasiness as one navigates new terrain. The strategy of systematically going through one's Top 5–7 character strengths and applying them into a sample coaching encounter is a way to build confidence and comfort in sessions. That is the approach I took with Chris – I remembered that each of the 24 character strengths was a potential resource he could use. He and I started with the top strength in his profile, and went through his Top 7 strengths one-by-one, brainstorming ways he could use each in his work coaching others. Like many clients, Chris resonated with the topic of taking on a character strengths mindset but he was concerned he would forget in the moment. Therefore, we created some "mindset catalysts" that would be practical and easy for him to remember to embody the particular strength. Table 3.8 offers some of the examples that emerged from Chris's signature strengths and the mindsets he could embody, or, at the least, remember in the moment that he had within him to potentially call forth.

Table 3.8. Character Strength Mindsets When With a Client

Character Strength	Mindset for Session	Catalyst to Prompt Mindset in Session
Curiosity	Take an exploratory and questioning approach	Ask a question
Kindness	Think and act from a caring and supportive perspective	Offer client a glass of water
Judgment	Allow rationality/reason to guide me	Touch my head subtly with my finger as a reminder to think and reason
Gratitude	Allow heartfelt appreciation to permeate my attitude and behavior	Spot a strength and share my appreciation for it
Honesty	When in doubt, be myself	Self-disclose a relevant story; share my newness to coaching to my client
Spirituality	Find meaning/sense of calling in working as a practitioner/helper; explore what gives my client meaning, if appropriate	Place a spiritual icon or sacred object on desk/wall in my office in the line of my view
Forgiveness	Let go of biases, offensive remarks, differing opinions	Take a deep breath and on the exhale "let go" of thinking and embrace gentleness

This approach of bringing forth signature strengths in sessions is a way practitioners can be true to their own message – and to practice what one preaches as a strength-based practitioner. It is a way of taking care of oneself during experiences that can, at times, be draining and stressful. Strengths use can manage the harsh inner critic and move practitioners in the direction of self-fairness, self-forgiveness, and self-compassion. Specifically, strengths use can be targeted before, during, or after a meeting or a session with a client. Table 3.9 offers an overview of three practitioner techniques and guiding questions across time orientation that can contribute to practitioner self-care and practitioner strengths activation. Each of these techniques is detailed out in Chapter 8.

Table 3.9. Character Strengths Activities Across Time Orientation

Time Orientation	Positive Psychology Strategy	Question(s) for Exploration
Before a session	Resource priming	What are my best qualities as a helper?
During a session	The mindful pause	What character strength am I using in session right now?
		What strength might I consciously bring forth right now?
After a session	Positive reminiscence	What went well in the session?
		What strengths did I successfully deploy?

Chapter Summary

- The practice of character strengths starts with ourselves. Spot strengths in yourself and in your life stories. Notice, understand, confirm, and appreciate your signature strengths.
- Character strengths are social: Recognizing, labeling, and appreciating character strengths in others, through their actions, nonverbal communication, and their stories is important for building strengths knowledge and strengthening relationships.
- Align character strengths with work tasks and life activities to deepen meaning and personal fulfillment.
- Use the AEA model, which is a metaprocess for working with another person's character strengths.
- Character strengths can be integrated into any theoretical orientation, change process, or disciplined approach in helping others, cutting across clinical psychology, coaching, management, and teaching.
- Practitioners are encouraged to deliberately use their own character strengths in sessions and meetings.

Chapter 4

Behavioral Traps, Misconceptions, and Strategies

Introduction

I have emphasized core concepts relating to character strengths (Chapter 1), key practices that have served practitioners well when it comes to signature strengths work (Chapter 2), and shown how character strengths can be integrated into practice (Chapter 3). Now, let's look at where practitioners frequently get stuck or hung up on when working with character strengths. I've seen the very best practitioners, researchers, and educators (some of which are recognized leaders in positive psychology) make these missteps when engaging in the education and practice of character strengths.

This chapter addresses troubleshooting with strengths work and is my attempt to bring the various practitioners and their differing levels of experience on a similar page with character strengths work. For the purposes of this chapter, the "behavioral traps" are actions that strengths-based practitioners take that may not be optimal, are misguided, or are not adhering to the science. I use the term "misconception" to refer to biased beliefs or mindsets that are incorrect, unhelpful, and/or wrong-minded. In psychological terms, thinking and behaving greatly influence one another, thus there is the potential that these phenomena can mutually impact one another and create vicious circles. These traps, misconceptions, and approaches emerged from my coaching and teaching positive psychology practitioners, observations of research in the field, and conversations with thought leaders and advanced practitioners/researchers across cultures.

Behavioral Traps and Suggested Strategies

Many, if not most, practitioners refer to themselves as strengths-based. However, the word "strengths" has become a generic term that does not have universal meaning. No practitioner is perfect, and there is no exact, agreed-upon strengths-based approach, but there are many bad habits and common errors that well-intentioned practitioners make and which could impact the client. I'll review seven of these common missteps and how each might be corrected or improved upon by deploying a character strengths-based approach.

Just Show Up

Behavioral Trap

Because the field of strengths is an amorphous and subjective area in which most practitioners do not give much attention to the different types of strengths, the dimensionality of strengths, and the models of strengths-based work, it is easy, and therefore common, for practitioners to wing it. By knowing a couple of strengths-based activities and taking a positive-minded approach, many practitioners feel confident they've got strengths covered. Many feel further credence for this approach because they place the onus of the work on the client, and, therefore, believe being armed with a few questions on strengths will be sufficient as the client is the one doing the work. In reality, this is not a sign of an intuitive and competent helper but more an indication of the fast-paced busyness of helping professionals that often leads us unprepared to do our best.

Suggested Strategy: Prepare With Resource Priming

It was Alexander Graham Bell, one of the most successful inventors the world has known, who said "Before anything else, preparation is the key to success." Research studies support this showing that if a therapist focuses on their client's strengths prior to a therapy session (called "resource priming") that a number of positive outcomes unfold such as improved outcomes, a higher use of strengths in the session, a stronger practitioner–client relationship, and more experiences of mastery/accomplishment (Fluckiger & Grosse Holtforth, 2008; Fluckiger, Casper, Grosse Holtforth, & Willutzki, 2009; Fluckiger, Wusten, Zinbarg, & Wampold, 2010). The task is fairly simple for the practitioner: Take a few minutes to reflect on the strengths of the client you are about to meet with. What are their signature strengths? What strength-based discussions have you had with them already? What strengths do they overuse? What strengths are they using in their daily life? In meetings with you? Resource priming allows the practitioner to tailor the work to the individual client.

The main study on resource priming was done with psychotherapists; however, therapy encounters shouldn't be the only population to benefit. No doubt coaching relationships can benefit as well as supervisor–supervisee, teacher–student, and so forth. Here are some examples of extending this practice across professions:

- Teachers might reflect on the strengths of their students and the strengths of their classroom-as-a-whole before walking in to teach a lesson. Further, they can consider how they will help the students explore and use their strengths during classroom lessons and projects.
- Managers might reflect on the strengths of their employees before entering a weekly meeting with them, before an employee review, or prior to a team meeting. In addition, these employers can take a moment to remember the best qualities of each employee before sending them an e-mail or phone message.
- Parents might reflect on the strengths of their children before their next interaction with them. While driving home, working parents could spend time considering ways in which they can validate and encourage their child's strengths later that day.
- Couples might consider the strengths of their spouse or partner before engaging in a conflict or confrontation. Couples can reflect on the signature strengths of their loved one that they most cherish and appreciate.

Remediate Lower Strengths, Deficits, and Weaknesses

Behavioral Trap

What's one of the first things a person does when they receive their rank-order results on the VIA Survey? They look to the bottom of their profile, and exclaim they want or need to boost one or more strengths. This is an automatic reaction and comes from our ingrained nature to fix or correct what's wrong. It's fascinating that we take this approach, bypassing about 20 positive qualities in order to get to the bottom! Why are we so focused on weakness and deficit? There are many reasons including our fight or flight biology that wires us to see inconsistencies, flaws, and potential danger very quickly. Research has shown over and over that bad is stronger than good (Baumeister, Bratslavsky, Finkenaeuer, & Vohs, 2001), meaning that the impact of the negative aspects of our psychology has more substantial and enduring effects than the good. And, other research shows that people perceive their weaknesses as more malleable than their strengths and, in turn, view their strengths as constant (Steimer & Mata, 2016). People also expect their weaknesses to improve and have a greater desire to correct or change their weaknesses.

Part of the reason clients believe their strengths are constant and thereby not malleable to change is the "taking-strengths-for-granted effect," which occurs as mindlessness and automaticity take hold of the individual rather than an open-minded mindfulness that pursues growth and possibility (Dweck, 2006; Niemiec, 2014a). Others have described this as seeing strengths as ordinary rather than extraordinary (Biswas-Diener et al., 2011), which misses the true reality and potential of our strengths.

Whether it be weaknesses, deficits, or lesser strengths, practitioners are equally vulnerable to being biased toward what's less strong and they will be pulled into the energy of the negative or the emotionality around a struggle. My colleague and I were a perfect example of this. Several years ago, we began consulting to local Boys and Girls Clubs in the region we lived. These clubs serve at-risk kids with programming, skill-building, and after-school resources for further learning, play, and connections. The entire staff at each club participated; we gathered the staff in a circle and engaged in exercises around signature strengths and strengths-spotting. Part of our approach involved the staff identifying and describing a child that was struggling, isolated, or difficult, in other words, a "lost child." When we asked each person to describe their examples we heard stories of fire-starting, selfish behavior, rude behavior, and disrespect; it was easy for us as the facilitators to get caught up in the stories and thinking about how difficult or problematic the child was. The deficit-based thinking and discussion was contagious for the staff and it even fed our own deficit-based thinking, despite the topic being character strengths! (I'll return to this story in the next section).

There's nothing inherently wrong with focusing on lower strengths and research has revealed there are benefits in targeting lesser strengths too (Proyer et al., 2015). However, if what is less strong in the individual is the starting point of a conversation, then perhaps the strengths-based approach is not as strong as it could be. A tactic that practitioners can take is to get clarity on the client's perspective and hopes at the onset of the interaction. After reviewing their character strengths profile (the rank-order of strengths from 1 to 24), many clients will immediately hyperfocus on their bottom strengths and comment on how they want to improve one of them. Consider this interaction I had with a coachee around getting clarity:

Coach: What would you like to focus on today?
Coachee: I want to elevate my lowest character strength.
Coach: At the expense of which other strengths?
Coachee: What do you mean?
Coach: If you lift a lower strength in your rank-order then that means it will rise above other strengths. Therefore, one or more strengths will go down in your rank order.
Coachee: That's true. I don't know if I like that so much. I was thinking I didn't like how some of my strengths were down at the bottom.
Coach: Right, some strengths might be lower because you have given less attention to them or simply don't perceive them especially strong in yourself. It's fine to consider that

as an option. But, you might frame it for yourself as "which strength do I want to bring to the forefront of my attention more consistently?"

Coachee: Yes, that gets at it. I'd like to give more attention to my strength of self-regulation.

Suggested Strategy: Educate and Then Go With the Resistance

What can you do with a client who has this misconception? In short, it is alluring for professionals to talk about "weaknesses" with clients, so it's important to embody some open-mindedness and flexibility in one's approach and in considering the suggestions in this section.

Inform the client that the VIA Survey is not a measure of weakness or deficit, therefore it's incorrect to use those terms. An improved albeit imperfect phrase is "lower strengths," which are just that, strengths that according to the individual's self-perception are lower within them in comparison to other strengths. Education can also come in the form of sharing that some research is showing it's better to target strengths than to remediate deficits (e.g., Cheavens et al., 2012; Meyers et al., 2015), although lower strengths are not technically considered deficits or weaknesses.

In addition, there's a time to do what's called psychojudo (Cummings & Sayama, 1995) and go with the resistance rather than fight with the client to adhere to the expert's opinion. Instead, the practitioner follows the client's lead, knowing that this is not a time to resist, disagree, and argue for the approach you believe is optimal for the situation. Finding the balance on this continuum of "allowing" and "resisting" can be challenging. The issue of lower strengths brings up this tension. As an example, when clients refer to their lowest strengths as weaknesses, I first inquire what they mean by this, and if it appears they are defining themselves by the term weakness then I am generally quick to move to the "resistant" side of the continuum and educate them on how the VIA Survey does not formally measure weaknesses. However, when a person insists on targeting their lower strengths, rather than fight them on the terminology and attempt to push them to focus on signature strengths, I go with the resistance and the client's inclination and at the same time look for opportunities to educate and move the client forward. Here's an example:

Coachee: I want to work on my lower strengths.

Coach: OK, but I want you to know that signature strengths are where many people find the most benefit. We have a natural inclination to want to correct what's wrong or change a problem or deficit within us. Often that's how people approach their VIA strengths profile – to go toward the bottom where they are not as strong. There's nothing wrong with that but research is showing there is benefit to shifting our mindset to study, understand, and build upon what's at the top.

Coachee: I disagree with you that the signature strengths are more important. Building up my lower character strengths will make me more complete.

Coach: [Educating] Let me share a bit about signature strengths. These are strengths that are most core to who you are and likely where your highest energy is. They are no doubt a driving force in your life. Understanding and building upon these unique strengths in you can help you reach your goals, become happier, and get more in flow at your work. Signature strengths are what really matter.

Coachee: I already know my signature strengths. They did not surprise me. Lower strengths are what I need. I was surprised that some of these were so low in my profile. I think that's where I will benefit.

Coach: [Going with the resistance] OK. Have you found benefit in working on your lower strengths before?

Coachee: Yes, I have.

Coach: What did you focus on?

Coachee: My lowest strength of perseverance.

Coach: What did you do?

Coachee: I set small goals so that I could keep accomplishing little things each day. I felt better getting things done – more in control.

Coach: Excellent. How did you do that?

Coachee: I took an approach of being gentle with myself. I can be pretty harsh at times, especially when I don't succeed with a project I'm working on. So, what I did is I tracked my little goals each day and if I didn't meet one or two then I remembered to be gentle to myself. I had the word "gentleness" written on the top right-hand corner of my tracking sheet. I then just picked up where I left off the day before.

Coach: That sounds like a solid approach you took. What character strengths do you hear yourself sharing as you describe the approach?

Coachee: Well, my approach with the tracking sheet certainly involved being disciplined and self-regulated.

Coach: Yes, I heard that. I also spotted kindness turned inward as you emphasized being gentle with yourself.

Coachee: That's right.

Coach: Where do those character strengths sit in your rank order?

Coachee: Kindness is Number 1 and self-regulation is Number 4.

As this case shows, ultimately, we never stray far from our core. This coachee was using signature strengths, quite automatically, in an important way. Our signature strengths are always nearby, and, as this person showed, signature strengths can be a successful avenue to boost a lowest strength. This is referred to as the "towing principle." If we, as practitioners, really believe this point, then we have no reason to fear an approach of "going with the resistance" or of handing the reigns of the session over to a client. With the ubiquity and power of the client's signature strengths, there is likelihood that whatever their intentions, stories, directions, or viewpoints our clients bring up, their signature strengths will be lurking nearby for us to point out and integrate.

I'll conclude this section by returning to the story of my colleague and I consulting at local Boys and Girls Clubs and running into our own "negativity bias" as we were swept up in the vicious circle of staff critiques of a "lost child" at the club. When we noticed ourselves falling into the trap, we were able to shift the conversation with one simple statement and question: "OK, it sounds like there are many challenges you're facing as a staff with Billy. But, we'd like to ask you another question now – What do you like about Billy? What is best about him?" The staff quickly shifted in their perception of Billy, offering observations of his helpfulness at the front desk, teamwork on the basketball court sharing the ball, praising of other kid's artwork in art class, and a myriad of other examples. We were then caught up in the strengths "positive contagion." And, the staff was left surprised and pleased that they were not only able to do the simple task of strengths-spotting but that they were able to transform their perceptions of this child who clearly had suffered a lot in his life.

Jump to Action Before Understanding

Behavioral Trap

Practitioners, especially those in the positive psychology domain, get very excited about the exercises and interventions that might benefit their clients, students, and employees. This leads them to sometimes jump to action before generating deeper client understanding. In the lingo of the aware-explore-apply model, this is equivalent to skipping the explore phase and going from awareness immediately into action. The classic example is the practitioner getting the client to take the VIA Survey and then immediately telling them what action they should take with their strengths or how to pursue their goals.

There are many reasons a practitioner might skip the explore phase of strengths work. There may be impatience on the part of the practitioner who wants to please the client right away and wants to show some expertise by offering a solution. Impatience, can also be driven by the client, who wants a quick remedy to their problem, and is not eager to reflect, journal, and answer various questions about their strengths. And, some practitioners may not know how to "go deep" with strengths and so jump from aware to apply.

Suggested Strategy: Before Activation, Consolidate Knowledge and Explore

There are exceptions to each suggested strategy for these traps. There will be times when it's good for a client to "jump first" and understand later. This is particularly true for depressed clients who often need behavioral activation more than anything else. They may not understand the connection or believe that it will be helpful but the action taken alone can begin to make an impact and pave the way for future cognitive-emotional work.

Spending time in exploring and helping clients understand, validate, and appreciate their strengths is often an important step between awareness of strengths and action with strengths. This helps clients consolidate their knowledge, taking stock in where they have come and where they are headed.

Practitioners might make an honest audit of themselves and their strengths work. In addition to considering the various questions in Appendix D, as many of these deal with exploration work, practitioners can ask themselves: Where do I, as the practitioner, place my emphasis with my strengths work? If I only examine the questions I ask, are my questions more aware-oriented, explore-oriented, or apply-oriented?

Practitioners can learn to make time to not only help the client explore their strengths more thoroughly but also to learn more about the client as an individual so that the exercise being deployed can be properly individualized and contextualized. Sufficient exploration of strengths helps the client draw connections between who they are and why this strengths work matters for them.

Start With "What Went Wrong?"

Behavioral Trap

There's a deeply ingrained perception many practitioners have that to talk about problems and struggles – "the hard stuff" – adds credibility. But, who says that character strengths work isn't equally challenging? In reality, it's quite easy to find the flaws – what didn't go well, what mistakes were made, and when did things turn sour. We do this negativity-first approach with ourselves so it's only natural this would transfer to our clients.

Many times after a business or work meeting, especially those involving one-on-one interaction, I would leave the meeting and a voice in my head would say:
• You should have said _____.
• Why didn't you bring up _____? Why did you hold back?

- You could have been smoother when you were discussing ____.
- The other person wasn't receptive to my idea about ___. I should have explained it better.

And on and on my thinking would go. My thoughts would immediately focus on what is wrong and then tirelessly replay the parts that went wrong. My mind would then attempt to solve what was wrong. But how can I fix something that already happened? I would deliberately think of what went right, but it always seemed to take a back-seat. In other words, I seemed to automatically put what was right in the trunk. And what was the result of replaying what went wrong and trying to find a solution? Little to nothing gained. In addition, I was left feeling worse about the meeting.

Suggested Strategy: Start With "What Went Well?"

To continue with the example about my approach after meetings, one day I took a different approach from recounting the negatives and what I could improve upon. While driving back to my office after a business lunch meeting, I immediately asked myself, what went well? Then, my second question: What character strengths did I bring forth in the meeting? I carefully listened to what my mind had to say. I observed my mind as it traveled through a panoply of strengths. This meeting was no different than the previous meetings. What was different was my follow-up thinking. The character strengths that were used swelled and swelled to the point where there was almost no room to even consider what went wrong!

My mind considered how my basic approach was one of humility linked with curiosity because I placed the focus on the other person, allowed them to share widely and deeply, and encouraged them to continue sharing by asking them a variety of questions. I used love of learning to gather knowledge about the person's organization and the various programs and outreach. I deliberately used self-regulation and perseverance together (some might call this patience) to not interrupt or quickly share my reaction. Instead I persistently held back this natural impulse. When I did share my comments and experiences, it was from my signature strengths of love and hope. These core strengths were my drivers – or the motor – that fueled what I said. In other words, warmth, genuineness, future-minded planning, and positivity drove the conversation from my end.

And, what went wrong? I did leave a little bit of focus in my thinking to consider the meeting from a deficit perspective. I had already mentally processed many dimensions of the conversation from the positive view that only one new area popped up. There was one point in the conversation where I felt I could have been a bit smoother in the transition, namely when I introduced a discussion point around how our two organizations might collaborate in the future. I considered I might bring forth greater strength of social intelligence in future scenarios during transition points. For example, rather than blurting out a general question of how might we work together more, I could shift to context-driven comments such as: "Wow, we sure do seem to have a lot in common. I appreciate our similar vision and hard work. This makes me wonder about how we might collaborate in the future. Do you have any thoughts about this?"

In graduate courses with students and in mindfulness-based strengths practice (MBSP; Niemiec, 2014a), I've embedded a "what went well?" activity at the beginning of each week. This is a time to discuss the homework exercises and activities. Clearly, there will be discussions of what didn't go well, what obstacles got in the way, what didn't get done – and those are important to address. But, if that's the totality of the experience then it's a one-dimensional experience. Bringing in a focus on the positive and good at the onset ensures that strengths get attention. This helps to set a good foundation for the discussion.

Be Rigid About Top Strengths

Behavioral Trap

You'll hear plenty about the value of signature strengths in this book – and despite my frequent mentioning of signature strengths, I'm probably still underselling their potential. That said, it is possible to get locked into the top strengths (e.g., the Top 5) and neglect the others. To become locked in is to conflict with the "all 24 matter" principle and reflects more of a rigid or naïve approach to strengths work than anything else.

Suggested Strategy: Prioritize Top Strengths but Attend to All

There are always many balancing points to keep in mind when working with the new science and practice of character strengths and the broader field of positive psychology. One of these balance points is to attend simultaneously to the principles of "all 24 character strengths matter" and "signature strengths often matter most." Despite the robustness of the character strengths work, getting hyperfocused on any one intervention or construct is probably unwise. This is where the wider view offered by the strength of perspective is important.

When interpreting character strength profiles, the VIA Institute has recommended caution by suggesting that people review their strengths profiles (or any interpretative reports on character strengths) with "broad brushstrokes" rather than fine-tuned, precise paint-strokes. An example of how this approach can be seen with a client of mine named Joan. After taking the VIA Survey, I asked Joan about what she thought of her results. She looked at her profile and had an immediate reaction, exclaiming, "Yes, creativity and curiosity are my top two strengths. I use those all the time." After talking about these two strengths and how she uses them in her life, I then asked about her other top strengths and which might be "signature" to her. She declined interest in talking about other top strengths. I offered the observation that she has many strengths to which she quickly resisted. I'll pick our dialogue up at that point.

Ryan: Those are some great examples of creativity and curiosity in your life. And, looking at your profile here, it is clear you have many other strengths too, Joan.

Joan: No, I just have creativity and curiosity. The others aren't me. Take a look at the bottom. There's perseverance at number 24 and that's correct. I'm not at all perseverant.

Ryan: Actually, we all have all of these strengths to some degree. You might not be accustomed to using one or more of them.

Joan: Nah, not me. That's not part of me.

Ryan: I'm sure there are times when you have used this strength a little bit in your life?

Joan: Not perseverance or persistence. I'm not that way.

Ryan: How does the word capacities strike you? You have each of these strengths as a capacity, or a potential, that can be developed and expanded upon. That's true for numbers 1 through 5 and numbers 20 through 24.

Joan: No, I don't see that. All you psychologists are the same. Always trying to find the positive. I'm telling you, I don't have perseverance.

Ryan: I should point out that you're persevering with your views in this conversation. You're showing perseverance quite strongly with me right now. You don't give up easily.

Joan: That's true. I am perseverant when I think I'm right.

For Joan, she struggled to understand her qualities until they were pointed out in-the-moment (i.e., strengths-spotting). While subtle, her lowest strength of perseverance was strong and clear in some situations. It was a bit rough around the edges in that she could be quickly opinionated and narrowly stick with a mostly uninformed perspective but she showed good willingness to adapt when the facts were presented clearly. Joan and I spent more time targeting her best qualities of creativity and curiosity but from time to time it was important to remind her of this conversation and that she had many qualities she could draw from, smooth out, and wield in her life.

Overplay Overuse

Behavioral Trap

The overuse of character strengths is discussed in Chapter 5 but is also mentioned here as a trap practitioners frequently fall into. To overuse a character strength is to express it too strongly for the situation, which leads to increased tension, a particular problem, a relationship conflict, etc. The concept of overuse offers a great way to reframe problems (e.g., instead of calling someone stubborn and hard-headed, one might say they are overusing their strength of perseverance). This makes overuse a truly fascinating and provocative topic.

The problem is not whether to address overuse of strengths or not, the issue is when and how much. Some competent practitioners address overuse very early on and many clients, upon learning about the topic, want to start with overuse. The problem with this is it's starting with a deficit-based approach, using the guise of strengths. An overuse of strengths is an interpretation made by the practitioner that means something is not right or is imbalanced. What frequently follows is a client preoccupation with overuse or a practitioner neglect of the basics of expanding, celebrating, and appreciating character strengths. Overuse is a deep and rich topic and one that's easy to get lost in.

I recall helping a counselor who was using character strengths as an approach to help a stressed-out client. She reviewed her client's character strengths profile and had discussions with him around exploring and building his strengths. In these conversations, the client honed in on his higher strength of humility and concluded that he was overusing his humility, being too self-servient and self-sacrificing, and that that was the cause of his problems. The counselor bought into this argument and began to target the overuse of humility. She became preoccupied with managing the overuse which did not gain any traction. She didn't know what to do. I asked her about her client's use and benefits of humility, which she resisted at first, but upon taking a closer examination of the true nature of healthy humility (i.e., someone with a good self-concept who is good at placing attention on others and prioritizing others' successes) she realized she and her client had never explored or understood the strength to begin with. And, they never spent time discussing the value of humility and the concrete benefits it brought to her client and others. Finding new ways to work with this robust concept of humility was all that her client needed, not finding ways to correct an overuse of it. The counselor was now able to offer her client a new way to see himself and the world around him through the lens of his signature strength.

Even though the desire will often be stronger to focus on the overuse of strengths rather than the building up of an underused strength, new research actually points to underuse, not overuse, as the bigger problem people face (Freidlin, Littman-Ovadia, & Niemiec, 2017). The underuse of character strengths has stronger relationships with lower flourishing, lower life satisfaction, and higher depression than the overuse of character strengths does.

Suggested Strategy: Understand, Expand, and Appreciate Before Reviewing Overuse

Understanding, expanding, appreciating, and celebrating strengths can be a good remedy for those who display the fetish for character strengths overuse. It's simply a matter of first things first. Help clients connect with their best qualities in a meaningful way before delving into different ways to deal with deficits, which there will always be time for.

I was coaching a business consultant who wanted to work on her character strengths and described her focus as "I want to stop overusing my prudence." I looked at her character strengths profile and saw that prudence was in her Top 5 strengths. I asked her to first describe her prudence and how she actually "uses" it before digging into how she "overuses" it. She was unable to come up with a single example of how she used her prudence (one of her signature strengths!). I felt sad for her as she was quick to self-criticize, dis-endorse, avoid, and pass over a quality that had no doubt served her well in many ways over the decades. Knowing that prudence is about planfulness, thinking before acting, and thinking decisions through, I asked her to share a time in her life when she had made an important decision. She quickly recounted her decision from a year ago when she changed companies. She went on to share how she took 2 years to think about the decision, wrote out cost–benefit analyses, asked the opinions of trusted colleagues, went to several interviews, and mapped out her finances. She spent time examining her values and how her strengths and values might play out together at multiple possible jobs. She ultimately made the decision to switch jobs, and even though it resulted in a substantial pay decrease it was an increase in her level of "meaning" at work. Her description of her process was the epitome of the prudence strength in action. It was one of the best decisions of her life and was orchestrated and managed by prudence. When I pointed this out to her, she had an "ah-ha" moment. She finally understood prudence and the value it played for her. We then took a look at her daily life and the ways she used her prudence throughout her days, such as being planful packing her two children's lunches for schools, each morning carefully watching them get on the bus and not leaving until the bus was out of sight, planning action items for each of the subordinates on her team, and so on. As her prudence strength became clearer to her, rather than turning to discussing overuse, I asked her as a homework assignment to list 100 ways she has used her strength of prudence in her life.

In order to not miss the forest for the trees by prioritizing overuse and forgetting the basics, practitioners can make a conscious decision to target use before overuse.

Take the Prescriptive/Authoritarian Approach

Behavioral Trap

Targeting strengths instead of exploring strengths is an authoritarian approach of telling a person what is most important for them to build up, rather than coexploring strengths. This approach is rampant in schools.

Over the decades, the field of character science has been dominated by approaches that are underlined by an authoritarian approach. Character, character psychology, and character education have a long history and an extensive review of this work goes beyond the scope of the intentions of this chapter (see Lapsley & Power, 2005, for a nice review of some of the best insights in these areas; and see Berkowitz & Bier, 2007, for the results of a meta-analysis of what works in character education).

The word, character, comes from the Greek word meaning "engraved mark" and "symbol or imprint on the soul." These phrases imply an unchanging or immutable quality as well as a sense of permanence. These descriptions are reinforced by programs that attempt to train or teach "good" character. Such character education programs are widely found in education and athletic programs, and many are outgrowths of a religious, political, or educational agenda.

Often when people speak of the word "character," such as "he is a man of good character" or "she has a lot of character," they are meaning that the person has a lot of integrity or that they are an honest person. This means that character is being viewed as encompassing a single trait or quality. Others advocate that the most essential feature of character is restraint or the control of one's personal appetites (i.e., similar to the character trait of self-regulation; Hunter, 2000). The result of such an approach to character is likened to an "all-or-nothing" mentality – either you have character or you don't. You are a good person or a bad person. Therefore, the dishonest man or woman is doomed. Consider golfer Tiger Woods and former US President Bill Clinton: Are these men of "bad" character because of their philandering? What about the exemplary perseverance and self-regulation of Woods on the golf course and the leadership and writings on kindness/generosity by Clinton (2007)? And, what about Marion Jones and Tonya Harding, each of whom were Olympic athletes that cheated at some point in their careers; are these incredibly talented and hardworking women to be labeled and cast aside as those with bad character? Albert Einstein might be viewed by many as a man of great character but it's not for his honesty, rather it's for his creativity, love of learning, perspective, and insights on spirituality.

Suggested Strategy: Practice Being an Authoritative Gardener

Nurture seeds, don't mold clay! Let me explain: As discussed in Linkins and colleagues (2015), Neal Mayerson offers a metaphor for how teachers approach their students in traditional and nontraditional character education programs. First, there is the prescriptive approach which is traditional character education, usually authoritarian-driven and analogous to the process of seeing children as clay to be molded. The "potter" (school, educator, or other authority figure) works to transform the "clay" (student's character) into a predetermined form. The potter dictates that they'd like to build up certain qualities in every child as they or the system has deemed those qualities most important, such as respect, kindness, responsibility, fairness, perseverance, and so on. Then, there is the descriptive and individualized approach, usually authoritative-driven and analogous to the process of seeing children as seeds to be developed. No two seeds are identical; each is genetically unique and contains certain traits and potential, which may or may not ultimately be expressed, depending upon environmental factors. The gardener's task is not to determine how growth will unfold, but rather to create optimal conditions for growth and development to occur. Like an individual seed, each child possesses a unique constellation of predispositions and possibilities. Under favorable conditions, this potential will find expression. The role of the educator – like that of the gardener – is to provide favorable conditions that will stimulate, encourage, and nurture growth.

This might seem obvious but virtually every character education program I have come across takes some version of this "clay" approach. This is especially true for those in the field of positive psychology, where prescriptive approaches are dominant. Even people that should know better such as prominent authors, expert researchers, and leading figures in positive psychology, are often clay-makers. Each, in some way, is acting as "the authority," eager to instill particular traits or other prescriptions into another person, usually an impressionable young person (i.e., student). This is surprising because most people seem to identify with the "seed" approach as the better choice when these approaches are articulated to them. It's hard to argue with the explanation that each child is an individual and that the role of the educator is to help a student first reveal his or her strengths of character (referred to as signature strengths) and then create an environment where those strengths can shine.

This metaphor can clearly be expanded to the approach of any practitioner (not just teachers/ educators) who is working with a client or employee. Practitioners can prioritize approaches that plant seeds and create a growth environment by focusing on the following:

- Ask questions often and as the default.
- Give opportunity for creative expression of unique strengths.
- Emphasize personal and meaningful exploration of the good.
- Notice and spot positive qualities in the moment.
- Nurture and develop positive qualities.
- Give appreciative feedback when strengths are expressed.
- Create an environment where unique expressions of strengths are desired and reinforced.
- Arrange an environment for open, mutual dialogue about strengths.
- Cocreate an environment of strength expression and growth.

Misconceptions, Realities, and Tips

There are eight common misconceptions or biases that are faulty patterns of thinking that can occur when taking a strengths-based approach. Both practitioners and their clients may operate under these misconceptions. For each misconception presented in the following, a more balanced "reality" is presented, which reflects what is known from the research and practice at the present time. Finally, a tip for practitioners (and their clients) to manage or avoid the faulty belief pattern is given as a possible point of action. Understanding these can help us deepen our understanding of what is meant by strengths-based practice.

Practitioners who are steeped in character strengths work probably would not hold many of these misconceptions because they have seen the depth and challenges of strengths-based work first-hand. These misconceptions will be most applicable to those practitioners new to positive psychology or unfamiliar with it.

Misconception 1: Focusing on Strengths is Pollyannaish

Reality

Character strengths not only accentuate what's best but what is used to face, manage, and overcome problems. Research shows that character strengths help to buffer problems (e.g., Huta & Hawley, 2010), diminish problems (e.g., Gander et al., 2013), and contribute to resilience (e.g., Martinez-Marti & Ruch, 2016; Shoshani & Slone, 2016).

Many make the case that if someone is advising another to "use their strengths" or is trying to help an organization be strengths-based then this automatically means that individual is neglecting what is wrong or problematic, and that that individual is narrowly focusing only on strengths. This is, of course, untrue. Practitioners who prioritize strengths work deserve far more credit than that.

This misconception is a symptom of the suffering of the field of positive psychology. The label of "positive" brings the assumption that positive psychology only examines the positive and does not address the "negative." Any serious positive psychology practitioner or leader knows this is an unfair statement. In fact, some scholars in positive psychology have gone out of their way to refute this and have labeled a "second wave positive psychology" that emphasizes the challenges, struggles, and problems that people have and how the science of positive emotions, strengths, and internal processes are part of suffering and can also help manage and transcend that suffering (Ivtzan, Lomas, Hefferon, & Worth, 2016).

At a recent workshop at a large university, I asked participants (mostly professors) to talk about their character strengths results with one another. During a debrief of the opening activity, a distinguished professor stood up and exclaimed that his group discussed the need for a focus on the negative. His comment is, of course, partly accurate; however, he was assuming that a presentation on strengths will solely be about the positive. This is far from reality as character strengths are quickly catalyzed at times of struggle, tragedy, and stress.

It amazes me to see how quickly we defend our negative mindset and our bias toward talking about problems. Never is this clearer than in a workshop exercise I offer to coachees and presentation attendees called "the 5-minute challenge." For this exercise, I give participants 1 minute to talk about each of the Top 5 strengths (5 minutes in total) with one other participant. Across hundreds of people from different cultures and professions there is a common reaction that emerges: 1 minute is too long to talk about one strength (yes, 1 minute!). People struggle to come up with ways to describe each of their best qualities, examples of previous use for each, and why each strength is important to them. However, when I ask the same people how much time they'd like to talk about 5 of their problems, there is immediate agreement that far more time would be needed and desired.

Practitioner Tip

Use character strengths to not only build well-being but also as an adjunct to manage and understand problems. Explain to clients that character strengths are applied to all the vicissitudes of life – the ups, downs, and in-between periods. They are characteristics that make us human, present at the best and worst of times, and can explain many of our errors as well as help us overcome them.

Misconception 2: Working With Strengths Is Easy

Reality

If all a practitioner does is ask a client occasionally about their top strengths and instructs them to use them more often, then that's true, strengths work is easy. When one considers the plurality of strengths, the multidimensional nature of each strength, the complexity of the myriad of situations one faces each hour to use strengths, AND the interaction of strengths with one another internally and in interaction with others, suddenly there is substantial depth and complexity. This depth is also reflected in research trying to understand the roles character strengths play in understanding and managing psychopathology (Freidlin et al., 2017; Kashdan, Julian, Merritt, & Uswatte, 2006), exposure to war (Shoshani & Slone, 2016), and disability (Niemiec et al., 2017).

Practitioner Tip

Teach, demonstrate, and discuss the various core themes on character strengths education. Teach clients to develop a growth mindset around character strengths in that there is important learning and growth with their character for the rest of their lives.

Misconception 3: All Strengths Are Created Equal

Reality

Not true. As outlined in Chapter 1, you have many different types of strengths: strengths of talent/intelligence, skill, values, interests, and resources. You also have strengths of character and many subcategories therein (e.g., signature, phasic, and lower strengths). Each of these categories is important and offers different benefits. Character strengths can serve as pathways to each of the strength categories; for example, zest and signature strengths can fuel interests, perseverance and self-regulation help make natural abilities and talents soar, and interpersonal-type strengths help us make the most of our resources. Despite varying levels of intercorrelation with one another, each of the 24 character strengths is unique from one another and offers distinct and novel contributions to well-being.

Practitioner Tip

Make an effort to understand the differences between the different strengths categories. Ask assessment questions to evaluate each in your clients. Be sure to understand less obvious distinctions such as the differences between kindness and love or between curiosity and love of learning.

Misconception 4: Character Strengths Are Static

Reality

Character strengths are dynamic, multidimensional, and capable of being developed (see Chapter 1). Character strengths are part of our personality, and decades of research on personality shows that although this is quite stable over time it can be impacted and can change. A number of factors can impact our personality, for example, changes in our life role (e.g., having a child or joining the military), atypical events (e.g., a traumatic experience), and deliberate interventions (e.g., a goal to focus on building curiosity). Hudson and Fraley (2015) offered an intervention study showing that stable traits of personality are malleable and can be changed by an individual's volition. A couple years later, Roberts and colleagues (2017) conducted a meta-analysis of 207 studies in clinical psychology research and found that marked change in personality traits can occur from clinical and nonclinical interventions (and persist longitudinally!). Further longitudinal studies are needed to give greater insight into the developmental changes and factors that influence our character strengths over the decades.

Practitioner Tip

Be prepared to offer examples to your client about how you have positively impacted or changed two or three of your character strengths.

Misconception 5: Knowing Your Strengths Is Enough

Reality

Strengths knowledge is necessary but not sufficient in order to reap all the benefits we can from our strengths. Research shows that it is indeed important and beneficial to have greater strengths awareness, but research also shows that greater benefits occur for those that use their strengths in their personal life and work (Hone et al., 2015; Littman-Ovadia & Steger, 2010). Those that use their strengths are more likely to be happier and engaged in what they are doing.

Practitioner Tip

Teaching strengths exploration and strengths use leads to understanding and better positive outcomes. Have a set of "go-to" questions memorized that will help you explore the strengths use of your client.

Misconception 6: Most People Already Know Their Character Strengths Well

Reality

Strengths blindness is pervasive; however, this is improving in society.

Practitioner Tip

Test this misconception. With each new client (or each new person you meet at a party), ask them to name their strengths or their character strengths, without giving them prompts or a "common language." Study the reactions you receive after you do this 10 or more times. Do people respond quickly? Is there depth and substantial meaning in their response? Do you get to know who they are at their core? Are VIA character strengths words used intuitively?

Misconception 7: "Character" Refers to a Handful of Traits

Reality

What is character? Character is plural and idiosyncratic to each human being. The field of character – and many organizations that teach character – has long argued that character can be boiled down to one core attribute (e.g., honesty or integrity) or to a select handful of attributes (e.g., kindness, respect, fairness, and responsibility). The new science of character challenges this antiquated thinking and observes that character is far more idiosyncratic and can be viewed as plural (Linkins et al., 2015; Peterson, 2006a). We are composed of many character traits and the expression of these come in strength combinations or constellations rather than as isolated traits.

Practitioner Tip

Look at the 24 character strengths on the inside-cover of this book. Are there any strengths that you would eliminate from your "character"? Any that you don't value at times in different situations?

Misconception 8: Talking About Character Strengths Is Bragging and Egotistical

One workshop participant explained it this way: "If I tell people about my strengths, they will think I am cocky and narcissistic. They will see me as different, but different in a bad way. Then, they will not include me in their regular social outings after work."

Reality

Talking about character strengths is a method of self-disclosure and promotes intimacy in relationships. Several research studies now support talking about the good and how it can be beneficial for the person sharing and the receiver (Gable et al., 2004; Lambert, Gwinn, Fincham, & Stillman, 2011; Reis et al., 2010). In addition, many of the strengths are inherently other oriented, such as kindness, fairness, and teamwork, and to bring these forward is to be unselfish. It's important to remember that talking about strengths helps people to see themselves more fully and completely. An egotistical approach would involve taking an approach of superiority in which the person believes they are better than others because of their character strengths. Such an approach of narcissism is the antithesis to someone who is sharing their strengths in a genuine and balanced way.

Many people will report this misconception as a reason they cannot talk about their strengths to others. People will often blame their inability to talk about strengths on their culture saying "We don't do that in our culture." Such views should be explored with open-mindedness. In addition, practitioners need to understand whether there is some level of misunderstanding about the intention of strengths work (e.g., the individual thinking they are being asked to one-up another person), some avoidance of discomfort, and/or a playing of the "humility card." Certainly, there exists a level of awkwardness in doing something new, like talking about one's strengths of character, and this awkwardness can lead to anxiety and avoidance. Hence claiming humility is a way to avoid discomfort.

Practitioner Tips

This is a complex misconception so I offer four tips to address it.
1. Practice nonavoidance of strengths talk and teach clients nonavoidance. I'm not saying to be culturally insensitive or socially unintelligent. Instead, I'm arguing that our ways of communicating with others needs to be more balanced and we need to deploy social intelligence. When you share strengths – or anything else for that matter – the demands of the situation are important. It matters what you say, when you say it, and how you say it. It's true that it is immodest if your approach is to directly or indirectly present your strengths as superior to others' strengths or that because of your many strengths you are a better person than others. It is not immodest, however, to name and share your strengths.
2. Reap the positive well-being benefits by sharing your strengths and give others well-being benefits through the engagement of a strengths-based conversation. If we only share what is wrong (e.g., "My kids stressed me out yesterday!") or neutral (e.g., "What is the weather forecast for this evening?"), then we are not revealing the whole picture.
3. Don't deprive others of knowing who you are. When we do not share our strengths, good qualities, or positive experiences, we are depriving others of learning about us. Instead, others see a façade. They only see a piece of your personality but not the full view. This can place a limitation on relationships. I have a friend whose highest strength is humility.

From time to time, she overuses her humility. The result is that people do not get a chance to know her. I tend to not know about her many accomplishments and positive experiences because she does not readily share them. Thus, I feel as if I don't know her as well as my other friends.

4. Offer education on humility and how talking about one's own strengths benefits others. Humility scientists have found that a true humility is not captured by degrading ourselves, berating ourselves, keeping ourselves shut up, or being subservient, rather a true humility involves having a confident, strong self-esteem in which we can easily prioritize and turn the attention toward others. A humble person does not rely on the praise of others in order to feel better. For years, I have emphasized the importance of this character strength and the sharing of our strengths from a perspective of deep humility. Occasionally, groups laughed when I have argued for the importance of humility and the finding that it is one of the least common strengths around the world. As researcher Everett Worthington (2007) refers to it, humility is the quiet virtue. Instead of creating a false humility, prioritize a true humility that represents a strong sense of self where self-disclosure is strong and comfortable and also places emphasis on the other person, helping them to express their best qualities.

Avoidance, Nonavoidance, and Culture

This last point leads to a deeper discussion of avoidance. Avoidance is at the core of many human problems. It is almost always, by definition, a contributing factor to anxiety- and fear-based disorders. If you are terribly afraid of something – public speaking, elevators, eating in restaurants, talking to someone – most likely you avoid the feared object completely or as much as you can. When you avoid that fear stimulus, you do not get the opportunity to face the fear, use your coping skills, challenge yourself, or overcome the fear. Instead, the anxiety/fear builds. This is why the strongest evidence-based treatment for anxiety disorders (in vivo exposure and response prevention) has the management of avoidance at its core.

It is only natural for many individuals to attempt to avoid the topic of character strengths because they don't have a substantive understanding of what is meant by strengths or a working knowledge of their own strengths. It is much easier to attempt to avoid the discomfort that comes from sharing something new or that comes from worry about how others might perceive them.

Some may say that this reaction to strengths sharing is cultural. Yes, it is true that some cultures are less likely to self-disclose as a whole and it is true that there is groupthink at play toward those who do talk about themselves in a one-dimensionally positive way. Many argue that people from certain countries are more likely to report that humility prevents them from discussing their strengths: people from many Asian countries; people in Scandinavian countries where the Law of Jante is a cultural phenomenon; and those in Australia where tall poppy syndrome is an underlying phenomenon. I, too, have encountered these responses in each of those regions of the world. However, at the same time, I've also heard the exact same comments from people in every Western city I have presented strengths to. Playing the "humility card" seems to be more of a gut reaction that is universal than something that is *solely* culturally based.

For those less familiar with phenomena such as the Law of Jante and tall poppy syndrome these refer to the approach that people who attempt to rise above others should be resented, attacked, or "brought down" to everyone else's level. Indeed, this thinking can pervade the consciousness, customs, and behaviors of many people. The renowned Brazilian author Paulo Coelho (2012) seems to agree with these points saying that he believes the Law of Jante is not prominent just in Brazil, France, and Scandinavia but in every country across the globe. Coelho then goes on to argue for an anti-Law of Jante that would be something as follows: "You are worth far more than you think. Your work and presence on this Earth are important, even though you may not think so."

Chapter Summary

Table 4.1 and Table 4.2 provide summaries of the behavioral traps and potential solutions as well as the common misconceptions explored in this chapter.

Table 4.1. Behavioral Traps With Suggested Strategies

Behavioral Trap	Suggested Strategy
Just show up	Prepare with resource priming.
Remediate lower strengths, deficits, weaknesses	Educate about signature strengths and biases, then go with the resistance.
Jump to action before understanding	Before activation, consolidate knowledge and explore.
Start with the negative, the struggles (what went wrong?)	Start with the positive, the strengths (what went well?).
Be rigid about top strengths	Prioritize top strengths but attend to all.
Overplay overuse	Understand, expand, celebrate, and appreciate signature strengths before reviewing how they are overused.
Take the prescriptive/authoritarian approach	Practice being an authoritative gardener.

Table 4.2. Common Misconceptions and Reality-Based Reframes

Common Misconception	Reality-Based Reframe
Focusing on strengths is Pollyannaish	Character strengths accentuate what is best and help us face, manage, or overcome problems.
Working with strengths is easy and therefore doesn't require new learning	Understand the depth of character strengths by studying plurality, multidimensionality, context-based application, and use with psychopathology, trauma, and disability.
All strengths are created equal	We have many types of strengths and many subsets of character strengths, with overlapping and unique benefits.
Character strengths are static and unchanging	Character strengths are dynamic, multidimensional, and capable of being developed.
Knowing your strengths is enough	Self-awareness of strengths is pivotal, but strengths use brings more substantial benefits.
Most people already know their character strengths well	While potentially improving, strengths (especially character strengths) blindness is pervasive and context-based.
"Character" refers to a handful of traits	Character is plural and idiosyncratic.
Talking about character strengths is bragging, selfish, self-promoting, or egotistical	Talking about character strengths is a method of self-disclosure and promotes intimacy in relationships.

Chapter 5

Advanced Issues in Applying Character Strengths

Introduction

Albert Einstein notably said, "The more I learn, the more I realize I don't know." Each of the topics in this chapter could fill separate books in their own right, which points to the fact that there's far more we don't know about character strengths than what we know. As people come to know their strengths and the strengths of others, complexity arises, new questions emerge, and integration opportunities unfold. Practitioners begin to question the application of character strengths among various populations and nuances in using strengths in relationships and in managing problems. This leads to important concepts that arise when understanding strengths application in these areas, such as overuse, underuse, hot buttons, synergies, collisions, morality, and the integration of mindfulness, savoring, flow, and hypnosis. These will be examined in this chapter as advanced issues and dynamics that are relevant for practitioners helping clients, students, and employees.

Overuse, Underuse, and the Golden Mean

Context is king, as the common phrase goes. The application of character strengths is contextualized where each situation we are in matters and can contribute to the expression of our character strengths. Strengths can be brought forth too strongly for a given situation (strength overuse) or too lightly or not at all in a particular situation (strength underuse) and oneself or others are then negatively impacted in some way. Any of the 24 VIA character strengths can be overused or underused (Grant & Schwartz, 2011; Niemiec, 2014b), points which have been recognized in regard to other categories of strength over the years as well (Biswas-Diener et al., 2011; Kaiser & Overfield, 2011; Linley, 2008). The overuse of curiosity can lead someone into a dangerous part of a city while the underuse of fairness may lead to problems in one's relationships, or the underuse of hope to feeling unfulfilled. This points to the importance of finding balance with virtue and character strengths expression. Scholars have discussed how virtues can be *corrective* and *expressive* (Goleman, 1997; Yearley, 1990) in that virtues and character strengths can serve to correct a temptation or a vice (e.g., self-regulation can counterbalance impulsivity; zest can correct sloth; humility can counterbalance hubris). At the same time, virtues and character strengths are often an expression of what is best in the individual.

The importance of finding balance with strengths use is clear and has been emphasized theoretically by researchers (e.g., Biswas-Diener et al., 2011; Fowers, 2008; Grant & Schwartz, 2011; Schwartz & Sharpe, 2006). In addition, empirical benefits of character strengths balance have been found. For example, researchers have framed having strengths balance as "jack of all strengths" and that this was a unique predictor of higher well-being (Young, Kashdan, & Macatee, 2014). In another study revealing the importance of character strengths balance, Allan (2014) found that some pairs of character strengths predicted life meaning when both strengths in the pair were high (e.g., honesty/kindness, love/social intelligence, hope/gratitude), while the opposite was true for a fourth pair – bravery/fairness – in which a wider discrepancy between these strengths predicted meaning only when bravery was higher.

Most strengths researchers credit Aristotle (4th BCE/2000) as being the first philosopher to articulate the concept of balance in regard to virtue expression. Aristotle was a practical philosopher who believed that all virtues were a balance of excess and deficiency, where "the golden mean" is the desirable middle between the vices, e.g., the virtue of courage is the mean between rashness (excess) and cowardice (deficiency). This golden mean is similar to "the middle way" of the Buddha, "the doctrine of the mean" of Confucius, and "the goldilocks principle" (something that is "just right," from the popular fairytale). Expanding this to character strengths, "the golden mean of character strengths" means to apply the right combination of character strengths to the right degree in the right context (Niemiec, 2014a). Snapshot 5.1. outlines 10 core principles for understanding character strengths overuse. A symphony orchestra is commonly used as a metaphor for understanding the golden mean. Here is this metaphor offered as a description for a client:

> You are the maestro who is conducting the performance of a variety of powerful instruments (i.e., character strengths). You call forth one or more instruments when the time is right during the movement. Some instruments you might point to regularly such as the violin section (i.e., signature strengths), others you'll call forth at the right time and on a semiregular bases such as the trombones (i.e., middle strengths), and still others you'll turn to less frequently but you'll certainly need them as part of the overall musical score, such as the drums (i.e., lower strengths). Remember, this is your symphony and the expression is unique to you, and the amount of music from each instrument will be determined by you at each moment. This combination of instruments creates a beautiful and inspiring performance (i.e., it's a manifestation of who you are; your character).

Snapshot 5.1. Ten Principles of Character Strengths Overuse, as Adapted From Niemiec (2014b)

1. Any of the 24 character strengths can be overused or underused.
2. Each of the 24 character strengths can be viewed along a continuum in terms of its expression in a given situation, where the center is a balanced, optimal use in terms of the right amount for the situation.
3. When a character strength is overused or underused it is no longer a strength. For example, the overuse of curiosity in a particular situation is no longer curiosity, it becomes something else, e.g., nosiness.
4. Overuse and underuse vary by the individual's expression and the contextual fit.
5. It is more likely that individuals will overuse their highest strengths and underuse their lowest strengths, although that should be viewed as a starting point for self-understanding, not as a prescription.
6. Overuse and underuse become a problem when they negatively affect oneself or others.
7. Overuse and underuse can be managed by bringing forth other character strengths or reworking the strength in question to use it in a new way.
8. Overuse and underuse offer additional language for reframing problems so that clients see themselves from a different perspective.
9. Overuse and underuse reflect elements of a deficit-based approach as they emphasize what is wrong, although they also retain important strength-based elements as core positive qualities within the individual are being examined.
10. Overuse and underuse can facilitate new avenues of exploration and intervention for clients.

Chris Peterson (2006b) offered a framework for character strengths to assist in the mapping out of psychological disorders and serve as an improvement (or paradigm shift) to the *DSM*'s categorical, deficit-based model. Peterson suggested that each character strength can be mapped as an exaggeration, absence, and opposite. For example, fairness can be viewed as partisanship (absence), prejudice (opposite), and detachment (exaggeration). Hope might be classified as present orientation (absence), pessimism/despair (opposite), and Pollyannaism (exaggeration). In 2009 and 2010, with Peterson's support, I offered the language of this framework to large groups of practitioners in different cultures who were attending extensive trainings in character strengths. The response, generally speaking, was that it was confusing and unwieldy, from a practical perspective. Practitioners reported it was difficult to internalize and to apply with their students, clients, and employees. Therefore, with the help of leading character strengths researchers and practitioners and the VIA Institute, I simplified the model to a continuum model that reflected overuse, optimal use, and underuse for each of the character strengths, attempting to retain as much of Peterson's original thinking (Niemiec, 2014a). See Table 5.1 for the language of overuse, underuse, and optimal use across the 24 character strengths. This conceptually-clean, practical approach has been well-received, utilized by other researchers in the field (e.g., Rashid, 2015), and initial research finds it not only holds up conceptually but appears to be useful and accurate in predicting psychological disorders, specifically social anxiety disorder (Freidlin et al., 2017).

Table 5.1. The Language of Character Strengths Overuse, Underuse, and Optimal Use

Strength	Overuse	Underuse	Optimal Use
Creativity	Eccentricity	Conformity	Originality that is adaptive
Curiosity	Nosiness	Disinterest	Exploration/seeking novelty
Judgment	Narrow-mindedness, cynicism	Unreflectiveness	Critical thinking & rationality
Love of learning	Know-it-all	Complacency	Systematic deepening (of knowledge)
Perspective	Overbearing	Shallowness	The wider view
Bravery	Foolhardiness	Cowardice	Facing fears, confronting adversity
Perseverance	Obsessiveness	Fragility	Keeping going, overcoming all obstacles
Honesty	Righteousness	Phoniness	Being authentic
Zest	Hyperactive	Sedentary	Enthusiasm for life
Love	Emotional promiscuity	Emotional isolation	Genuine, reciprocal warmth
Kindness	Intrusiveness	Indifference	Doing for others
Social intelligence	Overanalyzing	Obtuse or clueless	Tuned in, then savvy
Teamwork	Dependant	Selfishness	Collaborative, participating in a group effort
Fairness	Detachment	Partisanship	Equal opportunity for all
Leadership	Despotism	Compliant	Positively influencing others
Forgiveness	Permissive	Merciless	Letting go of hurt when wronged

Table 5.1. Continued

Strength	Overuse	Underuse	Optimal Use
Humility	Self-deprecation	Baseless self-esteem	Achievement does not elevate worth
Prudence	Stuffiness	Sensation seeking	Wise caution
Self-regulation	Inhibition	Self-indulgence	Self-management of vices
Appreciation of beauty & excellence	Snobbery or Perfectionism	Oblivion	Seeing the life behind things
Gratitude	Ingratiation	Rugged individualism	Thankfulness
Hope	Pollyanna-ism	Negative	Positive expectations
Humor	Giddiness	Overly serious	Offering pleasure/ laughter to others
Spirituality	Fanaticism	Anomie	Connecting with the sacred

Reproduced with permission from Niemiec, R. M. (2014a). *Mindfulness and character strengths: A practical guide to flourishing.* Boston, MA: Hogrefe Publishing.

The language framework outlined in Table 5.1 has been tested by researchers (Freidlin et al., 2017). These researchers found that character strengths can indeed be overused or underused and may even be harmful to mental health. Character strengths overuse and character strengths underuse were each linked with less flourishing, less life satisfaction, and higher depression, while optimal use of character strengths was linked with significantly higher flourishing, higher life satisfaction, and less depression. It is interesting to note that the more substantial problem (i.e., higher correlations) across these three variables was character strengths underuse, not overuse. This study also took a fresh look at psychopathology, specifically social anxiety disorder, through these lenses. A particular combination of six overuse/underuse phenomena correctly sorted 87.3% of people with or without social anxiety disorder. This combination was the overuse of social intelligence and humility, and the underuse of social intelligence, self-regulation, zest, and humor.

In practical terms, the overuse of any character strength is often a loss of the bigger picture, where the individual has become boxed into a modus operandi, such as the person high in perseverance that does not know when to quit, to accept that they tried hard but that a particular project is not going to come to fruition. The underuse of any character strength is often a function of being on autopilot, lost in unawareness, going through the motions in life. For example, a person oblivious to a friend who is crying and in need is potentially underusing social intelligence or kindness. Underuse can reflect a loss of courage in which the individual does not express who they are for fear of being judged or not accepted. While the ways we can overuse or underuse our character strengths are numerous, Table 5.2 offers a nonexhaustive list of types and accompanying examples to further flesh out the constructs. Underuse can be distinguished from the strengths blindness types discussed in Chapter 2 in that the latter is conceptual and the former addresses the practicality of strengths in action/inaction. That said, reviewing and understanding strengths blindness can add to the array of strengths underuse examples. In her study of the virtuous actions of Mahatma Gandhi, virtues scholar Nancy Snow (2016) identified types of "striving," or trying too hard, which I translate into overuse terminology in Table 5.2.

Table 5.2. Examples of Overuse and Underuse

Type of Imbalance	Name	Explanation	Character Strength Example
Overuse	Forcing	Pressuring oneself to act before one is ready.	Gabriel forces forgiveness towards Negan and it feels artificial and ingenuine.
	Impulsivity	Springing forward without first thinking how to act or assessing our emotional readiness.	Tara was impulsive with her zest agreeing to new projects before realizing she was already overcommitted.
	Overthinking	Thinking and rethinking a decision or scenario too many times.	Enid overthinks plans (prudence) for a birthday party to the point where this small event takes over her life to an abnormal extent.
	Unrelenting standards	Holding oneself to too high a standard; perfectionistic striving toward an unbalanced standard.	In working on a creative project, Sasha feels as if the project is never good enough; she says "there's always more."
Underuse	Oversight	Not thinking to use a character strength in a particular context or in a regular situation within a context.	It never occurred to Glenn that his signature strengths of kindness and gratitude were relevant at work, not just his relationships.
	Lost or eroded	The strength has faded over time; the person has lost touch with the strength they once clearly used.	After being in a stifling, high-intensity job at her last place of employment, Michonne has "lost" her sense of humor.
	Omission	The individual is strong with the strength across contexts and situations, however, on a particular occasion, mistakenly omits it.	Eugene's signature strength of prudence was overridden by his signature strengths of zest and perseverance while cheering at the sporting event.
	Undervalued	The strength is not appreciated or not viewed as a strength therefore is chronically underplayed.	Dwight does not view humility as a strength and therefore makes no effort to show modesty or a sense of humbleness, instead dwelling in narcissism at work and home.
	Lesser strength	The strength has never been very strong or focused on.	Rosita is low in creativity and makes no effort to try to improve this strength, therefore she offers very little at team brainstorming meetings.

A school psychologist was working with a gifted boy from Central America who had attention-deficit disorder and was high in self-regulation. She was concerned about his overusing self-regulation and becoming too rigid, controlling, and perfectionistic with his school-work and that he would therefore become overwhelmed. She decided to take the approach of prioritizing signature strengths discovery, exploration, and use before overuse (see Chapter 4). This offered the boy increased resources and greater freedom to be himself and felt like an authentic approach for her as the practitioner. She successfully took the following steps with him:

1. Fully explore self-regulation as his character strength. Understand how it relates to his management of impulses and emotions, how he has used the strength successfully over the years, and what goes through his mind (i.e., thoughts) when he is in a self-regulation zone.
2. Gather additional feedback from his mother, father, and teachers. Learn about not only his struggles but also his positive behaviors (especially those relating to self-regulation).
3. Examine balance with self-regulation with her client. In session, collaboratively map out behaviors/thoughts/feelings relating to the overuse of self-regulation, the underuse of self-regulation, and balanced use, especially in the context/situation of completing school homework.

Strengths-Based Practitioner Tip

Underuse
- *Key insight.* For managing strengths underuse, clients (and practitioners!) should be encouraged to take a growth mindset to their strengths development – that they are always the student who is learning, not the master that knows all.
- *Underuse exploration.* Describe a situation in which you underused one of your strengths. What might you do to become more mindful of this strength? In what situations might you use it more?
- *Tip.* Keep a diary/log of strengths use during the week. You will become more mindful of underused and underacknowledged strengths.

Overuse
- *Key insight.* For managing strengths overuse, clients (and practitioners!) should be encouraged to seek feedback from trusted others in regard to how they come across with their strengths, especially their signature strengths.
- *Overuse exploration.* Describe a situation in which you overused one of your strengths. How might you temper the overuse or build in another strength to better balance yourself?
- *Tip.* Consider a problem you are struggling with today. Examine it through the lens of strengths overuse. What strength are you bringing forth too strongly, even a little bit, that is contributing to the problem?

Synergies and Collisions: The Four-Quadrant Model

Character strengths are dynamic and relational. From this view, two or more character strengths can come together and create a synergy in which the new whole is greater than the sum of the strengths. Or, two or more character strengths can collide with one another leading to a whole that is far less than the sum of the strengths. These are character strengths synergies and character strengths collisions, respectively, and they can occur within oneself or between people. Therefore, a four-quadrant model assists in understanding these dynamics. The four quadrants are as follows, and also outlined with examples in Figure 5.1.
- Intrapersonal synergy
- Interpersonal synergy
- Intrapersonal collision
- Interpersonal collision

Character Strengths	Synergies (1 + 1 = 3)	Collisions (1 + 1 = 0)
Intrapersonal	Rick's love of learning and self-reg-ulation come together to help him focus and write a good paper.	Carl's appreciation of beauty en-joying a nature walk collides with his judgment/critical thinking that pulls him from the moment and gets him too much into his head.
Interpersonal	Daryl's curiosity and Maggie's honesty connect to create a great therapy session.	Carol's zest wanting to tell stories at the morning meeting collides with Morgan's prudence (he has a specific and packed-full agenda planned).

Figure 5.1. The four-quadrant model outlining character strengths synergies and collisions.

Examine Intrapersonal Synergies

To deepen awareness around the powerful swirl of character strengths at play within you across a myriad of situations, start by mapping out three examples of situations/domains when you were at your best: when you were engaged and productive at work, making a positive contribution in your closest relationship, and when helping out in your community. There you will find three sets of intrapersonal synergies to cherish and celebrate. One of the times I'm at my best is when leading a live workshop with a group. My hope – positive expectations for each attendee's future – merges with my love (and curiosity) for the topic at hand. This then facilitates a strong intrapersonal synergy, filling me with zest and energy as I express myself to participants.

Examine Interpersonal Synergies

Start your discussion with a colleague, relationship partner, or friend by acknowledging and labeling the synergy that took place or is taking place. Describe the strengths at play in the synergy and how each strength was boosting the other. Celebrate and appreciate this dynamic together. Like most couples, my wife and I can easily turn to quibbling about petty things in our day-to-day life. Thus, it is particularly insightful and helpful for us to remember, talk about, and celebrate our positives as a couple, especially our (interpersonal) synergies. One example is when we take stock on the reality of our present life. I bring forth my high perspective strength of seeing the big picture and she brings forth her high judgment/critical thinking strength to examine the details. We then converse about how we are both working at busy, full-time jobs and raising/nurturing three very young children who have a host of needs, interests, and activities. My perspective strength holds this bigger picture, especially through challenging times, while my wife's judgment strength brings forth subtle details and different ways of acknowledging this reality.

Experimenting With Intrapersonal Collisions

Since collisions occur when the use of one strength might limit, lessen, or negatively impact another strength(s), there is a moment of choice for individuals to discern for themselves when they notice the emergence of an intrapersonal collision: Which character strength should I bring forth more strongly? The answer is not always clear and will involve a number of factors the individual must weigh, including factors relating to their own personality as well as the demands of the situation.

As a way of more closely understanding the individual and contextual factors at play with intrapersonal collisions, consider the following 10 scenarios depicting collisions. How would you optimally handle each scenario?

Prudence and Bravery

The expression of caution or the expression of courage is the classic collision. Prudence that is underused in some situations is bravery, while bravery that is overused in some situations is a lack of prudence. For example, consider a business person who is passionate about opening a new business but is concerned about the struggling economic times. They hear about a new, somewhat risky opportunity in which they must act quickly with their business plans. Does he/she express high prudence and decide to wait until the economy turns around? Does he/she decide to enact bravery by taking the risk with the new investment because they are passionate about the idea despite the poor economic climate?

Self-Regulation and Bravery

You have a unique opportunity to meet with an entrepreneur who potentially can help your dream business soar. Your business will help a lot of people. The entrepreneur makes some very direct offensive religious and political comments – not only do they offend you but they appear to attack your special needs child (who is not present). You know that once you receive the entrepreneur's help, you won't have to work with them again.

Do you use bravery and make a point to challenge this offensive behavior (knowing that your comments will inevitably fall on deaf ears)? Do you use self-regulation – controlling your urge to say something driven by your "hot" emotions – and bite your tongue? The strength of honesty and particularly the dimension of integrity may come into play here.

Kindness and Fairness

Note that it's probably more common for these strengths to work together in tandem than to collide. But, a good example of a collision is the following: You are waiting in a long line and you see someone cut in front of you in line a few feet away. Do you use kindness and just assume the person is struggling or suffering in some way and just altruistically let it go? Do you express fairness and explain that many people have been waiting for a long time? The situation becomes more complex if you are already running late for an event that your daughter has to be on time for; then, does this impact the kindness or fairness level? Or, what if the person that cuts in line is in a wheelchair – then do you allow kindness to take precedence over fairness?

Honesty and Kindness

Another classic example often noted is a wife turning to a husband and asking "Do I look fat in this dress?" Let's say the husband perceives his wife as slightly looking fat. Should he be completely honest and say "Yes"? Should he be kind and dishonest and say "No"? While there might be a middle ground that is supported by social intelligence, does this compromise the integrity of one strength or the other? Which other character strengths might help to manage this collision?

Self-Regulation and Zest

Do I take control of my impulses and emotions or do I let them out with enthusiasm? Let's say you are at a funeral and you encounter an old friend you haven't seen in 10 years. You had been hoping to get in touch with the friend but had lost their contact information. You realize your time with the friend might be limited. Do you place more effort on controlling your excitement and joy because of the situation you are in? Or, do you allow you zest and energy to be unleashed explaining how much you have missed the friend?

Leadership and Teamwork

You are working on a team project with eight people. You are assigned a particular task and are working hard on it but there is much more you still need to do. Another team member is assigned to the task of "getting the project out the door" and while they are working on the task you are not pleased with the work they are doing. You could employ your leadership strength and offer to help (thus exerting your leadership in helping them organize it, manage the group, and get the project out the door). Or, you could stay focused on the task you are working on for the team as this is what you agreed to focus on and you still have more work to do.

Perspective and Perseverance

You are working on a long-term project that has had many hurdles and obstacles. It seems to be going on forever and some people whom you'd been working with are dropping off the project because they do not think the outcome is a viable reality. Data begins to show that the original goal, while still feasible, is diminishing in the likelihood of success. But you continue to believe it is possible. Do you give greater preference to your perspective strength by stepping back and seeing the bigger picture that "enough is enough" and stop the project? Do you stay true to your determination and gritty nature and keep plugging along despite the odds (perseverance)?

Bravery and Humility

You are someone who prefers not to speak up in groups. At the same time, you realize the value of being vulnerable and transparent with others, especially in situations where it is appropriate to do so. You are attending a fundraising event for a particular disease. You soon learn that the group might benefit from your offering a personal example that offers ideas for prevention of the disease. You see that there are several other people who are offering their knowledge and experiences. Do you join the others and share your experiences in front of the group (bravery)? Do you use your humility and allow the focus to stay on the others who are already sharing in the group?

Spirituality and Social Intelligence

You had a recent spiritual experience that was particularly inspiring and meaningful. You feel so positive about the experience and the benefits it has brought you that you want to share it with everyone you meet. From the lens of your social intelligence strength, you realize not every situation will be appropriate. Do you share the experience with any of the following people?
- Your best friend who is a strong atheist and doesn't like to talk about spirituality.
- Your coworker who is suffering and needs ideas for new coping skills.
- A greeter at Wall-Mart who seems to be a religious person.
- The employees who work for you.

Creativity and Humility

You have a lot of ideas and you love to share them. Also, you realize that when you start talking about your ideas it is at the expense of other people having an opportunity to speak. In considering this potential, in what situations might you use creativity and let your ideas "fly" and in what situations might you exert more humility to limit your expression of ideas to allow others more time to share?

Experimenting With Interpersonal Collisions

Reflect on the following five interpersonal collisions. These are offered to show what a collision might look like in action. As each collision unfolds, it becomes clear that there is a different "energy" coming from each person. These energies are different strengths being expressed; however, in a collision, the "strength" element is lost. Picture each scenario/collision and consider how you might resolve each one taking a strengths-based approach. How might you feel or act differently if you were one of the people in the scenario versus being the coach/mediator for the people in the scenario?

Creativity and Judgment

In this collision, the out of the box thinker clashes with the reflective discerning person. The former is looking to share more ideas, while the latter is looking for reasoned ideas and rationale. The person high in judgment offers challenges to each idea. This leads the person high in creativity to feel as if they are being placed in a box, contained, and slightly rejected, therefore, they express frustration in return. This leads the person high in judgment to feel confused as they were merely expressing their signature strength involving rationale and constructive critiques.

Humility and Humor

In this collision, the expressive playful person clashes with the low-key modest person. The person high in humor walks into the room of colleagues and engages several in conversations with a funny story. Laughter abounds in the room but the person high in humility only smiles and continues focusing on their work. The person high in humor notices this lack of involvement and walks over to the humble person and delivers some playful teasing. The person high in humility views this as an intrusion and feels angry as they had given plenty of space for the person with humor to joke and laugh and now it is being taken a step further to affect them personally. The person high in humor was attempting to use their strength of playfulness and laughter to involve others, while the person high in humility was attempting to give space and place the attention on others.

Self-Regulation and Curiosity

Two friends spontaneously connect at a gym, and following the initial check-in, there is a collision. The person high in self-regulation begins to step away as they are eager to get back to their workout which is closely mapped out in terms of timing. The person high in curiosity is excited by the energy of the conversation and asks a few more question, which annoys their friend. The person high in self-regulation is focused on their disciplined regimen and wanting/needing to draw inward, while the person high in curiosity is focused on exploring more in the situation at hand and wanting/needing to focus outward, hence the collision.

Kindness and Perspective

Two board members collide interpersonally with their character strengths. One board member is passionate about a new idea that could help a lot of people. He advocates for the implementation of a new program that has evidenced-based effects and is aligned with the organization's mission. Another board member refutes the idea, saying that the wider view is a dwindling budget and many other community needs that must be taken care of. The member high in kindness retorts that the program being proposed would be an exemplar that could later extend widely throughout the community. The result is the kindness of one person clashes with the perspective of another.

Prudence and Fairness

In a parenting scenario in which a young child is wanting to finish watching a television show that they are excited about, two parents collide in the optimal approach. One parent, high in prudence, says the show needs to be turned "off" now in order to stay aligned with the bedtime ritual and hence getting enough sleep before school the next morning. The other parent, high in fairness, sees how important finishing that show is to the child and advocates to be fair to the child emotionally, to let them finish watching the show they are enthused about ("only 15 more minutes") and then go to bed. The two parents feel "unheard" by one another and clash.

Resolving Interpersonal Collisions

As the concept of character strengths collisions is new, there is not an abundance of strategies designed to resolve such collisions. Anecdotally speaking, it appears that awareness of these collisions can go a long way. Many of these collisions occur as part of an unconscious dynamic within a dyad and therefore bringing awareness to how these strengths are operating in each individual offers not only new information but opportunities for discussion and then appropriate action.

An example of how this played out with one couple, Abe and Sasha, is offered using the aware-explore-apply model, along with questions to assist the practitioner at each phase:

Aware

Building insight around the character strengths at play in the collision.
- Name the conflict clearly and the action/inaction of each member of the couple.
- What character strength(s) is each member using as a lens to see the situation or to act from?
- Example: Abe and Sasha became aware of their interpersonal collision. Sasha would ask Abe for help in fixing something in or around the house (e.g., a leak in the sink, handling a large fallen tree branch) and Abe would not do it in a timely fashion. Sasha did not understand this as she knows Abe likes to keep busy and likes to "fix" things. Abe would explain that he was busy doing other things around the house and would get to it when he could. They described the character strengths collision as Abe's perseverance (desire to complete the task he was currently working on) clashing with Sasha's hope (positive expectations,

desire to reach a goal). Sasha was viewing her husband as a stick-in-the-mud, while Abe was viewing his wife as annoying and unappreciative.

Explore

After the insight of awareness, exploration of the collision can take the form of self-reflection, discussion, or other methods.
- How does each member of the couple's top character strengths play a role in the conflict?
- Is this a pattern in their communication as a couple or a one-off experience?
- For each strength in the collision, what is the underlying intention or the driving force?
- How strong (from 1–10, where 10 is the strongest) is each member expressing this particular strength? Is this an overuse of the strength in this situation? What number would represent optimal use of the strength?
- How might each individual move closer to optimal use of the strength in a future similar situation? What steps might they need to take to get there?
- How does knowing this dynamic assist the couple in the future?
- Example: Abe and Sasha discussed their tension. Abe explained that once he starts a new project, he wants to finish it and not get distracted by new projects. This fuels Abe with energy when he can see the finished project and can recognize the obstacles and challenges he had to overcome to get it done. Sasha explained how she gets fueled by doing new things and by entertaining others. For this, she needs to set up the house properly and have things in working order and looking nice, thus seeing things undone triggers her. Her strengths of creativity and appreciation of beauty/excellence further enliven her approach to the house. Sasha and Abe each rate their character strength expression strongly, around an 8 out of 10.

Apply

Following discussion, action planning can be taken by each member of the couple, with the intention to use a character strengths-based approach in future similar situations.
- What action might be taken in future similar situations?
- Example: Sasha reframed her mindset around her husband's actions as a strong use of his signature strength of perseverance, a quality she has always admired in him. She would take this fresh perception of him rather than seeing him as a stick-in-the-mud. In addition, she expressed her genuine appreciation to him for all his hard work around the house. Abe reframed his perception of Sasha as being annoying to being energetic, eager, and optimistic (i.e., hopeful and zestful) for wanting to find ways to take action and to get things done and have a beautiful, presentable home to others. As he enjoyed being part of the "entertaining couple," his gratitude for Sasha and her uniqueness was renewed. He stated he would be more open to interruptions during his focused work on part of the house and would certainly direct his perseverance to take a break on one task to go get a simpler task done.

Hot Buttons

Everybody has character strengths "hot buttons" or sensitive areas in which another person's strengths use is perceived by an observer to be strengths overuse or strengths underuse and triggers discomfort/frustration. Typically, this stems from one's own character strength beliefs, preferences, or expectations. In these situations, the person's character strength has been affronted or offended. The affront may feel personal and deliberate. Anger, frustration, or other upset emotions may be the result. Hot buttons can be the source of conflicts, of strengths collisions, and/or may even explain why a problem is happening. Hot buttons often emerge from one of these two overarching phenomena:

1. *You perceive underuse and are triggered.* There are numerous reasons a person can be triggered, such as another person does not share your highest strengths which you highly value or you perceive that they are displaying low levels of a particular strength for the situation at hand (and that strength may or may not be your signature strength). Viewing someone underplaying a strength that you highly value can be disappointing, frustrating, and even anxiety-provoking. Sometimes we place high standards and expectations on others to express certain strengths. A few examples include: a parent wanting their child to display more perseverance when faced with adversity at school or more bravery on the football field; a manager demanding high levels of appreciation of excellence with a work project; a spouse wanting more support (e.g., teamwork or love) in the home environment. In any of these situations, the underuse of that character strength is a hot button or trigger.

2. *You perceive overuse and are triggered.* In these instances, you perceive someone is displaying an intense behavior that could be noted as an overplay of a character strength (and you may or may not have it as a signature strength). This perceived overuse might be annoying to you, be an affront to your personal beliefs, cause you anxiety, or, for a myriad of other reasons, it is a hot button for you. Examples include: the person who always seems to be in critical thinking mode, a person being overly sappy with their expression of love, a person acting like the annoying "zesty" energizing bunny before you've had your morning coffee, and a person behaving like a religious zealot.

Where do these perceptions of overuse and underuse and their resulting hot buttons come from? This would depend on the theoretical orientation of the person you ask and how they believe people change, whether it is based in family of origin issues, faulty cognitions, problematic environment conditions, or other reasons. One theorist not explored among those mentioned in Chapter 3 is Albert Ellis (Ellis & Dryden, 1987) and his massive quantity of practical work on irrational beliefs. Ellis explains that common beliefs people occupy internally include "Life should be fair," "Life should be easier," "I shouldn't have to work so hard," "You must treat me well," "I must be approved by everyone," and "I must always do well." When people experience an affront to these beliefs, this forms a hot button; thus, an affront to fairness might be an offense to the belief that "Life should be fair," while an affront to gratitude might be an offense to the belief that "I must be approved by everyone." Ellis argued in his rational-emotive-behavior therapy approach that people can become aware of these (and many more) automatic beliefs and learn to challenge and overcome them, with astute thinking and behavior change.

Two of the best ways for practitioners to boost astute thinking and mindful understanding around hot buttons and the substantial role they can play in a client's everyday life are to not only label and understand one's own hot button issues but to witness the behavior of others. For the latter, here are some examples of character strength hot buttons from some of my past clients and students:

- A young woman high in *kindness* and generosity feels upset by the lack of giving at a group meeting.
- A man high in *curiosity* feels frustrated by a colleague's apparent lack of mutual interest and lack of reciprocal questions.
- A woman high in *fairness* feels angered by an individual's blatant disregard of the welfare of others.
- A colleague high in *teamwork* feels frustrated by one team member's lack of participation and contribution, and their letting the rest of the team do the work.

- A young man high in *honesty* is triggered by people who make excuses, blame, exaggerate, and dance around the truth without being direct, especially politicians!
- A subordinate high in *gratitude* feels disappointed when she is not acknowledged at work by her boss for going the extra mile on work projects week after week.

Hot Button Management – Overarching Strategies

In order to take control of these sensitive issues, there are a couple tactics you and your clients can try.

1. *Retrospective management.* This occurs when you've acknowledged the reality of the hot button issue – it is essentially *your* issue.
   - What would you do different next time you are in a similar situation?
   - What character strength might you use to temper what was triggered?
2. *Prospective management.* This refers to looking to the future to a situation in which you believe you might get triggered and taking preventative action. Perhaps you will soon be in a meeting with a difficult person, have to confront a family member, or do a project with a lazy person. To prepare yourself for optimal functioning in the heat of the moment, consider these questions:
   - What is the outcome you're looking for with this situation/interaction? What do you hope will happen?
   - How might you take an approach of understanding/learning rather than changing the other's view?
   - What character strengths will you need to deploy? How will you bring them forth?
   - When you are managing a hot button with someone whom you want to stay in relationship with, then the situation can be particularly sensitive. In such cases, preparation and reflection on strengths is helpful.
     - What character strengths will you need to use to stay in relationship with the person without trying to change them (for example, using forgiveness in small doses)?
     - What character strengths might you need to let go of (e.g., affronts to my fairness strength) as a sacrifice for the betterment of the relationship?
     - Would a planful deployment of a particular character strength be useful? Which one? How will you use it in the situation?

Hot Button Management – Specific Strategies

1. *Mindful listening and mindful speech.* Listening to someone with mindful attention by placing full focus in the present moment, and by listening and observing rather than judging, analyzing, or getting caught in emotion, can transform the moment (Nhat Hanh, 2001). Interactions involve a collection of moments that can be transformed. When we speak, we can practice mindful speech – from the heart – that is clear, direct, specific, and empathic (Niemiec, 2012).
2. *Be especially strong for "the first 3 minutes."* Couples relationship researcher, John Gottman (Carrere & Gottman, 1999) calls the first 3 minutes of an argument a critical period for setting up conflict discussions and is predictive of successful/unsuccessful marital outcomes. Gottman suggests deploying a softened start-up where there is a gentle opening for discussions around the conflict. He offers reasons why these initial minutes are crucial to the conversation (I've added the hypothetical character strengths that align with each in parentheses):

- It's about managing the potentially "hot" emotions and heightened bodily physiology (self-regulation).
- Having tact when starting the conversation (prudence).
- Displaying an open rather than constricted mental state (curiosity and judgment/open-mindedness).
- Managing emotional reactivity (self-regulation and social intelligence).

3. *Practice compassion-focused reappraisal.* This refers to a specific practice and way of perceiving someone who has offended you. It involves emphasizing the complex humanity of the offender and interprets the offense as evidence that the offender needs to experience positive growth or transformation (Witvliet, DeYoung, Hofelich, & DeYoung 2011; Witvliet, Knoll, Hinman, & DeYoung, 2010). This can bring benefit, both physical and mental, to the person who was offended.

4. *Tailor the use of character strengths to manage the hot button in the situation.* Here are a few examples from my clients or students:

- I recall a client who was particularly high in forgiveness and was triggered by family members who were not as forgiving and quite resentful. She attempted to use kindness and love toward them (i.e., "kill them with kindness") but that did not seem to temper the forgiveness. Social intelligence in acting appropriately and prudence in being cautious with words and actions helped to prevent conflict but did not remedy the pit in her stomach around her forgiveness hot button. Then, she realized it, she could circle back and use her own strength of forgiveness – the very strength that was causing her suffering! She deliberately "forgave" her family members for their actions, ignorance, and poor choices. Although much of this was internal and not interpersonally expressed, she felt she had a tool she could use each time her hot button was fired up.
- A new employee had her creativity hot button pressed regularly at work when she was talking about an interesting topic and someone interrupted her or changed the subject. She utilized humility to place greater attention on others and forgiveness to let go of any regrets about this. She added that in order to restore further balance, her strengths of fairness and kindness toward others also needed to be elevated a bit.
- A young man had a new, exciting insight he went to share with his wife who was watching television. She looked at him but she wasn't listening. He left the room upset because he did not receive the empathy or engagement he had hoped for. He paused, looked for a hot button, and realized his fairness was being activated. He went on to say that he discovered it was *he* who was being unfair to his wife because he had interrupted her flow by barging in on her and placing expectations on her. He explained the strength of perspective was helpful in seeing his wife's situation more clearly and his strength of self-regulation helped him to manage his feelings and find balance in the situation.

Strength-Based Practitioner Tip

Apply hot button exploration to yourself as a self-study and then explore it with a client. Try out this activity: Consider one of your signature strengths. Describe a situation in which you felt your strength was affronted. What was your reaction in the situation? Have there been similar situations in which this same strength of yours has been offended? Stepping back with a wider view of this situation, what is the best way to handle it? Do you need to consciously bring other character strengths into play? What are the character strengths of the other individuals involved in the situation?

Morality

Many years ago, I had the urge to write a book about these character strengths that attempted to summarize them in one word or phrase – "goodness" or "being good." I recall Chris Peterson mentioning something similar to this before he passed away. Still, to talk about goodness with such directness is to appear to be making a claim about what is best for other people and what it means for them to be a good person. This work with character strengths is not about proclaiming the line of where goodness lies, a hotly debated topic within moral philosophy and theology. To be clear, I personally believe that the authentic application of these character strengths and these concepts is an important element of being good (i.e., moral) and expressing goodness (i.e., morality) to others and the world. That said, there remains an abundance of important work to be done that examines the connections between character strengths and morality, the myriad of ways that character strengths can cause goodness (I suspect many of them can be found in this book), and reflects new opportunities for people to express goodness to others. In this section, I look at some of the work going on in this area.

The link between morality and character strengths is an important area to explore. The moral intelligence of human beings has been increasing over the centuries and some scholars argue this is being driven by science and reason (Shermer, 2015). The moral character scholar Christian Miller (2013) argues that the moral importance of character strengths is critical to the following: understanding ourselves, understanding family and friends, role models, ethical theory, education, and societal problems. In addition, many would add the role of the helping professional/practitioner to this list. For purposes of this book, it is worth noting that some argue that every encounter of counseling is a moral one, that, whether admitted or not, there is a moral vision, a reflection of values, and a discussion of the good life and being a good person (Christopher, 1996). By this token, the work of practitioners (managers, educators, coaches, psychologists), and many nonpractitioners (family members, friends, coworkers) is moral work.

Perhaps this book can be interpreted in some ways as what virtues philosopher Andre Comte-Sponville (2001) referred to as "applied morals" – as I describe many ways we can bring our best qualities forward to bring benefit to others. As discussed in Chapter 1, one of the three *refractions* of the VIA classification is not only the contribution of character strengths to personal identity and instrumental benefits but also the promotion of the greater good for others or the collective good of society. Indeed, there are many ways to be good and these character strengths represent 24 platforms from which one can be good from. Research has found that *doing good* is an important avenue for people to create meaningful and satisfying lives (i.e., *being good*) (Steger, Kashdan, & Oishi, 2008). Similarly, other research found that moral views of oneself capture some but not all character strengths and predicted moral concerns, life goals, adjustment (to early college years), and integrity (Noftle, 2014). It is also true that in any "story" of morality or goodness these character strengths can be found at the center of the story. Table 5.3 offers 24 examples of "ways to be good," one for each character strength, to help the practitioner see how easily character strengths tap into an expression of goodness, no matter how small, to bring benefit to others. This table is also offered to highlight the point that this conceptual application is important for each of the character strengths, not solely those strengths where morality is an obvious element.

Table 5.3. 24 Ways to Be Good

Character Strength	Examples of Behavioral Acts of Goodness
Creativity	Create a surprise gift for someone that might be in the form of a poem, thank you card, or a unique meal.
Curiosity	Ask a person follow-up questions when they share good news with you so you can help them capitalize on the positivity.
Judgment/critical thinking	Evaluate your own level of goodness toward one person in your life; use your reasoning to consider another way to be good to them.
Love of learning	Read a book or article on kindness, and, while putting one thing you learned into action, reflect on your growth in learning on that topic.
Perspective	Call someone in your life you know who has been struggling lately and offer your direct or indirect/supportive counsel.
Bravery	Challenge a person (in an appropriate, balanced way) about a wrong you are seeing perpetrated in your community, at work, or at home.
Perseverance	Start and finish a project, today, in a way that brings benefit to another person.
Honesty	Be honest with someone about their best qualities. Tell them directly and clearly what you notice about them.
Zest	Notice a person or group in your community that is lacking energy; deliberately spend time with that person or group in an enthusiastic way so that your energy is contagious.
Love	In your next two conversations, express an attitude of warmth and genuineness in your body language and words with the other person, giving them your undivided attention.
Kindness	Commit a random act of kindness for someone you've never met.
Social intelligence	Initiate a positive conversation with someone who appears lonely or shy, who lacks good social skills, or who is emotionally upset.
Teamwork	Offer to help support a teammate on a work project.
Fairness	Express your fairness with a group (e.g., your children, your colleagues, your friends); take action to bring balance and fair treatment to everyone in the group.
Leadership	Organize an activity, trip, or volunteer experience for a small group that contributes positively to your community or helps raise awareness in your group about an important issue.
Forgiveness	Be merciful and supportive to someone who has wronged you. See their vulnerability, see your strength, and if you're ready and if appropriate, tell them you forgive them.
Humility	Spend time talking with a homeless person on the street (or someone whom you know is struggling). Place your attention on them, giving them the stage to talk and share.
Prudence	Plan out in detail a special event for your child, spouse, or friend. Plan ahead and map everything out so that the other person is sure to be surprised and feel good.
Self-regulation	When someone is expressing anger toward you, pause with a couple slow breaths, instead of reacting with anger in return. See the humanness of the other person and that they are suffering.
Appreciation of beauty & excellence	Experience the emotion of elevation by observing moral goodness in an inspiring movie character and follow up with your own motivation to do good because of this.
Gratitude	Write a note of gratitude that shares why you are grateful for the person on a sticky-note. Place it on your colleague's desk or in your relationship partner's space that will offer a surprise to go along with your gratitude.
Hope	Sit down with your partner or friend and envision a positive future; talk about how you both can bring benefit to the lives of others with your vision.
Humor	Offer a smile and a funny story or joke to someone who is feeling stressed and needs some levity.
Spirituality	Recall something that one person in your life considers to be meaningful to them. Find a way to contribute to that meaning in some way, perhaps creating an experience with or for them.

The *Character Strengths and Virtues* text (Peterson & Seligman, 2004) explains that one of the ten criteria for a character strength is that the strength be morally valued: "Although strengths can and do produce desirable outcomes, each strength is morally valued in its own right, even in the absence of obvious beneficial outcomes" (p. 19).

Character strengths have been found to predict behavior in the moral domain and to both complement and provide incremental validity above the trait of honesty/humility in studies of economic games (Ruch, Bruntsch, & Wagner, 2017). Moral character is a realistic, agreed-upon lens by which people view themselves and others, as supported in research findings showing agreement of different peer-ratings along with self-ratings of character strengths (Helzer, Furr, Barranti, & Fleeson, 2014).

Some character strengths have an obvious, strong loading around morality such as the value of being kind or fair to others. Other character strengths have a less obvious moral connection such as judgment/critical thinking and humor. To address this, Peterson and Seligman (2004) explain these as "value-added strengths," in that the strength is *most* praiseworthy when it is combined with one or more character strengths. Humor with leadership or humor with teamwork become "the humorous leader" or the "playful teammate," respectfully, and each conjures up insights around the added value of the combination. Another example is humor with kindness. A typical comedian on the stage who is high in humor is probably not offering exemplary work in the "morally valued" category; however, when that comedian puts on a clown suit and walks into the pediatric cancer unit at a children's hospital to cheer up kids who are suffering (i.e., humor combined with kindness) then humor becomes exemplary in terms of moral value.

One character strength that has been given unique attention around moral goodness over the last decade is the strength of appreciation of beauty and excellence, and more specifically one of its dimensions referred to as "elevation." Elevation is an emotion people experience when they witness an act of moral goodness, feel physiological sensations in the body (e.g., warming of chest, tingling in extremities), and are motivated to do good (Algoe & Haidt, 2009; Haidt, 2000). Several studies now show that this emotion leads people to greater goodness as measured by prosocial acts and altruism (see Aquino, McFerran, & Laven, 2011; Cox, 2010; Diessner, Iyer, Smith, & Haidt, 2013; Landis et al., 2009; Schnall, Roper, & Fessler, 2010; Schnall & Roper, 2011; Siegel, Thomson, & Navarro, 2014; Thomson, Nakamura, Siegel, & Csikszentmihalyi, 2014). Interventions have targeted elevation, also known as "moral beauty," by encouraging students to engage with moral beauty in order to increase their desire to become better persons and to do good, because engagement with this form of beauty is uniquely predictive of caring for, being empathic of, and loving others and of someone showing benevolence toward others (Diessner et al., 2013).

The motivational elements of elevation are aligned with the thinking of Aristotle (4th BCE/2000), who viewed the core of moral character as comprised not only of externally acquired knowledge (e.g., moral principles), but also the emotions, reasons, and intentions that move an individual to act in accordance with those principles (moral sentiments). The latter, it can be argued, are guided by "internal" means of character strengths, especially the development of self-awareness, reflection, and the expression of strengths. Virtue theorist Matt Stichter (2007; 2015) adds to this by arguing for a "skill model of virtue," and explains that virtues are skills that deal with morality matters. Thus, the skill model of virtue is having both a practical know-how and a commitment to act well combined with practical wisdom to evaluate the moral purpose with respect to living well. For Stichter, this skill model of virtue is neo-Aristotlelian and the practical activity of acting well aligns with being well. Personality researchers have also discussed the potency of "acting well" in order to be well as an intervention to help people change (Blackie et al., 2014).

Virtuous character is guided by a clear vision of what is good and admirable, from which the individual is able to act consistently in a way that fits the situation (Fowers, 2008). As one of eight central features of mindfulness-based strengths practice (MBSP, Niemiec, 2014a), participants are asked to explore the connection of character strengths with their goals in relation to two overarching areas of personal purpose – authenticity and goodness. While it's argued that one leads to the other and the two interrelate, participants usually resonate with one or the other and are hence encouraged to use that as a starting point. Participants often have a sense as to whether their personal goals and drive toward virtuous character are aligned with striving toward "being a better me" (authenticity) or "being a better person" (goodness). An example of the former is focusing on widening and deepening one's expression of signature strengths, while the latter is viewed as deliberately targeting particular character strengths to benefit others or society (e.g., trying to improve one's kindness or bravery). In either case, the deliberate expression of character strengths/signature strengths for purposeful, virtuous ends takes mindful effort and practice. With such effort, these examples show how character emerges from the inside to the out, rather than something that infiltrates from the outside-in (Diessner et al., 2013).

The movement of the outside to the in is also clear in character development. The expression of character in the moral domain can be learned from the observation of others. As Bandura (1977), the father of observational learning, argued perhaps better than anyone, most of human learning occurs through observation, as what is observed is coded within us for future use. Character strengths and virtues can be observed in paragons and moral exemplars for their expression of goodness and excellence. Moral exemplars of strengths can be found in one's social circle (Laham, 2013) as well as through the influence of mentors and role models (Moberg, 2008). Moral exemplars show a strong motivational theme of agency and communion and often depict action in challenging situations (Walker & Frimer, 2007). There is not one pathway of virtuous expression for a moral character (Walker & Hennig, 2004), therefore, it is useful to look to multiple examples to understand the breadth. Extreme exemplars, referred to as paragons, was one of the criteria used to define the inclusion of a character strength in the VIA classification, and Peterson and Seligman (2004) also offer one example for each of the 24 strengths (e.g., Gandhi for fairness). Indeed, role models and mentors are one of the most common, recurring themes in terms of "enabling factors" that engender these character strengths (Peterson & Seligman, 2004). Niemiec and Wedding (2014) offer over 1,500 examples from movies organized by the 24 character strengths. The deployment of character strengths to reach moral ends (e.g., goodness, betterment of others/society) was specifically articulated in relation to the central characters of Rea, Finn, and Han Solo in *Star Wars: Episode VII – The Force Awakens* (Sansom et al., 2016).

Strengths-Based Practitioner Tip

As a practical exercise, clients can be encouraged to name their biggest influencers or the positive role models in their life. They can be encouraged to name someone who is living or deceased, real or fictional, old or young. The biggest impact is often found for those who consider someone personal – e.g., a family member, close friend, neighbor, teacher – who has directly impacted the client. If the client is unable to name someone personal they might consider either a person in the public eye or even a person who has been depicted in some form in the media (e.g., from a movie, television program, or book). When I was presenting character strengths workshops to officers and cadets at the United States Air Force Academy, I asked the group to reflect on an activity similar to this one. During the debriefing, one particularly stoic and tough officer raised his hand to share that his exemplar was Mr. Rogers (from the popular children's television show Mister Rogers' Neighborhood). He explained that he recalled often being in battle and other challenging situations with his unit and would say to himself: "If Mr. Rogers was in this situation, what would he do?" He then considered Mr. Rogers' likely actions and what his advice might be, as well as turning to those character strengths of Mr. Rogers. He then attempted to do what was right and best in the situation.

We can also learn about moral goodness through individuals showing a deficiency of character strength. This may occur in immoral or bad behavior but also in the absence of good or bad behavior, as the avoidance of bad behavior alone does not necessarily reflect strong character strength expression. Fowers (2008) addresses this when he describes Aristotle's five character types, particularly when explaining how an individual can be of a continent or incontinent character type, which are types that fall short of virtuous (good) character because they are characterized by a conflict or struggle to express a virtuous good, yet they are not in the domain of the vicious or beastly domain of character. The latter categories would fall in the area of what I call "character strengths misuse," which is the use of character strengths for manipulative or malevolent purposes. For example, creativity can be misused as evidenced in email spamming in which one receives a message from a Nigerian prince who informs you that you are an heir to a large sum of money and if you simply pass along your bank account number to the prince, he can make the confirmation and you and he will happily split the funds. Creativity research has termed this misuse of creativity as "malevolent creativity" and several studies have examined the dangers and moral complexity and ambiguity therein (Cropley, Kaufman, White, & Chiera, 2014). Researchers in creativity have even gone on to distinguish malevolent creativity (e.g., deliberate intention to harm, such as an employee stealing company secrets to bring down a company) from negative creativity (e.g., an employee who thinks of creative ways to steal office supplies from their employer, which may not have the intent to harm the company). The misuse of courage/bravery has been explored by Pury, Starkey, Kulik, Skjerning, and Sullivan (2015), who explain that "bad courage" occurs when an individual sees a particular goal as good, whereas society views that particular goal as bad. A terrorist expressing bravery as a suicide bomber would be one example of bad courage or its misuse. Some of these are obvious examples showing a lack of morality. It is important for practitioners to remember that morality is typically a highly nuanced area that, as discussed in Chapter 1 about the nature of "character," is not an all-or-none/black-or-white, categorical view. As humans, we like categories and boxes to place people in as this helps us understand them, but limiting a person to good or bad, moral or immoral, is usually not a sophisticated or accurate approach.

I suspect the themes I mention here, which are of varying levels of integration, will be enhanced by a cohesive theory of good character that examines character from the perspective of these 24 ubiquitous strengths. To this end, David Rand at Yale University is making important strides in experimental paradigms studying why character strengths may have evolved to serve humanity's interests to survive and thrive.

Mindfulness, Savoring, Flow, and Hypnosis

In this section, I'll offer some distinctions between states of mindfulness, savoring, flow, and hypnosis and discuss ways that each interface with character strengths. While there is overlap between each, important distinctions can be drawn. There are different ways to discuss and examine each of these, for example, mindfulness can be viewed as a trait, state, or process (Niemiec, 2014a) and savoring can be viewed as an experience, process, or response/strategy (Bryant & Veroff, 2007). This section will not examine such nuances nor will it discuss their relationship with one another. Rather, this section places emphasis on practical utility, especially focused on how each might enhance character strengths and how character strengths, in turn, might impact each phenomenon.

Mindfulness

In the early 2000s, a group of diverse mindfulness scientists collaborated together to offer an operational definition for mindfulness. This was particularly important because the field of mindfulness was growing substantially and researchers, practitioners, and thought leaders were often defining mindfulness in different ways. This distinguished group arrived at a two-part definition for mindfulness: (1) the self-regulation of attention (2) with an attitude of curiosity, openness, and acceptance (Bishop et al., 2004). From this definition, it is clear there are two character strengths (self-regulation and curiosity) that are already embedded in the essence of what mindfulness really is, at its core.

But the integration of mindfulness and character strengths does not stop there (Baer & Lykins, 2011). Niemiec (2014a) explained that there are two ways to integrate these constructs. These are highlighted in Table 5.4, which offers definitions for "strong mindfulness" and "mindful strengths use" and the rationale for their importance. As all people struggle from time to time to create any form of self-regulation practice – and some people struggle mightily and then quit – would it therefore not make sense to turn to one's best internal qualities for support? The all-too-common obstacles of mind wandering, forgetting to practice, and not having time can be confronted and overcome with strengths, especially signature strengths. Indeed, the practice of mindfulness or of character strengths can unleash a positive contagion – an internal virtuous circle that brings benefit intrapersonally or an external virtuous circle in which the more centered practitioner then interacts in a positive way with another person and this positivity carries forward (because of a recent mindfulness or strengths practice).

Table 5.4. Two Ways to Integrate Mindfulness and Character Strengths

Integration Concept	Definition	Rationale	Practical Activity
Strong mindfulness	Bringing character strengths to mindfulness CS → M	Manage your meditation obstacles. Improve mindful living (e.g., driving, walking, eating). Supercharge your meditation by bringing more of "you" to the practice.	1. Name one meditation obstacle. 2. Write one way that each of your Top 3 signature strengths could help you face the obstacle. 3. Make a plan and try it out.
Mindful strengths use	Bringing mindfulness to character strengths M → CS	Combat strength blindness by using signature (and other) strengths more. Discover an optimal strengths zone between overuse and underuse. Increase savvy toward context nuances. Reframe problems with strengths.	1. Pause with whatever you are doing. 2. Find your breathing in the moment for 10–30 seconds. 3. At the end of the pause, ask yourself: What character strength might I bring forth right now? 4. Bring the strength forward in your behavior, speech, feelings, or thinking. (the mindful pause)

Savoring

Savoring involves the deliberate cultivation of positive experience in the here and now. Although people are mindful of their experience during savoring, the process of savoring is more restrictive as the individual targets internal or external positive stimuli and maintains that focus (Bryant & Veroff, 2007), whereas mindfulness approaches involve being open to whatever arises in the present moment – positive, negative, or neutral. In short, savoring means to try to prolong the positive, whether that be a positive feeling of joy or peace or whether it be the presence of a character strength. Indeed, mindfulness gets us through the doorway to seize an opportunity to savor.

There are many connections between character strengths and savoring. As with mindfulness, we can examine the integration in three important ways (see Table 5.5): Strong savoring refers to deliberately strengthening your savoring capacity by turning to one or more character strengths. In turn, savoring can be brought to character strengths in at least two important ways: a focus on appreciating a character strength (of oneself or others) in the moment and a focus on noticing the strengths that emerge as a result of any savoring practice. Many savoring practices have been established and center around the past, present, or future, such as positive reminiscence, savoring the present moment, and positive mental time travel, respectively (e.g., Bryant & Veroff, 2007; Hurley & Kwon, 2012; Quoidbach, Berry, Hansenne, & Mikolajczak, 2010; Quoidbach, Wood, & Hansenne, 2009; Smith, Harrison, Kurtz, & Bryant, 2014).

Table 5.5. The Integration of Savoring and Character Strengths

Integration Concept	Definition	Rationale	Practical Activity
Strong savoring	Bringing character strengths to savoring CS → S	Manage your savoring obstacles. Improve savoring in your daily living (e.g., driving, walking, eating). Supercharge your savoring by bringing more of "you" to the practice.	1. Name one savoring obstacle (e.g., forgot to practice, don't have time, mind wandered). 2. Write one way that each of your Top 3 signature strengths could help you face the obstacle. 3. Make a plan and try it out.
Savored strength	Bringing savoring to character strengths S → CS	Enhance appreciation for one of your character strengths. Enhance appreciation for a character strength of someone else.	1. Select any established savoring practice, e.g., positive reminiscence. 2. Choose one of your character strengths as the target of the experience, e.g., perseverance. 3. Reminisce about one memory in which your perseverance was strong and positive (or substitute a difference character strength or different savoring strategy).

Table 5.5. Continued

Integration Concept	Definition	Rationale	Practical Activity
			4. Allow yourself to be immersed in the positive thoughts, feelings, words, and actions involved with savoring your memory of perseverance. Feel the sensations associated with this strength in the moment. Prolong the experience for at least 10 minutes.
The strength that rises	Bringing savoring to character strengths S → CS	Attend to a strength that is an outcome of savoring. With new awareness, the strength might be used in postsavoring as a beneficial experience in and of itself, or as a method for further prolonging and remembering the savored experience.	1. Engage in any established savoring practice (e.g., positive reminiscence). 2. After the practice concludes, notice which of your 24 character strengths is most elevated. 3. Consider expressing that strength in your life, or pause to savor the strength.

Distinguishing Between Mindfulness and Savoring

What follows are two meditation activities, using the same scenario, but shifted to be either a formal mindfulness activity or a formal savoring activity. For each activity, begin by going outside in nature and sitting down. This is not an imagery activity so you'll need to literally go outside!

1. *Mindfulness strategy.* Notice the nature scene. Be attentive to your senses, your feelings, and your thoughts as you sit there. Be attentive to the myriad of details surrounding you. Allow yourself to feel whatever it is you are feeling from moment to moment. You might feel peace. Maybe agitation? Lingering stress or emerging calm? Be open to all feelings and allow them to be there. Continue to watch them. Be open to new feelings or thoughts that arise. Do the best you can to not get "caught up" in any detail or any feeling. Instead, take an approach of exploring and noticing, more and more. You might even say to yourself over and over "What else can I notice?" Take in further details as you look around your environment and as you observe your inner experience.

2. *Savoring strategy.* Notice the nature scene. Allow yourself to be immersed in its beauty – the sounds, visual details, and pleasant smells. Take notice of something particularly positive – something that makes you feel good. It might be the sound of babbling water, the majesty of a giant tree, or the chirping of birds as they fly around. Absorb yourself in the details. Notice any positive feelings present within you – such as peacefulness, energy, love, awe, gratitude, hope, interest, or other feelings. Tune in closely to one of these feelings. Feel it fully as you enjoy the nature scene. Stick with that positive emotion. Appreciate how good it feels. Extend it by breathing with it. It might feel as if your breath is enhancing your feeling, deepening it. If the feeling fades, turn to another positive feeling or to another pleasurable part of the nature scene.

Flow

Flow is a mental state people experience when they engage in an activity that provides a persistent, nonoverwhelming challenge and the person is able to use their strengths or skills (Csikszentmihalyi, 1997). When a person is in flow, they are fully engaged in the activity at work, in sport, in conversation, etc. Many have described that when we are engaged in this way we are, by definition, using our strengths, including character strengths (Seligman, 2002, 2011). When we use our bodily-kinesthetic strength/talent in playing basketball we might find ourselves in the zone of flow, making multiple shots in a row, or when we are using our talent for interpersonal relating, we become (positively) lost in an engaging conversation. Character strengths, in retrospect, can easily be spotted in these examples and undoubtedly play an important role in enjoying and maintaining the flow experience. As character strengths are identified when a person is in flow, such as using creativity doing an engaging work project or the process of painting, this can be termed "character strengths flow." In addition to flow states facilitating character strengths use, the reverse can occur as well.

We can create opportunities and situations to enable flow, such as job crafting so we can engage in meaningful work or activities we are interested in (e.g., tennis, cooking, painting) so that we are likely to find flow. Thus, we can use our character strengths to arrange such situations. For example, a person might use their leadership strength to organize a group tennis outing where the likelihood of flow will be high; use love of learning to take a painting class; or curiosity as the person searches and reads engaging food recipes online. The deliberate use of character strengths, especially signature strengths, to catalyze flow or at least create potential opportunities for flow is another angle of "character strengths flow."

Hypnosis Trances

Hypnosis trances are states of absorption, attention, and concentration. There are volumes of research studies and texts outlining the efficacy of hypnosis as a valuable intervention for various clinical, medical, and everyday problems. While hypnosis enjoys a strong scientific base and is well-accepted as a psychological and medical intervention (e.g., American Medical Association), it engenders a number of misconceptions, fears, and confusion in the general public. An important truism to understand hypnosis is that all hypnosis is self-hypnosis. It is not a loss of control or loss of will, rather it is the using of a deep state of concentration and healing within oneself (Hammond, 1988, 1990). There are countless examples of what's referred to as the "everyday trance" in which a person is driving in their car, and operating their vehicle fine, and suddenly realizes they have missed their exit. The capacity of people to enter into trance states is utilized in a purposeful way during an experience of self-hypnosis or in the context of a helping professional using hypnosis, in order to alleviate a problem or enhance an internal quality such as self-efficacy. Hypnosis, as an approach, is most similar to mindfulness (especially "guided mindfulness meditations"), as they share a common practical foundation, methodology, therapeutic orientation, structure, and suggestive nature (Yapko, 2011). Therefore, many of the points raised earlier about the integration of mindfulness and character strengths apply to hypnosis, albeit with some tweaking.

Character strengths can be used to elicit a deep mental state, such as a hypnosis state. A client may initially use self-regulation to focus their attention, creativity to engage with visual imagery, perseverance to stay connected with their breathing while looking inward, and perspective to see the bigger picture (i.e., the insights) that the hypnosis experience is offering, such as new wisdom from their "inner advisor." On the other hand, hypnosis states might generate character strengths. Experiencing a calm, deep state – especially for any extended period – can conceivably lead to the awareness or boosting of any of the 24 character strengths. I witnessed this in my previous practice leading hundreds of clients in hypnosis experiences. Examples include the man who garnered improved critical thinking/judgment as he looked at the conflict with his father from different angles; the woman with severe irritable bowel syndrome who achieved complete relief from her symptoms and who elevated her self-regulation and prudence; and the many men and women who used hypnosis as a way to create greater bravery by facing their problem directly and in a safe way.

An Integration of Everything?

Participants in my mindfulnes courses will often say that they enjoyed being mindful because they relished really "tasting" one piece of chocolate or they became fully absorbed in the calmness they felt when they paid attention to their breathing. The example with tasting chocolate is more complex than it seems. Such individuals are using mindfulness initially to attend to the experience, then they turn to savoring to prolong the positive sensations involving taste. Simultaneously, some might be spontaneously entering a trance state where they are free from distraction and are suggestible, absorbed, and highly concentrated. Meanwhile, participants are using self-regulation with their attention, curious about the food object, grateful to have the experience they are having, persevering with the task at hand, and perhaps using other character strengths. If the task were particularly challenging and they were using their skills to engage, then we could add flow too!

Chapter Summary

- Overuse and underuse of character strengths are phenomena that reflect an imbalance of our character strengths use in that we either come across too strong or too soft (or not at all) with our strengths in a particular situation. When we find the strengths zone between overuse and underuse, and are expressing the right combination of character strengths to the right degree for the right situation, then we have found the golden mean.
- Synergies and collisions of character strengths occur when two or more character strengths combine to be greater than the sum of the strengths or far less than the sum of their parts, respectfully. Character strengths synergies and character strengths collisions occur on the intrapersonal and interpersonal levels.
- Hot buttons are sensitive areas in which another person's overuse or underuse of strengths triggers frustration or discomfort within us.
- Morality and character strengths are deeply linked. Character strengths offer many ways to be good and to do good in the world.
- Mindfulness, savoring, flow, and hypnosis trances can be integrated with character strengths. Each can be used to facilitate the expression of character strengths and each can be enhanced or brought about through the use of character strengths.

Chapter 6
Character Strength Spotlights
24 Practitioner-Friendly Handouts

Introduction

The breadth and depth of each of the 24 character strengths is substantial. For this reason, I have created "spotlights" on each of the character strengths to help practitioners practically access, keep track of, and assimilate character strengths into their work with clients, students, and employees, or into their personal lives. Each character strength receives the full spotlight of attention for a single page – a page that is loaded with research and practice. Following the virtue category for each character strength, each page offers core features, a circumplex snapshot (how the strength fares on dimensions of heart/mind and intra/interpersonal), the Top 5 character strength correlations, questions for building the strength, research highlights, research-based interventions, and the overuse/underuse language for the strength. I explain more about each here.

Core Features

Definition

These are the definitions offered by Peterson and Seligman (2004) and continue to be championed by the VIA Institute on Character (https://www.viacharacter.org).

Essence

This is viewed as the core of the character strength. For some spotlights, a second "catchy" phrase that captures the strength is added. These were derived from studying the research in character science, examining the items on the VIA Survey, and discussions and feedback from experts in the field.

Dimensions

Here synonyms are offered from the VIA classification and the original conception of Peterson and Seligman (2004). They reflect concepts that are similar and related to the particular strength. In other words, kindness is multidimensional: kindness is being nice and caring, and it is also having compassion, altruism, and/or generosity. Not all of the character strengths have noteworthy dimensions offered in this way. As discussed in Chapter 1, each of the character strengths are "dimensional" in that they are expressed in degrees, are capacities for thinking, feeling, and behaving, are expressed outwardly and inwardly, and so forth. Some studies have specifically examined a dimension for a particular character strength and found support for it, for example, modesty has indeed been found to be a subdomain of humility (Davis et al., 2016).

Circumplex

This is also referred to as the two-factor graph or the balance graph. This graph, uniquely created for each character strength, was created from a revised data analysis by Robert McGrath in 2014, and is originally based on the two-factor model of Peterson (2006a). It depicts a clustering of character strengths mapped across two continua: strengths that are heart-oriented (e.g., feeling, body, emotion, intuition) or head-oriented (e.g., thinking, logic, analysis, reasoning), and strengths that are interpersonal-oriented (expressed with others) or intrapersonal-oriented (expressed when alone). See Figure 2.1 in Chapter 2 for the full mapping of the 24 character strengths and for a practical exercise to work with the graph.

Correlations

The Top 5 character strength correlations are offered for each character strength. These come from a massive data set of 458,854 subjects from the VIA Institute data pool from the VIA Survey for adults, which was analyzed by Robert McGrath in May, 2013. The strengths are ordered from highest correlation down to fifth-highest correlation (McGrath, 2013). There were no perfect ties beyond the level of hundredth when decimal points were considered.

Questions for Strengths Building

This section offers a handful of questions to help a practitioner explore the character strength with a client or to assist a client in self-exploration. They are meant to catalyze self-awareness, insight, and behavior change.

Research Highlights

These general highlights are a sampling of three to five important or interesting findings relating to the specific character strength. Space limitations prevent more than this. The avid researcher can check out many sources in addition to this book for more details on the research highlights and other studies (go to the research tab on the VIA Institute site at https://www.viacharacter.org; also see Niemiec, 2013, 2014a; Niemiec & Wedding, 2014; Peterson & Seligman, 2004).

Interventions

While there is not an abundance of randomized trials on each of the 24 character strengths, there are good or reasonable interventions for each strength. Research is used as a guide and base for each strength in an effort to best inform practice. Therefore, the two or three specific interventions described are among the best we know for boosting the specific character strength. Where an intervention study does not exist for a particular strength, the most important findings from exisiting correlational research are presented. In every case, the citation is given so that readers can turn to the original work for more information. The practitioner needs to use their own judgment to discern usability and adaptability for their unique client and the unique context at hand.

Continuum of Overuse and Underuse

This is a reworking by Niemiec (2014a) with support from the VIA Institute. I credit Chris Peterson (2006b) for making the initial argument that each of the 24 strengths might be expanded, for theorizing about mental illnesses, as well as proposing strength opposites, excesses, and absences. In testing the latter approach around the world with leading practitioners and educators, this approach fell flat, repeatedly, from a practice perspective. The transition to a continuum of overuse and underuse, which aligns with Aristotle's (4th BCE/2000) conception of virtues having two points of imbalance and a golden mean, has proven to have a strong and improved fit for practitioners around the globe. Recent research has supported this model and even found it to be useful in understanding a population with psychopathology (Freidlin et al., 2017).

Strengths-Based Practitioner Tip

- Learn a lot about the 24 character strengths in 24 pages! There is an 800-page book (Peterson & Seligman, 2004), a 400-page book (Niemiec & Wedding, 2014), and a 350-page book (Niemiec, 2014a) on character strengths. While these pages don't replace those works, they offer you a quick spotlight on what is particularly helpful for you to know.
- Spend time examining the "spotlights" for your Top 5 strengths and familiarize yourself with these five as lenses describing who you are. Answer the questions. Try out the interventions.
- As you review the sections of a given "spotlight," which section strikes you most? Which would you like to spend more time with in building your knowledge?
- If a client is interested in building up a particular strength, turn to the "spotlight" on that strength as a catalyst for your conversation.
- If a client is struggling to understand a particular strength, use the questions for strengths building, interventions, and other sections to give you several different ways to help them deepen their knowledge and practice around the strength.
- Don't know much about humility or prudence? Use these sheets as an easy reference guide to bring you up to speed.

Virtue: Wisdom

Spotlight on
Creativity

Core Features

Definition: Thinking of novel and productive ways to conceptualize and do things; includes artistic achievement but is not limited to it.

Essence: Uniqueness that is practical. Seeing and doing things in different ways.

Dimensions: Originality, ingenuity.

Highest Correlations With Creativity

1. Curiosity
2. Bravery
3. Perspective
4. Zest
5. Judgment/critical thinking

Research Highlights

- One of the most common strengths in young children.
- Enhanced by supportive, open, informal, and reinforcing environments.
- Limited by time pressure, close supervision, and critical examination.

Questions for Strength Building

- In what situations are you most creative?
- How does creativity help you solve problems?
- What holds you back from expressing your creativity?

Creativity Interventions

- Encourage an individual to "be creative" before a thinking task or problem-solving activity. This is one of the oldest findings in the science of creativity (Nusbaum, Silvia, & Beaty, 2014).
- Develop divergent thinking, which means to generate multiple alternate solutions, instead of searching for one "correct" solution (Scott, Leritz, & Mumford, 2004). After you name a problem, brainstorm a list of ideas of potential solutions.

Conformity	Creativity	Eccentricity
Underuse	Strength Zone	Overuse

Virtue: Wisdom

Spotlight on
Curiosity

Core Features

Definition: Taking an interest in ongoing experience for its own sake; finding subjects and topics fascinating.

Essence: Exploration.

Dimensions: Interest, novelty-seeking, openness to experience.

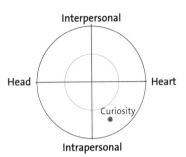

Highest Correlations With Curiosity

1. Zest
2. Love of learning
3. Creativity
4. Hope
5. Perspective

Questions for Strength Building

- How does your curiosity present across the different domains of life?
- Where do you feel most comfortable being curious?
- In what situations does your curiosity get you in trouble?
- What blocks or interferes with your curiosity?

Research Highlights

- One of the five strengths most connected with happiness/life satisfaction.
- One of the five most frequently endorsed strengths around the world.
- One of the strengths most aligned with a life of engagement.
- Connected with intelligence, life longevity, meaning, and good relationships.

Curiosity Interventions

- Consider an activity that you dislike. Pay attention to three novel features of this activity while you do it (Langer, 2006).
- Practice active curiosity, in which you actively explore your environment, rather than passive curiosity, in which you are only curious when something new pops up in your environment (Kashdan, 2009).

Disinterest	Curiosity	Nosiness
Underuse	Strength Zone	Overuse

Virtue: Wisdom

Spotlight on
Judgment/Critical Thinking

Core Features

Definition: Thinking things through and examining them from all sides; not jumping to conclusions; being able to change one's mind in light of evidence; weighing all evidence fairly.

Essence: Analytical; seeing a 360-degree view of the details.

Dimensions: Critical thinking, open-mindedness, rationality.

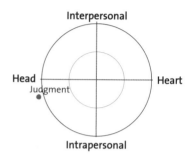

Highest Correlations With Judgment/Critical Thinking

1. Perspective
2. Prudence
3. Honesty
4. Love of learning
5. Fairness

Questions for Strength Building

- What are some ways you use judgment/critical thinking in an automatic way that is also productive for you?
- As judgment is a strong "mind" strength, in what situations is it best to combine it with a "heart" strength?
- When are you most vulnerable to overusing this strength?

Research Highlights

- One of the five highest endorsed strengths around the world.
- It's a "corrective virtue." It counteracts faulty thinking and biased opinions, which can help with decision-making.
- Helps in resisting suggestion and manipulation.

Judgment/Critical Thinking Interventions

- Challenge your personal biases and opinions by seeking information that runs counter to your beliefs, attitudes, and behaviors (Hart et al., 2009). This will help you expose yourself to different vantage points and information and expand your thinking.
- When in an argument, practice taking an approach that embodies the belief that truth emerges from a process of critical inquiry in which all important sides should be considered (Peterson & Seligman, 2004).

Unreflective	Judgment	Narrow-minded
Underuse	Strength Zone	Overuse

Virtue: Wisdom

Spotlight on
Love of Learning

Core Features

Definition: Mastering new skills, topics, and bodies of knowledge, whether on one's own or formally; related to the strength of curiosity but goes beyond it to describe the tendency to add systematically to what one knows.

Essence: Going deep with knowledge.

Highest Correlations With Love of Learning

1. Curiosity
2. Appreciation of beauty/excellence
3. Judgment/critical thinking
4. Creativity
5. Zest

Questions for Strength Building

- What is a new area you could apply this strength to (e.g., gardening, philosophy, cooking, painting, woodworking)?
- In what situations does your curiosity lead you to dig deeper and systematically learn a new skill/topic and in what situations is curiosity not a driving force?
- What topic areas of your learning are most important to you?

Research Highlights

- Been shown in several studies to be linked with academic success.
- Supports positive experiences, which can then predispose you to well-being.
- Leads to the development of a deeper base of knowledge, enhancing efficacy and competency.

Love of Learning Interventions

- Choose a subject matter that you are most curious about learning more (Covington, 1999). Pursue this interest area as you dig deeper and wider on the topic.
- When faced with learning something that might be boring, consider how the learning might benefit both you and the world beyond you (what researchers call "having a self-transcendent purpose"; Yeager, Henderson et al., 2014). Focusing on both can enhance motivation, learning, and meaning.

Complacency	Love of Learning	Know-it-all
Underuse	Strength Zone	Overuse

Virtue: Wisdom

Core Features

Definition: Being able to provide wise counsel to others; having ways of looking at the world that make sense to oneself and to other people.

Essence: The wider view.

Dimensions: Integrating viewpoints beyond one's own.

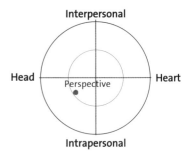

Highest Correlations With Perspective

1. Social intelligence
2. Judgment
3. Hope
4. Bravery
5. Honesty

Research Highlights

- One of the strengths most connected with a life of engagement.
- Linked with successful aging and well-being in older adults.
- Shown to buffer against the negative effects of stress and trauma.

Questions for Strength Building

- In what situations do you feel most comfortable (and least comfortable) in sharing your perspective?
- How has this character strength helped you in your relationships and work?
- Name instances when you have missed opportunities to share a bigger picture view. How might you learn from these?

Perspective Interventions

- Name a life problem. Imagine yourself traveling around the world speaking about the problem with people from different cultures and gathering information about differences in life contexts and different values and perspectives (Baltes & Staudinger, 2000).
- Have a conversation with a wise person (or imagine the conversation). If imagined, visualize the full dialogue in terms of questions asked, responses given, the nuances of the discussion, and any advice that would be offered (Baltes & Staudinger, 2000). This boosts wisdom-related knowledge.

Shallow	Perspective	Overbearing
Underuse	Strength Zone	Overuse

Virtue: Courage

Core Features

Definition: Not shrinking from threat, challenge, difficulty, or pain; speaking up for what is right; acting on convictions even if unpopular.

Essence: Facing fears, confronting adversity.

Dimensions: Valor, physical-psychological-moral bravery.

Highest Correlations With Bravery

1. Perspective
2. Social intelligence
3. Honesty
4. Creativity
5. Hope

Questions for Strength Building

- How best do you use your bravery (with a physical challenge, a psychological hurdle, a moral dilemma)?
- How does bravery cause others to both admire you and worry about you?
- In the past, which strengths have combined best with bravery for you? To what end?

Research Highlights

- General courage (something that would be courageous for anyone) is associated more with the presence of strengths than personal courage (something courageous for the individual, such as facing a fear of heights).
- Lowers anxiety, which in turn enhances the ability to tolerate ambiguous situations.
- Builds resilience as challenges are overcome and active coping skills are built.

Bravery Interventions

- Focus on the outcomes of courageous acts; for example, thinking of the person being helped, reminding oneself of the goodness of the action, or thinking about an obligation to act (Pury, 2008).
- Labeling others (or oneself) as courageous or brave, if there's appropriate reason to offer that observation, is a way to boost psychological bravery (Hannah et al., 2007).

Cowardice	Bravery	Foolhardy
Underuse	Strength Zone	Overuse

Virtue: Courage

Core Features

Definition: Finishing what one starts; persisting in a course of action despite obstacles; "getting it out the door;" taking pleasure in completing tasks.

Essence: Keep going, overcome all obstacles.

Dimensions: Industry, persistence.

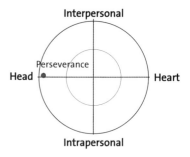

Highest Correlations With Perseverance

1. Self-Regulation
2. Honesty
3. Hope
4. Zest
5. Bravery

Questions for Strength Building

- What fuels your persevering behavior?
- Is there a bad habit or personal vice you'd like to apply your perseverance to in order to better manage it?
- What blocks your perseverance? How might you use your strengths to overcome that obstacle blocking you?

Research Highlights

- Involves two vectors: effort for a task and duration to keep going with that task.
- One of the strengths most associated with a life of engagement.
- Shown repeatedly across studies to be connected with success and various types of achievement.

Perseverance Interventions

- Being adaptable when confronted with negative events is crucial in building perseverance. One important factor in determining whether a person will adapt or not is their ability to make positive reappraisals of adverse events (i.e., practice seeing the good, the positive, the meaningful, and/or what can be learned from it) which maintains a mentality of "keep going" (Diener et al., 2006).
- Give positive feedback around focus, effort, and energy put forth on a task or in a challenging situation rather than focusing on a desired outcome. In other words, distinguish between low effort and low ability, and reward and reinforce effort (Dweck, 2006; Peterson & Seligman, 2004).

Helpless	Perseverance	Obsessive
Underuse	Strength Zone	Overuse

Virtue: Courage

Core Features

Definition: Speaking the truth but more broadly presenting oneself in a genuine way and acting in a sincere way; being without pretense; taking responsibility for one's feelings and actions.

Essence: Being true to yourself and authentic to others.

Dimensions: Authenticity, integrity.

Highest Correlations With Honesty

1. Perseverance
2. Perspective
3. Kindness
4. Fairness
5. Bravery

Questions for Strength Building

- In what situations do you find you need to temper your honesty or avoid the full truth?
- Examine the way you give constructive feedback to others. What are the best ways you do this?
- When you make a mistake, how easy is it for you to take responsibility?

Research Highlights

- Linked with self-concordance: The extent to which your goals accurately represent your implicit interests and values.
- One of the five character strengths most endorsed around the world.
- Allows for a more accurate self-assessment of your intentions and commitments, both to others and yourself.

Honesty Interventions

- When possible, encourage others to behave with a full sense of choice and self-expression which supports authenticity/honesty (Sheldon, Ryan, Rawsthorne, & Ilardi, 1997).
- One should be encouraged to express oneself consistently across settings and roles rather than acting in a particular manner at home and dramatically different at work (Sheldon et al., 1997).

Phoniness	Honesty	Righteousness
Underuse	Strength Zone	Overuse

Virtue: Courage

Core Features

Definition: Approaching life with excitement and energy; not doing things halfway or half-heartedly; living life as an adventure; feeling alive and activated.

Essence: Enthusiasm for life.

Dimensions: Vitality, vigor, energy.

```
                    Interpersonal


         Head  ─────────┼───────── Heart
                     Zest
                      ●

                    Intrapersonal
```

Highest Correlations With Zest

1. Hope
2. Curiosity
3. Gratitude
4. Perseverance
5. Humor

Questions for Strength Building

- How is zest blocked or inhibited for you and what can you do to manage this?
- What strengths best combine with zest to help you be at your best?
- As you examine the routines and activities of your day, which experiences bring you the most energy and enthusiasm? Might you create more of these?

Research Highlights

- Consistently one of the top two character strengths most associated with life satisfaction.
- One of the least endorsed character strengths around the world.
- Highly connected with engagement, meaning, work-as-a-calling, health behaviors, and work satisfaction.

Zest Interventions

- Research has found that sharing positive events with others (compared to not sharing) boosts energy and vitality. And, more frequent sharing of positive events has led to greater vitality 3 weeks later (Lambert, Gwinn, Fincham, & Stillman, 2011).
- Going outside, especially in nature, boosts zest and vitality (Ryan et al., 2010). Individuals can be encouraged to take breaks outdoors and arrange their day to spend some time in nature.

Sedentary	Zest	Hyperactive
Underuse	Strength Zone	Overuse

Virtue: Humanity

Core Features

Definition: Valuing close relations with others, in particular those in which sharing and caring are reciprocated; being close to people.

Essence: Genuine, reciprocal warmth.

Dimensions: Loving others, being loved by others.

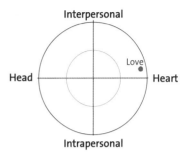

Highest Correlations With Love

1. Gratitude
2. Kindness
3. Zest
4. Hope
5. Social Intelligence

Research Highlights

- One of the top five character strengths most associated with life satisfaction.
- One of the most prevalent character strengths in very young children.
- Facilitates empathy, tolerance, and forgiveness in relationships, which contributes to the health and longevity of those relationships.

Questions for Strength Building

- How do you express love in a healthy way at work, at home, and with friends?
- Do you feel you have a balance in that you equally give *and* receive love from others?
- How do you combine this strength with each of your top strengths?

Love Interventions

- Practice spontaneous, in-the-moment loving acts that don't require extensive planning, memory, or forethought as a way of expressing and boosting this strength (Kammrath & Peetz, 2011).
- Develop a loving-kindness meditation practice in which you consciously tap into your inner resources of love through mental focus, imaging, and statements that focus on feeling and expressing love. This boosts love and is associated with a host of mental and physical benefits (Cohn & Fredrickson, 2010).

Emotional Isolation	Love	Emotional Promisuity
Underuse	Strength Zone	Overuse

Virtue: Humanity

Core Features

Definition: Doing favors and good deeds for others; helping them; taking care of them.

Essence: Doing for others.

Dimensions: Generosity, nurturance, care, compassion, altruism, and niceness.

Highest Correlations With Kindness

1. Gratitude
2. Teamwork
3. Leadership
4. Fairness
5. Love

Questions for Strength Building

- How is your kindness received by others?
- Do you notice a difference in the ease of which you express the different dimensions of kindness, e.g., generosity, care, compassion, being nice?
- When is it most important for you to turn your kindness inward, toward yourself?

Research Highlights

- One of the top five most prevalent character strengths across the globe.
- Helps buffer against the negative effects of stress and trauma.
- Kindness toward oneself can have numerous benefits including optimism, social connectedness, and goal mastery, and less anxiety, self-criticism, and perfectionism.

Kindness Interventions

- Keep track of each kind behavior you perform each day by writing it down and counting the kind acts at the end of the day (Otake, Shimai, Tanaka-Matsumi, Otsui, & Fredrickson, 2006).
- Offer the gift of your time to benefit a person you were not planning on giving time to (Gander, Proyer, Ruch, & Wyss, 2013).
- "Pay forward" a random act of kindness that brings benefit to others and does not generate a favor back to you (Baker & Bulkley, 2014; Pressman, Kraft, & Cross, 2015).

Virtue: Humanity

Core Features

Definition: Being aware of the motives and feelings of other people and oneself; knowing what to do to fit into different social situations; knowing what makes other people tick.

Essence: Tuned in, then savvy.

Dimensions: Emotional intelligence, personal intelligence.

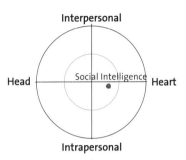

Highest Correlations With Social Intelligence

1. Perspective
2. Leadership
3. Bravery
4. Humor
5. Zest

Research Highlights

- One of the strengths most associated with a pleasurable life.
- An important strength that contributes to positive classroom behavior.
- Helps to buffer against the negative effects of stress and trauma.

Questions for Strength Building

- In what situations is your social intelligence strongest? How might you apply that social savvy to other situations?
- Which of your character strengths best complements and supports your social intelligence?
- When have your "reads" of social situations been inaccurate and how can you learn from them?

Social Intelligence Interventions

- Practice identifying a range of emotions as they occur within you and express them in a balanced way to others (Nelis, Quoidbach, Mikolajczak, & Hansenne, 2009).
- The practice of mindfulness and emotional intelligence has been connected scientifically (Schutte & Malouff, 2011). It is possible that mindfulness can help with the awareness and labeling of emotions as well as social awareness of nonverbal behavior and the details of the social context.

Clueless/Obtuse	Social Intelligence	Over-analyzing
Underuse	Strength Zone	Overuse

Virtue: Justice

Core Features

Definition: Working well as a member of a group or team; being loyal to the group; doing one's share.

Essence: Participative, contributing to a group effort.

Dimensions: Citizenship, social responsibility, loyalty.

Highest Correlations With Teamwork

1. Leadership
2. Kindness
3. Fairness
4. Love
5. Honesty

Questions for Strength Building

• How might you bring your teamwork strength into play beyond the work sphere ... into your relationships, family, or parenting?
• How does teamwork support you when stress is high?
• What strength do you combine most with teamwork?

Research Highlights

• Those high in this strength experience a higher level of social trust and have a more positive view of others.
• One of the strengths that predicted fewer depression symptoms in high school students.
• One of the strengths most associated with sustainable behavior, which is defined as behavior aimed to protect the social/physical environment.

Teamwork Interventions

• Encourage positive self-talk about one's team (not oneself) such as "we will perform well," "we are focused and ready," and "we believe in our ability" (Son, Jackson, Grove, & Feltz, 2011).
• Encourage an approach-oriented mindset among team members that is positive and proactive (Kilduff & Galinsky, 2013).
• Develop team optimism, efficacy, and resilience by encouraging members to be optimistic about the likelihood of success, confident in their capabilities, and capable of rebounding from setbacks, respectively (West, Patera, & Carsten, 2009).

Selfish	**Teamwork**	**Dependent**
Underuse	Strength Zone	Overuse

Virtue: Justice

Spotlight on
Fairness

Core Features

Definition: Treating all people the same according to notions of fairness and justice; not letting personal feelings bias decisions about others; giving everyone a fair chance.

Essence: Equal opportunity for all.

Dimensions: Care-based; justice-based; moral reasoning.

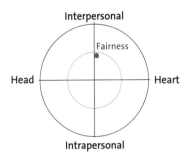

Highest Correlations With Fairness

1. Leadership
2. Teamwork
3. Forgiveness
4. Kindness
5. Honesty

Questions for Strength Building

- What situations at work or home challenge your capacity to be fair?
- When you perceive an injustice, how might you take action (or appropriate inaction) in a productive way that uses many of your strengths?
- What are three small examples in which you use fairness each day?

Research Highlights

- One of the five most frequently endorsed character strengths across the globe.
- Fair-minded individuals are more likely to engage in positive, prosocial behavior and less likely to engage in immoral behavior.
- Three types of fairness: *procedural* justice (the methods used are fair); *distributive* justice (the ultimate resolution is fair); *interactional* justice (individuals are treated with dignity and respect when policies and procedures are implemented).

Fairness Interventions

- Increase your fairness by involving others in decisions that impact them and allow others to disagree and refute ideas and assumptions (Kim & Mauborgne, 1997).
- Offer clear explanations for final decisions that are made and ensure understanding of the expectations for any new rules/policies (Kim & Mauborgne, 1997).
- Facilitate discussions around moral dilemmas or stories that present conflicting perspectives where tolerance, open-mindedness, and perspective-taking can be practiced (Berkowitz, 1985).

Detached	Fairness	Partisanship
Underuse	Strength Zone	Overuse

Virtue: Justice

Core Features

Definition: Encouraging a group of which one is a member to get things done and at the same time maintain good relations within the group; organizing group activities and seeing that they happen.

Essence: Positively influencing others.

Highest Correlations With Leadership

1. Fairness
2. Teamwork
3. Kindness
4. Social Intelligence
5. Gratitude

Questions for Strength Building

- In what specific ways do your express leadership at work and in your close relationships?
- What clues/signs do you pick up from others that you might be overplaying your leadership?
- How do you know when it's best to lead and when it's best to follow?

Leadership Interventions

- To improve this strength, one should be aware of and use one's strengths while watching out for overuse and underuse (Kaiser & Hogan, 2011).
- Improve your leader behavioral flexibility, which means to adapt your leadership style to be able and willing to respond in significantly different ways based on what the situation may require or to meet the individual needs of the people you are managing/leading (Sumner-Armstrong, Newcombe, & Martin, 2008).

Research Highlights

- Leadership can be distinguished as a *practice* (defining, establishing, or identifying direction; facilitating collective processes) or as a *personal quality* (the motivation and capacity to seek out, attain, and carry out leader roles).
- *Transactional* leaders clarify responsibilities, expectations, and the tasks to be done, while *transformational* leaders motivate others to perform at an extremely high level, fostering a climate of trust and commitment.
- One of the strengths substantially related to fewer problems (e.g., anxiety and depression).

Compliant	Leadership	Despotism
Underuse	Strength Zone	Overuse

Virtue: Temperance

Core Features

Definition: Forgiving those who have done wrong; accepting the shortcomings of others; giving people a second chance; not being vengeful.

Essence: Letting go of hurt when wronged.

Highest Correlations With Forgiveness

1. Fairness
2. Leadership
3. Teamwork
4. Kindness
5. Love

Questions for Strength Building

- Can you think of a time when you truly forgave someone but did not forget their transgression?
- How does it feel in your body when you fully forgive someone?
- Consider a time when you forgave someone who did not first apologize to you. What character strengths did you use to do that?

Research Highlights

- Forgiveness is distinct from denial, condoning, pardoning, forgetting, and reconciliation.
- Forgiveness is associated with many physical and psychological health benefits, such as emotional well-being, healthy lifestyle behaviors, social support, and spiritual well-being.
- People who are forgiving experience less anger, anxiety, depression, and hostility than less-forgiving people.

Forgiveness Interventions

- Practice compassion-focused reappraisal: After someone offends you, take time to think about how the offender is a complex human being who needs to experience positive growth and transformation, rather than seeing them in all-or-none/good-or-bad terms (Witvliet et al., 2011, 2010).
- Engage in cognitive processing following a minor offense by someone by writing about the personal benefits that resulted from the offense (McCullough, Root, & Cohen, 2006).
- Remind yourself that forgiveness is an ongoing process to be repeated with sustained effort over time (Baskin & Enright, 2004).

Merciless	Forgiveness	Permissive
Underuse	Strength Zone	Overuse

Virtue: Temperance

Spotlight on
Humility

Core Features

Definition: Letting one's accomplishments speak for themselves; not regarding oneself as more special than one is.

Essence: Achievement does not elevate worth. I'm OK but let's keep the positive focus on you.

Dimensions: Modesty.

Highest Correlations With Humility

1. Prudence
2. Fairness
3. Honesty
4. Teamwork
5. Kindness

Questions for Strength Building

- Can you think of a time when you regret being humble? Is there a way you could make a slight change yet retain humility?
- What are the obstacles to your expressing greater humility in your life?
- How do you balance humility with ego-driven desires for recognition and praise?

Research Highlights

- Humility is consistently one of the least endorsed strengths across the globe.
- Humility involves an accurate self-assessment, recognition of limitations, and a forgetting of the "self."
- Humility strengthens social bonds.
- Humble people are more helpful than less humble people.

Humility Interventions

- Write about a time in your life when you felt humility. How did you feel and what did you think? Be sure to make the humility experience genuine and not self-deprecatory (Exline & Geyer, 2004; Kesebir, 2014).
- Look for exemplars or heroes of humility and write about their characteristics to help you "starve" your arrogant nature and "feed" your humble nature (Worthington, 2007).

Arrogance	Humility	Self-deprecation
Underuse	Strength Zone	Overuse

Virtue: Temperance

Core Features

Definition: Being careful about one's choices; not taking undue risks; not saying or doing things that might later be regretted.

Essence: Wise caution.

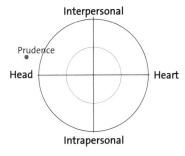

Highest Correlations With Prudence

1. Judgment/critical thinking
2. Humility
3. Honesty
4. Self-regulation
5. Fairness

Questions for Strength Building

- If prudence involves being respectful, careful about choices, conscientious, and setting goals, why does it get a bad rap?
- When do you combine bravery with prudence and when do you minimize bravery in order to express prudence?
- In what situations do people most appreciate your prudence?

Research Highlights

- One of the least endorsed character strengths across the globe.
- One of the strengths most associated with positive classroom behavior.
- Associated with physical health, job performance, and productivity.
- Substantially related to having fewer externalizing behaviors such as aggression.

Prudence Interventions

- When planning an activity, stop and consider potential obstacles and reflect on two components: your past experience with the activity (i.e., how long did it take last time?) and the steps or elements that make up the task (i.e., how much time will I need for each part) (Weick & Guinote, 2010).
- Make specific plans for one goal at a time on your to-do list while considering the constraints to achieving the goals; you might consider one "virtuous activity" as a goal to focus upon (Dalton & Spiller, 2012).

Sensation-Seeking	Prudence	Stuffiness
Underuse	Strength Zone	Overuse

Virtue: Temperance

Spotlight on
Self-Regulation

Core Features

Definition: Regulating what one feels and does; being disciplined; controlling one's appetites and emotions.

Essence: Self-management of vices. Appropriate control of impulses/emotions.

Dimensions: Self-control.

Highest Correlations With Self-Regulation

1. Perseverance
2. Zest
3. Hope
4. Prudence
5. Honesty

Questions for Strength Building

- What habit or behavior are you best at self-regulating?
- Recall a situation in which you tried hard and overcame a vice. What strengths did you use to do that?
- How has self-regulation contributed to your best successes in life?

Research Highlights

- One of the least endorsed character strengths across the globe.
- Self-regulation is like a muscle – it can be fatigued by over-exertion or strengthened with practice. It can take only 7 minutes in the laboratory to deplete.
- Parent self-regulation has been associated with their child's happiness.
- Connected with more health behaviors than any other strength.

Self-Regulation Interventions

- Starting a daily self-control exercise increases your general capacity for self-regulation. Practice monitoring yourself in one self-control domain (e.g., food intake, mood control, posture control, physical exercise, financial management, meditation practice) and this will likely improve your management of the other domains (your whole capacity) as well (Baumeister et al., 2006).
- Another technique: (1) Identify an important behavior change you expect to make; (2) imagine the most positive outcome of successfully changing your behavior; (3) imagine the most critical obstacle that stands in the way of fulfilling your wish; and then (4) set a specific plan accordingly (Stadler, Oettingen, & Gollwitzer, 2010).

Virtue: Transcendence

Core Features

Definition: Noticing and appreciating beauty, excellence, and/or skilled performance in various domains of life, from nature to art to mathematics to science to everyday experience.

Essence: Seeing the life behind things. Experiencing awe in the presence of beauty or greatness.

Dimensions: Awe, wonder, elevation, admiration.

Highest Correlations With Appreciation of Beauty & Excellence

1. Gratitude
2. Curiosity
3. Love of learning
4. Kindness
5. Creativity

Questions for Strength Building

- Do you resonate more with the appreciation of excellence or of beauty? Why?
- What are examples or experiences that lead you to feel awe vs. admiration vs. elevation?
- How does this strength impact your work and relationships?

Research Highlights

- Involves appreciating natural or abstract beauty (produces awe or wonder); excellence/skill/talent (produces admiration); virtue or moral goodness (produces elevation).
- One of the strengths most associated with a variety of health behaviors.
- Elevation has been shown in several studies to lead to more prosocial or altruistic behavior.

Appreciation of Beauty and Excellence Interventions

- Take time each day to notice beauty in either nature, art, or in the moral goodness of others and then write briefly about the beauty and what you experienced in a journal (Diessner, Rust, Solom, Frost, & Parsons, 2006).
- Go on "beauty walks." Research shows that a directed-attention walk in nature can lead to greater mindfulness of beauty (Diessner, Woodward, Stacy, & Mobasher, 2015).

Oblivion	Appreciation of Beauty/Excellence	Snobbery/Perfectionism
Underuse	Strength Zone	Overuse

Virtue: Transcendence

Spotlight on
Gratitude

Core Features

Definition: Being aware of and thankful for the good things that happen; taking time to express thanks.

Essence: An attitude of thankfulness.

Highest Correlations With Gratitude

1. Kindness
2. Love
3. Hope
4. Spirituality
5. Zest

Questions for Strength Building

- What are the situations in which you are most likely to express gratitude?
- How might you remember to think from a perspective of gratitude for the "little things" throughout your day?
- Are there certain people whom you struggle to express gratitude to? How might you use other strengths to help you in these situations?

Research Highlights

- One of the five strengths most associated with life satisfaction/happiness.
- One of the strengths most connected with a meaningful life.
- Contributes to a number of psychological and physical health benefits.
- Associated with achievement, work satisfaction, and work "callings."

Gratitude Interventions

- At the end of each day for the next week, write down three things you are grateful for and explain why they occurred (Gander et al., 2013; Seligman et al., 2005). Be sure to not repeat the examples from day to day.
- Write a gratitude letter to someone to whom you are especially grateful and who you have not properly thanked. If appropriate, make a gratitude visit and deliver the letter face-to-face (Gander et al., 2013; Seligman et al., 2005).

Entitlement	Gratitude	Ingratiation
Underuse	Strength Zone	Overuse

Virtue: Transcendence

Core Features

Definition: Expecting the best in the future and working to achieve it; believing that a good future is something that can be brought about.

Essence: Positive expectations.

Dimensions: Optimism, future mindedness, future orientation.

Highest Correlations With Hope

1. Zest
2. Gratitude
3. Perspective
4. Perseverance
5. Love

Questions for Strength Building

- What leads you to sustain your hope levels?
- How does hope help you at challenging times?
- How do you balance what is realistic and what is unrealistic in terms of your hope and optimism?

Research Highlights

- One of the five strengths most associated with life satisfaction/happiness.
- Strongly linked with meaning, engagement, and pleasure.
- Involves two types of thinking: (1) agency thinking: perceiving you can keep up the energy and motivation to follow through with goals; (2) pathways thinking: perceiving you can create goals and follow any of multiple ways to reach them.

Hope Interventions

- Visualize and write about your best possible self at some point in the future. Clearly see your life positively developed across three domains: personal, relational, and professional (Meevissen, Peters, & Alberts, 2011; Peters; Flink, Boersma, & Linton, 2010).
- Set a goal and boost your hopeful thinking by writing down many pathways to reach the goal and write down the many reasons you will be able to reach it (Feldman & Dreher, 2012; Snyder, Rand, & Sigmon, 2002).
- Journal about good and bad events. Write about why the good events will last and spread, and how they relate to your actions. Write about why bad events will pass quickly, are limited in their effect, and why you aren't completely to blame (Seligman, 1991).

Negative	Hope	Pollyannaism
Underuse	Strength Zone	Overuse

Virtue: Transcendence

Spotlight on
Humor

Core Features

Definition: Liking to laugh and tease; bringing smiles to other people; seeing the light side; making (not necessarily telling) jokes.

Essence: Offering pleasure/laughter to others.

Dimensions: Playfulness.

Highest Correlations With Humor

1. Social intelligence
2. Zest
3. Kindness
4. Hope
5. Love

Research Highlights

- One of the five strengths most associated with life satisfaction/happiness.
- One of the strengths most connected with pleasure/positive emotion.
- Connected with a number of health benefits.

Questions for Strength Building

- What situations promote your use of humor?
- What strengths do you use to be sensitive to the context in order to express humor at the right time?
- How do you initiate playfulness with others? How do others initiate it with you?

Humor Interventions

- At the end of each day for the next week, write down the three funniest things you experienced or did and explain why those things happened (Gander et al., 2013).
- Cultivate a playful attitude and a sense of fun. Suggestions include: Consider situations where you're serious and those where you're playful and spend more time in the latter; reflect on the benefits of adopting a more playful outlook on life; spend time playing with young children; do at least one fun thing each day; remind yourself to be playful (McGhee, 2010).

Overly Serious	Humor	Giddiness
Underuse	Strength Zone	Overuse

Virtue: Transcendence

Core Features

Definition: Having coherent beliefs about the higher purpose and meaning of the universe; knowing where one fits within the larger scheme; having beliefs about the meaning of life that shape conduct and provide comfort.

Essence: Connecting with the sacred.
Life is small amidst the grand design.

Dimensions: Purpose, meaning, faith, religiousness.

Highest Correlations With Spirituality

1. Gratitude
2. Hope
3. Zest
4. Love
5. Kindness

Questions for Strength Building

- How do you define spirituality for yourself?
- How can you best "practice what you believe" in a way that brings benefit to others and does not proselytize?
- How might you bring spirituality to your work in a way that doesn't intrude upon others (e.g., seeking meaning/purpose, keeping a sacred object close by, taking breaks to engage in a spiritual practice?

Research Highlights

- Spirituality is defined by scientists as the search for or communion with the sacred.
- One of the five strengths most associated with life meaning.
- Linked with compassion, altruism, volunteerism, and philanthropy.
- Associated with lower levels of marital conflict, greater spousal support, more consistent parenting, and more supportive relationships between children and their parents.

Spirituality Interventions

- Build your sense of purpose by proactively engaging more in life, e.g., taking on a new volunteer position that contributes positively to your community (Hill, Sumner, & Burrow, 2014).
- Sanctify a sacred object that is tangible or nontangible by turning your attention to it for a few minutes each day to reimbue it with what you consider to be precious, holy, or dear to you (Goldstein, 2007).
- Learn from a spiritual role model who is an exemplar in a spiritual quality, such as compassion. Consider what you appreciate most about this person and any positive attributes you might want to emulate (Oman et al., 2007, 2009; Oman & Thoresen, 2007; Plante, 2008).

Anomie	Spirituality	Fanaticism
Underuse	Strength Zone	Overuse

Chapter 7

How to Apply Character Strengths Interventions

Introduction

Chapters 7 and 8 continue the practical emphasis of this book and perhaps represent the culmination of this practicality. Chapter 8 includes 70 evidence-based interventions explicitly on character strengths. Each intervention is accompanied by an overview, purpose, step-by-step approach, research description, and in some cases troubleshooting, tips, and an example are provided. The interventions have been numbered with thumb tabs for ease of use.

A practitioner might view these interventions as "intentional activities" with character strengths on behavioral, interpersonal, emotional, and/or cognitive levels. The activities are written as handouts for practitioners to use personally with themselves or to copy for a client, student, employee, or workshop participant to boost their well-being. The user-friendly nature of these handouts makes them ideal for practitioners to assign to clients and students as homework between meetings.

Well-being is the overarching outcome of these interventions. For organizational purposes, the character strengths interventions (CSIs) are placed in one of eight categories, each an outcome (or an "end" in its own right) and a pathway to greater well-being (e.g., some clients want more meaning in life and at the same time, meaning in life is a pathway to greater well-being). These categories offer an initial focal point for practitioners even though most can be linked with several outcomes/pathways. Strengths-based practitioners are interested in boosting the following in their clients:

1. Character strengths awareness
2. Character strengths use
3. Meaning and engagement
4. Specific character strengths (e.g., gratitude, love, spirituality)
5. Positive relationships
6. Resilience (problem management)
7. Goal-setting/achievement
8. Mindfulness

The science of positive psychology and character strengths has not reached a point where nuanced statements can be made about these kinds of interventions (e.g., being able to say that one particular exercise will definitively and positively impact cognitive but not affective happiness). As research on interventions becomes more fine-grained, we will know more about differentiating the various positive outcomes that can emerge from different CSIs. For example, is a given CSI more adept at boosting the three dimensions of meaning: purpose, coherence, or significance (Martela & Steger, 2016)? Which exercises boost specific elements of physical health (e.g., improved sleep)? If a character strength exercise boosts one area of PERMA, and knowing that the PERMA elements are interrelated (Seligman, 2011), are all areas positively implicated? Do outcomes of character strengths use, such as improved self-efficacy and enhanced self-esteem, get a boost regardless of the CSI? At this point in time, the categorizations for the exercises should be considered general, not fine-grained.

Following these eight categories/sections, there is a final section that offers short descriptions of several additional character strengths activities that practitioners, clients, workshop leaders, educators, and employers might consider using. Less detail is provided on these for a number of reasons: they might not have leant themselves to the structure used in Chapter 8, might not have had good face validity, or may have had minimal research support. Some are quite strong conceptually, and all of them have been found to be beneficial at least anecdotally.

Optimal Conditions for Successful CSIs

These interventions, despite having a research base, are all starting points! They should not be applied blindly in a vacuum. Without individualization and contextualization, interventions cannot reach their maximum benefit. This means that each intervention can be further advanced by considering the uniqueness of the individual and the situation they are in.

As the study of positive interventions has received increasing attention (e.g., Parks & Schueller, 2014), researchers in positive interventions have begun to examine the "how" of interventions; in other words, what makes them work to boost well-being? Lyubomirsky (2008) originally suggested five important factors, which I have formulated into five questions that can serve as a quick guide to help you or your client select or continue with a particular intervention. I frame these as yes/no responses but they could also be rated with more nuance, such as using a 1–10 scale.

1. *Natural:* Do you find that this activity comes naturally to you as you engage in it?
2. *Enjoyment:* Do you find this activity to be enjoyable and interesting, like a fun challenge?
3. *Value:* Do you value this activity for its own sake and not because of some outcome it brings?
4. *Guilty:* Do you engage in this activity because you'd otherwise feel anxious, guilty, or ashamed if you didn't do it? (reverse-rated)
5. *Situation:* Do you engage in this activity because you feel forced to do it or want to please someone else? (reverse-rated)

In examining factors within individuals in a longitudinal study, researchers found that both motivation and effort (i.e., the will and the way) were critical (Lyubomirsky, Dickerhoof, Boehm, & Sheldon, 2011). Lyubomirsky and Layous (2013) took this a step further and developed a model that outlines important aspects of positive interventions – what matters are the features of the activities themselves (dosage, variety, sequence), features of the individual/client (motivation, effort, efficacy beliefs, social support, personality), and the fit between the person and activity. Proyer, Wellenzohn and colleagues (2014) applied this research to the myriad of positive psychology exercises they were studying in participants over several years. They outline four key elements that are good predictors of greater happiness and less depression in the (very) long-run of 3.5 years. These include continued voluntary practice, effort to keep working on the intervention, preference in regard to liking and perceiving benefit from the intervention, and early reactivity in regard to whether people experience immediate positive emotions from the activity. In addition, they found that combining these four elements was the most successful approach in the long-run for participants.

Another lens for looking at CSIs is through one, albeit loaded, question: Is the intervention wise? Wise psychological interventions as articulated by scientist Gregory Walton from Stanford University are a new class of interventions that are ordinary, brief, and more precise in that they rest on good psychological theory (Walton, 2014). Walton explains that wise interventions are very much like everyday experiences, and that the most important question is "What is the psychological process at hand?" He advises that in order to create a wise intervention, an aspect of the individual's "psychology" that is contributing to a problem and/or preventing flourishing is identified and then targeted as a point of correction. The focus is often aimed at altering the individual's self-reinforcing processes and aligning these with the context (wise interventions are context-dependent, not silver bullets). Although this class of interventions is geared toward social problems, offering a small lever to impact change in a complex system, the impetus of the concept of wise interventions offers an important dimension for practitioners to consider. Some of the interventions in Chapter 8 come directly from Walton and his research pointing to studies deploying these kinds of wise interventions.

In addition to factors that increase the likelihood of success with a CSI, practitioners should be mindful of cautions. It is generally suggested to not apply interventions without knowledge and clarity of the purpose of the intervention and what it is precisely targeting, as well as taking into account other areas of well-being that might change for better or for worse (Blackie et al., 2014). Safety of the intervention for the client is one of the most important considerations practitioners should evaluate for each client (Rashid, 2009).

Putting It All Together: Tailoring CSIs

Considering the findings in the previous section, how might practitioners create optimal CSIs using the activities in Chapter 8? I offer several important tips for optimal application of a given intervention with a client.

* *Try it yourself first.* Nothing can replace the adage of making improvements and positive change with oneself prior to using it with clients. Despite how a given intervention appears, it is always a different experience to play the intervention out for oneself. New insights, details, surprises, and strategies will often emerge.
* *Action, before judging.* Sometimes practitioners and clients have a negative reaction to the description or steps of an exercise. Specific aspects of the exercise might be judged, such as "I don't like journaling" or "That will be too uncomfortable" or "I don't see the point of doing that." The concept here is to challenge yourself to action – try it out. In some of these instances, you will surprise yourself.
* *Safety first.* Any practitioner should be qualified to deliver the intervention and handle the variety of possible results that might emerge when offering it to a specific individual or group. Practitioners should also do any troubleshooting to ensure the intervention and its delivery will be safe for the client.
* *Find the will and the way.* The deploying of good motivation (the will) and effort (the way) cannot be understated for intervention success. Motivation involves the client feeling *confident* they can do the activity and that the activity is *important* for them. Part of the latter involves the client understanding why they are being asked to do the intervention, while an important part of confidence involves the client understanding the steps – if the practitioner asks the client to "teach back" the intervention to the practitioner, can the client do it? If so, this builds confidence. As motivation, interest, and seeing value in the activity build as a synergy, the client's effort will follow.
* *Make the activity wise.* Adjust the activity to the individual and their situation. Practitioners might ask themselves the following questions:
    – Is there a simple adjustment I might make to tailor this to my client's preferences or values? I've written about how CSIs tend to fall across one of seven general modalities,

using the acronym ROAD-MAP (Niemiec, 2014a). These include: reflect on past use of strengths, observe others' strengths, appreciate others' strengths, discuss strengths with others, monitor one's own strengths, ask others about one's strengths, and plan strengths goals. Many of the interventions in Chapter 8 might be shifted to another modality of these seven to best fit a client. For example, a "writing exercise" could become a discussion exercise or a reflecting/meditative exercise might shift to an inquiry to ask others for feedback on the particular topic.

- How might I tailor this activity to my client's unique goals and their signature strengths?
- What is the situation/context my client might best benefit from applying this exercise?
- Is the timing right for using this intervention with this individual in their situation right now? (Schwartz & Sharpe, 2006; Waterman, 2012).
- Does the sequence of steps or character strengths integration play an important role? For example, one client of mine received feedback that she was being distracting and unproductive at team meetings. When she used her signature strengths of zest or humor at meetings, this further contributed to her problem as team members thought she was hijacking the meeting with jokes or her various high-energy stories. I suggested she might consider the sequence by which she expresses her character strengths. I wondered whether another strength might appropriately precede her signature strength expression. She decided to start with her judgment/critical thinking strength. This meant that she took a thinking-oriented approach of gathering details, collecting information, and listening to new directions teammates were sharing. She then offered this summary using her rational-minded, judgment/critical thinking strength. After that, she turned to her zest and humor. This sequence led to her team being more receptive to her style and to better appreciating her contribution as well as her zest and humor strengths.

Research Evidence: Strengths and Limitations

The interventions in Chapter 8 come from the research literature. Research was my guide for the activities selected and their placement in categories. I attempted to keep the intervention as exact as the researcher(s) originally reported it. Some activities were reviewed in positive intervention meta-analyses or other comprehensive analyses/reviews (e.g., Boiler et al., 2013; Hone, Jarden, & Schofield, 2014; Quinlan et al., 2011; Quoidbach, Mikolajczak, & Gross, 2015; Sin & Lyubomirsky, 2009). In some cases, I made the intervention more practical, attempted to improve it, or added in character strengths elements. In rare instances (e.g., character strengths hot buttons), there was no research literature and the intervention was drawn from expert opinion.

I could not include only randomized, controlled trials as my criteria for inclusion as that would have shortened this section considerably and would have excluded strong and promising interventions. I believe this would have been a disservice to practitioners looking for ideas of likely impact and it would have been a disservice to researchers who are looking for promising activities with an underlying rationale to test. Below are the categories I used as a basis for collating information about the research on interventions.

1. Intervention from controlled intervention study.
   Example: CSI 20: Strengths Alignment.
2. Variation of a successful intervention from a controlled study on strengths.
   Example: CSI 16: Holistic Strengths Use.
3. Intervention from a controlled study, but with character strengths as an integrated element.
   Example: CSI 64: Best Possible Self.

4. Intervention discussed in peer-reviewed or scholarly papers/chapters.
   Example: CSI 43: Turn Your Strengths Other-Oriented.
5. Intervention extrapolated from a correlational study.
   Example: CSI 41: Character Strengths Appreciation.
6. Intervention extrapolated from a theoretical concept.
   Example: CSI 59: Managing Your Strength Hot Buttons.
7. Intervention within an overall program that has research support.
   Example: CSI 70: Strengths Gatha.

Table 7.1 is offered as a guide to understanding the evidence. Readers might mark this page with a tab of some kind for ease of returning to it while reviewing the various character strengths interventions. The numbers used come from the preceding list of one to seven. The numbers are *not* meant to represent a rank-order of research strength. Each intervention should be reviewed, practiced, studied, and evaluated independently for its own merit and its own application potential. In some cases, more than one number is provided when multiple categories can be argued for goodness-of-fit.

Table 7.1. CSIs and Corresponding Research Background

CSI	Research Evidence Guide
CSI 1: Getting Started: Introducing and Exploring Character Strengths	6
CSI 2: Take the VIA	1, 4
CSI 3: Affirm/Value Your Strengths	3
CSI 4: Boost Your Motivation	3
CSI 5: Subtract a Signature Strength	3
CSI 6: Character Strengths Genogram	6
CSI 7: Character Strengths 360°	2, 7
CSI 8: Self-Monitor for Your Strengths	3
CSI 9: Stories and Character Strengths (Develop Strengths-Spotting)	1, 3
CSI 10: Mentors/Role Models	4, 6
CSI 11: Use a Signature Strength in a New Way	1
CSI 12: Acting "As If" (Acting From Strength)	3
CSI 13: Turn a Strength Inward	2
CSI 14: Create a Strengths Habit	4
CSI 15: Signature Strengths Across Domains	2
CSI 16: Holistic Strengths Use	2
CSI 17: Pathways to Virtue Use	2, 6
CSI 18: Head, Heart, and Hands: Living a Virtuous Life	5, 6
CSI 19: Boost a Lower Strength	1
CSI 20: Strengths Alignment	1
CSI 21: The Deathbed Test	4
CSI 22: Life Summary	1
CSI 23: What Matters Most?	3
CSI 24: Cultivate Inner Self-Worth	4

Table 7.1. Continued

CSI	Research Evidence Guide
CSI 25: Defining Moments Exercise	4, 7
CSI 26: Positive Action Through Movies	1, 4
CSI 27: Boosting Curiosity Through Novelty	1
CSI 28: Imagined Conversation	1
CSI 29: Activate Your Zest!	1
CSI 30: Loving-Kindness Meditation	1
CSI 31: Gift of Time	1
CSI 32: Pay it Forward	1
CSI 33: Prosocial Spending	1
CSI 34: Enhance Teamwork Through Role Matching	5, 6
CSI 35: Boosting Humility	1, 2
CSI 36: Engaging With Beauty	1
CSI 37: Three Good Things	1
CSI 38: Gratitude Letter/Visit	1
CSI 39: Three Funny Things	1
CSI 40: Cultivating Sacred Moments	1
CSI 41: Character Strengths Appreciation	4, 5
CSI 42: Love Letter	1
CSI 43: Turn Your Strengths Other-Oriented	4
CSI 44: Mindful Listening and Speaking	4, 7
CSI 45: Healthy, Fair Fighting	5
CSI 46: Subtract Then Add	2, 3
CSI 47: Perspective-Taking	1, 3
CSI 48: Compliment Review	1, 3
CSI 49: Positive Reminiscence With Strengths	1, 3
CSI 50: Counting the Good in Your Relationship	2
CSI 51: Believing Change Is Possible	1
CSI 52: Resource Priming	2
CSI 53: Benefit-Finding With Strengths	1
CSI 54: Open Your Character Strength Doors	1
CSI 55: Positive Reappraisal With Strengths	1, 3
CSI 56: Helping or Harming?	6
CSI 57: Overcome Stress With Humor	1
CSI 58: Managing Character Strengths Overuse	6, 7
CSI 59: Managing Your Strength Hot Buttons	6
CSI 60: Goal-Setting With Character Strengths	3
CSI 61: Hope for Your Goals	3
CSI 62: Mental Contrasting	1

Table 7.1. Continued

CSI	Research Evidence Guide
CSI 63: Implementation Intentions	1
CSI 64: Best Possible Self	3
CSI 65: The Mindful Pause	4, 7
CSI 66: Strong Mindfulness	4, 7
CSI 67: Fresh Look Meditation	5, 7
CSI 68: From Mindless to Mindful	7
CSI 69: Meditation Targeting a Character Strength	1, 7
CSI 70: Strengths Gatha	7

A Word About Programs

There are several successful programs that offer a number of character strength exercises or that target one specific character strength with several activities. Such programs are too lengthy to fit in the framework of Chapter 8. However, central exercises have been extracted or condensed from a program when there is good reason. For example, an activity in positive psychotherapy called "gift of time" has proven to be beneficial in the research in its own right, and the fresh look meditation from mindfulness-based strengths practice has a research base in the positive reappraisal literature. In addition, there are positive psychology workbooks found to be efficacious in the literature, such as for humility (see Lavelock, Worthington, & Davis, 2014a). Rather than replay the numerous activities from this 84-page workbook, I summarize those that seem most essential to theory, research, and good practice and integrate them for that humility activity. In terms of comprehensive programs targeting single character strengths, there are several additional examples, including appreciation of beauty (Martinez-Marti, Avia, & Hernandez-Lloreda, 2014), humor (McGhee, 2010), kindness (Neff & Germer, 2013), and forgiveness (Griffin et al., 2015), to name a few.

Tailored Intervention Packages

At the risk of being too prescriptive, I offer the following packages for practitioners and clients to consider. These packages are likened to the many intervention programs just mentioned that offer a collection of activities designed to boost one character strength or designed to boost well-being or another positive outcome. Research has shown that packaging groups of interventions together and finding optimal pairings between positive interventions can be beneficial for people (Schueller, 2010, 2011; Schueller & Parks, 2012).

The following 15 packages using the intervention pages throughout Chapter 8 are offered for practitioners to use in a variety of ways, such as with individual clients, group experiences, workshop settings, as classroom material, and as parts of seminars or lunch-and-learns in workplace environments, to name a few examples. These are not "validated packages," rather they are examples of tailored intervention combinations to offer you a jump-start in matching interventions with clients, context, and the problem/goal being addressed.

- *Introducing VIA and moving forward.* For clients new to character strengths work.
  CSI 1: Getting Started: Introducing and Exploring Character Strengths
  CSI 2: Take the VIA
  CSI 3: Affirm/Value Your Strengths
  CSI 15: Signature Strengths Across Domains
  CSI 11: Use a Signature Strength in a New Way

- *VIA's program* "creating a strengths-based mindset." An abridged version is made up of the package that follows. After clients take the VIA Survey, engage them in the following:
  CSI 1: Getting Started: Introducing and Exploring Character Strengths
  CSI 9: Stories and Character Strengths (Develop Strengths-Spotting)
  CSI 11: Use a Signature Strength in a New Way
  CSI 19: Boost a Lower Strength
  CSI 53: Benefit-Finding With Strengths

- *Boost happiness.* Five character strengths are more highly correlated with happiness, consistently across studies than the other strengths; and some evidence shows you can target these strengths to boost happiness. Try it yourself or offer the package to a client over a couple or few weeks for a supercharge to well-being.
  CSI 29: Activate Your Zest!
  CSI 38: Gratitude Letter/Visit
  CSI 30: Loving-Kindness Meditation
  CSI 27: Boosting Curiosity Through Novelty
  CSI 64: Best Possible Self (for hope)

- *Aware-explore-apply.* There are many ways to put the character strengths model into action, here is one example.
  CSI 8: Self-Monitor for Your Strengths
  CSI 16: Holistic Strengths Use
  CSI 60: Goal-Setting With Character Strengths

- *General strengths use – your ROAD-MAP.* As discussed earlier in the chapter, this acronym offers seven general ways of developing character strengths that could be applied to any strength. The following interventions offer examples of matches for each part of the acronym, although an individual might not necessarily deploy them in the order below.
  Reflect   – CSI 9: Stories and Character Strengths or CSI 25: Defining Moments Exercise
  Observe   – CSI 66: Strong Mindfulness or CSI 26: Positive Action Through Movies
  Appreciate – CSI 41: Character Strengths Appreciation
  Discuss   – CSI 44: Mindful Listening and Speaking
  Monitor   – CSI 8: Self-Monitor for Your Strengths
  Ask   – CSI 7: Character Strengths 360°
  Plan   – CSI 60: Goal-Setting With Character Strengths

- *Widen your character strengths savvy.* Go to the Specific Character Strengths section and practice at least five of the 11 character strengths directly addressed (some character strengths have more than one activity designed to enhance them). Here's an example you might do across 5 days or spread out over 5 weeks.
  CSI 36: Engaging With Beauty
  CSI 35: Boosting Humility
  CSI 28: Imagined Conversation (for perspective)

CSI 39: Three Funny Things
CSI 40: Cultivating Sacred Moments

- *Lead a workshop for people learning about character strengths.* These are some exercises that do particularly well in group settings, led by a seasoned practitioner/presenter.
  CSI 9: Stories and Character Strengths (practicing strengths-spotting in dyads)
  CSI 5: Subtract a Signature Strength (for the whole group)
  CSI 44: Mindful Listening and Speaking (in dyads)
  CSI 23: What Matters Most? (in small groups)
  CSI 59: Managing Your Strength Hot Buttons (in small groups)

- *Lost in languishing.* To be lost in subpar mental and social functioning – simply going through the motions in life, day after day – is commonplace. But, you and your clients can shift out of languishing.
  CSI 2: Take the VIA
  CSI 3: Affirm/Value Your Strengths
  CSI 24: Cultivate Inner Self-Worth
  CSI 51: Believing Change Is Possible
  CSI 12: Acting "As If" (Acting From Strength)
  CSI 54: Open Your Character Strength Doors

- *Deeper dive.* For general work with a counseling client or coachee who is fairly advanced in their understanding of VIA character strengths.
  CSI 7: Character Strengths 360°
  CSI 25: Defining Moments Exercise
  CSI 58: Managing Character Strengths Overuse
  CSI 67: Fresh Look Meditation

- *Work engagement.* Working as a manager trying to support an employee to engage more in their work? Try this package.
  CSI 2: Take the VIA
  CSI 11: Use a Signature Strength in a New Way
  CSI 20: Strengths Alignment
  CSI 62: Mental Contrasting

- *School engagement.* Teaching or helping a group of students that will be learning together for several months? Try this package.
  CSI 2: Take the VIA
  CSI 9: Stories and Character Strengths
  CSI 10: Mentors/Role Models
  CSI 27: Boosting Curiosity Through Novelty
  CSI 39: Three Funny Things
  CSI 51: Believing Change Is Possible
  CSI 52: Resource Priming

- *Relationship growth.* Take healthy action in a close relationship.
  CSI 41: Character Strengths Appreciation
  CSI 49: Positive Reminiscence With Strengths
  CSI 50: Counting the Good in Your Relationship
  CSI 45: Healthy, Fair Fighting
  CSI 43: Turn Your Strengths Other-Oriented
  CSI 44: Mindful Listening and Speaking

- *Improve health.* Take action to improve your physical health with strengths-based lifestyle adjustment.
  CSI 29: Activate Your Zest!
  CSI 14: Create a Strengths Habit
  CSI 68: From Mindless to Mindful
  CSI 62: Mental Contrasting
  CSI 63: Implementation Intentions

- *Stressed out?*
  CSI 52: Resource Priming
  CSI 59: Managing Your Strength Hot Buttons
  CSI 57: Overcoming Stress With Humor
  CSI 65: The Mindful Pause
  CSI 70: Strengths Gatha
  CSI 63: Implementation Intentions

- *Turn self-development into flourishing.* Wanting to grow in self-development, on your own, without support from a helping professional?
  1. Try systematically going through each of the "character strengths awareness" exercises (e.g., one per week).
  2. Then, move on to the "character strengths use" exercises (e.g., one per week).
  3. Finally, review the topics and see what either intrigues you most or where your greatest need might be (e.g., if you are wanting to overcome a problem, turn to the resilience section, or if you are wanting to build a stronger relationship, turn to the positive relationships section).

Chapter 8

Research-Based Interventions for Character Strengths

Character Strengths Awareness

Introduction

This section focuses on interventions that lay the foundation of awareness of character strengths. Insight and change follow awareness; hence practitioners should give extra attention to this section. These activities are diverse in their approach and clients find them especially engaging and relevant for their life.

Content

CSI 1: Getting Started: Introducing and Exploring Character Strengths
CSI 2: Take the VIA
CSI 3: Affirm/Value Your Strengths
CSI 4: Boost Your Motivation
CSI 5: Subtract a Signature Strength
CSI 6: Character Strengths Genogram
CSI 7: Character Strengths 360°
CSI 8: Self-Monitor Your Strengths
CSI 9: Stories and Character Strengths (Develop Strengths-Spotting)
CSI 10: Mentors/Role Models

Getting Started: Introducing and Exploring Character Strengths

CSI 1

Overview
Each strengths-based practitioner will use a unique approach in terms of how and when they introduce character strengths to their clients, employees, or students. Therefore, rather than offer a script, you'll find a potential structure for introducing character strengths and exploring them.

Purpose
Be prepared for strengths work!; get started in helping someone with character strengths; use a framework to introduce character strengths; understand important questions for opening a conversation and delving deeper into strengths work.

Steps
Introducing character strengths:
1. Start by answering "why strengths?": In general, why do strengths or character strengths matter? What's the point of strengths?
   - This might involve explaining the negativity bias, the brain's wiring for seeing flaws/problems/dangers (e.g., fight or flight system), the research around how bad is stronger than good, research around the high percentages of strengths blindness, high disengagement levels at work, and low flourishing levels in the population, as well as research connecting character strengths with numerous kinds of positive outcomes and research showing that it can be better to target what's best over remediating a deficit.
2. Narrow the question to the client: Why might character strengths matter for this particular client?
   - This involves linking strengths to the client's reason for meeting with you and if known, linking character strengths with the client's goals (e.g., character strengths are unique pathways to reaching any goal) and their personal values.
3. Delve into the "what?": What are strengths of character?
   - This might involve comments around the definition of character strengths, the new science of character, signature strengths, examples of strengths in the VIA classification, how character strengths are different from other types of strengths.
   - If not already completed, encouragement can be made for clients to take the VIA Survey as an initial test of strengths and as a frame for early conversations, exploration, and interventions. Note that many practitioners have clients/students take the VIA Survey prior to the first session/meeting.
4. Explain the "how?": How will you be taking a strengths-based approach? How will you help the client work with character strengths? Give an overview of 1–2 activities.
   - This might involve an explanation of strengths-spotting (including examples of the client's use of character strengths in the session), signature strengths use, the targeting of specific character strengths, the application of character strengths for boosting well-being and relationships and for managing problems/challenges.

Opening questions:
- To start, I'd be curious to hear what your emotional reaction was to your character strengths profile? When you originally looked at your rank-order results from the VIA Survey, can you pinpoint your feeling(s) back then and explain why you might have felt that way?
- Look closely through your profile again. What are you mindful of now within yourself as you read the rank-order, the strength names, and their descriptions? What strikes you?

CSI 1

Digging into your top strengths:
- For each of your Top 10 character strengths, ask yourself this: Is this character strength central to who I am as a human being? Is the character strength energizing for me and natural/easy to use?
- For each of the 10 strengths you say a strong YES to (this will probably be four to seven strengths, with seven being the suggested limit), reflect upon and answer the following three questions:
  1. How does this character strength describe the real me? In what ways is it a true description of me?
  2. How is this strength of value to me? Why is it important for me?
  3. What are the costs of this strength for me? In what way(s) does it not serve me well?

Supporting follow-through:
The latter questions may be offered in session or given as a homework activity between sessions, therefore, practitioners might try to maximize adherence to this activity by asking the client what their preferred "mechanism" of reflection/learning is. Typical approaches are: journal (handwritten or typing) responses; formal discussions with a loved one (family member or friend); sitting in meditation or quiet reflection with the questions; querying others for input on the questions.

Research

This activity is provided here, less as a science-based intervention, but more as a way for any practitioner to get started and dig into the work. Certainly, books and articles in the science of coaching, the art of psychotherapy, mindful listening/mindful speaking, and many more could be cited here.

Take the VIA

Overview

Understanding one's best qualities, or character strengths, is at the heart of positive psychology, and has become a starting point for practitioners and clients alike to better know themselves and one another. Prior to 2004, there was not a common language to converse about these topics. The VIA Institute on Character has brought this scientifically generated, cross-cultural language to the world and has developed multiple surveys with multiple translations to assess these positive attributes in human beings.

Purpose

Assess character strengths; become aware of one's strongest qualities; become familiar with the language of character strengths.

Steps

1. Go to the VIA Institute website (https://www.viacharacter.org), the world headquarters for all-things-character-strengths, select the test desired, and answer the questions assessing your 24 character strengths. Note: The VIA Youth Survey is for youth ages 10 to 17. Youth aged 13 and under will need parental consent in order to take the test.
2. After completing the test, print up the results, which offer a rank-order of your character strengths from 1 to 24, with definitions. Take notice of what strikes you most in the results. Be especially aware of insights that emerge and any immediate inclinations toward positive action.
3. *Optional.* Consider obtaining an individualized, interpretive report on your VIA Survey results. Versions are available for consumers, professionals, team consultants, and youth.

Troubleshooting

While the majority of the world is online, there are some cultures and parts of the world with limited or no online access. In addition, many people do not have access to a computer/laptop/device to take the VIA Survey (for example, many who are in prisons, psychiatric hospitals, etc.). And, some people are resistant to taking any test about themselves or are resistant to using electronic devices. In all of these situations, the individual deserves to learn and work with their character strengths. Paper copies of the VIA Survey can be given out to researchers for specific studies. Nonresearchers might start by having the client review the VIA classification list with definitions and inviting them to circle the five to seven strengths that best describe who they are.

Tip

When offering feedback on the results of a character strengths profile, it's important to take an approach of exploration rather than offering conclusive interpretations. One of the best questions to consider as a starting point is: As you look at your profile, what is your reaction to the results? Some people will be happy, proud, excited, or interested, whereas others will be dismissive, frustrated, or disappointed. If appropriate, discussing these feelings and normalizing any reaction is important. Often, there is an opportunity for education (e.g., a client reaction of "I don't like my weaknesses" necessitates education about the test and what it reveals). It is also important to place the VIA Survey results in the context of self-awareness, self-growth, client goals, benefit to others, and valued outcomes.

Research

Research in different settings has found that taking the VIA Survey is a positive experience. This ranges from the general population (Seligman et al., 2005), to veterans (Resnick & Rosenheck, 2006), and to people with several mental illnesses (Huffman et al., 2014; Sims et al., 2015). For many clients, simply the act of answering a variety of positive questions is a new experience – sometimes a wake-up call – that helps them realize or remember their many positive qualities.

Affirm/Value Your Strengths

Overview
People want to view themselves globally as good, moral, and capable people. It is one thing to take the VIA Survey and receive a rank order of results but it is another thing to understand and acknowledge the qualities as describing who you are and appreciating the importance of each in your life.

Purpose
See your highest strengths as values in your life; endorse and affirm your highest strengths; understand the importance of your strengths to your life.

Steps
1. Identify one of your top character strengths that you value.
2. Write about why this character strength is meaningful and important to your life.
3. *Optional.* Consider doing this activity immediately before going into a stressful or high-pressured situation.

Tip
This intervention often involves the individual affirming themselves in a life domain *different* from where a stressor is occurring (Cohen & Sherman, 2014). For example, if a stressor is happening at school, focusing on the value of love in a family relationship could be a good focal point.

Research
Reflecting on personal qualities can lead to reliable and important changes in behavior. Self-affirmation theory postulates that the affirmation of personal values expands the person's view of themselves, their resources, and what is most important (Steele, 1999). Exercises involving values affirmation have been well documented (e.g., Harackiewicz, Canning, Tibbetts, Giffen, & Hyde, 2014; Legault, Al-Khindi, & Inzlicht, 2012; Sherman, Nelson, & Steele, 2000). They have been shown to increase self-clarity (Stapel & van der Linde, 2011), support adolescents' sense of belonging during challenging times (Cook, Purdie-Vaughns, Garcia, & Cohen, 2012), to protect against various stressors, and to improve education, health, and relationship outcomes (Cohen & Sherman, 2014). In particular contexts, values affirmation has been shown to boost resilience to criticism or rejection, to boost performance, and to curb aggression. It was also shown to buffer the physiological stress response (Creswell et al., 2005). In these studies, many of the values commonly written about by subjects in the intervention groups are VIA character strengths such as kindness, creativity, humor, and spirituality. Of course, any of the 24 character strengths could be chosen as a core value to be explored (remember that VIA originally was an acronym for "values in action").

Boost Your Motivation

Overview

CSI 4

Making changes is both simple and challenging. Change happens naturally and almost effortlessly (i.e., simple), yet habits and problem behaviors can be very resistant to being tampered with (i.e., challenging). There is wisdom to the adage of "ready, willing, and able." An individual must be willing in that they see the importance of change, able in that they have confidence they can change, and ready in that the timing is right for them to make the change now (Miller & Rollnick, 2002).

To the latter point, the popular stages of change model articulates a series of five phases of behavior change that individuals progress through – precontemplation, contemplation, preparation, action, and maintenance (Prochaska & DiClemente, 1982).

Purpose

Enhance motivation; take steps toward change; apply motivation to character strengths work.

Steps

This example focuses on enhancing motivation around using character strengths more often.

1. *Importance.* On a 1–10 scale (where 10 is very high importance and 1 is very low importance), how important is it to you that you learn more about your character strengths? How important is it that you use your character strengths? What is the value of using your strengths more?
2. *Confidence.* On a 1–10 scale (where 10 is very high confidence and 1 is very low confidence), how confident are you that you can learn more about your character strengths? How confident are you that you can use your character strengths more in your life?
3. *Readiness.* Using the following five phases that people typically go through when making a change, what phase are you in?
   a. Precontemplation: There's no reason and no value for me to make this change.
      "I won't" work on using my character strengths or "I can't" work on using my character strengths.
   b. Contemplation: I see the value but am not ready to take any action.
      "I can" and "I may" work on using my character strengths someday.
   c. Preparation: The change is important. I am getting ready to make a change.
      "I will" make a change and use my character strengths more soon, so I am preparing for it by planning my activities and thinking about the situations I'll use my strengths in.
   d. Action: The change has taken place and I am making progress.
      "I am" making changes by using my character strengths more.
   e. Maintenance: The change has continued for 6 months or longer.
      "I still am" making this change as I seamlessly use my character strengths more at work and at home each day.
4. *Review and action.* Examine your findings from the three steps.
   a. Appreciate the positive: What do you have to celebrate and appreciate? Maybe you see a higher value in the change than you realized? Feel more confident than you thought you were? See that you have moved beyond precontemplation? What specific character strengths account for these positives?
   b. Impact your growth area: Choose one of the three areas (importance, confidence, readiness) you'd like to improve on. Consider what you need to do to move up one point on the scale *or* to move toward or reach the next stage of readiness. One example to boost importance is to connect the change more with your intrinsic values, while an example to boost confidence is to offer yourself an encouraging affirmation.

c. Build in strengths support: Dialogue with someone (e.g., a counselor) about ways you might target your area of growth with one of your character strengths.

CSI 4

Tip

Find your character strength "driver" or impetus. Are there one or two core signature strengths that drive your actions forward and naturally elicit motivation in you across many situations? For some people, it is the character strength of love or kindness that gives them reason to act, whereas for others it is spirituality guiding and motivating them. What is your character strength driver?

Research

Many parts of this activity around importance, confidence, readiness, affirmations, and change talk were drawn from elements of motivational interviewing, a collaborative approach that emphasizes helping others become more motivated and committed to a goal by compassionately exploring their reasons for change. Motivational interviewing has amounted an impressive body of research evidence on helping people work through resistant problems (Miller & Rollnick, 2002). The emphasis here is in the direction of self-guidance, although it's important to be clear that the approach of motivational interviewing is a process that occurs between the client and practitioner, where change is drawn from the client and not imposed by a practitioner.

Personality researchers have found there are naturally motivating features of our personality traits that can be useful in spurring people to accomplish their goals (McCabe & Fleeson, 2016). The VIA character strengths offer important clusters of natural motivation that exist in each human being.

Subtract a Signature Strength

Overview

Many of us are living a decent or good life but often do not realize it as we get caught up in petty issues and challenges and do not take time to "smell the roses." And, when we attempt to break from our routines and seek well-being, we are essentially adding more "things," such as possessions, relationship experiences, and achievements, in an attempt to be happier. This intervention takes a different tactic to help us break through our autopilot mind: take something away. It involves seeing what your life would be like without one of your best qualities.

Purpose

Help individuals appreciate what they have; enhance gratitude and positive action; deepen appreciation for a signature strength.

Steps

1. Choose one of your signature strengths – the one you see as most core to who you are.
2. Image this strength for a moment. Picture it in action and take notice of how important it has been for you. It has probably helped you build important relationships in your life, achieve many things, and feel happiness and contentment in countless moments. See these benefits clearly.
3. Now, imagine something else. Imagine that you are not able to use this strength for 1 month. For 1 month, you cannot bring forth this strength in any way. What would that be like? How would that feel? As an example, if you chose curiosity, that would mean you *cannot* pursue new activities, explore or investigate anything, ask anyone any questions, try new foods, go anywhere new in your city, search on the Internet or your phone, or pursue anything novel or different for the next month.
4. Take a few minutes to write down your observations.

Research

This activity involving taking away something positive and important in one's life is called mental subtraction in research studies, and is shown to boost well-being when compared with people who do not engage in the activity (Koo, Algoe, Wilson, & Gilbert, 2008). Mental subtraction has also been shown to be a happiness booster when used in regard to material possessions (Ang, Lim, Leong, & Chen, 2015).

Examples

In leading this exercise with thousands of workshop participants, it is remarkable how people consistently are struck by the loss of a core quality. Here are the typical reactions people describe in regard to what it would be like to take away a signature strength: empty, lost, depressed, impossible, can't breathe, panicky, indecisive, hopeless, confused, devastated, hollow, not me, loss of joy, de-energized, disoriented, self-loathing, bereft, useless, deprived, aimless, scared, unknown to themselves, and stressed.

Character Strengths Genogram

Overview
A family genogram is a formal way of mapping out family relationships over generations, and often it is kept to one page so that everything can be seen at a glance. Genograms have been a staple of many family therapists and counselors for several decades, especially since family therapy become popular in the 1950s.

Purpose
Awareness of family relationships; boosting insight into family dynamics; bringing a strengths-based approach to families.

Steps
1. Write down your nuclear family, writing male names in squares and female names in circles, drawing horizontal lines to connect these symbols if they are in a relationship and vertical lines to show generational differences (going upward for previous generations such as your parents and grandparents and down for your children).
2. Write down two to three signature strengths next to each individual (you might use abbreviations such as "Z" for zest, "Cu" for curiosity, and "SR" for self-regulation). If the family member has taken the VIA Survey, then write down their Top 3 strengths. If they have not and are alive then invite them to take the VIA Survey or review the list of 24 character strengths with them. If not, take an educated guess — perhaps with the wisdom of people who knew them best — as to what qualities best described them.
3. Continue to extend this exercise to as many family members, relatives, and generations as you wish.
4. Review the genogram as a whole. Share and discuss it with others.

Tip
Start simple with this activity, such as examining just your nuclear family. If you are familiar with genograms then you can probably make it complex very quickly with several generations of family members and relatives, while using a variety of common genogram symbols.

Troubleshooting
This has the potential to be a highly impactful and emotional activity, especially if an individual has had a troubled family background and is not accustomed to this type of reflection. Some people may benefit from discussions with a helping professional.

Research
Genograms are used across a variety of fields including medicine, social work, family therapy, genealogy, and sociology. In the helping professions, they serve as an important awareness-building activity for family relationships. Numerous studies on genograms have been conducted across professions; for example, Rempel, Neufeld, and Kushner (2007) found that genograms helped to uncover unrealized potential in people's social networks and facilitated greater understanding of social networks as opportunities for caregiving. A shorter version of this exercise (the "family strengths tree") is part of the 14-week positive psychotherapy program, which has overall benefits for well-being and depression, and clients invite family members to take the VIA Survey and then compile the results for the family (Rashid, 2015; Seligman et al., 2006).

Examples
Search the Internet for "create a genogram online" for a variety of free options to explore this activity and to see examples of how genograms are structured.

Character Strengths 360°

Overview
The 360° form of feedback has become a standard in top organizations across the globe. In organizational settings, this involves each employee receiving feedback from multiple sources and contexts, including their boss/superior, subordinates, fellow colleagues, and customers, and provides the individual with important insights into their performance. Feedback on character strengths can work in a similar way and of course extend far beyond the workplace.

Purpose
Learn the perceptions of others in regard to your core strengths; integrate others' insights into your life; attain new ways of looking at yourself through a strengths lens.

Steps
For this exercise, use the tool on the following page.
1. Distribute this tool to people who know you (they don't have to know you very well). Gather feedback from 10 or more people. Make an effort to gather people across the domains of your life, e.g., personal/home (e.g., parents, siblings, spouse/partner, children), work, school, social, spiritual, community.
2. Ask each person to honestly fill the form out by selecting only those character strengths that they perceive most strongly describe you. It's generally a good idea to limit the quantity of strengths selected to five or seven at the most.
3. Emphasize the second step on the page which invites the person to offer a concrete example or story for each strength they spot.
4. Gather the feedback from everyone. Look for common themes across the stories and character strengths.
5. Compare your VIA Survey results with your Character Strengths 360° results.
   - *Strong signature strengths.* What strengths were highly noted by both you and others?
   - *Possible blind spots.* What strengths were noted highly by others but not you?
   - *Potential opportunities.* What strengths were noted highly by you but not others?
6. Take action: Review your insights and put one of your new insights to use!

Research
This activity is one of the favorite exercises reported by participants in mindfulness-based strengths practice (MBSP; Niemiec, 2014a) because of the insights and sometimes connections it brings about. It has been widely used in workshops and university courses around the globe. It is being used in the education context with students and teachers (Linkins et al., 2015). A more complex version has been studied called "reflected best self-portrait," This exercise involves participants recruiting about 30 people to gather stories about "my greatest strengths" and "how I could improve or grow" from friends, family, teachers, teammates, coworkers, or anyone with extended contact with the individual. The person then collects the stories and examines them for recurring behaviors, values, and character strengths. Then, the individual compiles an integrated portrait of these patterns in the form of a summary of a couple of paragraphs or a more creative form, such as an essay, presentation, video, or set of images. This activity promotes self-development through positive emotion resources, agentic resources (beliefs about our capability to exert control over events in our life), and relationship resources (Roberts et al., 2005; Spreitzer, 2006). In one study with adolescents, researchers compared feedback on strengths only with feedback on strengths plus growth areas from groups of personal and professional contacts or professional contacts only, and the best benefits were found for strengths plus growth areas solicited from the broadest range of contacts (Spreitzer et al., 2009).

Step 1

Below are 24 character strengths. Which of these **most strongly** describes who this person is and how they operate in their life? Check off those strengths that you **most clearly** see in them. Choose about 5 strengths (no more than 7).

____ **Creativity:** ingenuity; sees & does things in new/unique ways; original & adaptive ideas

____ **Curiosity:** novelty-seeker; takes an interest; open to different experiences; asks questions

____ **Judgment:** critical thinker; analytical; logical; thinks things through

____ **Love of learning:** masters new skills & topics; passionate about knowledge & learning

____ **Perspective:** wise; provides wise counsel; sees the big picture; integrates others' views

____ **Bravery:** valorous; does not shrink from fear; speaks up for what's right

____ **Perseverance:** persistent; industrious; overcomes obstacles; finishes what is started

____ **Honesty:** integrity; truthful; authentic

____ **Zest:** enthusiastic; energetic; vital; feels alive and activated

____ **Love:** gives and accepts love; genuine; values close relations with others

____ **Kindness:** generous; nurturing; caring; compassionate; altruistic; nice

____ **Social intelligence:** aware of the motives and feelings of oneself & others, knows what makes other people tick

____ **Teamwork:** a team player; community-focused, socially responsible; loyal

____ **Fairness:** acts upon principles of justice; does not allow feelings to bias decisions about others

____ **Leadership:** organizes group activities; encourages and leads groups to get things done

____ **Forgiveness:** merciful; accepts others' shortcomings; gives people a second chance

____ **Humility:** modest; lets accomplishments speak for themselves; focuses on others

____ **Prudence:** careful; wisely cautious; thinks before speaking; does not take undue risks

____ **Self-regulation:** self-controlled; disciplined; manages impulses & emotions

____ **Appreciation of beauty & excellence:** awe-filled; quickly moved to wonder; marvels at beauty & greatness

____ **Gratitude:** thankful for the good; expresses thanks; feels blessed

____ **Hope:** optimistic; future-minded; has a positive outlook

____ **Humor:** playful; enjoys joking and bringing smiles to others; lighthearted

____ **Spirituality:** religious and/or spiritual; practices a faith; purpose- & meaning-driven

Step 2

On the back of this page, give a brief rationale or example of how you have seen this person display *each strength* you checked off.

Self-Monitor Your Strengths

Overview

Much of our behavior operates on autopilot in which we are not particularly aware of our existing thoughts, feelings, and behaviors in the moment. Self-monitoring is an intervention that can help us bring a mindful awareness to our strengths-related thoughts, feelings, and behaviors, which can, in turn, catalyze us into positive action.

Purpose

Enhance awareness of strengths that are operating outside of awareness; link internal character strengths with behavioral action.

Steps

1. Create a tracking sheet like the example on the next page or use an app on one of your devices.
2. Set a reminder alert for every hour or set up an intermittent alarm that will cue you to pause and check in on the behaviors you are monitoring.
3. In your tracking log, be sure to note the activity you are doing, the strengths you are using and how you are using the strengths. This will help you draw connections between your internal processes and your actual behaviors.

Tip

Research has found in some studies that it is important to be honest and consistent with self-monitoring in order to have a greater impact. Honest tracking and consistent tracking are behaviors that you can control.

Research

Self-monitoring is a solid tool that has been used in assessment and treatment (see Korotitsch & Nelson-Gray, 1999). It is used to understand and improve behaviors ranging from mood management, improving eating behaviors, and managing addictions. It is used as a weekly exercise and special activity (called strengths-activity mapping) in the mindfulness-based strengths practice (MBSP) program (Niemiec, 2014a).

CSI 8

Day of the Week/ Time	Current Activity	Character Strength(s)	How I'm Using My Strengths	Any Comments (e.g., emotions felt, obstacles to using strengths, strength intentions)
Day: Time:				
Day: Time:				
Day: Time:				
Day: Time:				
Day: Time:				
Day: Time:				
Day: Time:				

Stories and Character Strengths
(Develop Strengths-Spotting)

Overview
Human beings are a collection of stories – ranging from the seemingly unimportant story of brushing your teeth this morning to the seemingly superimportant story of the birth of your child, and then there are all the stories of routines, events, and conversations that happen in between. Character strengths are part of these life experiences and therefore can be noticed in any story.

Purpose
Develop strengths-sight – the attentional focus on our own or others' character strengths (Lottman, Zawaly, & Niemiec, 2017), also known as practicing strengths-spotting in others and in yourself; become more familiar with the "language" of character strengths; become more comfortable sharing positive stories and good news with others.

Steps – Version 1
1. Think of a specific time, recently or awhile back, when you were at *your* best – you were functioning strongly. This could be a time at work, school, home, or other place and you were behaving in a way that was true to who you are.
2. Develop this out as a story with a beginning, middle, and end.
3. Write out the story.
4. Review the story and take careful notice of the character strengths you used throughout the story.

Steps – Version 2
1. Share with someone a recent positive experience you had in which you contributed to the experience in a meaningful way.
2. After you tell this story, ask the person to offer feedback to you about the character strengths they heard you express in the story. Hint: you might give them a handout on the VIA classification to assist them in spotting your character strengths.

Tip
"Don't put the cart in front of the horse," as the saying goes, in relation to not getting ahead of oneself. Applied to this exercise, don't put specific strengths ahead of the story; it's typically easier for clients new to strengths to share a general story about something positive than to ask them to come up with a story about prudence or love of learning on the spot. As clients become experienced with the language, ask for stories about specific strengths.

Troubleshooting
Some people struggle with the extreme language of at one's "best." This can be easily adjusted in the instructions to a more modest framing and to fit the context, such as "a time when you were happy at work," "a time when you were functioning strongly at school," or "something positive that happened this week in your relationship."

Research
An early version of this intervention was called "you, at your best" and offered some benefits, although not long-lasting benefits, in a gold standard intervention study (Seligman et al., 2005). This does not mean the exercise isn't useful; quite the contrary, it has been used now by thousands of practitioners across the globe with success. It's a useful and practical entry point for strengths fluency (Linkins et al., 2015). In addition, several studies now show the benefits of sharing something positive, such as good news with others (Gable et al., 2004; Reis et al., 2010), bringing gains to happiness, positive emotions, and life satisfaction (Lambert et al., 2011). These benefits to positive emotions were even stronger if the listener offered an enthusiastic response.

Mentors/Role Models

CSI 10

Overview
Mentors are a type of role model who can positively influence the character of their protégés. This occurs through many pathways, such as when mentors relate character to goal-setting, building knowledge, reflecting about the good life, solving practical problems, and role model identification (Moberg, 2008).

Purpose
Understanding your character strengths through the eyes of a role model; practice spotting strengths in your mentor/role model.

Steps
Explore the role of one or more mentors/role models, past or present, in your life.
1. Name a person who has served as a mentor or role model to you. The individual might become clear as you think about a time in your life when you were struggling and someone stepped in to help you.
2. What was their core belief about you and your strengths? What did they see in you? How did they communicate this with you?
3. What impact did this have on you at the time? What is the impact on you today?
4. Looking back, what were their character strengths? How did they use their strengths to help you?

Troubleshooting
Keep the mentor/role model as someone personal, if possible. If it's difficult to name a living role model, then consider an important person who is now deceased and approach the exercise that way. If that also is a challenge then consider people in the public eye, living or deceased, such as leaders, actors/actresses, whom have positively influenced your character. Finally, turn to fictional characters such as characters from movies and books (e.g., Niemiec, 2017).

Tip
Extend this exercise to other people in your life, such as finding the "hero" or "heroine" in an imperfect father, a mother who struggled but had perseverance, a sibling you've lost touch with, or a close friend. What do you admire in these individuals? How have they positively influenced you? How do they see the real you?

Research
Most people can identify at least two personal heroes and usually a half-dozen more (Allison & Goethals, 2011). Mentoring and role modeling is a research supported practice in character education (Berkowitz, 2011), and learning from mentors has been described as one of three major paths for developing wisdom (Gluck & Baltes, 2006). Turning to the observation of others has long been discussed as a pivotal learning pathway (Bandura, 1977), but can be especially influential when the model is a character/person of virtue (Bandura, 2003, 2008). For 1,500 movie examples of characters displaying strong virtue and character strength to serve as potential role models, see Niemiec and Wedding (2014).

Character Strengths Use

Introduction

This section offers interventions around taking action with character strengths. Many clients will ask their practitioner: "What do I do with my strengths?" While any of the interventions in this book could potentially be offered in response to this question, those in this section are particularly important for jumping into action.

Contents

CSI 11: Use a Signature Strength in a New Way
CSI 12: Acting "As If" (Acting from Strength)
CSI 13: Turn a Strength Inward
CSI 14: Create a Strengths Habit
CSI 15: Signature Strengths Across Domains
CSI 16: Holistic Strengths Use
CSI 17: Pathways to Virtue Use
CSI 18: Head, Heart, and Hands: Living a Virtuous Life
CSI 19: Boost a Lower Strength

Use a Signature Strength in a New Way

Overview
The identification and use of signature strengths is a quintessential exercise in positive psychology and has been shown to be successful across cultures and populations in studies comparing signature strengths groups with placebo groups or several other intervention groups.

CSI 11

Purpose
Take strengths awareness to the next level; widen your knowledge and use of your best qualities; act in accordance with who you are – your authentic self.

Steps
1. Take the VIA Survey or VIA Youth Survey at https://www.viacharacter.org
2. As you review your rank-ordered results, select one of your top strengths.
3. Use the strength in a new and different way each day for 1 week.

Tip
Take notice of how you felt using each strength and when, where, and how you used the strength in each instance (Duan et al., 2013). This will help you make further connections between your actions, feelings, and the context.

Troubleshooting
Some participants are unable to come up with ways they might use their strengths in new ways. It can be helpful to offer a handout of examples for each of the 24. Table 2.1 in Chapter 2 offers examples for this exercise. Other tables and figures that might spur ideas include Table 1.2 in Chapter 1, Figure 2.2 in Chapter 2, and Table 3.1 in Chapter 3.

Another tactic in approaching this activity, although not explored from a scientific standpoint, is to use a different signature strength in a new way each day for one week. This requires less demand on any one signature strength but requires the user to put forth some effort for each of their signature strengths. While this variation has not been studied rigorously, it's hypothesized that this would add to one's versatility with strengths use and offer more options for future strengths use.

Research
In a gold standard study – a randomized, double-blind, placebo-controlled study of five positive interventions – participants who were assigned to use their signature strengths in new ways experienced elevations in happiness and decreases in depression for 6 months (Seligman et al., 2005). This was fully replicated in another study (Gander et al., 2013) and similar results have been found with various populations in different countries, as described in Chapter 2.

Acting "As If" (Acting From Strength)

Overview
A common refrain around character strengths from individuals is to exclaim, "If only I could…" (be more creative, have courage, have more hope, etc.). Alfred Adler (1963), creator of the influential psychotherapy called "individual psychology," created the "acting as if" technique as a way to counteract "if only" beliefs with actual action. The power of trying out new behaviors to create reality out of practice has long been championed by those working in psychodrama, an approach articulated by Jacob Moreno (Blatner, 1988). Modern personality researchers are confirming that individuals can be instructed to take on behaviors of a trait, such as a character strength, and this can boost the trait and well-being (Blackie et al., 2014).

CSI 12

Purpose
Boost your use of a character strength; shift from wanting a strength to behaving with a strength; build your symphony of strengths.

Steps
1. Select the strength you wish to improve.
2. Select the situation (including any person) you want to bring the strength more strongly to (e.g., curiosity on a date, bravery at a work meeting, creativity with a difficult family member, humor with a friend while out for the night).
3. Behave in a way that is consistent with that strength in that situation, e.g., act brave or creative, or approach a situation with gratitude or hope. Use the synonyms and definitions in the VIA classification (see inside cover) to help you act consistently with that strength. For example, if you choose zest, act not only with zest but explore being enthusiastic, full of energy, living with vigor and vitality, approaching life with excitement, doing things wholeheartedly, and viewing life as an adventure.

Tip
This activity can be catalyzed by reading aloud a speech or inspiring passage that exemplifies the strength, as suggested by Polly and Britton (2015), who offer an example of a poem, monologue, or famous speech for each of the 24 strengths. For example, for perspective they suggest reading aloud an excerpt from the "Gettysburg Address" speech by Abraham Lincoln, a Shakespearean sonnet for love, and an excerpt from a speech by Mother Teresa for humility. A practitioner might practice this "acting as if" reading in a session with a client.

Troubleshooting
If the exercise is too intimidating for clients and they refuse to partake, then one option is to soften it by engaging in "reflecting as if" (Watts, 2013). With this approach, the client reflects on the above steps and explores possibilities and then the client and practitioner co-construct a list of "as if" behaviors before taking a small action.

Research
Personality researchers argue that by shifting in our state in the moment we can also change our traits (Fleeson, 2001), and also note that enacting the behaviors of a trait can enhance well-being (Fleeson et al., 2002). Personality researchers have shown that this strategy can be used with the creativity strength, which can be fostered by building from what consistently predicts creativity, e.g., openness to experience, and then behaving in a way that is open by acting inquisitive, philosophical, curious, and/or imaginative (Blackie et al., 2014). The same researchers offer an example for conscientiousness (which we might replace with the strength of prudence) and note that if someone wants to increase their "prudence" at work, they can act planfully, carefully, and responsibly.

Turn a Strength Inward

Overview
Some character strengths are explicitly viewed as characteristics to be expressed to other people (e.g., kindness, forgiveness, fairness). However, each character strength can be directed inwardly – toward oneself.

CSI 13

Purpose
Self-care; self-understanding; self-improvement.

Steps
1. For each of the questions below, consider a specific situation in which something has gone wrong, you have made an error, or you are suffering in some way. Rate yourself on the following using a scale of 1–10, where 1 is the lowest amount of inward application and 10 is the highest amount of inward application.
   - What is your level of self-kindness/self-compassion? How kind are you with yourself?
   - What is your level of self-fairness? How fair are you with yourself?
   - What is your level of self-forgiveness? How forgiving are you with yourself?
   - What is your level of self-leadership? How much do you apply self-leadership, taking control, and leading/organizing yourself to action?
   - What is your level of self-bravery? How brave are you in facing what's going on within yourself (e.g., inner struggles, flaws, limitations, troubling memories)?
   - What is your level of self-honesty? How honest are you with yourself?
   - What is your level of self-perspective? How often do you turn to and follow your own inner wisdom?
   - Consider other character strengths not mentioned and rate yourself the same way.
2. Select your highest rating. What are you doing best at? How can you learn from this positive approach you are taking?
3. Select your lowest rating. What would you benefit most from improving? What are you in most need of? Which resonates most with you?
4. Consider how you express the character strength chosen in Step 3 to other people. Reflect on what you say, think, and do. Apply these thoughts, words, and actions toward yourself.

Research
The research on turning character strengths inward is mounting and particularly strong for kindness, often termed self-compassion (see Neff & Germer, 2013), self-forgiveness (e.g., Cornish & Wade, 2015; Griffin et al., 2015), and perspective/wisdom (e.g., Baltes & Staudinger, 2000). The concept of turning bravery inward, also known as "psychological courage" has been discussed by Putnam (1997).

Create a Strengths Habit

Overview

Most of our habits – both good and bad – are created automatically, beyond our conscious awareness. Making a small change in your behavior sounds straightforward. Yet many people are so overwhelmed that even when they understand how developing their strengths will make their job easier and more enjoyable, they lack the daily mental space and energy to start. Quite simply, it's easy to get lost in autopilot mode and daily habits.

CSI 14

Purpose

Bring the process of habit-making into greater conscious control; enhance strength use.

Steps

1. Consider a character strength you would like to build up.
2. *Cue.* Choose a brief cue (e.g., 30 seconds).
3. *Routine.* Create a new routine (e.g., 5 minutes).
4. *Reward.* Give yourself a reward (e.g., 30 seconds).

Research

Neuroscientific research around habit-making behaviors has revealed this three-part process, called the habit loop, at play in creating and automatizing habits (Duhigg, 2012). Applying this research to strengths, Michelle McQuaid studied over 2,000 employees across 65 countries. She found that people could create an 11-minute strengths habit. More specifically, she found that 41% improved their ability to name their own strengths, 60% became better at setting weekly strength-based goals, and 41% improved their feeling of having the opportunity to do what they did best each day. In addition, 39% improved the likelihood of having a meaningful strengths conversation with their supervisor, and 32% felt their organization was more committed to developing their strengths (McQuaid & VIA Institute on Character, 2015). Numerous additional benefits included greater flourishing, engagement, and feeling valued, energized, and like they were making a difference. Strengths habit-making is discussed at length in McQuaid and Lawn (2014).

Examples

- Cue (for the character strength of *humor*): Turn on my computer to start my day.
- Routine: Watch 5 minutes of funny videos online.
- Reward: Take my first sip of coffee.

- Cue (for the character strength of *appreciation of beauty*): Walk my dog.
- Routine: Take pictures and short videos of nature.
- Reward: Post one or two pictures on Facebook or Instagram.

- Cue (for the character strength of *self-regulation*): Hear the mindfulness bell sound on my computer (set to sound every 2 hours).
- Routine: Practice mindful breathing in and out for a few minutes.
- Reward: Play a 1-minute game on my smartphone.

Signature Strengths Across Domains

Overview
People are susceptible to using their signature strengths narrowly, which limits their potential. Some will find many ways to use their strength of prudence at work but then struggle to see its application in the domains of family or social relationships. In contrast, others will readily bring forth new ways to use their strength of love with family and friends but claim (incorrectly) that it cannot be applied in the workplace.

Purpose
Practice and apply top strengths; expand the range of situations in which strengths are used; enhance awareness and use of signature strengths.

Steps
1. Choose one of your signature strengths. You might consider choosing a signature strength you'd like to better understand and improve upon.
2. Choose three domains in your life that you regularly partake in. Domains you might consider include: family, relationship, social, spiritual, community, sport, school, work.
3. Write about how you can use this particular signature strength in the three domains. Some of what you write about might reflect past use in that domain and some might be new or retooled ways of using the strength.
4. Develop a concrete plan to put the strength into action in each setting. Set a designated period of time to take action.

Research
This activity is a variation of the established exercise called use your signature strengths in new ways, which can lead to substantial, long-term benefits for happiness and depression (e.g., Gander et al., 2013; Seligman et al., 2005). Research in the education context has applied this exercise to students (Linkins et al., 2015).

Holistic Strengths Use

Overview
The circumplex mapping of the 24 character strengths across two continua (mind–heart; intrapersonal–interpersonal) has received considerable attention and interest, especially among practitioners (see Figure 2.1 in Chapter 2 for the most current circumplex). It was originally developed from the research of Chris Peterson (e.g., see Peterson, 2006a) and was updated and revised by Robert McGrath in 2014 (VIA Institute, 2014, where you can see a sample report with the circumplex mapping). Some character strengths are clearly more heart-oriented than mind-oriented (e.g., love), some are more mind-oriented (e.g., judgment/critical thinking), some are more interpersonally based (e.g., teamwork), and some are more intrapersonally based (e.g., curiosity). Nevertheless, character strengths can be expressed through all four dimensions. The VIA Institute has included this as a graph in personalized character strengths reports for hundreds of thousands of people since 2009. Practitioners who have been working with it are interested in its practical utility. This activity offers one example of the practical use.

CSI 16

Purpose
Widen the use of character strengths expression; express the strength in a complete, holistic way.

Steps
1. Identify one of your signature strengths (or one you wish to work on).
2. Write about how the strength might be expressed in each of the following:
   a. *Mind: logic, analysis, thinking.* What are the thoughts that accompany the strength? What thoughts go through your mind when you are using it? How might you express it in a "heady" way? Example: perseverant thoughts might include "I can do it," "I will keep pushing forward," "I'll try my best."
   b. *Heart: feeling, intuition, body.* How do you feel when you use the strength? Where do you feel it in your body? How can you express it in a heart-based way? Examples: feeling gratitude in the heart region; tingling in the hands and fingers when feeling zest.
   c. *Intrapersonal.* Turn the strength inward. How do you express the strength when you're alone? What does it look like outside the context of an interaction? Examples: curiosity when doing an Internet search; gratitude use in prayer; self-kindness to oneself when feeling down and self-critical.
   d. *Interpersonal.* Turn the strength outward. How do you express the strength to others? What does it look like in the context of an interaction? Examples: curiously asking someone questions; sharing gratitude to someone who did a favor; doing a kind and thoughtful act for another.
3. Develop a concrete plan to put the strength into action in a new way across one or more of these areas. Set a designated period of time you can commit to.

Troubleshooting
If focus on any area is a challenge, combine areas such as "interpersonal" and "heart" in which the strength might be expressed deeply and emotionally in a close relationship.

Research
A version of this exercise is discussed in Niemiec (2014a). This activity is a variation of the established exercise called use your signature strengths in new ways, which has been shown to lead to substantial, long-term benefits for happiness and depression (e.g., Gander et al., 2013; Seligman et al., 2005). Components of this exercise have been suggested from analyses with couples, such as making a character strength interpersonally oriented (Veldorale-Brogan et al., 2010).

Pathways to Virtue Use

Overview
In the VIA classification, the virtues are the higher-order, broader attributes and the character strengths are defined as "pathways" to the virtues (Peterson & Seligman, 2004).

Purpose
Builds virtues; offers a different lens for self-development and strengths development; widens the use of strengths/virtues work.

Steps
1. *Select a virtue.* What virtue do you want to give greater attention to or enhance (wisdom, courage, humanity, justice, temperance, or transcendence)? Choose one.
2. *Examine the strengths.* As you view the VIA classification of character strengths and virtues (see inside cover), examine the character strengths that nest under the virtue you chose.
3. *Determine the pathway.* Which of those strengths under that particular virtue are you highest in? How might you use the highest strength as "your unique pathway" to building the virtue? (e.g., using curiosity as a path to greater wisdom or forgiveness as a pathway to more temperance). This step involves using a high strength in a new way.
4. *Consider other strengths.* If needed, bring in a second or third strength to help clarify and solidify the pathway to virtue expression. And, consider character strengths outside of those listed under the virtue you selected.
5. *Reexamine your virtue.* Take another look at your virtue. Does it need additional work or are you ready to turn to another virtue?

Troubleshooting
If you are trying to decide which virtue to focus on, consider "expanding" (building upon) your highest virtue or "enhancing" (building up) a lower virtue. As the virtues are framed holistically, consider the following questions:
- Are you wanting to become more "thinking-oriented" or "knowledge-based" (wisdom)?
- Are you wanting to become more volitional or "gut-oriented," digging deep within yourself to take action (courage)?
- Are you wanting to become more interpersonally focused (humanity)?
- Are you wanting to become more community-oriented or group-focused (justice)?
- Are you wanting to become more focused on managing your vices, protecting yourself from over-doing things (temperance)?
- Are you wanting to become more spiritually oriented or meaning-based (transcendence)?

Tip
Put this exercise into perspective. The six virtues have been championed by many of the greatest thinkers throughout history. You are focusing on enhancing one of those great virtues!

Research
As scientists reviewed the classic works of virtue and human goodness across religions, philosophies, and classifications – across cultures and nations – they found parallel themes (Dahlsgaard, Peterson, & Seligman, 2005) which became the virtues of the VIA classification (Peterson & Seligman, 2004). Some research has found that the strengths fit quite well under the assigned virtue categories (e.g., Ruch & Proyer, 2015), while others have found that some re-arranging is useful to determine an ideal fit (e.g., McGrath, 2014). Some character strengths do not ideally fit under one but under several virtue categories, such as humor (Ruch & Proyer, 2015), and some may fit better under other categories, such as hope under courage (Pury, 2008). This exercise, which includes the core step of using a high strength in a new way, can be viewed as a variation of the exercise used in research studies that was found to boost happiness and lower depression for as long as 6 months (e.g., Gander et al., 2013; Seligman et al., 2005).

Head, Heart, and Hands: Living a Virtuous Life

Overview
There is evidence that character can be described as having three basic elements, or virtues, which could be referred to as caring, inquisitiveness, and self-control. Scholars argue that all three must be valued and nurtured for a well-lived life. None is sufficient by itself: A life well-lived requires heart, head, and hands (positive action).

CSI 18

One avenue for the development of good character is to learn to simultaneously manage and control yourself, care for others, and be interested in, exploring, appreciating, and engaging with the world.

Purpose
Increase your virtue use; engage in virtuous, authentic living; expand goodness toward yourself, others, and the world.

Steps
1. Take a look at the self-control strengths listed below. These relate to virtuous living in regard to managing yourself. Reflect on these strengths individually and as a group. Using these strengths as a catalyst, write down one way you could bring greater goodness to yourself. What would it look like to bring further goodness to you?
2. Take a look at the caring strengths listed below. These relate to virtuous living of being good and caring to others. Reflect on these strengths individually and as a group. Using these strengths as a catalyst, write down one way you could bring greater goodness to others. What would it look like to bring further goodness to others?
3. Take a look at the inquisitiveness strengths listed below. These relate to the virtue of bringing goodness to the environment or the world in general. Reflect on these strengths individually and as a group. Using these strengths as a catalyst, write down one way you could bring greater goodness to the environment or the world in general. What would it look like to bring further goodness to the world?
4. Review the three examples of virtuous action you have written. Consider making a plan that includes action with all three. Bring forth your head, heart, and hands in a strong way. What is the first step you might take right now?

Research
There are multiple lenses to view the character strengths (e.g., heart/mind; intra/interpersonal; six virtue categories; and so forth). This activity reflects another important lens that has emerged from research. McGrath (2015c) studied over one million individuals across four samples and multiple measures of character strengths and found support for the character strengths splitting into three groups, which he named caring, inquisitiveness, and self-control. Here's how the character strengths loaded onto each of these groups:
- *Self-Control:* honesty, judgment, perseverance, prudence, and self-regulation.
  - humility (included here but not as central as the others).
- *Caring:* fairness, forgiveness, kindness, gratitude, love, and spirituality.
  - teamwork and leadership (included here but not as central as the others).
- *Inquisitiveness:* appreciation of beauty & excellence, curiosity, creativity, love of learning, and perspective.
  - bravery, zest, social intelligence, hope, and humor (included here but not as central as the others).

Examples

Self-control. I'm going to push myself to take more control of my life. I could be more honest with myself about my ego needs for attention and affection. I could challenge my inner critic that is quick to judge me. I could be better to my body by watching the food and drink I put in it.

Caring. How can I stretch my service to other people? Not just those who are part of my personal circle, but all people? I will show greater compassion for those who are suffering, whether that be a homeless person, my colleague who had a bad day, or my child who fell on the playground. I will appreciate the sacredness of each interaction with people today – seeing them and my conversation with them as a gift.

Inquisitiveness. I will focus on challenging my set beliefs and will learn more about how other people think and feel. I will take an interest in how I can give back to my community, such as local volunteering, becoming active in civic work, or cleaning up my neighborhood street once a month. I will deliberately learn new topics and skills and then teach these to others so that my building of new knowledge spreads in the world. I will take time each day to marvel outside in nature or watch with appreciative admiration the skills of one of my colleagues in action or the skills of athletes on television.

Boost a Lower Strength

Overview

A common and perhaps even universal behavior after a person takes the VIA Survey is to look at their bottom strengths. People have a natural inclination to judge these as weak areas and therefore want to improve them. Lower strengths are not referred to as weaknesses since the VIA Survey does not measure weaknesses; it measures relative strengths. Lower strengths might be less developed strengths, strengths not valued as highly, or strengths not as natural and easy to deploy; these are working hypotheses to explore in oneself or in others as the reason why a strength is lower in one's profile is unique to each person. While research has shown support for working on signature strengths, there has also been support for working on other character strengths, such as the lower strengths, in one's profile.

CSI 19

Purpose

Improve strengths use; boost a strength you are less familiar with; widen your overall character strengths savvy.

Steps

1. Take the VIA Survey or VIA Youth Survey at https://www.viacharacter.org
2. Choose one of your lower strengths, one of those that appear in the Bottom 5 of your character strengths profile.
3. Use your lower strength in a new way each day.

Troubleshooting

Some people will struggle to implement ways to use a lower strength as these strengths are likely to be unfamiliar, not particularly energizing, and may seem inauthentic to use. One should remember the "towing effect," which refers to the use of a signature strength to "tow along" or bring forward a lower strength. One person's signature strength of curiosity can be used to tow along a lower strength of humility by using an interested, questioning orientation with different people at a party, thereby placing the attention on others.

Research

One randomized trial found that a group of participants who worked on one higher strength and one lower strength had benefits for happiness compared to placebo (Rust et al., 2009). Other studies have found benefits for groups who have focused on boosting a lower strength (e.g., Proyer et al., 2015; Rashid, 2004). In the study by Proyer and colleagues, participants experienced benefits to well-being when they focused on their lower strengths, and this effect was particularly strong for participants who were not high in terms of their overall strengths endorsement.

Meaning and Engagement

Introduction

Meaning and engagement are foundational elements in positive psychology and more specifically in well-being theory. Character strengths offer clear and direct routes to these important outcomes and can be viewed as central to processes involving meaning-making and engagement-creation.

Contents

CSI 20: Strengths Alignment
CSI 21: The Deathbed Test
CSI 22: Life Summary
CSI 23: What Matters Most?
CSI 24: Cultivate Inner Self-Worth
CSI 25: Defining Moments Exercise
CSI 26: Positive Action Through Movies

Strengths Alignment

Overview
One of the most significant and practical themes of strengths work is that your top strengths can be consciously aligned with any activity, conversation, task, or routine in day-to-day living. Nowhere is this more apparent than in the workplace. Workers can deliberately connect their signature strengths with their work task to reach outcomes employers are interested in, such as employee engagement, employee sense of calling, and employee productivity.

Purpose
Improve energy and engagement at work; discover more meaning and sense of calling at work.

CSI 20

Steps
1. List the five tasks that you do most frequently at work (e.g., filing, leading team meetings, emailing clients, making sales calls, etc.).
2. Review your Top 5 strengths in your character strengths profile from the VIA Survey.
3. Write down one way you can use any *one* of your top strengths with *each* of the five work tasks (e.g., using creativity to lead a team meeting by ending it with a new quote each time; using creativity to offer different perspectives when making a sales call, etc.) Explain how you will bring the character strength forth in the given task.
4. When you are ready, repeat Step 3 with a different top strength. Repeat until you go through all five of your signature strengths.

Research
This exercise (described in Littman-Ovadia & Niemiec, 2017) examines current work tasks and the potential of greater signature strengths use when engaging in these tasks. The intervention was studied in a controlled trial of workers who specifically used four of their signature strengths with work tasks over 4 weeks, which, relative to a control group, led to significant improvements in calling 6 months later and life satisfaction 3 months later (Harzer & Ruch, 2016). This research draws from other research finding the use of signature strengths at work is important for building a calling (Harzer & Ruch, 2012), as well as the relevance of character strengths for vocation irrespective of the content of the strength (e.g., whether it's creativity, prudence, or hope that is signature) (Harzer & Ruch, 2013). Other character strengths researchers are drawing many important connections between the use of strengths, especially signature strengths, at work as they relate to performance (Dubreuil, Forest, & Courcy, 2013), organizational citizenship behavior and less counterproductive work behaviors (Lavy & Littman-Ovadia, 2016), flourishing (Hone et al., 2015), and ambitious work behavior (Gander et al., 2012). In addition, perseverance has been found to be a key character strength in the work setting (Littman-Ovadia & Lavy, 2016). Research in organizational psychology refers to this type of activity as "job crafting" in which employees make proactive changes that are physical, relational, cognitive, or emotional to improve their jobs, and it has been associated with various positive outcomes, including improved job satisfaction and greater meaning at work (Wrzesniewski et al., 2013).

The Deathbed Test

Overview

In outlining the criteria for character strengths, one of the essential elements of a character strength is that the strength is fulfilling. In order to identify this criterion, Peterson and Seligman (2004) offer the example of the deathbed test as a testament to qualities that contribute to fulfillment and meaning rather than simply activities that are fun. They explain:

> "A strength contributes to various fulfillments that constitute a good life, for oneself and for others. Although strengths and virtues determine how an individual copes with adversity, our focus is on how they fulfill an individual" (p. 17).

CSI 21

Purpose

Build perspective; appreciate life in the present; tap into life fulfillment.

Steps

1. Imagine you are lying at your deathbed.
2. Finish this sentence: I wish I would have spent more time _____.
3. What character strengths might you use to help you accomplish what you have written about in Step 2.

Research

This engaging activity was described in Peterson and Seligman (2004). The exercise also received praise from Wong (2015), who has written extensively on meaning interventions. A similar exercise called temporal scarcity offered by Kurtz (2008) has shown to boost well-being. This exercise involves reflecting and writing about a situation that emphasizes how little time one has left, for example, a student considering they only have 6 months left before graduation. Another example is an individual reflecting on their own mortality and their limited time remaining before death. These kinds of exercises increase the perceived value of one's current situation.

Examples

For Step 2, Peterson and Seligman (2004) offer sample responses such as "I wish I had spent more time making a mark on the world" and "I wish I had spent more time getting to know my children and being kind to my friends" or "spent more time praising God and giving thanks" (p. 17). In my workshops, common responses people have offered include: "doing more activities with people I love," "exploring other cultures," "being present with my children," "expressing my gratitude to people," "focusing on my health," and "volunteering."

Life Summary

Overview
Taking stock in life by looking to one's past and what is possible for the future is an intuitive approach some people take automatically. This exercise makes this fascinating mental activity more concrete and specific and, when infused with character strengths, it can easily fit into goal-setting approaches.

Purpose
Building life perspective; practicing strengths-spotting.

Steps
1. Write a short description of how you would like to have your life relayed to your grandchildren (or great-grandchildren).
2. A few days later, review the summary. What character strengths do you see embedded in the story (even if the exact VIA words are not used)?
3. Take stock in what is missing in your life and the changes that would be necessary to make the summary a reality.
4. What character strengths will you need to deploy to make these changes? How will you bring these strengths forward, starting today?

Research
The original life summary exercise has been studied by Schueller (2010) to understand how certain positive interventions might be packaged together. In this study, the people who benefited from the life summary activity also tended to benefit specifically from the counting blessings (i.e., gratitude practice) exercise as opposed to other activities. In another study looking at the packaging of this and other interventions (Schueller & Parks, 2012), results found that engaging in multiple exercises was beneficial to participants in decreasing depression; specifically, doing two or four positive interventions (but not six) over a 6-week period was found to be beneficial.

Example
From Jason, 25, who works in management:

> I would like my grandchildren to know that I was an active, contributing member of the community. I would want them to know I went through challenging times in the military and being unemployed for a period of time, but that I never gave up. I eventually got a job in a startup company, worked my way into management, and started a family. I took pride in being a good father and standing up for what I believed to be the right thing.

> I see several character strengths in my story – zest ("active"), teamwork ("being in the military"), perseverance, ("never gave up"), love and perspective ("good father"), and bravery ("standing up" for what's right). What is missing in my life right now is the long-term experience as a "good father." To reach that goal, I will use my strengths of love and zest to express daily care for my kids. My signature strength of gratitude will remind me of how lucky I am to be here today – this gratitude will motivate me to stay consistent as a good father. My spiritual beliefs and kindness toward others will help shape me to do the right thing.

What Matters Most?

Overview
This seemingly simple question becomes loaded with meaning and intentionality when it is examined closely. This exercise helps you look to the future to assist you in the present.

Purpose
Boost awareness of key source of personal meaning; tap internal mechanisms for reaching meaning; widen life perspective; develop and sustain meaning and purpose.

Steps

CSI 23

1. *Image what will matter most.* Picture in your mind the area of your life that will matter most to you 6 months or 1 year from now. Visualize that area of your life functioning even stronger at that time compared to today (even if the area is already doing well at the moment).
2. *Phrase your intention.* In order to strengthen the area, make a simple intention that will help you highlight the focal point for the area. Try to capture this intention in a phrase or a sentence. For example, increase happiness in marriage; graduate from college; become more productive at work, improve physical health.
3. *Signature strength pathways.* List one way each of your five strongest signature strengths could be used as a "pathway of meaning" to help you make your intention a reality and improve this area of meaning. Each of these strengths can therefore assist you in taking action and deepening your experience of what matters most.
4. *Action planning.* You now have five pathways to enhancing or staying strong with what matters most to you. Write down the steps you will take to make this improvement. Will you bring forth one strength pathway at a time? Combine pathways? How will you ensure you use all of your five strongest strengths?

Research
Originally outlined as an activity by Littman-Ovadia and Niemiec (2017), this exercise was created to target meaning and purpose. It is based on the science of meaning and is a variation of the best possible self exercise (King, 2001), which boosts optimism (Meevissen, Peters, & Alberts, 2011). Another variation boosted happiness and lowered depression (Shapira & Mongrain, 2010) and has been used with success with people who are seriously suffering (e.g., Huffman et al., 2014).

Cultivate Inner Self-Worth

Overview
The fulfillment of meaning matters more than people realize as we have only scratched the surface of its vast potential for healing, growth, and flourishing (Wong, 2015). An important place to start with meaning-making is ourselves – appreciating our uniqueness and potential. This lays the foundation for contributing to the improvement of others and our society.

Purpose
Cultivate personal meaning; improve self-worth and confidence; draw connections between character strengths and future potential.

CSI 24

Steps
To become aware of the intrinsic value of your life and every life, explore the following four domains through journaling, reflection, or discussion:
1. *Relationship.* What people do you matter most to? What character strengths do they see in you?
2. *Singularity.* You are unique, irreplaceable, and capable of making an important contribution. Explain how this is true. Explore how your character strengths contribute to each of these components.
3. *Growth.* Seeing challenges as opportunities to learn and grow is a quality you can develop and use. Which of your character strengths will help you develop this kind of growth perspective? How might you view your character strengths from a growth mindset perspective in which you overcome challenges to improve each strength?
4. *Spirituality.* Each person can connect with something greater, outside of themselves, which is sacred. Examples include nature, God, higher power, collective unconsciousness, and the pursuit of an ultimate concern. What is the sacred or the holy that you seek? How might your character strengths support you on your journey?

Troubleshooting
Some individuals may get stuck on one domain, unable to answer a question or challenged by the exploration task. They should be encouraged to move on to the next step as the steps do not have to be completed sequentially. That said, getting stuck might reflect a deep, core issue that needs meditation, reflection, and astute dialogue. Therefore, it is often useful to return to the skipped step with a fresh perspective days or weeks later.

Research
This is a tool at the core of meaning therapy, a theoretically grounded and integrative approach that helps clients navigate challenges by enhancing their capacity to seek and create meaning in life (Wong, 2010, 2015). The character strengths elements have been added to make the activity more personal and to empower the individual to take action at each step.

Defining Moments Exercise

Overview
Each moment of our life is a moment of potential meaning and importance. Although most moments are not memorable, some unexpectedly come to mean a great deal. A moment that becomes a "defining moment" can come from an experience of suffering or achievement. It might occur before, during, *or* after a life transition, traumatic experience, stressor, hardship, celebration, accomplishment, or relationship connection.

Purpose
Build positive memories; enhance self-understanding by connecting important moments with character strengths.

Steps
1. Name one moment in time that has had a positive effect on you. Choose a moment in which you took action in some way. This moment doesn't have to be dramatic, simply any moment that has had a meaningful impact on you.
2. List the character strengths you used in that situation. Which character strengths did you bring forth? How did you express them?
3. Explore how this moment has shaped who you are. How has this moment contributed to your identity? No matter how small, how has it affected your view of yourself today?
4. Step back and view the bigger picture. Were you enacting virtues that helped you mobilize your strengths in that moment? Courage to take action? Humanity, justice, or wisdom? Driven by temperance or transcendence?

Research
Narrative identity is linked with well-being. People with high levels of well-being tend to emphasize personal growth in their life stories and their challenges are often framed as transformative (Bauer, McAdams, & Pals, 2008). This activity invites individuals to explore their stories from a growth perspective. It has been used with success in mindfulness-based strengths practice (MBSP; Ivtzan et al., 2016; Niemiec, 2014a; Niemiec & Lissing, 2016). Research is needed to study its particular effects in isolation from the MBSP program, but it is hypothesized that it would increase savoring, build self-efficacy, improve positive memory recall, and enhance positive self-perceptions. Anecdotally, people respond that they give greater priority to memories that were fading, experience savoring, and feel more confident in the present moment.

Example
Turning points are opportunities for growth and some of the most powerful surround areas of health problems, work/career events, parenthood, marriage, sexual relationships, and illness/death of others (Wethington, 2003). While most people report defining moments where they are actively a participant in the experience, I recall one man who took a different approach. He shared how one of his defining moments occurred when he was in active duty during the Vietnam War. He recalls passively observing a fellow soldier rescue a young boy, pulling the boy away from an explosive device and bringing him to safety. This observed act of self-sacrifice and kindness shaped the observing man's identity and served as a model for the behaviors he strives to display today.

Positive Action Through Movies

Overview

The influential monk Thomas Merton said "Art enables us to find ourselves and lose ourselves at the same time." This describes the pastime of watching movies in which a good film generates full engagement and pleasure as we lose ourselves in the experience and brings us to look deep, discover who we are at our core, challenge and align our values, and discover or rediscover meaning and what matters most.

Purpose

Tap emotions of elevation and admiration; take positive action for others (prosocial activity) or oneself (self-development); practice strengths-spotting; bring the trifecta of movie enjoyment – experiencing pleasure, engagement, and meaning – to yourself.

CSI 26

Steps

1. Select a movie that has inspired you or choose one from the short list below.
2. Watch the movie with an openness to learn, to feel, and to understand yourself *and* others.
3. As the credits of the movie roll, be present to what is stirring inside you. What do you feel? What character strengths are bubbling within you? Take notice of any motivation to positive action that you sense that might benefit yourself or others.
4. Write down what you are most inspired by from the movie, whether that is a particular character, a dialogue or quote, a plot development, an interaction or scene, a cinematic element such as the scenery, lighting, music, etc. Write down the strengths of the character or those strengths that link with the cinematic element.
5. Consider a way you might translate one of your observations to your personal life.

Research

Movies might be the most powerful medium for depicting heroism as fictional heroes (e.g., movie characters) rate higher on heroism scales than nonfictional heroes (e.g., a parent) (Allison & Goethals, 2011). And, the viewing of positive psychology movies has been found to lead to increases in positive characteristics and positive behaviors (Smithikrai, 2016) and various indicators of well-being and personal motivation to be good (Smith, 2014). Indeed, movies offer the power of observational learning in that what is observed is coded within us for potential future use as a guide for action (Bandura, 1977). The most appreciated movies are those with the longest-lasting effects, which involved the experience of emotions in the moment and reflection following the film (Oliver & Bartch, 2010).

Cinematic elevation and cinematic admiration have been argued as being important factors of impact because of significant links between these emotions and prosocial behavior (e.g., Schnall & Roper, 2011). Building off emotions studied by Haidt (2000) and colleagues (Algoe & Haidt, 2009), cinematic elevation occurs when a person observes the portrayal of goodness or character strengths in action, experiences the tingling and warming sensations of inspiration, and is then motivated to do good; cinematic admiration differs in that the physiologic sensations are more likely "chills" and energizing sensations with an outcome of motivation toward self-improvement and copying of the character (Niemiec & Wedding, 2014).

Examples

Twelve exemplars meeting criteria for a positive psychology movie (Niemiec, 2007) follow: *Amelie* (2001), *American Beauty* (1999), *The Fault in Our Stars* (2014), *Frozen* (2013), *Groundhog Day* (1993), *Invictus* (2009), *It's a Wonderful Life* (1946), *Life is Beautiful* (1998), *Star Wars: Episode VII – The Force Awakens* (2015), *Wings of Desire* (1987), *The Wizard of Oz* (1939), and *Zorba the Greek* (1964). For 1,500 examples of character strengths, PERMA, mindfulness, and resilience, see Niemiec and Wedding (2014)

Specific Character Strengths

Introduction

This section of interventions involves specific character strengths from the VIA classification. Some character strengths lend themselves more to activities than others. For example, there are a number of exercises to boost gratitude and these are relatively simple to apply, whereas fairness is challenging and complex and interventions are hard to come by. Other sections in this chapter also include activities that target particular character strengths (e.g., compassion-focused reappraisal, which boosts specific strengths such as forgiveness and compassion/kindness, was placed under the resilience section).

Contents

CSI 27: Boosting Curiosity Through Novelty
CSI 28: Imagined Conversation
CSI 29: Activate Your Zest!
CSI 30: Loving-Kindness Meditation
CSI 31: Gift of Time
CSI 32: Pay it Forward
CSI 33: Prosocial Spending
CSI 34: Enhance Teamwork Through Role Matching
CSI 35: Boosting Humility
CSI 36: Engaging With Beauty
CSI 37: Three Good Things
CSI 38: Gratitude Letter/Visit
CSI 39: Three Funny Things
CSI 40: Cultivating Sacred Moments

Boosting Curiosity Through Novelty

Overview
All humans have a strong autopilot mind that operates much of our thoughts and actions during the day. Autopilot is particularly strong during routine activities we do without much thinking. Some of those activities might feel draining even to think about. Bringing a small dose of mindful attention can transform these routines. Curiosity is part of the core of mindful attention (Bishop et al., 2004) and is the focal point for this exercise.

Purpose
Build curiosity; discover renewed energy doing a mundane routine; break free from autopilot/routine mind.

Steps
1. Select a task that you do each week that you do not like. It is likely an activity you find boring and tedious.
2. While you do the activity this week, pay attention to three novel (unique) features of the activity. Be sure to uses your senses.
3. Write down your experiences or discuss them with a friend.

Research
This exercise was conducted as a scientific experiment by Ellen Langer at Harvard, who found that those who were in the curiosity group (relative to a control group) changed the way they viewed the activity and weeks later were more likely to have done the previously-disliked task again on their own (Langer, 2006). Similar curiosity exercises have been encouraged by Kashdan (2009), and a curiosity activity focusing on engaging in curious and absorbing activities during the week was part of a larger intervention study found to cause greater happiness (Proyer et al., 2013). The activity by Langer closely relates to an activity assigned in successful mindfulness-based programs such as mindfulness-based cognitive therapy (MBCT; Segal et al., 2013) and mindfulness-based strengths practice (MBSP; Niemiec, 2014a), in which participants are asked to select a routine activity that they do every day in a mostly mindless way (e.g., brushing teeth, washing hair, feeding pets) and conduct the routine activity each day mindfully, engaging their full attention and senses.

Example
Common examples people choose for this activity include washing the dishes, vacuuming, getting gas for their car, folding laundry, cutting the lawn, making dinner, and driving in traffic to work. For Step 2, a person who has selected vacuuming might say that while they vacuumed they attended to the whirling sound of the machine, noticed the smooth maneuvering of the vacuum around furniture, and observed the clean streaks that the vacuum cleaner left in the carpet.

Imagined Conversation

Overview
It is a cliché to say that you already have the answers to many problems within you. We think that we need expert advice or that we are deficient in knowledge of some kind; however, research is showing that we have the capacity within us to be wise and to solve problems – more than we realize.

Purpose
Boost the strength of perspective; reconnect with the wisdom within you.

Steps
1. Select a minor problem that you are experiencing.
2. Close your eyes and imagine yourself having an inner dialogue about the problem with a wise person in your life. Imagine the back and forth – your describing the problem, their response, and the back and forth of the conversation.
3. When you conclude the conversation, write down your reactions.

Troubleshooting
Practice having the conversation with a different (imagined) wise person. Notice the different advice, questions, or approach that this person offers you.

Tip
Another similar, effective approach is to do "imagined travel" in which you bring the problem to your mind and imagine yourself traveling around the world to different places, situations, and cultures and presenting your problem to people at each location. Learn from each place, reflecting on the differences in life context and values (Gluck & Baltes, 2006; and used in MBSP, Niemiec, 2014a).

Research
With over 20 years of wisdom research at the Berlin Wisdom Project, scientists have revealed a number of practical strategies for boosting wisdom, or what is also referred to as perspective. Researchers have found that direct, short-term interventions can be particularly effective, and these include the two mentioned here. In imagined conversation, researchers found that wisdom-related performance levels increased substantially (by almost one standard deviation) and equal to a group of people who had the real-life conversation with a wise person! (Gluck & Baltes, 2006). A similar exercise, referred to usually as the inner advisor technique in which the individual is encouraged to go on an inward journey to meet a wise person and have a conversation with them, is a particularly effective strategy in the scientific and clinical practice of hypnosis (e.g., Hammond, 1990).

Activate Your Zest!

Overview
Structuring your daily life to include more activity, such as movement, exercise, pleasure, or meaningful action is an important and successful way to feel good. In many instances of this zest activation, the individual experiences benefits from the engagement in the activity itself and from additional benefits that may happen to occur (e.g., if the person is with other people, in nature, etc.).

Purpose
Build your strength of zest; increase your movement/exercise.

Steps

CSI 29

1. Choose one physical activity you enjoy. There are a variety of types of activities that might appeal to you. Consider the following types of action:
   - *Balance:* yoga, tai chi.
   - *Cardiovascular:* swimming, running, biking, skating, rigorous walking, light walking.
   - *Strength-building:* lifting weights, Pilates.
   - *Sport:* tennis, basketball, soccer.
   - *Movement tracking:* use a pedometer to track the steps you take each day. Activate yourself to increase your steps each week.
2. Do the activity you choose according to a simple plan, for example, 15–30 minutes, 5 times a week. Adjust the frequency and intensity to more or less based on the activity, your previous level of exercise, and what best fits for you at this point in time.
3. Write about the experience, the feelings, and the benefit of doing the activity each time.

Troubleshooting
If the above activities do not resonate with you or you are already consistent with your level of movement/exercise, then consider targeting activities in life that are pleasurable, engaging, or meaningful (e.g., authentic happiness theory, Seligman, 2002). Other examples of behavioral activation discussed by researchers include monitoring daily behavior, reviewing daily behavior, scheduling daily activities, rating the degree of accomplishment during engaged activities, exploring alternative behaviors related to goal-achievement, and scheduling leisure activities (Mazzucchelli, Kane, & Rees, 2010).

Research
Zest is the character strength that moves us from depletion to vitality (Ryan & Deci, 2008), most predicts work-as-a-calling (Peterson et al., 2009), and is repeatedly in the Top 2 strengths most correlated with happiness (Buschor et al., 2013; Park et al., 2004; Proyer et al., 2011), and has been found to cause happiness when targeted (Proyer et al., 2013). This particular exercise, a form of behavioral activation, is one of the most established interventions in psychology. It has consistently been useful in lowering depression and boosting well-being in nonclinical populations (Mazzucchelli et al., 2010). A similar behavioral activation exercise was used to boost zest in an intervention study that was found to cause happiness (Proyer et al., 2013). Behavioral activation is such a successful approach it has been found to be superior to antidepressant medication for symptom outcome, attrition rates, and side effects, and behavioral activation has been shown to outperform cognitive therapy approaches (Dimidjian et al., 2006).

Loving-Kindness Meditation

Overview
Loving-kindness practice, often called "metta," is a type of meditation that involves generating and directing one's capacity for love/kindness toward oneself, toward other people, and toward all living beings. The origins of this practice date back over 2,600 years to Buddhism. Modern day scientists are just now beginning to uncover the benefits of this practice.

Purpose
Boost the strength of love; improve self-care; boost compassion for others.

Steps
Loving-kindness involves directing mindfulness toward a specific character strength within you (i.e., love), also referred to as "mindful strengths use" (Niemiec, 2014a). The standard practice (Salzberg, 1995) is as follows:

1. Think of someone in your life whom you have felt deeply loved by. Reflect on a specific situation in which you were fully and genuinely loved by that person.
2. Allow yourself to feel the love from that person in that situation as if it's happening right now. Open yourself to notice the feelings in your body.
3. Recite the following four lines of meditation, feeling and perhaps forming pleasant images associated with each line:
   - May I be filled with loving-kindness,
   - May I be safe from inner and outer dangers,
   - May I be well in body and mind,
   - May I be at ease and happy.

Tips
After you become comfortable using the strategy to direct love inward to yourself, practice the second level, which involves directing the love to a specific person (i.e., change the word "I" to "you"), and then the third level of directing the love to "all beings."

This is an important activity to use with clients in a counseling relationship and can help them forge connections with themselves and with others (Leppma, 2012).

Research
The science of loving-kindness and related practices such as self-compassion have exploded in the last two decades, in no small part to the work of Sharon Salzberg (1995) and Jack Kornfield (1993), early pioneers of these practices, and more recently Kristin Neff and Christopher Germer (2013). Neuroimaging studies suggest this meditation enhances brain regions dealing with empathy and emotional processing (Hofmann, Grossman, & Hinton, 2011). Loving-kindness meditation has been found to be beneficial in boosting positive emotions (Cohn & Fredrickson, 2010) and increasing personal resources, such as greater mindfulness, purpose, social support, and decreased illness symptoms, which then increased life satisfaction and reduced depression (Fredrickson, Cohn, Coffey, Pek, & Finkel, 2008). Brief loving-kindness meditation has also been shown to boost social connection and positivity (Hutcherson, Seppala, & Gross, 2008), and led to improvements in pain and psychological distress in chronic pain clients (Carson et al., 2005). The work of Kristin Neff (2003; Neff, Rude, & Kirkpatrick, 2007; Neff & Vonk, 2009) on similar practices around self-compassion has also revealed many positive results, such as feelings of happiness, optimism and curiosity; decreased anxiety, depression, and rumination; fewer feelings of failure and inferiority; less self-criticism, perfectionism, anger and closed-mindedness; more emotional intelligence and wisdom; and improved initiative and mastery of goals.

CSI 30

Gift of Time

Overview
Positive relationships are viewed as the royal road to happiness – they bring benefit to us and others, allowing us to express intimacy, tend to others' needs, and be cared for by others. They facilitate joy, playfulness, and a variety of other positive emotions and character strengths. This kindness activity opens the door of opportunity for enhancing relationship connections.

Purpose
Boost kindness; practice social intelligence; nurture positive relationships.

Steps
1. Name three people that you care about that you would like to connect with this week.
2. Offer each of these three people your gift of time by spending time with them. This might involve helping them, talking with them, or doing an activity with them. For each of these meetings, be sure that each is in addition to your already-planned activities for the week.
3. In each instance, express your signature strengths while you are offering the gift of time to the person.

CSI 31

Research
This activity was originally used in positive psychotherapy as championed by Tayyab Rashid (2015). Positive psychotherapy, as a 14-week program, has been shown to be beneficial in lowering depression in both individual and group psychotherapy compared to treatment as usual and a control group, respectively (Seligman et al., 2006). Several additional studies reveal positive effects (see Rashid, 2015, for a review). This intervention was separated out from positive psychotherapy and boosted happiness and decreased depression as a stand-alone intervention (Gander et al., 2013). Rashid (2015) argues that using signature strengths during the gift of time helps clients "pursue meaning and purpose by using their strengths, such as strengthening close interpersonal and communal relationships or pursuing artistic, intellectual, or scientific innovations or philosophical or religious contemplation" (p. 9).

Pay it Forward

Overview
Most people immediately understand that if they are being asked to "pay it forward" that it means to commit a random act of kindness for someone. This activity, popularized by a movie from 2000 of the same name, is viewed as an adaptive strategy that is mutually beneficial for the giver and receiver. Only recently has this activity undergone study by scientists.

Purpose
Boost kindness; contribute to the betterment of others.

Steps
1. Commit a random act of kindness that brings benefit to others and is not done so that you can receive a favor in return.
2. Set up a plan to regularly commit a kind act, e.g., once a day or once a week. Make an effort to vary your activities, allowing some to be spontaneous and some to be planned, in order to keep the actions fresh and energizing and not feel forced or contrived.

CSI 32

Tip
An additional feature to add to this exercise is to count your kindness. Counting kind acts has been the subject of intervention studies. In one study, participants (mostly Japanese women) were asked to keep track of their kindness behaviors toward others each day for 1 week and this led to increases in gratitude, happiness, and happier memories (Otake et al., 2006). In a randomized, placebo-controlled study, the counting kindness intervention increased happiness and decreased depression (Gander et al., 2013).

Troubleshooting
If your frequency of random acts of kindness no longer feels energizing or genuine, then consider taking a break for a week or a month and return to it in the future.

Research
Researchers argue that there is a reciprocal relationship between kindness and happiness (Otake et al., 2006). An important study by Baker and Bulkley (2014) examined the underlying motivation for reciprocity with paying it forward – in order words, do people pay kindness forward because they want to help or because they know others are watching and want to be seen as generous and then be more likely to receive help in the future? Positive emotion or reputation/self-interest? What they found was that paying it forward has stronger and more lasting effects, whereas kindness for self-interest benefitted in the short run but waned over time.

A study with children (aged 9–11 years) discovered that those who performed three acts of kindness per week for 4 weeks showed improved well-being and experienced significant increases in peer acceptance, i.e., popularity (Layous, Nelson, Oberle, Schonert-Reichl, & Lyubomirsky, 2012). In another study, students performed random kind acts for 1.5 hours and experienced a wide range of benefits, including higher positive emotions and lower negative emotions (Pressman et al., 2015). In addition, the majority of students who followed up having received kind acts reported that they would also perform a kind act and almost 40% stated that they already had. Lefevor and Fowers (2016) examined kindness (defined as the VIA trait) and agreeableness (defined as the Big 5 trait) in a "helping" situation and found that only kindness predicted the helping behavior.

Prosocial Spending

Overview
It is interesting to consider how spending money can be a booster for well-being. First and foremost, we spend money on basic necessities such as food, housing, clothing, caregiving for children, and gas for vehicles. Then, there is discretionary money or what some refer to as disposable money, such as money used for purchasing vacations, special events, extra electronic devices, jewelry, and other material possessions. This exercise relates to thinking through optimal strategies for the latter type of income.

Purpose
Kindness (generosity); money management; boosting well-being.

Steps
1. Determine a small amount of discretional money that you would like to spend.
2. Consider a way you can express kindness/generosity to another person and engage in a shared experience.
3. Spend the money on the experience with one or more people, e.g., going to a concert or sporting event together.

CSI 33

Tip
When in doubt about what to spend your money on, purchase experiences rather than possessions (Mann & Gilovich, 2016).

Research
Caprariello and Reis (2013) found across four studies that the inclusion of others was critical to the happiness people experience when they spend money. They found that spending money on shared social experiences was superior to spending money on experiences people have by themselves or spending money on material possessions. Other research has supported these findings, showing that well-being is boosted by spending a small amount of money on someone else, e.g., friend, stranger, charity (Dunn, Aknin, & Norton, 2008, 2014).

Enhance Teamwork Through Role Matching

Overview
Optimal teams can flourish when each team member is contributing from their capacity of energy and strength. To this end, a new model of role behavior on teams has been uncovered with the following seven team roles: idea creator, information gatherer, decision-maker, implementer, influencer, relationship manager, and energizer.

Purpose
Understand your unique role that can contribute to your team; align character strengths use with your team role; facilitate greater energy and productivity at work.

Steps
1. Review the descriptions of the seven roles below. Identify your two strongest roles. Be sure to consider the kinds of things you like doing as you carry out your job and your main function at work or volunteering.
2. Consider how you can more fully deploy your signature strengths to maximize each specific role.
3. How might you offer unique contributions on your team through one or both of these roles?
4. Speak with your supervisor or manager about potentially engaging in some job sculpting. Is there any adjustment to your work that can be done to maximize your use of these two roles?
5. As you work with your team, whenever possible and appropriate, try to focus your energy on your highest two roles.

Research
These seven roles were conceived by Neal Mayerson, chairman of the VIA Institute, as essential functions of a strong team, followed by expert review and feedback. An assessment tool was then created for these roles for the purposes of testing their existence, distinctiveness, and relation to the 24 character strengths (Ruch, Gander, Platt, & Hofmann, 2016). These researchers found these team roles were positively related to job satisfaction and to most of the character strengths. An algorithm was created looking at one's entire character strengths profile in order to predict the most engaging role to the least engaging role based on VIA Survey results. Successful role matching was achieved with the algorithm; however, it is done by examining the totality of one's character strengths profile and is not as simple as matching specific character strengths to specific roles.
- *Idea creator:* enjoys generating ideas to solve problems and facilitate growth. Innovates, reframes, renews, even revolutionizes.
- *Information gatherer:* enjoys learning about best practices, competitors, and information to help one's employer. Shares what is learned at team meetings, in writing/presenting.
- *Decision maker:* energized by analyzing information from various perspectives, weighing evidence, applying logic, and choosing a fruitful course of action.
- *Implementer:* executes decisions. Is the "doer" in the team and may be the one who manufactures, markets, sells, or delivers.
- *Influencer:* optimistic and enthusiastic, relishes the challenge of convincing others. Helps to weather opposition and rejection working to persuade customers, investors, etc.
- *Relationship manager:* helps to build networks of people, resolve team conflicts, and motivates and encourages people. Good listeners with caring hearts and practical advice.
- *Energizer:* infects others with the energy and enthusiasm to persevere. Hums briskly through obstacles, rarely burning out, quarter to quarter and year to year.

Boosting Humility

Overview
Humility is an underappreciated character strength, hence is often referred to as the quiet virtue (Worthington, 2007). But, since the publication of the VIA classification, research has exploded in the field of humility revealing a number of benefits to oneself and others, especially benefits to boosting social relationships in a positive way. Researchers have primed subjects to be humble with success over recent years but this activity offers more detailed exploration strategies for enhancing this "underdog" strength.

Purpose
Boost humility; build other character strengths; improve social relationships.

Steps
Researchers have tested and shown that the PROVE model (an acronym for the first letters of each of the 5 activities below; Lavelock et al., 2014a, 2014b) is effective in boosting humility, among other benefits. This model involves numerous exploration activities at each step (it usually takes 7.5 hours to complete). The steps below come directly from those used by these researchers; however, they have been substantially abbreviated to one activity per step.

CSI 35

1. *Pick a time when you weren't humble.* Describe a specific situation, in detail, in which you were not humble. Consider a 3rd party observer to offer some objectivity to your story and to get some distance on it. Elaborate on the details from the observer's perspective. What is different between the two stories?
2. *Remember the place of your abilities and achievements within the big picture.* Write about a time when you accomplished something. Describe your feelings, thoughts, and actions before, during, and after the accomplishment. Now, consider what you could have done before, during, and after the event to treat it with humility.
3. *Open yourself and be adaptable.* Write about a time when you did something humble in the interest of somebody else. Describe your feelings and actions. How did you feel afterward expressing humility (or after refraining from being prideful/selfish)? Would you describe your actions as "down to earth," level-headed, supportive, wise? How so?
4. *Value all things to lower self-focus.* Make a list of five things that you realize you should value more and describe why. Consider a situation that most people would view as negative. Write about why this situation could still be considered valuable.
5. *Examine your limitations and commit to a humble lifestyle.* Write a letter to yourself, about yourself. Write about your character strengths and write about your limitations and the barriers to your humility. Be as accurate as possible. Review the letter and your insights from the preceding steps and summarize how you will hold on to humility moving forward in your daily life, at times of achievement, and at challenging times.

Research
In a research study that randomly assigned participants to complete a humility workbook (Lavelock et al., 2014a), a longer form of the steps above, or to a control group, only the group that deliberately focused on humility was able to boost this strength, and, in addition, the humility group increased in forgiveness and patience and decreased in general negativity (Lavelock et al., 2014b). The researchers explain that the foundations for the workbook come from multiple sources, most especially from Tangney (2005) and from Peterson and Seligman (2004).

Engaging With Beauty

Overview
Many people go through life with blinders on, missing the details of life. There is a reason why the motto, "stop and smell the roses," is a well-worn phrase. Researchers have begun to examine the different types of beauty that inspire people. Beauty in nature can inspire the emotion of awe, beauty in art and skill can inspire admiration, and the witnessing of beauty in positive acts of human behavior can inspire elevation. Elevation, it turns out, can lead people to be motivated to do something good for others.

Purpose
Boost appreciation of beauty/excellence; improve engagement with the surrounding world.

Steps
Create what researchers refer to as a "beauty log." Identify and describe three aspects of beauty.
1. One time each day look for beauty in one of the following three forms of beauty.
   - Describe something you felt was beautiful that is from nature.
   - Describe something you felt was beautiful that is human-made (e.g., arts and crafts).
   - Describe something you felt was beautiful in human behavior (e.g., acts of goodness).
2. Describe the beauty you witnessed by writing a few sentences about it in a journal.

Research
Diessner and colleagues (2006) found that this intervention when compared with a control group boosted hope and engagement with moral beauty in those that kept the beauty log. Research also shows that daily beauty walks increase awareness of natural beauty (Diessner et al., 2015). Engagement with the third form of beauty noted above, also known as moral beauty, elicits the emotion of elevation, and has been shown to reveal many positive effects especially involving increases in altruism and prosocial behavior (e.g., Algoe & Haidt, 2009; Aquino, McFerran, & Laven, 2011; Cox, 2010; Thomson et al., 2014).

Three Good Things

Overview
This gratitude exercise involves counting one's blessings. People fall prey to habits and routines and can quickly overlook the good things that take place during the day. When we slow down to look at the details of our life, we begin to understand that it is the little things that matter. This exercise invites you to reflect on the little things – small, positive things that occur during the day.

Purpose
Boost gratitude; appreciate the nuances and details of daily interactions; take the "blinders" off to look more closely at life.

Steps
1. At the end of the day, reflect back on what went well.
2. Write down three things that went well and why they went well.
3. Maintain this as a gratitude journal for at least 1 week.

CSI 37

Tip
In order to get the most out of this exercise, commit to never repeating anything you write about in your gratitude journal. Then, if you engage in this activity each day for 1 year you will have well over 1,000 unique expressions of gratitude. That will certainly expand this character strength in you!

Research
This exercise helps people overcome adaptation/habituation and increases the meaning of good acts. In a randomized, double-blind, placebo-controlled study, this exercise led to increases in happiness and decreases in depression for 6 months (Seligman et al., 2005). This exercise was significantly beneficial in boosting happiness in older adults (Proyer, Gander, et al., 2014a), and in supporting health and decreasing negative emotions (Emmons & McCullough, 2003). An important factor with this particular exercise is the voluntary nature of the activity (i.e., participants wanting to do it on their own): One study showed that participants who engaged in the activity for 1 week and continued on their own fared better than those who were instructed to do the activity for 2 weeks (Gander et al., 2013). Another important factor is frequency: People who counted their blessings once a week reported being happier than those who counted their blessings three times a week (Lyubomirsky et al., 2005).

Gratitude Letter/Visit

Overview
The practice of gratitude has emerged as a character strength that can be boosted fairly easily and with several positive benefits. There are many activities surrounding gratitude. This is one of the most commonly discussed, researched, and applied.

Purpose
Boost gratitude; appreciate the contribution others have had on your life; boost a positive relationship.

Steps
1. Think of someone who has had a positive influence on your life and you are grateful to but you have not properly thanked.
2. Write a letter to them describing your feelings and why you are grateful for them.
3. *Optional.* If appropriate and plausible, deliver the letter to the person and consider reading it to them in their presence.

CSI 38

Troubleshooting
This is actually two interventions in one activity and each involves the use of multiple character strengths. The letter-writing activity alone is beneficial. To deliver the letter is another activity that requires bravery and probably many other strengths, such as zest, social intelligence, love, and perspective. Before delivering and reading your gratitude letter to someone, it is important to consider if this is necessary and appropriate for you to do. In addition, be prepared for any kind of reaction. While indeed the delivery and reading of a letter like this can be profoundly beneficial to the recipient, the writer, and the relationship, there is no guarantee that it will be positive. Some people expect nothing but a positive response to their heart-felt words but are left disappointed when they encounter a person who doesn't know how to handle such a novel experience. Discussing the pros and cons of delivering the letter with a trusted confidant or practitioner can be a good preliminary step to delivering it.

Research
In a gold-standard research study of five positive psychology interventions and a placebo group, those participants randomly placed in a group to write a gratitude letter experienced the strongest initial increase in happiness, although the levels of happiness returned to baseline as the study progressed (Seligman et al., 2005). Just like some people take an antianxiety pill when they need a quick dose of calmness (e.g., before going on an airplane), this exercise might be useful for those clients looking for a quick boost in happiness.

One study found that those who wrote a gratitude letter experienced a higher level of humility than those who performed a neutral activity (Kruse, Chancellor, Ruberton, & Lyubomirsky, 2014). Other studies have examined the conditions in which writing gratitude letters can be helpful. In one study, those who wrote gratitude letters each week for 8 weeks had a boost in happiness only if the person had an intrinsic desire to become happier (Lyubomirsky et al., 2011).

Three Funny Things

Overview
Humor is a character strength that is connected with life pleasure and happiness. It is frequently viewed as a lubricant for good social relationships.

Purpose
Boost humor; enhance a social relationship.

Steps
1. At the end of the day, reflect on the funniest things you experienced during the day.
2. Write about three funny things that happened to you during the day. Explain why these funny things occurred and describe your feelings in each instance.
3. Complete this exercise each day for 1 week.

Tip
Be sure to write about the details of each humor incident – the people who were involved, what you said or didn't say, nonverbal expressions, and the environment and circumstances you were in.

CSI 39

Research
In a gold-standard study, this intervention boosted happiness and decreased depression in participants (Gander et al., 2013). The reason for this, it was argued, is that humor boosts amusement which can help buffer negatives states and experiences. A later study found this exercise boosted happiness for 6 months and had a short-term effect on depression (Wellenzohn et al., 2016a). In a group of older adults, this particular exercise led to a reduction in depression (Proyer, Gander, et al., 2014a).

Cultivating Sacred Moments

Overview

Spirituality has been defined by scientists as the search for the sacred (Pargament & Mahoney, 2002). This inclusive definition refers to the many secular and nonsecular ways a person might connect with the transcendent, which might be nature, God, a higher power, all of life, and so on. Although sacred moments often emerge spontaneously, this activity takes the approach of deliberate cultivation of sacred moments. This is an exercise of "mindful strengths use" (Niemiec, 2014a), as mindfulness is directed toward a particular character strength, in this case, the strength of spirituality. Examples of the feeling of connection with the transcendent may be described as awe, elevation, compassion, gratitude, inner peace, amazement, purpose, meaningfulness, interconnection with others, union with God/higher power/nature.

Purpose

Enhance spirituality strength; experience the transcendent in everyday life; sanctify a special object.

Steps

1. Practice mindful breathing for at least 5 minutes per day for 3 days.
2. Choose an object that you can appreciate as precious, dear, blessed, cherished, and/or holy.
3. Spend a minimum of 5 minutes a day (5 days a week for 3 weeks), slowing down and practicing mindful breathing, and then shifting your attention to the sacred object. Be open to what is sacred in the moment.

Troubleshooting

If you have trouble selecting an object to focus on, choose something straightforward such as your wedding ring, necklace, religious icon, or other symbol of a ceremony you completed. Other common examples include small statues or figures, meaningful photographs, mementos from trips, spiritual books, and other jewelry. If you continue to struggle to choose a tangible object, choose a nontangible one, such as a personal mantra, a quotation, or a meaningful memory. Note that the object is meant not as an object of attachment but as a stepping stone for well-being (Goldstein, 2007).

Research

This cultivating sacred moments exercise was created by Goldstein (2007) and found to boost well-being. Researchers have studied sacred moments in the therapist–client psychotherapy relationship and found that 55% of therapists who described an important moment in their work with a client would describe the moment as "sacred;" this, in turn was strongly related to improvements in the therapeutic relationship, perceived client improvement, and work motivation (Pargament, Lomax, McGee, & Fang, 2014). Spiritual meditation using mantas has been found to boost positive mood and spirituality and to lower anxiety compared with a relaxation group and a group that practiced secular mantras (Wachholtz & Pargament, 2005).

Positive Relationships

Introduction

Positive relationships, often viewed as "the royal road to happiness," are emphasized in this section. Character strengths offer a pivotal pathway for creating, enhancing, and recovering positive relationships. Many of the activities in this section are framed toward an intimate, long-term relationship such as a marriage or committed, long-term relationship. But, these exercises are about building positive and healthy relationships, thus can be beneficial for any close relationship, in most cases with minor adjustments.

Contents

CSI 41: Character Strengths Appreciation
CSI 42: Love Letter
CSI 43: Turn Your Strengths Other-Oriented
CSI 44: Mindful Listening and Speaking
CSI 45: Healthy, Fair Fighting
CSI 46: Subtract Then Add
CSI 47: Perspective-Taking
CSI 48: Compliment Review
CSI 49: Positive Reminiscence With Strengths
CSI 50: Counting the Good in Your Relationship

Character Strengths Appreciation

Overview
The "Michelangelo phenomenon" refers to how people in close relationships influence and sculpt each other, bringing one another closer to his or her ideal self (Drigotas, Rusbult, Wieselquist, & Whitton, 1999; Rusbult, Kumashiro, Kubacka, & Finkel, 2009). This is named after the Italian painter/sculptor who famously described sculpting as a process of revealing and uncovering the figure(s) hidden in the stone. This "sculpting" occurs slowly with each interaction of the couple. Aligned with this is the value of couples understanding and appreciating one another's signature strengths, which can be viewed as core elements of the ideal self. This exercise takes a step beyond recognizing another person's strengths, extending this to offering an appreciation for that person's best qualities.

Purpose
Offering insights to others; boosting a positive relationship; signature-strengths-spotting and -appreciating.

Steps
1. Identify three of your partner's best character strengths.
2. Write down a recent admirable incident in which your partner displayed each of these strengths. How were you seeing the strength expressed?
3. Express appreciation. Share with your partner what you wrote, explaining why their character strength use is important to you and valued by you. For example, it may make you feel more emotionally attracted to them, more committed in the relationship, or happier in the relationship with them. Appreciation can also be expressed nonverbally.

Tip
Consider practicing this activity across the domains of your life, such as with your best friend, your teenager, and your work colleague.

Research
The first two steps were originally suggested for couples by Seligman (2002), who echoing the relationship research of John Gottman around fanning the embers of fondness and admiration (Gottman & Silver, 1999), stated that it was his version of his favorite exercise. The third step was added because of the importance of appreciation in close relationships.

The science of appreciation in relationships is gaining momentum revealing numerous benefits to concepts such as savoring and gratitude (Adler & Fagley, 2005; Bao & Lyubomirsky, 2013; Sheldon & Lyubomirsky, 2012). The foundation for this activity is studies by Kashdan and colleagues (2017) that have highlighted the value of character strengths appreciation, finding that those couples who recognized and appreciated one another's character strengths had higher relationship satisfaction, belonging, autonomy, sexual satisfaction, and relationship commitment. This research also found that less relationship satisfaction was associated with those who perceived their partner's strengths use as difficult or draining for the partner or causing problems/conflicts in the relationship. This finding speaks to the potential negative impact of strengths overuse/underuse.

Research on ideal self/real self is also relevant here, such as the work around the Michelangelo phenomenon, which found strong associations between perceived partner affirmation and movement toward the ideal self and the couple's well-being (Drigotas et al., 1999; Rusbult et al., 2009). In addition, correlational research on ideal self and real self also relates here. Researchers found that across cultures (US, Russia, and China) individuals' actual self-concept was closer to their ideal self when their autonomy was supported by their partners (Lynch, La Guardiab, & Ryan, 2009). In other words, it is important to have people in your life who affirm you and encourage you to be your true, best self.

Love Letter

Overview
The character strength of love is an obvious quality that applies in our close relationships; however, it is easy to assume this strength is present and to take it for granted. Finding ways to express warmth, care, deep positive regard, and authentic appreciation to those we love is important for us, the giver, to express, and for the receiver to hear and experience.

Purpose
Boost love; improve mood; boost a positive relationship.

Steps
1. Think about the love you have for your relationship partner.
2. Write a brief love letter to this person. In the letter, tell your loved one about your love for him or her, offering your thoughts, feelings, and examples. Also, consider linking your love to something that happened today or recently.

Tip
This exercise was originally broader than this, inviting people to consider any person that they loved (Lavy et al., 2014a). Consider this activity for other categories of love in addition to romantic love, such as family love, friendship love, parent–child love, and even agape love.

CSI 42

Research
In one study, participants were randomly assigned to this love letter intervention or to one of two control groups. The intervention group who engaged in this activity of strengths deployment experienced an enhancement of their mood the following day (Lavy et al., 2014a). These results emphasize the role of character strengths use in reducing negative affect and these researchers term this a "mood-repair strategy" because of the causal effect of daily strengths use on mood the following day. In another study of couples by these researchers, character strengths endorsement and use were found to contribute to both partners' life satisfaction (Lavy et al., 2014b). They suggest from this research that the lack of opportunity for strengths use can impair the health of a relationship and that therefore the discovery of new ways to use strengths in one's close relationship is of substantial importance.

The writing of love letters to family, friends, and even those whom one is in conflict with is an activity frequently discussed by the prolific mindfulness teacher Thich Nhat Hanh (2001) as a way to promote peace, understanding, and conflict resolution.

Turn Your Strengths Other-Oriented

Overview
A crucial factor in the success of a character strengths activity is matching the activity to the right context. This exercise aims to direct a character strength outward toward others and within the context of one's close, intimate relationship. It involves taking any character strength and conceptualizing it as a pathway that can be used to bring benefit to the relationship.

Purpose
Find new ways to express character strengths; prioritize character strengths over applying skills in a close relationship.

Steps
1. Choose one of your signature strengths.
2. Think about how you can direct this strength toward your relationship partner. How might you clearly express this strength in a way that they would appreciate? How might you understand your partner better or perceive their behaviors more accurately? What benefit might you bring them by using this strength?
3. Undertake an action that will make your strength other-oriented.
4. Repeat the process for a second signature strength.

CSI 43

Research
Researchers have found support for this exercise: If character strengths can be enacted as relationship virtues, there is a positive influence on relationship communication and adjustment (Veldorale-Brogan et al., 2010). Fowers (2000) has suggested that couples should move beyond learning skills (e.g., communication skills), which frequently do not translate into the home life, and instead bring forth character strengths such as generosity, fairness, forgiveness, acceptance, and appreciation.

Example
Some character strengths are automatically other-oriented, such as kindness, fairness, and teamwork, but explicitly working with questions from these "obvious" relationship strengths – how might you view your relationship as a "team"? or how might you deliberately bring kindness to your partner today? – can reveal new insights. Other strengths might be less clear to make other-oriented yet are equally important, for example, curiosity can be used to ask your partner new questions. Social intelligence, which can be tricky to apply, can be used by being on the lookout for your partner's emotions and by responding to their feelings with care and sensitivity.

Mindful Listening and Speaking

Overview

Mindfulness can be applied to any action we take in our daily lives, and one of the more challenging domains for mindfulness is our communication; namely, the practice of mindful speech and mindful listening. Mindful speech means to speak in an honest way that is concise, specific, direct, and from the heart. This involves letting go of speaking in tangents, disclaimers, hurtful comments, and repeating oneself. Mindful listening means to offer full attention to the speaker with genuine kindness/compassion. This involves setting aside the impulse to react or to think of what one wants to say next.

Purpose

Improve mindful communication; connect deeply with a loved one; practice really "seeing" and "hearing" another human being.

Steps

This exercise involves a couple carving out about 15 minutes for this practice. As a preliminary step, the couple is invited to agree on some basic rules: set aside all electronic devices, turn off or move any distractions, sit together in a quiet space where you can be alone together, and refrain from talking when the other person is talking. Flip a coin to determine who speaks first. A time-frame is given in parentheses for each part of this exercise.

CSI 44

1. Person A speaks while Person B listens. Person A practices the principles of mindful speech and shares something from his or her day that happened: some positive, negative, or neutral event; or some new awareness or use of character strengths. Person B practices the principles of mindful listening. (5 minutes)
2. Switch roles. Person B is the mindful speaker and Person A is the mindful listener. (5 minutes)
3. Open-ended practice of mindful communication back-and-forth. During this time, the couple continues the dialogue, practicing mindful speech and mindful listening. This phase more closely simulates typical, real-world interactions, but carries forward the practices from the previous steps. (5 minutes)
4. If desired by both parties, repeat the steps above or conclude for the day.

Research

The steps of this exercise are taken directly from *Mindfulness and Character Strengths*. Mindful speech and mindful listening are practiced each week in the mindfulness-based strengths practice (MBSP) program (Niemiec, 2014a), which has shown to improve well-being (Ivtzan et al., 2016; Niemiec & Lissing, 2016). This mindfulness approach is derived from the work and mindful living principles of Thich Nhat Hanh (1979, 1993, 2009).

Healthy, Fair Fighting

Overview
Conflicts and fights within intimate relationships are inevitable. To maintain a successful relationship, couples can learn different strategies based on how severe the particular problem is in their relationship. In other words, the management of little problems and of big problems seems to require very different approaches. Couples can learn to communicate and solve problems well (what some refer to as "fair fighting").

Purpose
Learn skillful responding rather than habitual reacting in your relationship; improve conflict management; find character strengths balance.

Steps
1. Identify a conflict or problem in your relationship.
2. Determine whether the conflict/problem is minor or major. Ultimately, is the problem trivial, such as your partner forgetting to put the dishes away or watching too much television the previous night, or is the problem serious, such as your partner has been unfaithful to you or has avoided facing their addiction?

3. Use your character strengths to take action that is balanced and appropriate.
   - Minor problem: Use forgiveness to "let go" of the little things. For trivial problems, it can be counterproductive to "fly off the handle," express strong anger, and place blame, especially if done every time.
   - Major problem: Use bravery to be direct and confrontational for the big things. For serious problems, sharing genuine and strong emotion for how the behavior impacted you and to directly confront the person about their behavior can be productive for the relationship.
4. Caveat: This exercise also begs for the use of a metastrength, such as perspective/wisdom and/or social intelligence, because the above formula won't fit every couple's unique situation, relationship history, and problem severity. Not every serious situation will benefit from confrontation, and, at the same time, not every trivial problem should be let go of. The preceding steps should be viewed as a starting point, offering some general advice and strategies to consider applying in your unique situation as appropriate.

Research
This activity is based on correlational research by McNulty and Russell (2010), who conducted two longitudinal studies of newlyweds investigating problem-solving behaviors. They found that the approach the couple used with a particular severity level of a given problem affected relationship satisfaction. Direct approaches predicted higher satisfaction if the problem was major; whereas those same approaches predicted relationship dissatisfaction if the problem was minor. They suggest that couples dealing with minor problems may benefit from *avoiding* direct negative behaviors, whereas couples handling more serious problems may benefit from *using* direct negative behaviors (which they noted with examples such as blaming – "You drink too much," commanding – "You have to stop drinking," and rejection – "You are selfish for drinking too much"). They found that indirect negative behaviors related to less relationship satisfaction, regardless of the severity of the problem. Examples of indirect communication they mention include: avoidance – "I'm not the one who drinks too much," insinuation – "Have you ever heard of drinking in moderation?," and presumption – "You must not love me."

Subtract Then Add

Overview
What would your life be like without one of your best relationships? Hard to imagine, perhaps even painful or unbelievable. Give it a try and then supercharge the activity with an extra dose of appreciation.

Purpose
Boost a positive relationship; deepen gratitude/appreciation; build perspective about a meaningful relationship.

Steps
1. Name an important, positive relationship in your life. This could be an intimate partner, a close friend, your child, or someone else you're close to.
2. Imagine your life without that person in it. Picture this clearly. Notice the impact of what this would be like. How would your life be different? How do you feel?
3. Write a letter to that person describing how important they are to you. What do they mean to you? Why and how are they important to you?
4. Be sure to name and explain their character strengths in the letter.
5. When you finish the letter, reflect back on the character strengths you personally activated.

CSI 46

Research
This activity combines two successful positive interventions. The first part, mental subtraction, has been shown to boost well-being (Ang et al., 2015; Koo et al., 2008), while the second part, the addition of a gratitude letter, was found to give a substantial boost to happiness in the short-run (Seligman et al., 2005).

Perspective-Taking

Overview
Wise interventions are simple interventions that target an underlying psychological issue in a specific context (Walton, 2014). This activity addresses the deeper issue while supporting couples in conflict management. It is referred to as a 7-minute relationship activity.

Purpose
Boost the strength of perspective; improve conflict management; preserve the quality of a close relationship.

Steps
1. Consider a conflict you have in your intimate relationship.
2. Reflect on how a neutral third party "who wants the best for all" would view the conflict in the relationship. Write down these views.
3. Discuss what you wrote about with your relationship partner. Discuss how you and your partner might adopt this perspective in future conflicts. If you each complete this exercise, then compare notes and look for synergies.
4. Discuss the character strengths each of you will need to deploy to take this perspective and to undertake the subsequent action.

CSI 47

Research
Finkel, Slotter, Luchies, Walton, and Gross (2013) studied this intervention, asking couples to take 7 minutes every 4 months (for 1 year) to discuss and plan around what a hypothetical, neutral third party might say to a relationship conflict. This exercise was intended to forestall the vicious circle of negative emotion (i.e., anger) that can occur between couples in conflicts. In their randomized, controlled trial, the control group declined in marital quality (level of love, satisfaction, intimacy, trust, passion), whereas the intervention group stabilized. The character strengths element is added here to offer a pathway for couples to take productive action.

Compliment Review

Overview
The giving and receiving of compliments is an important exchange in relationships. Some relationship partners will experience a stronger benefit from receiving a compliment than others. This is related to the importance of seeing the character strengths in your relationship partner and expressing appreciation for the strengths. There are benefits to character strengths appreciation but who benefits most, to what degree, in what way, and in what situation are underexplored areas.

Purpose
Create a balanced and positive relationship; a tool for those with low confidence or self-esteem; boost strengths appreciation.

Steps
1. Consider a compliment from your romantic partner.
2. Write about why your partner admired you and describe what the compliment meant to you and its significance for your relationship.
3. What specific character strengths was your partner seeing and appreciating in you (even if they didn't use the exact language of the VIA classification at the time)?

CSI 48

Research
Marigold, Holmes, and Ross (2007, 2010) theorized that those with low self-esteem are quick to dismiss compliments as not having meaning. This activity taps into that underlying psychological issue, offering a correction and a simple, positive pathway forward (hence, falling in the category of a wise intervention; Walton, 2014). Marigold and colleagues found that this activity led to an increase in feeling secure in the relationship in the short-run and long-run, which in turn helped to manage the fear of rejection. Participants also reported valuing their relationship more, behaved more positively toward their partners (as reported by the partners), and viewed the partner as behaving more positively.

In a study with dating couples, those with low self-esteem benefited from the spotting of new strengths in themselves or the spotting of faults in their partner. This increased their feelings of security in regard to their perception of their partner's commitment and positive regard as well as increased positive general feelings of their own worth (Murray et al., 2005).

There is also emerging research on the benefits to relationship satisfaction, sexual satisfaction, relationship commitment, and the meeting of psychological needs for those couples who recognize and appreciate the character strengths of one another (Kashdan et al., 2017). In addition, couples who endorse character strengths and deploy them in their relationship have higher relationship satisfaction (Lavy et al., 2014b).

Positive Reminiscence With Strengths

Overview
The science and practice of savoring is an important area within positive psychology. Savoring means to deliberately prolong the positive. You might be experiencing a positive emotion or a character strength and you take action to keep the emotion or strength present and strong. This exercise is one of many to develop savoring.

Purpose
Apply savoring to a close relationship; enhance positive memories.

Steps
1. Bring one positive relationship to mind. This can be a previous or current relationship. Choose someone that you are or were close to.
2. Allow yourself to reexperience pleasant memories you had with the person. Image clearly the memories and positive stories that involve the person.
3. Use your character strengths to intensify the memories, for example, using curiosity to explore, creativity to consider the positive memory from different perspectives, and love and gratitude to experience positive emotions in the moment.
4. Journal about your experience and thoughts on these questions:
   - What stood out most to you in your positive reminiscence?
   - What is it like to *savor* a relationship?
   - What are the elements that made the relationship strong?
   - How did you feel in the relationship?
   - What did the person see in you? (try to use character strengths in your description)
   - What character strengths did you see in them?

Research
The scientific support for savoring is outlined in the seminal book on the topic by Bryant and Veroff (2007). Savoring interventions can focus on the past (reminiscence), the present, and the future (anticipation). This particular exercise, focusing on the past, has revealed higher levels of well-being for those who savored compared with those who did not savor (Bryant et al., 2005). Also, Pinquart and Forstmeier (2012) showed that prompts can be used to catalyze positive reminiscence.

Counting the Good in Your Relationship

Overview
Little things matter. It is easy to repeat this adage but much harder to follow, especially when it comes to our close relationships.

Purpose
Build a positive relationship; boost gratitude for another person.

Steps
1. Observe and take note of the positive things that your partner does for you or others.
2. For 1 week, at the end of each day, write down (at least) one good thing your partner did that day. Write about the following:
   - Describe what they did.
   - What character strengths were they using? How did they express them?
   - How did your partner's action impact you or others?
3. Track these good things each day for 1 week.

Research
This exercise is a variation of the gratitude exercise called counting blessings, which has been shown to increase happiness and decrease depression (Gander et al., 2013; Seligman et al., 2005). Counting blessings has been shown to benefit well-being across different studies and in various populations, ranging from medical to psychiatric problems (Emmons & McCullough, 2003; Froh, Sefick, & Emmons, 2008; Huffman et al., 2014).

CSI 50

Resilience (Problem Management)

Introduction

The exercises in this section are captured well by the words of Helen Keller who observed, "When one door of happiness closes, another opens; but often we look so long at the closed door that we do not see the one which has been opened for us." Every client, whether a student, employee, coachee, or patient, has problems and life challenges. Often, it never occurs to clients to strategically involve their character strengths in seeking resolution or healing. Yet, research is showing that character strengths play an important role as coping strategies for stress (Gustems-Carnicer & Calderón, 2016; Harzer & Ruch, 2015). This section offers CSIs to help people manage problems and conflicts in life. Common exercises that seamlessly integrate strengths involve reframing challenges, finding benefit in struggles, perspective-taking, seeing the common humanity in others, and using character strengths to find balance.

Contents

CSI 51: Believing Change Is Possible
CSI 52: Resource Priming
CSI 53: Benefit-Finding With Strengths
CSI 54: Open Your Character Strength Doors
CSI 55: Positive Reappraisal With Strengths
CSI 56: Helping or Harming?
CSI 57: Overcome Stress With Humor
CSI 58: Managing Character Strengths Overuse
CSI 59: Managing Your Strength Hot Buttons

Believing Change Is Possible

Overview
Viewing our personality as fixed and unchanging can be a damaging vantage point in many ways. It tells us we are stuck with our traits, good or bad, and are destined to repeat the past. Research is now revealing that such views are not reality and that people can not only decide to change their personality traits and be successful doing it (Hudson & Fraley, 2015; Roberts et al., 2017), but that they can also develop a growth mindset in regard to their perceptions about the malleability of change for themselves and others (Dweck, 2006).

Purpose
Boost growth mindset and counteract fixed mindset; understand the changeable nature within you and others.

Steps
1. Consider a situation in which you felt excluded or felt like a "victim."
2. Consider the following insights from social science and neuroscience: People have the potential to change. Understand that feeling excluded or victimized is not a fixed, personal deficiency in you. Also, understand that those who are doing the excluding or victimizing are not fixed, bad people unable to change but instead have complicated motivations and are subject to change. Recent neuroscience studies reveal that pathways in the brain that handle negative behaviors can be changed.
3. Write a personal narrative that offers an example (past, present, or potential future) that draws from these insights. Consider your character strengths as you write this narrative.

CSI 51

Research
This activity comes from Yeager, Johnson, and colleagues (2014), who used it in a study of adolescents experiencing the challenging transition to high school where social adversity often heightens. The researchers tested this one-time, brief intervention that also included a brief article on the neuroscience and examples from upper grade-level students applying the insights. This intervention is supported by *incremental theory*, which views people as being malleable, growing and changeable and is based on the work of Carol Dweck (2006) on fixed and growth mindsets. The students in the study showed less negative reactions to an immediate experience of social adversity and, 8 months later, reported lower overall stress and physical illness, and better academic performance over the year (Yeager et al., 2014). These researchers also tested the *entity theory* of personality, which views people as fixed and unchanging, and found that this type of fixed mindset predicted more negative immediate reactions to social adversity and greater stress, poorer health, and lower grades at the end of the school year.

   This activity is a "wise intervention" (Walton, 2014) as the researchers used a targeted, simple intervention for a particular context and timed it to assist individuals psychologically when they needed it most (Yeager et al., 2014). This intervention can be viewed as a "saying is believing" activity because it enhances the internalizing of key insights and practices a form of self-persuasion, which has been found to be superior for helping people change their attitudes or behavior compared to direct forms of persuasion such as direct marketing and political speeches (Aronson, 1999).

Resource Priming

Overview
Preparation is crucial to success. Benjamin Franklin once said "by failing to prepare, you are preparing to fail." Resource priming is a systematic way that practitioners prepare for a meeting with a client, student, or employee by thinking about their strengths. This activity here offers resource priming as a valuable preparation approach for anyone to use in approaching a stressful situation or upcoming life issue.

Purpose
Boost preparation; activate internal resources; enhance the likelihood of success in the immediate future.

Steps
1. Consider an upcoming stressor that you will need to attend to or handle directly.
2. Think about your five best character strengths. Think about how much you have used them in the past and how they are an important part of you.
3. Draw connections between your character strengths and the stressful situation. Hypothesize ways you might use each strength in the situation.
4. Take action with your strengths in the situation.

Troubleshooting
Don't worry about giving yourself excessive praise. In a study of resource priming of therapists, only 6 minutes of 6,247 minutes were rated by trained observers as excessive praise, even when trained therapists were instructed to maximize strengths activation (Fluckiger et al., 2010).

Tips
Researchers in resource priming offer several examples of boosting strengths activation that are adapted to optimize this exercise (Fluckiger et al., 2010).
- Use a worksheet to write down and track your concerns or needs in regard to the upcoming situation; consider how your character strengths can be used to address each.
- Consider your best strengths, your motivating strengths, and your unused strengths.
- Consider the character strengths of those in your social network that might support you.

Research
Among psychotherapists who practiced resource priming before a meeting with a client, there were observable improvements by both therapist ratings and independent observers' ratings; strengths activation, attachment and mastery experiences for the client, and improved therapy outcomes were found (Fluckiger & Grosse Holtforth, 2008). This strengths-activating approach reinforces positive expectations for change and helps clients use strengths as a catalyst for change (Fluckiger et al., 2009). They argue that there should be an integration of a capitalization model (which highlights strengths) and a compensation model (which remediates weaknesses), explaining that "Focusing on activated strengths (resource activation) can initiate and maintain positive feedback circuits that foster the therapeutic alliance and increase patients' receptiveness" (Fluckiger et al., 2009, p. 213). This relates to another stream of research finding that values affirmation (in many cases, these are character strengths affirmations) prior to a stressor buffered neuroendocrine and stress responses (Creswell et al., 2005).

CSI 52

Benefit-Finding With Strengths

Overview
At first glance, it might seem counterintuitive to spend time focusing on the positive of having a problem or seeing the benefits of a personal affront from another person to you. However, researchers are seeing positive effects from this type of approach.

Purpose
Enhance self-growth from a difficult experience; widen perspective; become unstuck from all-or-none thinking.

Steps
1. Consider a situation in which someone offended you.
2. Focus on the personal benefits that resulted from this experience.
3. Spend about 20 minutes writing about these benefits that you gained.
   - What were the positive aspects of the experience?
   - What character strengths did this catalyze in you?
   - What have you learned as a result? How has this contributed to your growth in some way?
   - How might the experience help you face similar challenges in the future?
   - What character strengths will you call forth as you face similar situations in your future?

Tip
This exercise of using strengths with a problem can also be applied to the successful resolution of past problems. This involves the individual thinking of any problem or conflict they have successfully resolved and then naming the character strengths they used to resolve it. This approach involves finding benefit in past character strengths use that was likely forgotten about, unnoticed, or underappreciated, yet builds internal resources that can be capitalized upon for use in the present or future.

CSI 53

Research
McCullough and colleagues (2006) studied this exercise with people who experienced a conflict or offense from others (i.e., interpersonal transgression). They randomly assigned participants to the activity above, to a group that focused on the traumatic features of the offense they experienced, or to a control group. The researchers found that the group that focused on benefit-finding became more forgiving than the other two groups. Increases in benefit-finding and character strengths predicted positive changes in life satisfaction over time for children with a life-threatening illness (Chaves, Hervás, García, & Vázquez, 2016). Many studies have found there are gains for people that engage in benefit-finding on both a physical and psychological level (Bower, Low, Moskowitz, Sepah, & Epel, 2008); however, it is not always the case (e.g., see a study of women with breast cancer by Tomich and Helgeson, 2004). In order for benefit-finding to be a "wise intervention" (Walton, 2014), the timing must be right for the situation and context and the optimal underlying psychological components must be addressed.

Open Your Character Strength Doors

Overview
It is easy to view a hardship or life challenge as a door that has been shut in your face with no doorknob to open it. Maybe that door will eventually be opened, maybe not. This activity challenges us to look elsewhere – to look for other doors that can be opened or new doorknobs to be discovered or created – finding opportunities, catalyzing growth, and embracing new insights.

Purpose
Boost hope, practice reframing; manage a problem or overcome a hardship; develop perspective; find benefit in stress.

Steps
1. Write about a recent time in which you experienced a negative event.
2. Write about the positive consequences, not immediately apparent, that resulted from this event.
3. Write down and explain the character strengths that were catalyzed as a result of this event.

Tip
To take full advantage of the benefits of this exercise, do this activity each day for 1 week. This means reflecting on seven negative events in your life and the positive consequences and character strengths deployment with each.

CSI 54

Research
This activity was originally used in positive psychotherapy as championed by Tayyab Rashid (2015). Positive psychotherapy, as a 14-week program, has been shown to be beneficial in lowering depression in both individual and group psychotherapy compared to treatment as usual and a control group, respectively (Seligman et al., 2006). Several additional studies reveal positive effects (see Rashid, 2015, for a review). This intervention, one door opens another door closes, was separated out from positive psychotherapy, and as a stand-alone activity it boosted happiness and decreased depression (Gander et al., 2013).

Example
One client spoke of a negative event of getting diagnosed with breast cancer and then having to undergo chemotherapy and radiation. When I asked her to examine the other doors that had been opened as a result, she immediately had a lot to say. She spoke of her realization that she was braver than she realized, as she directly faced the grueling medication regimen. Teamwork was another strength-door that was opened as she consciously collaborated with many doctors, nurses, and medical staff to maintain an optimal lifestyle during the treatment. She experienced greater levels of her strength of love – opening herself more to experiencing the love offered by her family and friends, which was previously difficult for her to do. Many times, while lying down in her bed, she practiced gratitude. It became a daily ritual for her (that she continued posttreatment). She was grateful that she was making medical progress, grateful to have another chance at living fully, grateful for her relationship support, grateful for the caring medical staff (even though not every staff-person was outright compassionate, some were), and grateful for the little things such as a flower by her bedside, a bird flying by her window, and the warmth of a cup of soup.

Positive Reappraisal With Strengths

Overview
After you have been hurt or offended by someone else's actions, there is positive action you can take.

Purpose
Boost forgiveness; boost compassion; improve perspective-taking; generate a growth mindset; see the potential for change in others (malleability).

Steps
1. Bring the person that offended you and their offense to mind.
2. Write about the following: What character strengths did you show during the offense? What character strengths are you showing right now? What insights have you gained from this offense?
3. Practice seeing the complex humanity of the person. View them as a human being who has both imperfections/flaws and character strengths. What character strengths do you see in the person, however small? View them as someone who is in need of experiencing positive growth and transformation.

Tip
This activity merges two beneficial interventions in the context of an interpersonal offense. The first (Steps 1 and 3) is called compassion-focused reappraisal; Step 2 is a benefit-finding activity. You might find it useful to engage in one activity or the other, as each brings forth unique ways of viewing/managing the problem at hand and offers similar but also different benefits.

CSI 55

Troubleshooting
It is wise to practice this exercise first with small interpersonal offenses such as feeling snubbed by a friend or getting cut off in traffic. This will help you understand the exercise and its benefits and perhaps lead you to ways of making this exercise work for you personally, such as journaling the activity or discussing it with others.

Research
Positive reappraisal is a type of meaning-based coping that helps individuals reframe a stressful situation, event, or perception of a person as benign, valuable, or beneficial, offering more balance to one's perceptions. It has been found to be a substantial coping strategy even for those in very difficult circumstances (Folkman, 1997). Compassion-focused reappraisal offers a particular way of interpreting offenses, which has shown to lead to greater forgiveness, empathy, smiling, happiness, positive emotion, and positive social language, less negative emotion, and diminished physiological activity such as tension under the eye and slower heart beats (Witvliet et al., 2010, 2011). Part of the reason this exercise is beneficial is it helps people see others as complex individuals rather than in all-or-nothing terms (e.g., "that person is a liar and a bad person"). The other intervention, Step 2, is a benefit-focused reappraisal. This was found to boost gratitude and benefit-oriented language (Witvliet et al., 2010).

Helping or Harming?

Overview
Our thoughts and behaviors, however subtle, can be a friend or foe to us. Our thoughts can weigh us down, spiral us into the negative, and be a form of interior abuse. Our behaviors, even the innocent glass of wine, the reconnection with an ex, or the taking on of "one more" work project, can also lead to negative consequences. However, these are not guaranteed to be harmful as in some cases those behaviors might help us, and, in some cases, the negative thought gives us a new insight or idea. Similarly, our character strengths can nourish us or take us down the wrong path. This technique offers a way to navigate our strengths so we can manage them and make the most of them in any given moment.

Purpose
Self-care; taking healthy action; avoiding unhealthy behaviors; useful when feeling lost in worry or upset.

Steps
1. Notice a character strength you are using right now or are considering using in the near future.
2. Ask yourself: Is this character strength helping or harming me right now? Or, if I use this character strength, is it likely to help or harm me?
3. Pause; take a couple deep breaths as you reflect on your honest answer.
4. If the strength will help nourish you, then take action accordingly. If you determine it will hurt you or might harm you in some way, then consider a different course of action or the use of a different character strength.

CSI 56

Tip
This technique can be particularly helpful in evaluating potential strengths use in an upcoming conflict. Many people find it helpful in finding balance when in the midst of deep suffering.

Research
This technique is used in psychotherapies such as cognitive-behavior therapy and rational-emotive behavior therapy as a technique for managing troublesome thought patterns and worries (e.g., Reivich & Shatté, 2003). In addition, it has been used specifically in the context of resilience, as exemplified in the research and practice of Lucy Hone (2017) who discusses this as an essential strategy in relation to grief work, for example: Is this behavior helping me or harming me in my daily functioning? And when making decisions: Will that potential course of action help or harm me? This approach has also been used in resilience training of the US Army in which soldiers are challenged to examine their thought patterns and to decide if these are helping or hindering their resilience (Reivich, Seligman, & McBride, 2011).

Examples
"My kindness to others is hurting me because I'm focusing all my attention on helping others and not enough on taking care of myself." "My love of learning is helping me right now because I am exploring topics on the Internet and this is making me feel energized before I go to work." "My bravery is likely to harm me at the party I'm about to go to because I'll probably confront my co-worker there and that might lead to a spectacle; therefore, I'll use my social intelligence to attend to other people at the party."

Overcome Stress With Humor

Overview
Humor is a character strength that we all have the capacity to express, even if it is not particularly high in your character strengths profile. It involves being playful, finding humor in serious or challenging situations, smiling and laughing, finding ambiguity in the ironic or absurd, and so forth. This activity allows you to use and express humor in your thinking.

Purpose
Develop humor; use a specific character strength to manage stress.

Steps
1. Think about one minor stressful experience from your day.
2. Consider how the stressor was, or could have been, solved in a humorous way.
3. Evaluate your strategy for its potential future use. But, don't let your social intelligence or kindness fall too far astray!

Tip
The crux of this exercise is not to see problems as trivial but instead to examine the problem through a different lens. Consider the wisdom of comedians who regularly make light of the darkness, and often it is their own darkness they are making light of.

Troubleshooting
For those that feel awkward doing this activity, remember that the core of humor is playfulness. And, for those who feel they have lost their sense of humor upon entering the serious world of adulthood, the rediscovery of a playful attitude is a key element for change. Researchers have noted five different facets to playfulness (see Proyer & Ruch, 2011). How might you express any of these parts of yourself more?

- *Spontaneous.* Are you ever impulsive, adventurous, carefree, or free-spirited?
- *Expressive.* Are you ever animated and emotional, bouncy and open, or feel as if you are manifesting joy?
- *Creative.* Are you ever actively imaginative and original?
- *Fun.* Are you ever excitable and playful (the opposite of dull)?
- *Silly.* Are you ever childlike and whimsical?

CSI 57

Research
This exercise, referred to as "solving stressful situations in a humorous way," showed short-term benefits in a randomized, placebo control study of various humor interventions, including an increase in happiness and a decrease in depression (Wellenzohn et al., 2016a).

Managing Character Strengths Overuse

Overview
Each of our 24 character strengths can be plotted on a continuum of overuse and underuse in the extremes and optimal use in the center, where there's a context-based strengths zone (Niemiec, 2013, 2014a). This concept builds from Aristotle (4th BCE/2000), who described virtues as residing between two opposites, and was expanded upon by Peterson (2006a) in considering psychopathology, and reiterated by additional strengths researchers (Biswas-Diener et al., 2011; Linley, 2008; Rashid, 2015). Character strengths overuse occurs when the intensity of the strengths does not match the situation where it is being expressed. This references both degree/intensity of the expression and context (i.e., the individuals who are involved and the specifics of the situation). Overuse of strengths can be rebalanced into the strengths zone of a situation with the support of awareness, exploration, and practice.

Purpose
Enhance awareness of strengths overuse; self-empower to manage overuse.

Steps
1. *The situation.* Describe in writing a situation in which you overused a character strength. What was the situation or circumstance you were in? What were the consequences for you or others?
2. *Examine the overuse.* As you reflect on the strength overuse, were you aware of this at the time? What were your thoughts and feelings during the overuse? How would others describe your strength overuse?
3. *Examine past success.* Describe a situation in which you used this particular character strength in a way that was beneficial to yourself and others. What benefits did it bring? What were your thoughts, feelings, and actions as you used this strength at the time?
4. *Discrepancy.* What are the differences in your observations between your strengths overuse in this particular situation and your previous success with the strength (#3)? What adjustments might you make accordingly?
5. *The balancer.* How might you use one or more of your signature strengths to temper or balance the overused strength in this situation? How might you use one of your nonsignature strengths to support you in managing the overused strength?

Research
The existence of character strengths overuse has been shown to be linked with significantly lower flourishing and life satisfaction and higher depression (Freidlin et al., 2017). This overuse can negatively affect relationships and life in general in many ways (Grant & Schwartz, 2011). Although an assessment of character strengths overuse, underuse, and optimal use has been created (see Freidlin et al., 2017), interventions are only beginning to be developed. The mindfulness-based strengths practice (MBSP) program is the first to emphasize practical strategies for character strengths overuse and underuse through the practice of mindful strengths use (Niemiec, 2014a).

CSI 58

Managing Your Strength Hot Buttons

Overview
Our character strengths can act as "hot buttons" – as sensitive areas – for us in our inter-actions with others. When we get fired up by something someone says or does, it is often enlightening to pause and ask ourselves: Which of my character strengths is being triggered or affronted right now? Each individual's experience of hot buttons is unique and may get triggered because they perceive someone is overusing or underusing a particular character strength, and the individual getting triggered may or may not be high on that particular strength.

Purpose
Enhance awareness of a triggering situation; frame problems with strengths language; de-velop insights and positive action simultaneously.

Steps
1. Name a topic or situation that comes up in one of your relationships or in your life in gen-eral that triggers you – something that takes you off balance or upsets you.
2. What character strength is being triggered in you? Why?
3. Now that you've built some new insight into this hot button issue, consider the following: What might you do different next time? What character strengths could you use to tem-per what was triggered?
4. *Optional.* To dig a bit deeper, consider this: Is there a "strengths collision" at play? In other words, are there two strengths wanting to be expressed and are competing against one another? Explain.
5. *Optional.* Is there a "strengths synergy" you might bring forth? In other words, might you focus on two strengths that can work together strongly to balance the situation?

CSI 59

Research
It is an accepted phenomenon that people get triggered by other people and in particular situations – anger, sadness, and anxiety are common emotions that get triggered. What is less explored is the character strengths contribution to these triggering situations. In my on-line courses, educational programming, and live workshops, the topic of character strengths as hot buttons has been one of the more provocative and popular topics. Research is needed on this intervention to understand the nature, operationalization, and correlates of hot but-tons, as well as benefits and mechanisms of action for this intervention. While the phrase was not used, the hot button of fairness appeared to be at play in outlining the construct of civil courage, which, in a research review, was defined as brave behavior accompanied by anger and indignation that has the intention of enforcing social and ethical norms (Greite-meyer, Osswald, Fischer, & Frey, 2007). From a strengths perspective, those engaging in civil courage are taking action because their hot button of fairness has been affronted and they desire greater fairness for a particular group, which they do not perceive as existing in society.

Example
Martha gets upset when her husband teases her. She views this as an affront to her hot button of kindness, perceiving that he is overusing his humor and underusing his kindness, love, and social intelligence toward her. Upon reflection, she sees the important role of her perspective strength in this situation, admitting that her husband is not trying to hurt her emotionally and that he is merely using one of his signature strengths. She decides to use curiosity to ask him one question whenever he makes a joke and to use perspective to keep her wider view of his signature strength in mind.

Goal-Setting/Achievement

Introduction

The research is clear that people benefit from setting goals and striving to reach them. This is closely related to positive accomplishment, a central pathway toward well-being. Moreover, research in personality is showing that traits are useful for helping us accomplish our goals (McCabe & Fleeson, 2016). This section offers character strengths integration into goal-setting and achievement.

Contents

CSI 60: Goal-Setting With Character Strengths
CSI 61: Hope for Your Goals
CSI 62: Mental Contrasting
CSI 63: Implementation Intentions
CSI 64: Best Possible Self

Goal-Setting With Character Strengths

Overview

Character strengths can serve as *the means or the ends* in goal-setting. In other words, you might have a goal to improve your prudence or to boost your bravery at work; this is what is meant by "ends" – the end-point for the goal (even though working on character strengths is a life-long journey!). And, character strengths can, or better stated, *should*, be the means to reaching any goal. This is where character strengths are the pathways to reaching the goal.

Some character strengths in particular are inherently linked with goal-setting, especially hope, prudence, and perseverance. Consider this as a way to remember these crucial character strengths for goal-setting: *Hope* helps you envision the goal, *prudence* helps you plan the goal, and *perseverance* helps you carry the goal out.

The widely used acronym SMART applies to the setting of goals in a strategic way that has some basis in evidence. However, this acronym has experienced some "drift" in that each letter has taken on numerous synonyms and alternate meanings. Rubin (2002) found that the most common representation for SMART goals are that they are: specific, measurable, attainable, relevant, and time-bound.

Purpose

Improve goal-setting skills; boost well-being; make progress on goals; integrate character strengths seamlessly with goals; establish a framework for future goal-setting.

Steps

1. *Envision one goal that you would like to attain.* Use your *hope* strength to envision something that links with your interests and values (referred to as a self-concordant goal).
2. *Make the goal SMART.* Using this acronym, check to frame your goal to be specific, measurable, attainable, relevant, and time-bound. Use your *prudence* strength to plan it out thoroughly across these five elements.
3. *Weave in character strengths seamlessly.* How will your *signature strengths* serve as a means to help you reach your goal? Might other character strengths support you as pathways to your goal as well?
4. *Begin to take action toward your goal.* How will your *perseverance* strength support you in overcoming obstacles and staying focused on your goal ahead?
5. *Enlist support.* Might you include the help of family and friends to maintain your goal progress? This could involve deploying your strengths of *teamwork, curiosity*, and *love*.

CSI 60

Research

Researchers have found that signature strengths use is connected with well-being and that one of the explanations for this is that signature strengths help us make progress on personally relevant goals (Linley et al., 2010). Caroline Adams Miller has written extensively on evidence-based practices for goal-setting and argues that character strengths use is integral to the process (Miller & Frisch, 2009).

Goal pursuit and progress has been linked with a range of well-being outcomes (e.g., Sheldon & Elliot, 1999; Sheldon & Houser-Marko, 2001). The pursuit of self-concordant goals (those that are consistent with the individual's developing interests and values) is linked with more sustained effort in achieving those goals and thus there is an increased likelihood of attaining those goals. The attainment of self-concordant goals leads to greater well-being than does attainment of goals that are not self-concordant (Sheldon & Kasser, 1998).

Hope for Your Goals

Overview
Hope and goals go together like hand and glove as both are directed to the future. Hope is a character strength that revolves around being future-minded and having positive expectations about the future, while goals are what we strive toward in the future. Both hope and goals come from action taken in the present.

Purpose
Set your goals; reach your goals; build your strength of hope.

Steps
Building hope around goals is a three-step process of learnable skills (Lopez, 2014; Snyder, 2000):
1. *Goal*. Identify an idea of who you want to be, what you want to accomplish, and/or where you want to go in the short-term or long-term.
2. *Agency*. Build in thoughts that you can take responsibility for moving toward your goals, that you have the character strengths within you to motivate yourself.
3. *Pathways*. Create several routes to achieving your goal. Consider your character-strengths-oriented plans for navigating around the obstacles that can emerge at any time.

Research
The three elements of hope noted here are based on extensive research from scientist and thought-leader Rick Snyder (2000) and continued by Shane Lopez (2014), who argued that hope is built from the goals that are most important to us. Related is the approach of hope therapy, which builds from this model by emphasizing goal-pursuit skills – setting clear approach goals, producing pathways to attain them, and summoning the mental energy to maintain goal pursuit – over an eight-session program. A randomized trial found that hope therapy boosted agency, meaning, and self-esteem while lowering depression and anxiety, compared to a waitlist control group (Cheavens, Feldman, Gum, Michael, & Snyder, 2006).

CSI 61

Mental Contrasting

Overview
Turning behavior changes into good habits involves a number of important factors, including motivation, willpower, character strengths use, and simply good planning. Two exercises that have been successful individually but especially strong when they are combined are mental contrasting (MC) and implementation intentions (II) (together MCII). These are two distinct motivational techniques that have helped countless people improve their commitment to their goals and to find success with their new habits, from eating better to exercising more.

Purpose
Increase success with setting and reaching goals; make goals around your strengths.

Steps
1. Identify an important "behavior change" wish that you expect you can accomplish (e.g., use my top signature strength of kindness more at work with my colleagues).
2. Identify and imagine the most positive outcome of successfully changing your behavior (e.g., greater social connections at work).
3. Identify and imagine the most critical obstacle that stands in the way of fulfilling your wish (e.g., forgetting to take action each day).

Tip
Where possible, look for positive feedback from others as positive feedback about creative performance (whether genuine or not) has been shown to turn MC into improved performance (Oettingen, Marquardt, & Gollwitzer, 2012). In addition, individuals might add a fourth step that considers how they might use their character strengths to overcome the critical obstacle that stands in their way to fulfilling their wish.

Research

CSI 62

These three steps come directly from researchers who report that this particular sequence of steps is important for success (Stadler, Oettingen, & Gollwitzer, 2010). These three steps of MC boost goal commitment and success whereas any step alone does not lead to successful goal commitment and performance. MC appears to be particularly effective at increasing clarity about critical cues for unhealthy snacks (Adriaanse et al., 2010) and has been found to enhance not only the belief in the value of exercise but increase the actual rate of physical activity (Sheeran, Harris, Vaughan, Oettingen, & Gollwitzer, 2013).

Researchers have found that the combination of MC and II is a particularly successful combination. For example, Adriaanse et al. (2010) found that participants in MCII decreased unhealthy snacking habits compared to a group that thought about and listed healthy snacks. Moreover, their second study revealed that MCII was superior to MC and to II alone. In another study, MCII reduced meat consumption compared to an information-only control group (Loy, Wieber, Gollwitzer, & Oettingen, 2016), boosted consumption of fruits and vegetables compared to an information-only control group (Stadler et al., 2010), and MCII has been found to be a beneficial tool for other purposes, such as substantially improving time management across different populations (Oettingen, Kappes, Guttenberg, & Gollwitzer, 2015).

Implementation Intentions

Overview
Implementation intentions are the details that help you plan for a desired goal: when, where, and how you want to take action. They involve "if-then" plans that spell out in advance how you will strive toward the goal you set. For the if-component, a critical cue is selected (e.g., a likely obstacle to the goal or a good opportunity), and the then-component is the response to the cue (Gollwitzer & Oettingen, 2013). Using the terminology from the popular stages of change model (Prochaska & DiClemente, 1982), this exercise is particularly helpful for people in the preparation, action, or maintenance phases of behavior change.

Purpose
Increase success with reaching and maintaining goals; troubleshoot obstacles in goal-setting; improve health and strength behaviors.

Steps
1. *Goal details.* Name your desired goal clearly. Think about the details of the goal and the pathways of getting there. Be sure to consider *when* you want to take action, *where* you will take action, and *how* you want to take action.
2. *Obstacles and opportunities.* Try to anticipate all critical situations. What are the obstacles that might be in your way? What are the opportunities that might arise?
3. *Design the "if".* This can be internal (a feeling, a worry) or external (a person, situation, location, time, object). Be sure to consider your specific obstacles *and* opportunities!
4. *Design the "then."* This is the response you will make if the "if" happens (positive or negative).

Tip
Be specific and consider any goal! Implementation intentions teach us to turn our vague character strengths goals into real action. Instead of saying: "I want to use my curiosity more," use an if-then approach to say, "If it's 8 a.m. on a weekday, then I will turn my computer on to explore a new site." Instead of saying: "I don't want to underuse self-regulation with my child when they act out," use an "if-then" approach to say, "If I start feeling angry at my child, then I will self-regulate by taking 5 mindful breaths."

Research
Hudson and Fraley (2015) found that implementation intentions catalyzed people's ability to make desired changes to their personality traits, as exemplified in this exercise. Implementation intentions increase the rate of goal attainment and habit change by enhancing awareness of situational cues and empowering control and action that can be taken in an automatic way (Gollwitzer & Oettingen, 2013). Dalton and Spiller (2012) conducted a study in which participants had a to-do list of virtuous activities to complete over 5 days, where some had one activity and others had six activities to complete. The implementation intentions and plans were particularly helpful for having one goal but not for six goals.

Example
A client with a goal to boost their creativity detailed out the following: If I feel upset by someone rejecting my use of creativity (obstacle), then I will remind myself that it's good that I'm authentically expressing myself. If I feel like I'm bragging when I tell people about my creativity (obstacle), then I will smile and ask them a question about their strengths. If I hear of a new project my boss is working on (opportunity), then I will ask them if I can help contribute to it.

Best Possible Self

Overview
Looking to the future is an important pathway to setting goals that are personally meaning-ful. It can provide perspective on where you would like to direct your life. Linking character strengths with this imagined future is a crucial and empowering addition.

Purpose
Link character strengths with life goals, create pathways to a positive future.

Steps
1. Take a few minutes to select a future time period (e.g., 6 months, 1 year, 5 years from now) and imagine that at that time you are expressing your best possible self. Visualize your best possible self in a way that is pleasing to you and that you are interested in. Imagine the details closely. You might think of this as reaching your full potential, hitting an impor-tant milestone, or realizing one of your life dreams. Reach high *and* be realistic.
2. After you have a fairly clear image, write about the details. Writing your best possible self down helps to create a logical structure for the future and can help you move from the realm of foggy ideas and fragmented thoughts to concrete, real possibilities.
3. Write about the character strengths you observe in this image and in what you've written. And, what character strengths will you need to deploy to make this vision a reality?
4. Write down your specific goal(s) and action plan that result from this exercise.

Tips
Think of this exercise as having two basic steps: a visualization component and a character strengths component. After you visualize your future moment in time, be sure to closely con-sider your character strengths pathways. Also, consider narrowing the focus of "your best possible self" to a domain of life, such as relationships or work (e.g., as in Huffman et al., 2014). The exercise then becomes "your best possible self in a relationship." Many people ap-preciate this narrower focus.

CSI 64

Research
This exercise has been shown to boost people's positive emotions, happiness levels, opti-mism, hope, coping skills, and positive expectations about the future. (Austenfeld, Paolo, & Stanton, 2006; Austenfeld & Stanton, 2008; King, 2001; Meevissen et al., 2011; Peters et al., 2010; Shapira & Mongrain, 2010).

Example (shortened)
I can envision starting a family and we are spending quality time together vacationing and going to activities together in the city. I will need to use my *prudence* strength to map out my long-term finances, my *perseverance* strength as my spouse and I "keep trying" to have chil-dren, and my *forgiveness* strength which will help me "let go" of any blame I might impose on myself or my spouse as we encounter obstacles along the way.

Example (shortened)
I see myself doing work that is meaningful and fills me with a sense of purpose as I help people reach their dreams on a daily basis. I will use my *love of learning* strength to return to school to study new topic areas. I will use my *social intelligence* to network with people in the helping profession and stay open to emerging pathways that might broaden my experiences.

Mindfulness

Introduction

Character strengths and mindfulness are strong well-being boosters and their integration offers insight and depth to understanding and influencing human motivation and behavior (see Chapter 5 for a discussion). This section offers positive interventions that bring these areas together. These are some of the most popular activities found in the evidence-based, manualized, 8-week program mindfulness-based strengths practice (MBSP).

Contents

CSI 65: The Mindful Pause
CSI 66: Strong Mindfulness
CSI 67: Fresh Look Meditation
CSI 68: From Mindless to Mindful
CSI 69: Meditation Targeting a Character Strength
CSI 70: Strengths Gatha

The Mindful Pause

Overview
It is commonplace to hear phrases such as "Live in the moment," "Take it one moment at a time," "Just stop and breathe," "Look within," "Be in the here-and-now," and "Face your problems head-on." This activity offers a recipe for getting to these adages quickly and, at the same time, activating your best internal resources.

Purpose
Short-circuit worry, stress, and autopilot thinking; take advantage of present moment awareness; activate character strengths in the moment; shift your mindset to mindfulness and character strengths.

Steps
1. Pause and feel your inbreath and outbreath for 10–15 seconds. Let everything go except for your breath. Give your breath your full attention.
2. Conclude with a question: Which of my character strengths might I bring forward right now?

Tip
This exercise is about allowing whatever character strength is going to emerge to come forth. It's not about controlling for a particular strength or planting or hoping a certain strength will arise. Instead, trust yourself, remember you have 24 character strength capacities, and see which strength emerges. Whatever it is, go with it! Remember, you can express the strength in your thinking (e.g., labeling and generating "fairness" thoughts), in your feelings (e.g., noticing where you feel gratitude in your body and savoring it), or in your behavior/actions (e.g., an action directed toward others or an action for yourself). This means that any moment, literally, is a potential moment for your character strength expression.

Troubleshooting
If you have difficulty applying the mindful pause, try one of these 5 variations: (1) pause and review one of your signature strengths you might bring forth; (2) pause and remind yourself of your current role (parent, employee, friend) and take action consistent with the role; (3) decide on a strength you want to build up, pause, and see what action comes to mind to use the strength; (4) pause and consider how you might bring forth more goodness into the next moment; (5) pause and just be (nothing else, just breathe and be present).

CSI 65

Research
This exercise is based on my research and practice integrating and teaching mindfulness and character strengths (Niemiec, 2014a). The application of this activity has been discussed across different populations, such as parents and teachers (Lottman et al., 2017), gifted students (Sharp et al., 2016), the workplace (Niemiec & Lissing, 2016), and across a myriad of contexts that helping professionals engage in (Niemiec, 2016).

Examples
I use the mindful pause frequently during moments of transition during my day, especially as I transition from work to family. These are important moments for me to embrace, and I try to let go of the tension and positives of a full day at work and then become present for my family-time. The most common character strength to emerge for me (Step 2) is love, which is one of my signature strengths. I then take action by immediately and consciously bringing my full attention in a warm and interactive way to my young children as they play. One day, another strength came up for me during this activity – teamwork (a lower strength for me). I then used teamwork by helping my wife cook dinner (a task she typically loves to do independently). This led to the discovery of a new interest area for me and added a fun relationship connection point for the two of us.

Strong Mindfulness

Overview
Three of the most common obstacles that prevent people from engaging in meditation is they report their mind is wandering too much, they don't have time to practice, or they forget to practice. This leads people to feel disconnected from their practice and, as a result, their mindfulness practice wanes, and they conclude that meditation or mindfulness is not for them. What most meditation teachers forget to teach people is that the individual already has all the resources within them to succeed – they are called character strengths! Why not turn to our most energizing, innermost qualities during mindfulness practice to help invigorate and sustain our practice?

Purpose
Become more consistent with your meditation or self-regulation practice; energize your meditation and mindful living; bring more of "you" into your mindfulness practice; enhance motivation and meaning with your practice.

Steps
1. Name the primary obstacle that gets in your way of practicing mindfulness on a regular basis
2. Brainstorm how each of your Top 5 signature strengths could help you overcome, face, or better manage this obstacle.
3. Take action with one or more of these strength strategies at your next practice session.

Research
The concept of "strong mindfulness" is one of two main types of integration of mindfulness and character strengths (Niemiec, 2014a) and involves finding ways to take any of the 24 character strengths and weaving them into meditation, mindfulness practices, and mindful living (see Niemiec, Rashid, & Spinella, 2012).

Examples
In my *Psychology Today* blog, I've discussed examples for infusing all 24 character strengths into a mindfulness practice. Here are a few of those examples.
- *Humility.* At the onset of your practice, remind yourself of the impermanence of life as you reflect on your mortality and the mortality of those you love.
- *Self-regulation.* Follow a disciplined daily structure – same day, same time, same length, same practice – for a week.
- *Appreciation of beauty & excellence.* Engage in your mindful sitting or mindful walking practice outside, with your eyes open.
- *Gratitude.* Infuse a blessing component at the beginning and end of your meditation practice.

Fresh Look Meditation

Overview

The practice of reframing allows us to see a problem in a new way, with fresh eyes. With this kind of cleansed seeing, problems can, at best, be transformed or cured, or at least, managed better with a higher degree of empowerment. Reframing with character strengths is facilitated by considering each of the following:

1. Character strengths already present within the problem (that we have overlooked or underappreciated);
2. Character strengths that are being overused or underused contributing to the problem; and/or
3. Character strengths that are not strong enough alone and therefore need additional strengths to combine synergistically with them.

Purpose

Practice a new way to manage problems and stressors; enhance your ability to reframe challenges; improve your ability to spot character strengths overuse, underuse, and opportunities for strengths use.

Steps

These are the five steps outlined in Niemiec (2014a), which comes with an audio recording of this meditation.

1. Anchor your attention to your breathing. Spend a few minutes getting focused and grounded into the present moment.
2. Picture a *minor* life challenge or issue you are facing. See the details play out like a short movie.
3. Attend to your thoughts and feelings as they arise in the moment. Notice in your "movie" where you are overusing or underusing your character strengths.
4. Start your movie again but this time view yourself successfully using your character strengths to manage, balance, or resolve your life challenge/problem.
5. Return your attention to your breath anchor.

Research

This meditation activity is considered a centerpiece activity in mindfulness-based strengths practice (MBSP; Niemiec, 2014a), and is based on substantial research on the benefits of reframing from the science and practice of clinical hypnosis (for practical examples, see Hammond, 1990; Yapko, 2011), and from the research on positive reappraisal, which has found that mindfulness facilitates positive reappraisal (Garland, Gaylord, & Park, 2009), and these two phenomena are linked with an upward, positive spiral process (Garland, Gaylord, & Fredrickson, 2011).

CSI 67

From Mindless to Mindful

Overview
Habits, by definition, have a mindless component and can operate on their own, outside our conscious awareness. We can understand this with the metaphor of "autopilot": When an airline pilot has the plane at a nice cruising speed, he or she can turn on autopilot so the plane can fly itself. Our habits and vices work the same way. We mindlessly eat snacks out of the cupboard (a habit of behavior), watch hours of television at the same time every day (a habit of behavior), and replay the same worry-prone scenarios (a habit of mind) as tension arises. Our autopilot mind has taken over and flies our habits wherever our mind wishes to go. We can learn to catch our autopilot mind in the moment, learn from it, and create new habits of mind and behavior that are strengths-based.

Purpose
Shift toward cultivating strength; making strengths use more routine; use mindfulness to support new habits.

Steps
1. Select one of your "bad" habits or vices. Choose something you are struggling with or bothered by and that you do each day or nearly every day, such as tense discussions with a colleague or family member, overeating at lunch, overdrinking at night, staying up late, etc.
2. Consider your autopilot mind the next time you engage in this habit or vice. How much of your habit is done on autopilot? When does your mind wander off?
3. Using your autopilot mind as the target, the next time you engage in the activity, practice bringing mindful attention to what happens before, during, and after your activity. In addition, deliberately bring one of your character strengths to help you with your mindfulness.

Tip
When selecting a vice or habit, consider situations in which you typically display mindless behavior, where you are quick to react with anger or frustration, or behaviors you wish you could stop but feel you somehow cannot. Perhaps you notice that you seem to have a lot of arguments with your spouse? Numerous tense discussions with a colleague? A habit of overeating or overdrinking in the evening? Stress every time you drive to work?

Research
This activity is part of the mindfulness-based strengths practice (MBSP) program (Niemiec, 2014a) and builds from the various mindfulness exercises devoted to helping people shift from habitual reacting to skillful responding (Kabat-Zinn, 1990; Segal et al., 2013).

Example
Jodie selected her tendency to overeat and snack on high-calorie foods at night as her area of focus. In bringing attention to her autopilot mind while snacking at night, she noticed a large discrepancy between her mindlessness and mindfulness. The next evening, she engaged in mindful eating and deliberately brought her strength of curiosity to the process immediately before snacking (walking from her kids' bedroom to the kitchen), during the snacking (standing at her counter), and after her snacking (feeling bloated and lying on the couch). She reported that her mindful eating slowed her down to notice her feelings of anxiety about the tasks of the next day as well as eating as a reward ("I deserve to eat after a hard day"). Being ready and equipped with her curiosity strength helped her to face these thoughts and feelings directly. This slowed down the quantity of food she ate and gave her the opportunity to simply breathe and savor the bites of food, using all five of her senses. She also became curious about where the food came from and the experience of each bite of food flowing in her body. This led her to be curious about alternate approaches to handling her feelings and rewarding herself in future evenings.

Meditation Targeting a Character Strength

Overview
Mindfulness can be used as a type of meditation to facilitate awareness, exploration, and action. Each of the 24 character strengths can be the target of a meditation practice. Some character strengths are regularly the focus of popular meditations such as love, gratitude, and forgiveness, while other character strengths are rarely the subject of a meditation such as humor, fairness, and judgment/critical thinking.

Purpose
Boost one of your character strengths; integrate mindfulness with one of your strengths; practice a meditation that is naturally energizing for you.

Steps
These steps will help you get started with the character strength you choose.
1. Close your eyes and bring your attention fully to the present moment and attend to your inbreath and outbreath for 2–5 minutes.
2. Call to mind one character strength you would like to focus on. Breathe with this character strength, allowing it to be present within you.
3. Bring to mind one situation in which you brought this character strength forth strongly and positively in a way that was beneficial to yourself and/or others.
4. Take notice of your feelings as you focus on this character strength. Where do you locate it in your body?
5. Continue to breathe with your strength. Notice any image that is associated with your use of this character strength. Notice any insights, phrases, or positive thoughts that are connected with your use of this strength.
6. Select a cue that will connect your character strength with your feelings/body and image/thoughts. This will be a cue you can use in the future to remind yourself of the power of this character strength within you. The cue might be verbal (e.g., a word or phrase) or physical (e.g., placing your hand on your heart, pointing your finger upward, or tapping your head). Choose something that has personal meaning to you.
7. In the future, when you wish to draw from that character strength, simply activate your cue. You can practice this so that your cue becomes stronger and triggers your character strength automatically.

CSI 69

Tip
Consider moving through each of your signature strengths in a single meditation using the steps above. With each strength, sharpen your focus and allow your understanding to deepen.

Research
Meditations on virtues and character strengths have been done in different forms since the origins of meditation and across many traditions, such as in spiritual practices, hypnosis practices, guided imagery work, and mind–body medicine. The character strength that has probably been most targeted by practitioners and researchers is love and there are several studies on loving-kindness meditation (e.g., Hutcherson et al., 2008). Meditations can also be found on gratitude (Brach, 2003), forgiveness (Kornfield, 2008), and spirituality (Brahm, 2006), to name a few.

Strengths Gatha

Overview

A gatha is a Sanskrit term meaning song, poem, or verse. Gathas are intended to create an awareness in the present moment *and* a connection with the immediate future based on the gatha's contents. Gathas differ from mantras, in which individuals repeat a word or sound with the intention of creating a relaxed or oneness state. Instead, gathas help to catalyze moments of mindful living as well as positive action for the immediate future.

Purpose

Use strengths and mindfulness readily in good and challenging moments; take action with heightened awareness; deploy strengths purposefully; engage in mindful living.

Steps

1. Choose a character strength (e.g., gratitude) or character strength concept (e.g., signature strength, strengths overuse) that you would like to focus on.
2. Create a short gatha (e.g., two to four lines) that captures the essence of the character strength – of what mindfulness of that strength really looks like.
3. Weave in elements of mindfulness practice into the gatha, as appropriate, such as breathing, walking, slowing down, deepening awareness, clear seeing, widening perspective, using your senses, facing challenges in the now, and so on.

Research

Thich Nhat Hanh has written extensively about gathas (see Nhat Hanh, 1979, 2001). He has developed them for driving, working, eating, answering the phone, smiling, handling emotions, and a myriad of other daily actions, feelings, and situations. The strengths gatha intervention is part of mindfulness-based strengths practice (MBSP; Niemiec, 2014a) and has been recommended as an intervention for students in the classroom (Sharp et al., 2016).

Examples (3 gathas)

Breathing in, I calm my body,
Breathing out, I smile,
Dwelling in this present moment,
I know this is a wonderful moment. (Nhat Hanh, 1979)

Breathing in, I see my strengths,
Breathing out, I value my strengths,
Dwelling now in my strengths,
I express myself fully. (Niemiec, 2014a)

Breathing in, I see my fear,
Breathing out, I bow to my bravery,
Remembering to call it forth,
I grow my capacity.

Additional Character Strengths Activities

Introduction

This section offers 12 additional character strengths activities that practitioners might use with clients. Less detail is provided on these as some of these activities reflect emerging theories, and some do not lend themselves well to the handout format. Each offers a strong concept and, in some cases, a science-based intervention.

Polyvocality: Expanding Strength Voices

The inner critic can be harsh, overly negative, and unkind. A counterbalance is often needed, not to crush or exile the inner critic but to talk back to it and to accentuate the positive. We can expand the character strength voices in our head by reflecting on how other people describe us. How would your sport coach describe you? What good things do you think your teacher or boss has observed in you the last few months, even if they haven't said them out loud? If your parent or grandparent was sitting next to you right now, how would they describe you? This can be made practical even further by asking oneself to name five positive people in your life and then to write about how each would positively describe oneself in one sentence, using their words. The importance of expanding character strengths voices has been discussed in Wong (2006) and Niemiec (2014a), and can be particularly useful for people who are highly critical, self-blaming, or struggle with low self-esteem.

Identify and Label Character Strengths That Rise Up

Mindful attention means taking notice of whatever rises up in the present moment. Be particularly attentive to character strengths related material. These might be thoughts (e.g., a kind thought, a humble belief), emotions (e.g., a feeling of gratitude, a bodily sense of zest), or actions (e.g., speaking with social intelligence, walking with self-regulation). Label the character strength "fragment" that is present, file the insight away, and return the focus to the present moment (Niemiec, 2014a). This labeling has the potential to open up new energy resources. For example, it has been hypothesized that the act of forgiveness frees up additional resources, which might serve as extra mental energy that can be invested in mindfulness (Webb, Phillips, Bumgarner, & Conway-Williams, 2012).

Secret Strengths-Spotting

This is the most popular activity among my students at Xavier University. This activity involves a group of individuals having a basic understanding of the 24 character strengths. Early on in a workshop or a semester, each person draws the name of another person in their class/group from a hat. Students are asked to "secretly" observe the individual looking for character strengths. These can be spotted at any time, during or outside of class time. After a specified amount of time (e.g., for a university course, the midterm is a good amount of time), students reveal the person they observed and offer a formal verbal report to the person on the character strengths witnessed, the evidence for each strength, the observed outcome, and so forth. Students are encouraged to reflect on what it was like to take on a strengths lens for an extended period of time and what it was like to hear about their own strengths, through the eyes of another student. The activity builds awareness of strengths (in self and others) and, more generally, of positive events. A variation is discussed in Linkins and colleagues (2015) for younger students in the classroom.

Set Up "Bells of Awakening" in the Environment

Thich Nhat Hanh (1979, 2009) encourages individuals to create "bells" of mindfulness to break habitual mindlessness and awaken to the present moment. Bells are external cues that are set up that use naturally occurring sounds (e.g., an actual bell, a baby's cry) or self-created reminders (e.g., sticky notes). Whenever an individual sees a sticky note or hears the particular sound in their environment, it is a moment of awakening to return to the present moment where they can reconnect with their breath and with the character strengths already happening in the moment that might have been operating unconsciously (Niemiec, 2014a).

Engage the Full Psychology of Your Strengths

Name one of your signature strengths. List three healthy thoughts that you typically have (or could have) when you are experiencing that strength. Name the emotion/feeling you have when you are expressing that strength; make note of the sensations in your body that accompany the strength. Finally, what does the strength look like in action? This exercise, found in Niemiec (2014a), builds off the concept that each character strength is a capacity or potentiality that can be developed.

The Matrix of Strengths

This exercise helps you to understand and explore how your strengths are interconnected. When one expresses one strength strongly and completely other character strengths are necessarily involved. A character strength constellation is forming and being expressed. When you express a character strength, take notice of the connection between the first and second strength and between the second and third strength expressed, and so on. Robert McGrath (2013) has conducted intercorrelation matrices of the 24 character strengths and has found that all the character strengths relate to one another, some more than others.

Your Master Strength

Some researchers hypothesize that there is one "master strength" that operates the use of all the other character strengths. Examples include self-regulation (Baumeister & Vohs, 2004), perspective/wisdom (Schwartz & Sharpe, 2006), and love (Vaillant, 2008). Other researchers have proposed other strengths as the master, such as humility, honesty/authenticity, leadership, spirituality, and gratitude; however, often the strength being suggested is the given researcher's main area of study. I have suggested that the master strength concept can be individualized – tailored to the individual's highest signature strength (Niemiec, 2014a). Test this out for yourself. Make a habit of examining the action you take during highs and lows throughout each day, as well as times of neutrality. Examine each instance and each situation for a core strength driver operating the use of the other strengths, acting as a catalyzing strength, or seeming to be a higher order strength driving a deeper purpose. As this activity and concept is mostly unexplored, keep an open mind to possibilities.

Positive Mental Time Travel

Vividly imagine four positive events that could possibly happen the next day before going to bed. This is a future-oriented savoring activity that boosts positive emotions (Quoidbach et al., 2009). A key character strength that is involved in this activity is the building of perspective.

Letter From the Future

Write a letter from one's future self to one's present self. Describe important goals that have been reached and the wonderful life that has been achieved (Hoffman, Hinkle, & Kress, 2010). This exercise, a variation of the best possible self exercise, boosts well-being. In terms of character strengths, these exercises that engage the future and the reaching of goals closely involve the character strength of hope.

Break a Bad Habit or Vice

For a habit that has taken a strong hold, focus on stopping the behavior before it starts. This vigilant monitoring approach involves closely focusing attention on the unwanted behavior to make sure it is not engaged. Monitor oneself for slipups. This strategy is the opposite of a distraction strategy and it helps inhibit bad habits (Quinn, Pascoe, Wood, & Neal, 2010). A key character strength to involve in the vigilant monitoring is prudence.

Aerobic Laughter

Engage in group laughter that is not dependent on humor, jokes, or a formal comedy show. This might be a guided experience, a laughter club, laughter yoga, or simply laughing alone or with a partner. This type of guided approach to aerobic laughter has been found to generate positive emotions and well-being (Beckman, Regier, & Young, 2007).

Immediate Versus Delayed Positive Relationship Behaviors

To convey love to one's relationship partner, offer small, spontaneous acts of love, such as a quick back-rub, saying "I love you," a surprise dinner, or an act of kindness. These acts were found to convey "love" better than the longer-term, sustained behaviors such as doing chores each day or remembering to do an important, caring task in 5 days. The researchers concluded that in-the-moment, positive relationship behaviors are acts of the heart, whereas delayed, sustained positive relationship behaviors are acts of will (Kammrath & Peetz, 2011). The former behaviors involve using character strengths such as kindness and love, while the latter behaviors involve using character strengths such as self-regulation, prudence, and perseverance.

Chapter 9

Afterword

- Need more character strengths research or want to stay updated on new findings? We track it and disseminate it on the VIA Institute site. Here's the direct link: https://www.viacharacter.org/www/Research/Character-Research-Findings
- Want more books on character strengths? Go to the references and seek out Doman (2016), McQuaid and Lawn (2014), Niemiec (2014a), Niemiec and Wedding (2014), Polly and Britton (2015), and, of course, Peterson and Seligman (2004).
- Want a book on a specific character strength? Check out the following:
  Wired to Create (Kaufman & Gregoire, 2015) [Creativity]
  Curious? (Kashdan, 2009) [Curiosity]
  The Power of Mindful Learning (Langer, 1997) [Love of Learning]
  Thinking, Fast and Slow (Kahneman, 2011) [Judgment/critical thinking]
  Practical Wisdom (Schwartz & Sharpe, 2011) [Perspective]
  The Courage Quotient (Biswas-Diener, 2011) [Bravery]
  Mindset: How You Can Fulfill Your Potential (Dweck, 2006) [Perseverance]
  The Gifts of Imperfection (Brown, 2010) [Honesty/Authenticity]
  The Body and Positive Psychology (Hefferon, 2013) [Zest]
  Love 2.0 (Fredrickson, 2013) [Love]
  Self-Compassion (Neff, 2011) [Kindness]
  Social Intelligence (Goleman, 2006) [Social Intelligence]
  Effective Teamwork (West, 2012) [Teamwork]
  The Fairness Instinct (Sun, 2013) [Fairness]
  The Humanitarian Leader in Each of Us (LaFasto & Larson, 2012) [Leadership]
  Beyond Revenge (McCullough, 2008) [Forgiveness]
  Humility: The Quiet Virtue (Worthington, 2007) [Humility]
  Willpower (Baumeister & Tierney, 2011) [Self-Regulation]
  Awe (Pearsall, 2007) [Appreciation of Beauty & Excellence]
  Thanks! (Emmons, 2007) [Gratitude]
  Making Hope Happen (Lopez, 2014) [Hope]
  Humor as Survival Training for a Stressed-Out World (McGhee, 2010) [Humor]
  The Gospel of Happiness (Kaczor, 2015) [Spirituality]
- Want to experience, research, or learn about the first character strengths training program and the only strengths-based mindfulness program, peruse a variety of free resources on mindfulness-based strengths practice (MBSP), or be part of a growing network of MBSP leaders? Go to https://www.viacharacter.org/mindfulness.
- Need more practices and user-friendly observations on character strengths, check out my regular blog, "What Matters Most?," on the *Psychology Today* site at https://www.psychologytoday.com/blog/what-matters-most
- Want to engage in character strengths (and mindfulness) on the leading gamified, positive psychology website "Happify?" Check out my popular track called "Awaken Your Potential," which is an abridged version of MBSP, at this special link: https://www.happify.com/o/lp27/?tmp=38&srid=via&fl=1&trid=47

- Want to learn more about my family? Sure. At this book's publication, my son Rhys is 6, my son Ryland is 3.5, and my daughter Maya is 1.5. I won't share the age of my wife, who's a child psychologist. Rhys is prudent before he turns highly zestful in situations. Ryland is highly zestful, which unleashes his love and humor. Maya is socially intelligent. She smiles at each interaction, is unfettered by our loud family antics during our dance parties, and maintains a calm and steady curiosity about her world that at times merges with the most delightful of giggles.

References

Adler, A. (1963). *The practice and theory of individual psychology*. Paterson, NJ: Littlefield, Adams.

Adler, M.G., & Fagley, N.S. (2005). Appreciation: Individual differences in finding value and meaning as a unique predictor of subjective well-being. *Journal of Personality, 73*(1), 79–114. http://doi.org/10.1111/j.1467-6494.2004.00305.x

Adriaanse, M.A., Oettingen, G., Gollwitzer, P.M., Hennes, E.P., de Ridder, D.T. D., & de Witt, J.B. F. (2010). When planning is not enough: Fighting unhealthy snacking habits by mental contrasting with implementation intentions (MCII). *European Journal of Social Psychology, 40*, 1277–1293. http://doi.org/10.1002/ejsp.730

Algoe, S.B., Gable, S.L., & Maisel, N.C. (2010). It's the little things: Everyday gratitude as a booster shot for romantic relationships. *Personal Relationships, 17*, 217–233. http://doi.org/10.1111/j.1475-6811.2010.01273.x

Algoe, S.B., & Haidt, J. (2009). Witnessing excellence in action: The "other-praising" emotions of elevation, gratitude, and admiration. *Journal of Positive Psychology, 4*, 105–127. http://doi.org/10.1080/17439760802650519

Allan, B.A. (2014). Balance among character strengths and meaning in life. *Journal of Happiness Studies, 16*, 1247–1261. http://doi.org/10.1007/s10902-014-9557-9

Allan, B.A., & Duffy, R.D. (2013). Examining moderators of signature strengths use and well-being: Calling and signature strengths level. *Journal of Happiness Studies, 15*, 323–337. http://doi.org/10.1007/s10902-013-9424-0

Allison, S.T., & Goethals, G.R. (2011). *Heroes: What they do and why we need them*. New York, NY: Oxford University Press.

American Psychiatric Association. (2013). *Diagnostic and statistical manual of mental disorders* (5th ed.). Washington, DC: Author.

Andrewes, H.E., Walker, V., & O'Neill, B. (2014). Exploring the use of positive psychology interventions in brain injury survivors with challenging behavior. *Brain Injury, 28*(7), 965–971. http://doi.org/10.3109/02699052.2014.888764

Ang, S.H., Lim, E.A. C., Leong, S.M., & Chen, Z. (2015). In pursuit of happiness: Effects of mental subtraction and alternative comparison. *Social Indicators Research, 122*(1), 87–103. http://doi.org/10.1007/s11205-014-0681-z

Aquinas, T. (1989). *Summa theologiae: A concise translation* (T. McDermott, Ed. & Trans.). Westminster, MD: Christian Classics. (Original work completed 1265–1273)

Aquino, K., McFerran, B., & Laven, M. (2011). Moral identity and the experience of moral elevation in response to acts of uncommon goodness. *Journal of Personality and Social Psychology, 100*(4), 703–718. http://doi.org/10.1037/a0022540

Aristotle (2000). *Nicomachean ethics* (R. Crisp, Trans.). Cambridge, UK: Cambridge University Press. (Original work composed 4th century BCE)

Aronson, E. (1999). The power of self-persuasion. *American Psychologist, 54*, 875–884. http://doi.org/10.1037/h0088188

Asplund, J., Lopez, S.J., Hodges, T., & Harter, J. (2007). *The Clifton StrengthsFinder® 2.0 technical report: Development and validation*. Princeton, NJ: The Gallup Organization.

Atkinson, K.E. (2007). *Psychotherapists' views of using signature strengths in the workplace: An exploratory study* (master's dissertation). University of Lethbridge, Alberta, CA. Retrieved from https://www.uleth.ca/dspace/bitstream/handle/10133/959/Atkinson_Katherine_E.pdf?sequence=1

Austenfeld, J.L., Paolo, A.M., & Stanton, A.L. (2006). Effects of writing about emotions versus goals on psychological and physical health among third-year medical students. *Journal of Personality, 74*(1), 267–286.

Austenfeld, J.L., & Stanton, A.L. (2008). Writing about emotions versus goals: Effects on hostility and medical care utilization moderated by emotional approach coping processes. *British Journal of Health Psychology, 13*, 35–38. http://doi.org/10.1348/135910707X250857

Azañedoa, C.M., Fernández-Abascalb, E.G., & Barracac, J. (2014). Character strengths in Spain: Validation of the Values in Action Inventory of Strengths (VIA-IS) in a Spanish sample. *Clínica y Salud, 25*, 123–130. http://doi.org/10.1016/j.clysa.2014.06.002

Baer, R. (2015). Ethics, values, virtues, and character strengths in mindfulness-based interventions: A psychological science perspective. *Mindfulness, 6*, 956–969. http://doi.org/10.1007/s12671-015-0419-2

Baer, R. A., & Lykins, E. L. M. (2011). Mindfulness and positive psychological functioning. In K. M. Sheldon, T. B. Kashdan, & M. F. Steger (Eds.), *Designing positive psychology: Taking stock and moving forward* (pp. 335–348). New York, NY: Oxford University Press.

Baker, W., & Bulkley, N. (2014). Paying it forward versus rewarding reputation: Mechanisms of generalized reciprocity. *Organization Science, 25*(5), 1493–1510. http://doi.org/10.1287/orsc.2014.0920

Baltes, P. B., & Staudinger, U. (2000). Wisdom: A metaheuristic (pragmatic) to orchestrate mind and virtue toward excellence. *American Psychologist, 55*, 122–136. http://doi.org/10.1037/0003-066X.55.1.122

Bandura, A. (1977). *Social learning theory*. New York, NY: General Learning Press.

Bandura, A. (2003). On the psychosocial impact and mechanisms of spiritual modeling. *The International Journal for the Psychology of Religion, 13*, 167–174. http://doi.org/10.1207/S15327582IJPR1303_02

Bandura, A. (2008). An agentic perspective on positive psychology. In S. J. Lopez (Ed.), *Positive psychology: Exploring the best in people* (Vol. 1., pp. 167–196). Westport, CT: Praeger.

Banth, S., & Singh, P. (2011). Positive character strengths in middle-rung army officers and managers in civilian sector. *Journal of the Indian Academy of Applied Psychology, 37*(2), 320–324.

Bao, K. J., & Lyubomirsky, S. (2013). Making it last: Combating hedonic adaptation in romantic relationships. *Journal of Positive Psychology, 8*(3), 196–206. http://doi.org/10.1080/17439760.2013.777765

Baskin, T. W, & Enright, R. D. (2004). Intervention studies on forgiveness: A meta-analysis. *Journal of Counseling & Development, 82*, 79–90. http://doi.org/10.1002/j.1556-6678.2004.tb00288.x

Bates-Krakoff, J., McGrath, R. E., Graves, K., & Ochs, L. (2016). Beyond a deficit model of strengths training in schools: Teaching targeted strength use to gifted students. *Gifted Education International*. Advance online publication. http://dx.doi.org/10.1177/0261429416646210

Bauer, J. J., McAdams, D. P., & Pals, J. L. (2008). Narrative identity and eudaimonic well-being. *Journal of Happiness Studies, 9*, 81–104. http://doi.org/10.1007/s10902-006-9021-6

Baumeister, R. F., Bratslavsky, E., Finkenaeuer, C., & Vohs, K. D. (2001). Bad is stronger than good. *Review of General Psychology, 5*(4), 323–370. http://doi.org/10.1037/1089-2680.5.4.323

Baumeister, R. F., Matthew, G., DeWall, C. N., & Oaten, M. (2006). Self-regulation and personality: How interventions increase regulatory success, and how depletion moderates the effects of traits on behavior. *Journal of Personality, 74*(6), 1773–1802. http://doi.org/10.1111/j.1467-6494.2006.00428.x

Baumeister, R. F., & Tierney, J. (2011). *Willpower: Rediscovering the greatest human strength*. New York, NY: Penguin Books.

Baumeister, R. F., & Vohs, K. D. (Eds.). (2004). *Handbook of self-regulation: Research, theory, and applications*. New York, NY: Guilford.

Beck, A. T., Rush, A. J., Shaw, B. F., & Emery, G. (1979). *Cognitive therapy of depression*. New York, NY: Guilford Press.

Beck, A. T., Ward, C., & Mendelson, M. (1961). Beck depression inventory (BDI). *Archives of General Psychiatry, 4*(6), 561–571. http://doi.org/10.1001/archpsyc.1961.01710120031004

Beckman, H., Regier, N., & Young, J. (2007). Effect of workplace laughter groups on personal efficacy beliefs. *The Journal of Primary Prevention, 28*, 167–182. http://doi.org/10.1007/s10935-007-0082-z

Berg, I. K., & Dolan, Y. M. (2001). *Tales of solutions: A collection of hope-inspiring stories*. New York, NY: Norton.

Berkowitz, M. W. (1985). The role of discussion in moral education. In M. W. Berkowitz & F. Oser (Eds.), *Moral education: Theory and applications* (pp. 197–218). Hillsdale, NJ: Lawrence Erlbaum and Associates.

Berkowitz, M. W. (2000). Character education as prevention. In W. B. Hansen, S. M. Giles, & M. D. Fearnow-Kenney (Eds.), *Improving prevention effectiveness* (pp. 37–45). Greensboro, NC: Tanglewood Research.

Berkowitz, M. W. (2011). What works in values education. *International Journal of Educational Research, 50*. 153–158. http://doi.org/10.1016/j.ijer.2011.07.003

Berkowitz, M. W., & Bier, M. C. (2007). What works in character education. *Journal of Research in Character Education, 5*(1), 29–48.

Berthold, A., & Ruch, W. (2014). Satisfaction with life and character strengths of nonreligious and religious people: It's practicing one's religion that makes the difference. *Frontiers in Psychology, 5*. http://doi.org/10.3389/fpsyg.2014.00876

Biggs, E. E., & Carter, E. W., (2015). Quality of life for transition-age youth with autism or intellectual disability. *Journal of Autism and Developmental Disabilities, 46*(1), 190–204. http://doi.org/10.1007/s10803-015-2563-x

Bishop, S. R., Lau, M., Shapiro, S. L., Carlson, L., Anderson, N. D., Carmody, J., … Devins, G. (2004). Mindfulness: A proposed operational definition. *Clinical Psychology: Science and Practice, 11*, 230–241. http://doi.org/10.1093/clipsy.bph077

Biswas-Diener, R. (2006). From the equator to the North Pole: A study of character strengths. *Journal of Happiness Studies, 7*, 293–310. http://doi.org/10.1007/s10902-005-3646-8

Biswas-Diener, R. (2012). *The courage quotient: How science can make you braver.* San Francisco, CA: Jossey-Bass.

Biswas-Diener, R., Kashdan, T. B., & Minhas, G. (2011). A dynamic approach to psychological strength development and intervention. *Journal of Positive Psychology, 6*(2), 106–118. http://doi.org/10.1080/17439760.2010.545429

Blackie, L. E. R., Roepke, A. M., Forgeard, M. J. C., Jayawickreme, E., & Fleeson, W. (2014). Act well to be well: The promise of changing personality states to promote well-being. In A. C. Parks, & S. Schueller (Eds.), *The Wiley-Blackwell handbook of positive psychological interventions* (pp. 462–474). Oxford, UK: Wiley-Blackwell.

Blatner, A. (1988). *Foundations of psychodrama: History, theory, and practice.* New York, NY: Springer.

Bohart, A. C. (2007). An alternative view of concrete operating procedures from the perspective of the client as active self-healer. *Journal of Psychotherapy Integration, 17*, 125–137. http://doi.org/10.1037/1053-0479.17.1.125

Bohart, A. C., & Tallman, K. (2010). Clients: The neglected common factor in psychotherapy. In B. L. Duncan, S. D. Miller, B. E. Wampold, & M. A. Hubble (Eds.), *The heart and soul of change: Delivering what works in therapy* (2nd ed., pp. 83–111). Washington, DC: American Psychological Association.

Boiler, L., Haverman, M., Westerhof, G. J., Riper, H., Smit, F., & Bohlmeijer, E. (2013). Positive psychology interventions: A meta-analysis of randomized controlled studies. *BMC Public Health, 13*, 119. http://doi.org/10.1186/1471-2458-13-119

Borghans, L., Duckworth, A. L., Heckman, J. J., & ter Weel, B. (2008). The economics and psychology of personality traits. *Journal of Human Resources, 43*(4), 972–1059. http://doi.org/10.1353/jhr.2008.0017

Bower, J. E., Low, C. A., Moskowitz, J. T., Sepah, S., & Epel, E. (2008). Benefit finding and physical health: Positive psychological changes and enhanced allostasis. *Social and Personality Psychology Compass, 2*(1), 223–244. http://doi.org/10.1111/j.1751-9004.2007.00038.x

Brach, T. (2003). *Radical acceptance: Embracing your life with the heart of a Buddha.* New York, NY: Bantam.

Brahm, A. (2006). *Mindfulness, bliss, and beyond: A meditator's handbook.* Boston, MA: Wisdom Publications.

Brdar, I., & Kashdan, T. B. (2010). Character strengths and well-being in Croatia: An empirical investigation of structure and correlates. *Journal of Research in Personality, 44*, 151–154. http://doi.org/10.1016/j.jrp.2009.12.001

Bright, D. (2016). What is a virtue theory and why does it matter? *Positive Work and Organizations: Research and Practice, 2.* Available at: http://www.ippanetwork.org/wo-division/what-is-a-virtue-theory-and-why-does-it-matter/

Brown, B. (2010). *The gifts of imperfection: Let go of who you think you're supposed to be and embrace who you are.* Center City, MN: Hazelden.

Bryant, F. B., Smart, C. M., & King, S. P. (2005). Using the past to enhance the present: Boosting happiness through positive reminiscence. *Journal of Happiness Studies, 6*, 227–260. http://doi.org/10.1007/s10902-005-3889-4

Bryant, F. B., & Veroff, J. (2007). *Savoring: A new model of positive experience.* Mahway, NJ: Lawrence Erlbaum Associates.

Buckingham, M., & Clifton, D. O. (2001). *Now, discover your strengths: How to develop your talents and those of the people you manage.* New York, NY: Free Press.

Buschor, C., Proyer, R. T., & Ruch, W. (2013). Self- and peer-rated character strengths: How do they relate to satisfaction with life and orientations to happiness? *Journal of Positive Psychology, 8*(2), 116–127. http://doi.org/10.1080/17439760.2012.758305

Butina, B. L. (2016). *An investigation of the efficacy of the using your signature strengths in a new way exercise to enhance strengths use in work settings* (Doctoral dissertation). Northcentral University, Scottsdale, AZ. Manuscript submitted for publication.

Caprariello, P. A., & Reis, H. T. (2013). To do, to have, or to share? Valuing experiences over material possessions depends on the involvement of others. *Journal of Personality and Social Psychology, 104*(2), 199–215. http://doi.org/10.1037/a0030953

Carrere, S., & Gottman, J. M. (1999). Predicting divorce among newlyweds from the first three minutes of a marital conflict discussion. *Family Process, 38*(3), 293–301. http://doi.org/10.1111/j.1545-5300.1999.00293.x

Carson, J. W., Keefe, F. J., Lynch, T. R., Carson, K. M., Goli, V., Fras, A. M., & Thorp, S. R. (2005). Loving-kindness meditation for chronic low back pain: Results from a pilot trial. *Journal of Holistic Nursing, 23*(3), 287–304. http://doi.org/10.1177/0898010105277651

Carter, E. W., Boehm, T. L., Biggs, E. E., Annandale, N. H., Taylor, C. E., Loock, A. K., & Liu, R. Y. (2015). Known for my strengths: Positive traits of transition-age youth with intellectual disability and/or autism. *Research and Practice for Persons with Severe Disabilities, 40*(2), 101–119. http://doi.org/10.1177/1540796915592158

Chan, D. W. (2009). The hierarchy of strengths: Their relationships with subjective wellbeing among Chinese teachers in Hong Kong. *Teaching and Teacher Education, 25*(6), 867–875. http://doi.org/10.1016/j.tate.2009.01.010

Chan, J., Chan, F., Ditchman, N., Phillips, B., & Chou, C. (2013). Evaluating Snyder's hope theory as a motivational model of participation and life satisfaction for individuals with spinal cord injury: A path analysis. *Rehabilitation Research, Policy, and Education, 27*(3), 187–205. http://doi.org/10.1891/2168-6653.27.3.171

Chaves, C., Hervás, G., García, F. E., & Vázquez, C. (2016). Building life satisfaction through well-being dimensions: A longitudinal study in children with a life-threatening illness. *Journal of Happiness Studies, 17*(3), 1051–1067.

Chaves, C., Vázquez, C., & Hervás, G. (2016). Positive interventions in seriously-ill children: Effects on well-being after granting a wish. *Journal of Health Psychology, 21*(9), 1870–1883.

Cheavens, J. S., Feldman, D. B., Gum, A., Michael, S. T., & Snyder, C. R. (2006). Hope therapy in a community sample: A pilot investigation. *Social Indicators Research, 77*(1), 61–78. http://doi.org/10.1007/s11205-005-5553-0

Cheavens, J. S., Strunk, D. R., Lazarus, S. A., & Goldstein, L. A. (2012). The compensation and capitalization models: A test of two approaches to individualizing the treatment of depression. *Behaviour Research and Therapy, 50*, 699–706. http://doi.org/10.1016/j.brat.2012.08.002

Choubisa, R., & Singh, K. (2011). Psychometrics encompassing VIA-IS: A comparative cross cultural analytical and referential reading. *Journal of the Indian Academy of Applied Psychology, 37*(2), 325–332.

Christopher, J. C. (1996). Counseling's inescapable moral visions. *Journal of Counseling and Development, 75*, 17–25. http://doi.org/10.1002/j.1556-6676.1996.tb02310.x

Clifton, D. O., & Harter, J. K. (2003). Strengths investment. In K. S. Cameron, J. E. Dutton, & R. E. Quinn (Eds.), *Positive organizational scholarship* (pp. 111–121). San Francisco, CA: Berrett-Koehler.

Clinton, B. (2007). *Giving: How each of us can change the world.* New York, NY: Alfred A. Knopf.

Coelho, P. (2012, February 3). *The law of Jante* [Web log post]. Retrieved from: http://paulocoelhoblog.com/2012/02/03/the-law-of-jante-3/

Coghlan, A., & Filo, K. (2016). Bringing personal character strengths into the production of the leisure experience. *Leisure Sciences, 38*(2), 100–117.

Cohen, G. L., & Sherman, D. K. (2014). The psychology of change: Self-affirmation and social psychological intervention. *Annual Review of Psychology, 65*, 333–371. http://doi.org/10.1146/annurev-psych-010213-115137

Cohn, M. A., & Fredrickson, B. L. (2010). In search of durable positive psychology interventions: Predictors and consequences of long-term positive behavior change. *Journal of Positive Psychology, 5*(5), 355–366. http://doi.org/10.1080/17439760.2010.508883

Comte-Sponville, A. (2001). *A small treatise on the great virtues* (C. Temerson, Trans.). New York, NY: Metropolitan Books.

Consentino, A. C., & Castro, A. (2012). Character strengths: A study of Argentinean soldiers. *Spanish Journal of Psychology, 15*(1), 199–215. http://doi.org/10.5209/rev_SJOP.2012.v15.n1.37310

Cook, J. E., Purdie-Vaughns, V., Garcia, J., & Cohen, G. L. (2012). Chronic threat and contingent belonging: Protective benefits of values affirmation on identity development. *Journal of Personality and Social Psychology, 102*(3), 479–496. http://doi.org/10.1037/a0026312

Cooperrider, D., & Whitney, D. (2005). *Appreciative inquiry: A positive revolution in change*. San Francisco, CA: Berrett-Koehler.

Cornish, M. A., & Wade, N. G. (2015). Working through past wrongdoing: Examination of a self-forgiveness counseling intervention. *Journal of Counseling Psychology, 62*(3), 521–528. http://doi.org/10.1037/cou0000080

Cornum, R., Matthews, M. D., & Seligman, M. E. P. (2011). Comprehensive soldier fitness: Building resilience in a challenging institutional context. *American Psychologist, 66*(1), 4–9. http://doi.org/10.1037/a0021420

Covington, M. V. (1999). Caring about learning: The nature and nurturing of subject-matter appreciation. *Educational Psychologist, 34*(2), 127–136. http://doi.org/10.1207/s15326985ep3402_5

Cox, K. (2006). Investigating the impact of strength-based assessment on youth with emotional or behavioral disorders. *Journal of Child and Family Studies, 15*(3), 278–292. http://doi.org/10.1007/s10826-006-9021-5

Cox, K. S. (2010). Elevation predicts domain-specific volunteerism 3 months later. *Journal of Positive Psychology, 5*(5), 333–341. http://doi.org/10.1080/17439760.2010.507468

Crabb, S. (2011). The use of coaching principles to foster employee engagement. *The Coaching Psychologist, 7*(1), 27–34.

Creswell, J. D., Welch, W., Taylor, S. E., Sherman, D. K., Gruenewald, T., & Mann, T. (2005). Affirmation of personal values buffers neuroendocrine and psychological stress responses. *Psychological Science, 16*, 846–851. http://doi.org/10.1111/j.1467-9280.2005.01624.x

Crocker, J., Niiya, Y., & Mischkowski, D. (2008). Why does writing about important values reduce defensiveness?: Self-affirmation and the role of positive other-directed feelings. *Psychological Science, 19*, 740–747. http://doi.org/10.1111/j.1467-9280.2008.02150.x

Cropley, D. H., Kaufman, J. C., White, A. E., & Chiera, B. A. (2014). Layperson perceptions of malevolent creativity: The good, the bad, and the ambiguous. *Psychology of Aesthetics, Creativity, and the Arts, 8*(4), 400–412. http://doi.org/10.1037/a0037792

Csikszentmihalyi, M. (1997). *Finding flow: The psychology of engagement with everyday life*. New York, NY: Basic Books.

Cummings, N., & Sayama, M. (1995). *Focused psychotherapy: A casebook of brief, intermittent psychotherapy throughout the life cycle*. New York, NY: Brunner/Mazel.

Dahlsgaard, K., Peterson, C., & Seligman, M. E. P. (2005). Shared virtue: The convergence of valued human strengths across culture and history. *Review of General Psychology, 9*, 203–213. http://doi.org/10.1037/1089-2680.9.3.203

Dalton, A. N., & Spiller, S. A. (2012). Too much of a good thing: The benefits of implementation intentions depend on the number of goals. *Journal of Consumer Research, 39*(3), 600–614. http://doi.org/10.1086/664500

Davis, D. E., McElroy, S. E., Rice, K. G., Choe, E., Westbrook, C., Hook, J. N., … Worthington, E. L. (2016). Is modesty a subdomain of humility? *Journal of Positive Psychology, 11*(4), 439–446. http://doi.org/10.1080/17439760.2015.1117130

Davis, D. E., Worthington, E. L., & Hook, J. N. (2010). Humility: Review of measurement strategies and conceptualization as personality judgment. *Journal of Positive Psychology, 5*(4), 243–252. http://doi.org/10.1080/17439761003791672

Deci, E., & Ryan, R. (2000). The "what" and "why" of goal pursuits: Human needs and the self-determination of behavior. *Psychological Inquiry, 11*(4), 227–268. http://doi.org/10.1207/S15327965PLI1104_01

DeMaria, L., Andrew, G., & Leventhal, K. S. (2016, January). *Girls first and youth first: Building the evidence for personal resilience training for India's youth*. Conference presentation at Youth First: Fostering Youth Development From the Inside Out, New Delhi, India.

Dembkowski, S., & Eldridge, F. (2003). Beyond GROW: A new coaching model. *International Journal of Mentoring and Coaching, 1*(1), 1–6.

Diener, E., Emmons, R. A., Larsen, R. J., & Griffin, S. (1985). The Satisfaction With Life Scale. *Journal of Personality Assessment, 49*, 71–75. http://doi.org/10.1207/s15327752jpa4901_13

Diener, E., Lucas, R. E., & Scollon, C. N. (2006). Beyond the hedonic treadmill: Revising the adaptation theory of well-being. *American Psychologist, 61*(4), 305–314. http://doi.org/10.1037/0003-066X.61.4.305

Diener, E., Wirtz, D., Tov, W., Kim-Prieto, C., Choi, D., Oishi, S., & Biswas-Diener, R. (2009). New measures of well-being: Flourishing and positive and negative feelings. *Social Indicators Research, 39,* 247–266. http://doi.org/10.1007/978-90-481-2354-4_12

Diessner, R., Davis, L., & Toney, B. (2009). Empirical relationships between beauty and justice: Testing Scarry and elaborating Danto. *Psychology of Aesthetics, Creativity, and the Arts, 3*(4), 249–258. http://doi.org/10.1037/a0014683

Diessner, R., Iyer, R., Smith, M. M., & Haidt, J. (2013). Who engages with moral beauty? *Journal of Moral Education, 42*(2), 139–163. http://doi.org/10.1080/03057240.2013.785941

Diessner, R., Rust, T., Solom, R., Frost, N., & Parsons, L. (2006). Beauty and hope: A moral beauty intervention. *Journal of Moral Education, 35,* 301–317. http://doi.org/10.1080/03057240600874430

Diessner, R., Woodward, D., Stacy, S., & Mobasher, S. (2015). Ten once-a-week brief beauty walks increase appreciation of natural beauty. *Ecopsychology, 7*(3), 126–133. http://doi.org/10.1089/eco.2015.0001

Dimidjian, S., Hollon, S. D., Dobson, K. S., Schmaling, K. B., Kohlenberg, R. J., Addis, M. E., … Jacobseon, N. S. (2006). Randomized trial of behavioral activation, cognitive therapy, and antidepressant medication in the acute treatment of adults with major depression. *Journal of Consulting and Clinical Psychology, 74,* 658–670. http://doi.org/10.1037/0022-006X.74.4.658

Doman, F. (2016). *Authentic strengths.* Las Vegas, NV: Next Century Publishing.

Douglass, R., & Duffy, R. (2015). Strengths use and life satisfaction: A moderated mediation approach. *Journal of Happiness Studies, 16,* 619–632. http://doi.org/10.1007/s10902-014-9525-4

Drigotas, S. M., Rusbult, C. E., Wieselquist, J., & Whitton, S. W. (1999). Close partner as sculptor of the ideal self: Behavioral affirmation and the Michelangelo phenomenon. *Journal of Personality and Social Psychology, 77*(2), 293–323. http://doi.org/10.1037/0022-3514.77.2.293

Drozd, F., Mork, L., Nielsen, B., Raeder, S., & Bjørkli, C. A. (2014). Better days: A randomized controlled trial of an internet-based positive psychology intervention. *Journal of Positive Psychology, 9*(5), 377–388. http://doi.org/10.1080/17439760.2014.910822

Duan, W., & Bu, H. (2017). Randomized trial investigating of a single-session character-strength-based cognitive intervention on freshman's adaptability. *Research on Social Work Practice.* Advance online publication. http://dx.doi.org/10.1177/1049731517699525

Duan, W., Ho, S. M. Y., Tang, X., Li, T., & Zhang, Y. (2013). Character strength-based intervention to promote satisfaction with life in the Chinese university context. *Journal of Happiness Studies, 15,* 1347–1361. http://doi.org/10.1007/s10902-013-9479-y

Dubreuil, P., Forest, J., & Courcy, F. (2013). From strengths use to work performance: The role of harmonious passion, subjective vitality and concentration. *Journal of Positive Psychology, 9*(4), 1–15.

Dubreuil, P., Forest, J., Gillet, N., Fernet, C., Thibault-Landry, A., Crevier-Braud, L., & Girouard, S. (2016). Facilitating well-being and performance through the development of strengths at work: Results from an intervention program. *International Journal of Applied Positive Psychology.* Advance online publication. http://dx.doi.org/10.1007/s41042-016-0001-8

Duckworth, A. L., Peterson, C., Matthews, M. D., & Kelly, D. R. (2007). Grit: Perseverance and passion for long-term goals. *Journal of Personality and Social Psychology, 9,* 1087–1101. http://doi.org/10.1037/0022-3514.92.6.1087

Duckworth, A. L., Steen, T. A., & Seligman, M. E. P. (2005). Positive psychology in clinical practice. *Annual Review of Clinical Psychology, 1,* 629–651. http://doi.org/10.1146/annurev.clinpsy.1.102803.144154

Duhigg, C. (2012). *The power of habit: Why we do what we do in life and business.* New York, NY: Random House.

Dunn, E. W., Aknin, L. B., & Norton, M. I. (2008). Spending money on others promotes happiness. *Science, 319,* 1687–1688. http://doi.org/10.1126/science.1150952

Dunn, E. W., Aknin, L. B., & Norton, M. I. (2014). Prosocial spending and happiness using money to benefit others pays off. *Current Directions in Psychological Science, 23,* 41–47. http://doi.org/10.1177/0963721413512503

Duttro, K. (Ed.) (2003). Special issue: The influence of Bernard Haldane. *Career Planning and Adult Development Journal, 19*(3), 1–128.

Dweck, C. (1986). Motivational processes affecting learning. *American Psychologist, 41*(10), 1040–1048. http://doi.org/10.1037/0003-066X.41.10.1040

Dweck, C. (2006). *Mindset: The new psychology of success.* New York, NY: Random House.

Edelkott, N., Engstrom, D. W., Hernandez-Wolfe, P., & Gangsei, D. (2016). Vicarious resilience: Complexities and variations. *American Journal of Orthopsychiatry, 86*(6), 713–724.

Ellis, A., & Dryden, W. (1987). *The practice of rational-emotive therapy*. New York, NY: Springer.

Elston, F., & Boniwell, I. (2011). A grounded theory study of the value derived by women in financial services through a coaching intervention to help them identify their strengths and practice using them in the workplace. *International Coaching Psychology Review, 6*(1), 16–32.

Emmons, R. A. (2007). *Thanks!: How the new science of gratitude can make you happier*. Boston, MA: Houghton-Mifflin.

Emmons, R. A., & McCullough, M. E. (2003). Counting blessings versus burdens: An experimental investigation of gratitude and subjective well-being in daily life. *Journal of Personality and Social Psychology, 84*, 377–389. http://doi.org/10.1037/0022-3514.84.2.377

Ericsson, K. A., & Ward, P. (2007). Capturing the naturally occurring superior performance of experts in the laboratory: Toward a science of expert and exceptional performance. *Current Directions in Psychological Science, 16*(6), 346–50. http://doi.org/10.1111/j.1467-8721.2007.00533.x

Escandón, S., Martinez, M. L., & Flaskerud, J. H. (2016). Exploring character strengths: Forging a relationship between nursing students and community youth. *Issues in Mental Health Nursing, 37*(11), 875–877.

Exline, J. J., & Geyer, A. (2004). Perceptions of humility: A preliminary study. *Self and Identity, 3*, 95–114. http://doi.org/10.1080/13576500342000077

Feldman, D. B., & Dreher, D. E. (2012). Can hope be changed in 90 minutes? Testing the efficacy of a single-session goal-pursuit intervention for college students. *Journal of Happiness Studies, 13*(4), 745–759. http://doi.org/10.1007/s10902-011-9292-4

Ferragut, M., Blanca, M. J., & Ortiz-Tallo, M. (2014). Psychological virtues during adolescence: A longitudinal study of gender differences. *European Journal of Development Psychology, 11*(5), 521–531. http://doi.org/10.1080/17405629.2013.876403

Finkel, E. J., Slotter, E. B., Luchies, L. B., Walton, G. M., & Gross, J. J. (2013). A brief intervention to promote conflict reappraisal preserves marital quality over time. *Psychological Science, 24*(8), 1595–1601. http://doi.org/10.1177/0956797612474938

Fleeson, W. (2001). Toward a structure- and process-integrated view of personality: Traits as density distributions of states. *Journal of Personality and Social Psychology, 60*(1), 1011–1027. http://doi.org/10.1037/0022-3514.80.6.1011

Fleeson, W. (2004). Moving personality beyond the person-situation debate: The challenge and the opportunity of within-person variability. *Current Directions in Psychological Science, 13*, 83–87. http://doi.org/10.1111/j.0963-7214.2004.00280.x

Fleeson, W., Malanos, A. B., & Achille, N. M. (2002). An intraindividual process approach to the relationship between extraversion and positive affect: Is acting extraverted as "good" as being extraverted? *Journal of Personality and Social Psychology, 83*, 1409–1422. http://doi.org/10.1037/0022-3514.83.6.1409

Fluckiger, C., Caspar, F., Grosse Holtforth, M., & Willutzki, U. (2009). Working with patients' strengths: A microprocess approach. *Psychotherapy Research, 19*(2), 213–223. http://doi.org/10.1080/10503300902755300

Fluckiger, C., & Grosse Holtforth, M. (2008). Focusing the therapist's attention on the patient's strengths: A preliminary study to foster a mechanism of change in outpatient psychotherapy. *Journal of Clinical Psychology, 64*, 876–890. http://doi.org/10.1002/jclp.20493

Fluckiger, C., & Wusten, G., Zinbarg, R. E., & Wampold, B. E. (2010). *Resource activation: Using client's own strengths in psychotherapy and counseling*. Cambridge, MA: Hogrefe & Huber Publishers.

Folkman, S. (1997). Positive psychological states and coping with severe stress. *Social Science & Medicine, 45*, 1207–1221. http://doi.org/10.1016/S0277-9536(97)00040-3

Forest, J., Mageau, G. V. A., Crevier-Braud, L., Bergeron, L., Dubreuil, P., & Lavigne, G. V. L. (2012). Harmonious passion as an explanation of the relation between signature strengths' use and well-being at work: Test of an intervention program. *Human Relations, 65*(9), 1233–1252. http://doi.org/10.1177/0018726711433134

Forster, J. R. (2009). *Articulating strengths together: An interactive process to enhance positivity*. New York, NY: Booksurge.

Fowers, B. J. (2000). *Beyond the myth of marital happiness*. San Francisco, CA: Jossey-Bass.

Fowers, B. J. (2005). *Virtue and psychology: Pursuing excellence in ordinary practices*. Washington, DC: American Psychological Association. http://doi.org/10.1037/11219-000

Fowers, B. J. (2008). From continence to virtue: Recovering goodness, character unity, and character types for positive psychology. *Theory & Psychology, 18*(5), 629–653. http://doi.org/10.1177/0959354308093399

Fox Eades, J. (2008). *Celebrating strengths: Building strengths-based schools*. Warwick, UK: CAPP Press.

Franklin, B. (1962). *Autobiography of Benjamin Franklin*. New York, NY: MacMillan.

Franklin, S. S. (2009). *The psychology of happiness*. New York, NY: Cambridge University Press. http://doi.org/10.1017/CBO9780511819285

Fredrickson, B. L. (2001). The role of positive emotions in positive psychology: The broaden-and-build theory of positive emotions. *American Psychologist, 56*, 218–226. http://doi.org/10.1037/0003-066X.56.3.218

Fredrickson, B. L. (2013). *Love 2.0: How our supreme emotion affects everything we feel, think, and do*. New York, NY: Hudson Street Press.

Fredrickson, B. L., Cohn, M. A., Coffey, K. A., Pek, J., & Finkel, S. M. (2008). Open hearts build lives: Positive emotions, induced through loving-kindness meditation, build consequential personal resources. *Journal of Personality and Social Psychology, 95*(5), 1045–62. http://doi.org/10.1037/a0013262

Fredrickson, B. L., & Joiner, T. (2002). Positive emotions trigger upward spirals toward emotional well-being. *Psychological Science, 13*(2), 172–175. http://doi.org/10.1111/1467-9280.00431

Freidlin, P., Littman-Ovadia, H., & Niemiec, R. M. (2017). Positive psychopathology: Social anxiety via character strengths underuse and overuse. *Personality and Individual Differences, 108*, 50–54. http://doi.org/10.1016/j.paid.2016.12.003

Froh, J. J., Sefick, W. J., & Emmons, R. A. (2008). Counting blessings in early adolescents: An experimental study of gratitude and subjective well-being. *Journal of School Psychology, 46*, 213–233. http://doi.org/10.1016/j.jsp.2007.03.005

Fung, B. K. K., Ho, S. M. Y., Fung, A. S. M., Leung, E. Y. P., Chow, S. P., Ip, W. Y., … Barlaan, P. I. G. (2011). The development of a strength-focused mutual support group for caretakers of children with cerebral palsy. *East Asian Archives of Psychiatry, 21*(2), 64–72.

Gable, S. L., Reis, H. T., Impett, E. A., & Asher, E. R. (2004). What do you do when things go right? The intrapersonal and interpersonal benefits of sharing positive events. *Journal of Personality and Social Psychology, 87*(2), 228–245. http://doi.org/10.1037/0022-3514.87.2.228

Gander, F., Proyer, R. T., Ruch, W., & Wyss, T. (2012). The good character at work: An initial study on the contribution of character strengths in identifying healthy and unhealthy work-related behavior and experience patterns. *International Archives of Occupational and Environmental Health, 85*(8) 895–904. http://doi.org/10.1007/s00420-012-0736-x

Gander, F., Proyer, R. T., Ruch, W., & Wyss, T. (2013). Strength-based positive interventions: Further evidence for their potential in enhancing well-being and alleviating depression. *Journal of Happiness Studies, 14*, 1241–1259. http://doi.org/10.1007/s10902-012-9380-0

Gardner, H. (1983). *Frames of mind: The theory of multiple intelligences*. New York, NY: Basic Books.

Garland, E., Gaylord, S., & Park, J. (2009). The role of mindfulness in positive reappraisal. *Explore: The Journal of Science and Healing, 5*(1), 37–44. http://doi.org/10.1016/j.explore.2008.10.001

Garland, E. L., Gaylord, S. A., & Fredrickson, B. L. (2011). Positive reappraisal mediates the stress-reductive effects of mindfulness: An upward spiral process. *Mindfulness, 2*(1), 59–67. http://doi.org/10.1007/s12671-011-0043-8

Gayton, S. D., & Kehoe, E. J. (2015). Character strengths and hardiness of Australian army special forces applicants. *Military Medicine, 180*(8), 857–862.

Gibbs, T., & Larcus, J. (2015). Wellness coaching: Helping students thrive. *Journal of Student Affairs, 24*, 23–34.

Gillham, J. (2011, July). *Teaching positive psychology to adolescents: Three-year follow-up*. Paper presented as part of the symposium Positive Psychology in Schools, presented at the 2nd World Congress on Positive Psychology, Philadelphia.

Gillham, J., Adams-Deutsch, Z., Werner, J., Reivich, K., Coulter-Heindl, V., Linkins, M., … Seligman, M. E. P. (2011). Character strengths predict subjective well-being during adolescence. *Journal of Positive Psychology, 6*(1), 31–44. http://doi.org/10.1080/17439760.2010.536773

Gluck, J., & Baltes, P. B. (2006). Using the concept of wisdom to enhance the expression of wisdom knowledge: Not the philosopher's dream but differential effects of developmental preparedness. *Psychology and Aging, 21*, 679–690. http://doi.org/10.1037/0882-7974.21.4.679

Goddard, H. W., Olson, J. R., Galovan, A. M., Schramm, D. G., & Marshall, J. P. (2016). Qualities of character that predict marital well-being. *Family Relations: An Interdisciplinary Journal of Applied Family Studies, 65*(3), 424–438.

Goldstein, E. D. (2007). Sacred moments: Implications on well-being and stress. *Journal of Clinical Psychology, 63*(10), 1001–1019. http://doi.org/10.1002/jclp.20402

Goldstein, K. (1995). *The organism: A holistic approach to biology derived from pathological data in man.* New York, NY: Zone Books. (Originally published in 1934)

Goleman, D. (1997). *Healing emotions: Conversations with the Dalai Lama on mindfulness, emotions, and health.* Boston, MA: Shambhala.

Goleman, D. (2006). *Social intelligence: The new science of human relationships.* New York, NY: Random House.

Gollwitzer, P. M., & Oettingen, G. (2013). Implementation intentions. In M. Gellman & J. R. Turner (Eds.), *In Encyclopedia of behavioral medicine* (pp. 1043–1048). New York, NY: Springer.

Gordon, C. L., Arnette, R. A., & Smith, R. E. (2011). Have you thanked your spouse today? Felt and expressed gratitude among married couples. *Personality and Individual Differences, 50*, 339–343. http://doi.org/10.1016/j.paid.2010.10.012

Gordon, A. M., Impett, E. A., Kogan, A., Oveis, C., & Keltner, D. (2012). To have and to hold: Gratitude promotes relationship maintenance in intimate bonds. *Journal of Personality and Social Psychology, 103*(2), 257–274. http://doi.org/10.1037/a0028723

Gottman, J., & Silver, N. (1999). *The seven principles for making marriage work.* New York, NY: Three Rivers.

Gradisek, P. (2012). Character strengths and life satisfaction of Slovenian in-service and pre-service teachers. *CEPS Journal, 2*(3), 167–180.

Grant, A. M., & Schwartz, B. (2011). Too much of a good thing: The challenge and opportunity of the inverted u. *Perspectives on Psychological Science, 6*, 61–76. http://doi.org/10.1177/1745691610393523

Greitemeyer, T., Osswald, S., Fischer, P., & Frey, D. (2007). Civil courage: Implicit theories, related concepts, and measurement. *Journal of Positive Psychology, 2*(2), 115–119. http://doi.org/10.1080/17439760701228789

Griffin, B. J., Worthington, E. L., Lavelock, C. R., Greer, C. L., Lin, Y., Davis, D. E., & Hook, J. N. (2015). Efficacy of a self-forgiveness workbook: A randomized controlled trial with interpersonal offenders. *Journal of Counseling Psychology, 62*(2), 124–136. http://doi.org/10.1037/cou0000060

Güsewell, A., & Ruch, W. (2012). Are only emotional strengths emotional? Character strengths and disposition to positive emotions. *Applied Psychology: Health and Well-Being, 4*(2), 218–239. http://doi.org/10.1111/j.1758-0854.2012.01070.x

Güsewell, A., & Ruch, W. (2015). Character strength profiles of musicians. *Journal of Arts and Humanities, 4*(6), 1–17.

Guo, J., Wang, Y., & Liu, X. Y. (2015). Relation between marital satisfaction and character strengths in young people. *Chinese Mental Health Journal, 29*(5), 383–388.

Gustems-Carnicer, J., & Calderón, C. (2016). Virtues and character strengths related to approach coping strategies of college students. *Social Psychology of Education, 19*(1), 77–95.

Haidt, J. (2000). The positive emotion of elevation. *Prevention and Treatment, 3.* http://doi.org/10.1037/1522-3736.3.1.33c

Hall, L. (2013). *Mindful coaching: How mindfulness can transform coaching practice.* Philadelphia, PA: Kogan Page.

Halvorson, H. G. (2011). *Succeed: How we can reach our goals.* New York, NY: Penguin.

Hammond, D. C. (1988). *Hypnotic induction and suggestion: An introductory manual.* Des Plaines, IL: American Society of Clinical Hypnosis.

Hammond, D. C. (1990). *Handbook of hypnotic suggestions and metaphors.* New York, NY: W. W. Norton.

Hannah, S. T., & Jennings, P. L. (2013). Leader ethos and big-C character. *Organizational Dynamics, 42*, 8–16. http://doi.org/10.1016/j.orgdyn.2012.12.002

Hannah, S. T., Sweeney, P. J., & Lester, P. B. (2007). Toward a courageous mindset: The subjective act and experience of courage. *Journal of Positive Psychology, 2*(2), 129–135. http://doi.org/10.1080/17439760701228854

Harackiewicz, J., Canning, E., Tibbetts, Y., Giffen, C., & Hyde, J. (2014). Closing the social class achievement gap for first generation students in undergraduate biology. *Journal of Educational Psychology, 106*, 375–389. http://doi.org/10.1037/a0034679

Harris, M. A., Brett, C. E., Johnson, W., & Deary, I. J. (2016). Personality stability from age 14 to age 77 years. *Psychology and Aging, 31*(8), 862–874.

Hart, W., Albarracin, D., Eagly, A. H., Brechan, I., Lindberg, M. J., & Merrill, L. (2009). Feeling validated versus being correct: A meta-analysis of selective exposure to information. *Psychological Bulletin, 135*(4), 555–588. http://doi.org/10.1037/a0015701

Harzer, C., & Ruch, W. (2012). When the job is a calling: The role of applying one's signature strengths at work. *Journal of Positive Psychology, 7*, 362–371. http://doi.org/10.1080/17439760.2012.702784

Harzer, C., & Ruch, W. (2013). The application of signature character strengths and positive experiences at work. *Journal of Happiness Studies, 14*(3), 965–983. http://doi.org/10.1007/s10902-012-9364-0

Harzer, C., & Ruch, W. (2014). The role of character strengths for task performance, job dedication, interpersonal facilitation, and organizational support. *Human Performance, 27*, 183–205. http://doi.org/10.1080/08959285.2014.913592

Harzer, C., & Ruch, W. (2015). The relationships of character strengths with coping, work-related stress, and job satisfaction. *Frontiers in Psychology, 6.* http://doi.org/10.3389/fpsyg.2015.00165

Harzer, C., & Ruch, W. (2016). Your strengths are calling: Preliminary results of a web-based strengths intervention to increase calling. *Journal of Happiness Studies, 17*(6), 2237–2256. http://doi.org/10.1007/s10902-015-9692-y

Hefferon, K. (2013). *The body and positive psychology: The somatopsychic side to flourishing.* London, UK: McGraw-Hill.

Helzer, E. G., Furr, R. M., Barranti, M., & Fleeson, W. (2014). *Visible virtues: Agreement on perceptions of moral character.* Conference presentation: Annual Meeting of the Society for Personality and Social Psychology, Austin, Texas. http://dx.doi.org/10.1037/e578192014-023

Hill, P. L., Sumner, R., & Burrow, A. L. (2014). Understanding the pathways to purpose: Examining personality and well-being correlates across adulthood. *Journal of Positive Psychology, 9*(3), 227–234. http://doi.org/10.1080/17439760.2014.888584

Hodges, T. D., & Clifton, D. O. (2004). Strengths-based development in practice. In A. Linley & S. Joseph (Eds.), *Handbook of positive psychology in practice.* Hoboken, NJ: John Wiley and Sons.

Hoffman, R., Hinkle, M. G., & Kress, V. W. (2010). Letter writing as an intervention in family therapy with adolescents who engage in nonsuicidal self-injury. *The Family Journal, 18*, 24–30. http://doi.org/10.1177/1066480709355039

Hofmann, S. G., Grossman, P., & Hinton, D. E. (2011). Loving-kindness and compassion meditation: Potential for psychological interventions. *Clinical Psychology Review, 31*(7), 1126–1132. http://doi.org/10.1016/j.cpr.2011.07.003

Hone, L. (2017). *Resilient grieving: Finding strength and embracing life after a loss that changes everything.* New York, NY: The Experiment.

Hone, L. C., Jarden, A., Duncan, S., & Schofield, G. M. (2015). Flourishing in New Zealand workers: Associations with lifestyle behaviors, physical health, psychosocial, and work-related indicators. *Journal of Occupational and Environmental Medicine, 57*(9), 973–983. http://doi.org/10.1097/JOM.0000000000000508

Hone, L. C., Jarden, A., & Schofield, G. M. (2014). An evaluation of positive psychology intervention effectiveness trials using the re-aim framework: A practice-friendly review. *Journal of Positive Psychology, 10*(4), 303–322. http://doi.org/10.1080/17439760.2014.965267

Hudson, N. W., & Fraley, R. C. (2015). Volitional personality trait change: Can people choose to change their personality traits? *Journal of Personality and Social Psychology, 109*(3), 490–507 http://doi.org/10.1037/pspp0000021

Huffman, J. C., DuBois, C. M., Healy, B. C., Boehm, J. K., Kashdan, T. B., Celano, C. M., … Lyubomirsky, S. (2014). Feasibility and utility of positive psychology exercises for suicidal inpatients. *General Hospital Psychiatry, 36*(1), 88–94. http://doi.org/10.1016/j.genhosppsych.2013.10.006

Hunter, J. W. (2000). *The death of character: Moral education in an age without good or evil.* New York, NY: Basic Books.

Hurley, D. B., & Kwon, P. (2012). Results of a study to increase savoring the moment: Differential impact on positive and negative outcomes. *Journal of Happiness Studies, 13*, 579–588. http://doi.org/10.1007/s10902-011-9280-8

Huta, V., & Hawley, L. (2010). Psychological strengths and cognitive vulnerabilities: Are they two ends of the same continuum or do they have independent relationships with well-being and ill-being? *Journal of Happiness Studies, 11*, 71–93. http://doi.org/10.1007/s10902-008-9123-4

Hutcherson, C. A., Seppala, E. M., & Gross, J. J. (2008). Loving-kindness meditation increases social connectedness. *Emotion, 8*(5), 720–724. http://doi.org/10.1037/a0013237

Ivtzan, I., Lomas, T., Hefferon, K., & Worth, P. (2016). *Second wave positive psychology: Embracing the dark side of life.* New York, NY: Routledge.

Ivtzan, I., Niemiec, R. M., & Briscoe, C. (2016). A study investigating the effects of mindfulness-based strengths practice (MBSP) on wellbeing. *International Journal of Wellbeing, 6*(2), 1–13.

Jahoda, M. (1958). *Current concepts of positive mental health.* New York, NY: Basic Books. http://doi.org/10.1037/11258-000

Joseph, S., & Linley, A. (2006). *Positive therapy: A meta-theory for positive psychological practice.* New York, NY: Routledge.

Kabat-Zinn, J. (1990). *Full catastrophe living.* New York, NY: Dell.

Kaczor, C. (2015). *The gospel of happiness: Rediscover your faith through spiritual practice and positive psychology.* New York, NY: Penguin Random House.

Kahneman, D. (2011). *Thinking, fast and slow.* London, UK: Penguin Books.

Kaiser, R. B., & Hogan, J. (2011). Personality, leader behavior, and overdoing it. *Consulting Psychology Journal: Practice and Research, 63*(4), 219–242. http://doi.org/10.1037/a0026795

Kaiser, R. B., & Overfield, D. V. (2011). Strengths, strengths overused, and lopsided leadership. *Consulting Psychology Journal: Practice and Research, 63,* 89–109.

Kammrath, L. K., & Peetz, J. (2011). The limits of love: Predicting immediate vs. sustained caring behaviors in close relationships. *Journal of Experimental & Social Psychology, 47*(2), 411–417. http://doi.org/10.1016/j.jesp.2010.11.004

Kannangara, C. S. (2015). From languishing dyslexia to thriving dyslexia: Developing a new conceptual approach to working with people with dyslexia. *Frontiers in Psychology, 6.* http://doi.org/10.3389/fpsyg.2015.01976

Kannangara, C. S., Griffiths, D., Carson, J., & Munasinghe, S. (2015). The relevance of cybernetics for a positive psychology approach to dyslexia. *Kybernetes, 44*(8/9), 1284–1297. http://doi.org/10.1108/K-11-2014-0270

Kashdan, T. B. (2009). *Curious? Discover the missing ingredient to a fulfilling life.* New York, NY: HarperCollins.

Kashdan, T. B., Blalock, D. V., Young, K. C., Machell, K. A., Monfort, S. S., McKnight, P. E., & Ferssizidis, P. (2017). Personality strengths in romantic relationships: Measuring perceptions of benefits and costs and their impact on personal and relational well-being. *Psychological Assessment.* Advance online publication. http://dx.doi.org/10.1037/pas0000464

Kashdan, T. B., Julian, T., Merritt, K., & Uswatte, G. (2006). Social anxiety and posttraumatic stress in combat veterans: Relations to well-being and character strengths. *Behaviour Research and Therapy, 44,* 561–583. http://doi.org/10.1016/j.brat.2005.03.010

Kashdan, T. B., McKnight, P. E., Fincham, F. D., & Rose, P. (2011). When curiosity breeds intimacy: Taking advantage of intimacy opportunities and transforming boring conversations. *Journal of Personality, 79,* 1369–1401. http://doi.org/10.1111/j.1467-6494.2010.00697.x

Kauffman, C., Silberman, J., & Sharpley, D. (2008). Coaching for strengths using VIA. In J. Passmore (Ed.), *Psychometrics in coaching: Using psychological and psychometric tools for development* (pp. 239–253). Philadelphia, PA: Kogan Page.

Kaufman, S. B., & Gregoire, C. (2015). *Wired to create: Unravelling the mysteries of the creative mind.* London, UK: Vermilion.

Kern, M. L., & Bowling, D. S. (2015). Character strengths and academic performance in law students. *Journal of Research in Personality, 55,* 25–29. http://doi.org/10.1016/j.jrp.2014.12.003

Kesebir, P. (2014). A quiet ego quiets death anxiety: Humility as an existential anxiety buffer. *Journal of Personality and Social Psychology, 106*(4), 610–623. http://doi.org/10.1037/a0035814

Keyes, C. L. M. (2002). The mental health continuum: From languishing to flourishing in life. *Journal of Health and Social Behavior, 43,* 207–222. http://doi.org/10.2307/3090197

Keyes, C. L. M. (2003). Complete mental health: an agenda for the 21st century. In C. L. M. Keyes & J. Haidt (Eds.). *Flourishing: Positive psychology and the life well-lived* (pp. 293–312). Washington, DC: American Psychological Association.

Khumalo, I. P., Wissing, M. P., & Temane, Q. M. (2008). Exploring the validity of the Values-In-Action Inventory of Strengths (VIA-IS) in an African context. *Journal of Psychology in Africa, 18*(1), 133–142.

Kilduff, G. J., & Galinsky, A. D. (2013). From the ephemeral to the enduring: How approach-oriented mindsets lead to greater status. *Journal of Personality and Social Psychology, 105*(5), 816–831. http://doi.org/10.1037/a0033667

Kim, W. C., & Mauborgne, R. (1997). Value innovation: The strategic logic of high growth. *Harvard Business Review, 75*, 103–112.

King, L. A. (2001). The health benefits of writing about life goals. *Personality and Social Psychology Bulletin, 27*, 798–807. http://doi.org/10.1177/0146167201277003

Kirchner, J., Ruch, W., & Dziobek, I. (2016). Brief report: Character strengths in adults with autism spectrum disorder without intellectual impairment. *Journal of Autism and Developmental Disorders, 46*(10), 3330–3337. http://doi.org/10.1007/s10803-016-2865-7

Kobau, R., Seligman, M. E. P., Peterson, C., Diener, E., Zack, M. M., Chapman, D., & Thompson, W. (2011). Mental health promotion in public health: Perspectives and strategies from positive psychology. *American Journal of Public Health, 101*(8), e1–e9. http://doi.org/10.2105/AJPH.2010.300083

Koo, M., Algoe, S. B., Wilson, T. D., & Gilbert, D. T. (2008). It's a wonderful life: Mentally subtracting positive events improves people's affective states, contrary to their affective forecasts. *Journal of Personality and Social Psychology, 95*, 1217–1224. http://doi.org/10.1037/a0013316

Kooij, D. T., van Woerkom, M., Wilkenloh, J., Dorenbosch, L., & Denissen, J. J. (2017). Job crafting towards strengths and interests: The effects of a job crafting intervention on person–job fit and the role of age. *Journal of Applied Psychology.* Advance online publication. http://dx.doi.org/10.1037/apl0000194

Kornfield, J. (1993). *A path with heart.* New York, NY: Bantam Books.

Kornfield, J. (2008). *The art of forgiveness, lovingkindness, and peace.* New York, NY: Bantam Books.

Korotitsch, W. J., & Nelson-Gray, R. O. (1999). An overview of self-monitoring research in assessment and treatment. *Psychological Assessment, 11*(4), 415–425. http://doi.org/10.1037/1040-3590.11.4.415

Krentzman, A. R. (2013). Review of the application of positive psychology to substance abuse use, addiction, and recovery research. *Psychology of Addictive Behaviors, 27*(1), 151–165. http://doi.org/10.1037/a0029897

Kruse, E., Chancellor, J., Ruberton, P. M., & Lyubomirsky, S. (2014). An upward spiral between gratitude and humility. *Social, Psychological, and Personality Science, 5*(7), 805–814. http://doi.org/10.1177/1948550614534700

Kurtz, J. L. (2008). Looking to the future to appreciate the present: The benefits of perceived temporal scarcity. *Psychological Science, 19*, 1238–1241. http://doi.org/10.1111/j.1467-9280.2008.02231.x

LaFasto, F., & Larson, C. (2012). *The humanitarian leader in each of us: Seven choices that shape a socially responsible life.* Thousand Oaks, CA: Sage.

Laham, S. M. (2013). Ease of retrieval and the moral circle. *Social Psychology, 44*(1), 33–36. http://doi.org/10.1027/1864-9335/a000099

Lambert, N. M., & Fincham, F. D. (2011). Expressing gratitude to a partner leads to more relationship maintenance behavior. *Emotion, 11*, 52–60. http://doi.org/10.1037/a0021557

Lambert, N. M., Gwinn, A. M., Fincham, F. D., & Stillman, T. F. (2011). Feeling tired? How sharing positive experiences can boost vitality. *International Journal of Wellbeing, 1*(3), 307–314. http://doi.org/10.5502/ijw.v1i3.1

Landis, S. K., Sherman, M. F., Piedmont, R. L., Kirkhart, M. W., Rapp, E. M., & Bike, D. H. (2009). The relation between elevation and self-reported prosocial behavior: Incremental validity over the five-factor model of personality. *Journal of Positive Psychology, 4*(1), 71–84. http://doi.org/10.1080/17439760802399208

Langer, E. J. (1997). *The power of mindful learning.* Reading, MA: Addison-Wesley.

Langer, E. (2006). *On becoming an artist: Reinventing yourself through mindful creativity.* New York, NY: Ballantine Books.

Lapsley, D. K., & Power, F. C. (Eds.). (2005). *Character psychology and character education.* Notre Dame, IN: University of Notre Dame Press.

Larcus, J., Gibbs, T., & Hackmann, T. (2016). Building capacities for change: Wellness coaching as a positive approach to student development. *Philosophy of Coaching: An International Journal, 1*(1), 43–62. http://doi.org/10.22316/poc/01.1.05

Laska, K. M., Gurman, A. S., & Wampold, B. E. (2014). Expanding the lens of evidence-based practice in psychotherapy A common factors perspective. *Psychotherapy: Theory, Research, & Practice, 51*, 467–481. http://doi.org/10.1037/a0034332

Lavelock, C. R., Worthington, E. L., & Davis, D. E. (2014a). *The path to humility: Six practical sections for becoming a more humble person.* Retrieved from https://www.evworthington-forgiveness.com/diy-workbooks/

Lavelock, C. R., Worthington, E. L., Jr., Davis, D. E., Griffin, B. J., Reid, C. A., Hook, J. N., & Van Tongeren, D. R. (2014b). The quiet virtue speaks: An intervention to promote humility. *Journal of Psychology & Theology, 42*, 99–110.

Lavy, S., & Littman-Ovadia, H. (2016). My better self: Using strengths at work and work productivity, organizational citizenship behavior and satisfaction. *Journal of Career Development.* Advance online publication.

Lavy, S., Littman-Ovadia, H., & Bareli, Y. (2014a). Strengths deployment as a mood-repair mechanism: Evidence from a diary study with a relationship exercise group. *Journal of Positive Psychology, 9*(6), 547–558. http://doi.org/10.1080/17439760.2014.936963

Lavy, S., Littman-Ovadia, H., & Bareli, Y. (2014b). My better half: Strengths endorsement and deployment in married couples. *Journal of Family Issues, 37*, 1730–1745. http://doi.org/10.1177/0192513X14550365

Lavy, S., Littman-Ovadia, H., & Boiman-Meshita, M. (2016). The wind beneath my wings: The role of social support in enhancing the use of strengths at work. *Journal of Career Assessment.* Advance online publication.

Layous, K., Nelson, S. K., Oberle, E., Schonert-Reichl, K. A., & Lyubomirsky, S. (2012). Kindness counts: Prompting prosocial behavior in preadolescents boosts peer acceptance and well-being. *PLoS ONE, 7*(12), e51380. http://doi.org/10.1371/journal.pone.0051380

Lefevor, G. T., & Fowers, B. J. (2016). Traits, situational factors, and their interactions as explanations of helping behavior. *Personality and Individual Differences, 92*, 159–163. http://doi.org/10.1016/j.paid.2015.12.042

Legault, L., Al-Khindi, T., & Inzlicht, M. (2012). Preserving integrity in the face of performance threat: Self-affirmation enhances neurophysiological responsiveness to errors. *Psychological Science, 23*, 1455–1460. http://doi.org/10.1177/0956797612448483

Leppma, M. (2012). Loving-kindness meditation and counseling. *Journal of Mental Health Counseling, 34*(3), 197–204. http://doi.org/10.17744/mehc.34.3.955g218326616282

Leventhal, K. S., DeMaria, L. M., Gillham, J. E., Andrew, G., Peabody, J., & Leventhal, S. M. (2016). A psychosocial resilience curriculum provides the "missing piece" to boost adolescent physical health: A randomized controlled trial of Girls First in India. *Social Science & Medicine, 161*, 37–46. http://doi.org/10.1016/j.socscimed.2016.05.004

Leventhal, K. S., Gillham, J., DeMaria, L., Andrew, G., Peabody, J., & Leventhal, S. (2015). Building psychosocial assets and wellbeing among adolescent girls: A randomized controlled trial. *Journal of Adolescence, 45*, 284–295. http://doi.org/10.1016/j.adolescence.2015.09.011

Levitt, H. M., Pomerville, A., & Surace, F. I. (2016). A qualitative meta-analysis examining clients' experiences of psychotherapy: A new agenda. *Psychological Bulletin, 142*(8), 801–830. http://doi.org/10.1037/bul0000057

Linkins, M., Niemiec, R. M., & Gillham, J., & Mayerson, D. (2015). Through the strengths lens: A framework for educating the heart. *Journal of Positive Psychology, 10*(1), 64–68. http://doi.org/10.1080/17439760.2014.888581

Linley, A. (2008). *Average to A+: Realising strengths in yourself and others.* Coventry, UK: CAPP Press.

Linley, P. A., & Harrington, S. (2006). Strengths coaching: A potential-guided approach to coaching psychology. *International Coaching Psychology Review, 1*(1), 37–46.

Linley, P. A., Nielsen, K. M., Gillett, R., & Biswas-Diener, R. (2010). Using signature strengths in pursuit of goals: Effects on goal progress, need satisfaction, and well-being, and implications for coaching psychologists. *International Coaching Psychology Review, 5*(1), 6–15.

Littman-Ovadia, H., & Davidovitch, N. (2010). Effects of congruence and character-strength deployment on work adjustment and well-being. *International Journal of Business and Social Science, 1*(3), 138–146.

Littman-Ovadia, H., & Lavy, S. (2012). Differential ratings and associations with well-being of character strengths in two communities. *Health Sociology Review, 21*(3), 1378–1410. http://doi.org/10.5172/hesr.2012.21.3.299

Littman-Ovadia, H., & Lavy, S. (2016). Going the extra mile: Perseverance as a key character strength at work. *Journal of Career Assessment, 24*(2), 240–252. http://doi.org/10.1177/1069072715580322

Littman-Ovadia, H., Lavy, S., & Boiman-Meshita, M. (2016). When theory and research collide: Examining correlates of signature strengths use at work. *Journal of Happiness Studies*. Advance online publication.

Littman-Ovadia, H., Lazar-Butbul, V., & Benjamin, B. A. (2014). Strengths-based career counseling: Overview and initial evaluation. *Journal of Career Assessment, 22*(3), 403–419. http://doi.org/10.1177/1069072713498483

Littman-Ovadia, H., & Niemiec, R. M. (2017). Meaning, mindfulness, and character strengths. In P. Russo-Netzer, S. E. Schulenberg, & A. Batthyany (Eds.), *To thrive, to cope, to understand: Meaning in positive and existential psychology*. New York, NY: Springer.

Littman-Ovadia, H., & Steger, M. (2010). Character strengths and well-being among volunteers and employees: Toward an integrative model. *Journal of Positive Psychology, 5*(6), 419–430. http://doi.org/10.1080/17439760.2010.516765

Logan, D. E., Kilmer, J. R., & Marlatt, G. A. (2010). The virtuous drinker: Character virtues as correlates and moderators of college student drinking and consequences. *Journal of American College Health, 58*, 317–324. http://doi.org/10.1080/07448480903380326

Lomas, T. (2016). Towards a positive cross-cultural lexicography: Enriching our emotional landscape through 216 "untranslatable" words pertaining to well-being. *Journal of Positive Psychology, 11*(5), 546–558. http://doi.org/10.1080/17439760.2015.1127993

Lopez, S. J. (Ed.). (2008). *Positive psychology: Exploring the best in people. Volume 1: Discovering human strengths*. Westport, CT: Praeger.

Lopez, S. J. (2014). *Making hope happen: Create the future you want for yourself and others*. New York, NY: Atria Books.

Lottman, T., Zawaly, S., & Niemiec, R. M. (2017). Well-being and well-doing: Bringing mindfulness and character strengths to the early childhood classroom and home. In C. Proctor (Ed.), *Positive psychology interventions in practice*. New York, NY: Springer.

Louis, M. C. (2011). Strengths interventions in higher education: The effect of identification versus development approaches on implicit self-theory. *Journal of Positive Psychology, 6*(3), 204–215. http://doi.org/10.1080/17439760.2011.570366

Lounsbury, J. W., Fisher, L. A., Levy, J. J., & Welsh, D. P. (2009). An investigation of character strengths in relation to the academic success of college students. *Individual Differences Research, 7*(1), 52–69.

Loy, L. S., Wieber, F., Gollwitzer, P. M., & Oettingen, G. (2016). Supporting sustainable food consumption: Mental contrasting with implementation intentions (MCII) aligns intentions and behavior. *Frontiers in Psychology, 7*.

Lynch, M. F., La Guardiab, J. G., & Ryan, R. M. (2009). On being yourself in different cultures: Ideal and actual self-concept, autonomy support, and well-being in China, Russia, and the United States. *Journal of Positive Psychology, 4*(4), 290–304. http://doi.org/10.1080/17439760902933765

Lyubomirsky, S. (2008). *The how of happiness: A scientific approach to getting the life you want*. New York, NY: Penguin Press.

Lyubomirsky, S., Dickerhoof, R., Boehm, J. K., & Sheldon, K. M. (2011). Becoming happier takes both a will and a proper way: An experimental longitudinal intervention to boost well-being. *Emotion, 11*(2), 391–402. http://doi.org/10.1037/a0022575

Lyubomirsky, S., & Layous, K. (2013). How do simple positive activities increase well-being? *Current Directions in Psychological Science, 22*, 57–62. http://doi.org/10.1177/0963721412469809

Lyubomirsky, S., Sheldon, K. M., & Schkade, D. (2005). Pursuing happiness: The architecture of sustainable change. *Review of General Psychology, 9*, 111–131. http://doi.org/10.1037/1089-2680.9.2.111

Macdonald, C., Bore, M., & Munro, D. (2008). Values in action scale and the big 5: An empirical indication of structure. *Journal of Research in Personality, 42*(4), 787–799. http://doi.org/10.1016/j.jrp.2007.10.003

Madden, W., Green, S., & Grant, A. M. (2011). A pilot study evaluating strengths-based coaching for primary school students: Enhancing engagement and hope. *International Coaching Psychology Review, 6*(1), 71–83.

Mann, T. C., & Gilovich, T. (2016). The asymmetric connection between money and material vs. experiential purchases. *Journal of Positive Psychology, 11*(6), 647–658. http://doi.org/10.1080/17439760.2016.1152594

Marigold, D.C., Holmes, J.G., & Ross, M. (2007). More than words: Reframing compliments from romantic partners fosters security in low self-esteem individuals. *Journal of Personality and Social Psychology, 92*, 232–248. http://doi.org/10.1037/0022-3514.92.2.232

Marigold, D.C., Holmes, J.G., & Ross, M. (2010). Fostering relationship resilience: An intervention for low self-esteem individuals. *Journal of Experimental Social Psychology, 46*, 624–630. http://doi.org/10.1016/j.jesp.2010.02.011

Martela, F., & Steger, M.F. (2016). The three meanings of meaning in life: Distinguishing coherence, purpose, and significance. *Journal of Positive Psychology, 11*(5), 531–545. http://doi.org/10.1080/17439760.2015.1137623

Martinez-Marti, M.L., Avia, M.D., & Hernandez-Lloreda, J. (2014). Appreciation of beauty training: A web-based intervention. *Journal of Positive Psychology, 9*(6), 477–481. http://doi.org/10.1080/17439760.2014.920512

Martinez-Marti, M.L., & Ruch, W. (2014). Character strengths and well-being across the life span: Data from a representative sample of German-speaking adults in Switzerland. *Frontiers in Psychology, 5*.

Martinez-Marti, M.L., & Ruch, W. (2016). Character strengths predict resilience over and above positive affect, self-efficacy, optimism, social support, self-esteem, and life satisfaction. *Journal of Positive Psychology, 12*(2), 110–119. http://doi.org/10.1080/17439760.2016.1163403

Maslow, A. (1970). *Motivation and personality* (2nd ed.). New York, NY: Harper & Row.

Maslow, A.H. (1973). *The farther reaches of human nature*. New York, NY: Viking.

Matthews, M.D., Eid, J., Kelly, D., Bailey, J.K.S., & Peterson, C. (2006). Character strengths and virtues of developing military leaders: An international comparison. *Military Psychology, 18*(Suppl.), S57–S68. http://doi.org/10.1207/s15327876mp1803s_5

Mayerson, N.M. (2013, June). *Signature strengths: Validating the construct*. Presentation at Third World Conrgress on Positive Psychology, Los Angeles, CA. Abstract retrieved from http://psycnet.apa.org/?fa=main.doiLanding&doi=10.1037/e574802013-112.

Mayerson, N.M. (2015). "Characterizing" the workplace: Using character strengths to create sustained success. *Kognition & Paedagogik, 96*, 14–27.

Mayerson, N.M. (2016). Creating sustained organizational success: An application of character science. *Positive Work and Organizations: Research and Practice, 2*. Retrieved from http://www.viacharacter.org/blog/strengths-at-work/

Mazzucchelli, T.G., Kane, R.T., & Rees, C.S. (2010). Behavioral activation interventions for well-being: A meta-analysis. *Journal of Positive Psychology, 5*(2), 105–121.

McAdams, D.P., Anyidoho, N.A., Brown, C., Huang, Y.T., Kaplan, B., & Machado, M.A. (2004). Traits and stories: Links between dispositional and narrative features of personality. *Journal of Personality, 72*(4), 761–784. http://doi.org/10.1111/j.0022-3506.2004.00279.x

McCabe, K.O., & Fleeson, W. (2016). Are traits useful?: Explaining trait manifestations as tools in the pursuit of goals. *Journal of Personality and Social Psychology, 110*(2), 287–301. http://doi.org/10.1037/a0039490

McCullough, M.E. (2008). *Beyond revenge: The evolution of the forgiveness instinct*. San Francisco, CA: Jossey-Bass.

McCullough, M.E., Root, L.M., & Cohen, A.D. (2006). Writing about the benefits of an interpersonal transgression facilitates forgiveness. *Journal of Consulting and Clinical Psychology, 74*(5), 887–897. http://doi.org/10.1037/0022-006X.74.5.887

McGhee, P.E. (1999). *Health, healing, and the amuse system: Humor as survival training*. Dubuque, IA: Kendall/Hunt.

McGhee, P.E. (2010). *Humor as survival training for a stressed-out world: The 7 humor habits program*. Bloomington, IN: AuthorHouse.

McGrath, R.E. (2013). *Intercorrelation matrix of VIA Survey results of 458,854 respondents*. Unpublished data of the VIA Institute.

McGrath, R.E. (2014). Scale- and item-level factor analysis of the VIA Inventory of Strengths. *Assessment, 21*(1), 4–14. http://doi.org/10.1177/1073191112450612

McGrath, R.E. (2015a). Measurement invariance in translations of the VIA inventory of strengths. *European Journal of Psychological Assessment, 32*(3), 187–194. http://doi.org/10.1027/1015-5759/a000248

McGrath, R.E. (2015b). Character strengths in 75 nations: An update. *Journal of Positive Psychology, 10*(1), 41–52. http://doi.org/10.1080/17439760.2014.888580

McGrath, R. E. (2015c). Integrating psychological and cultural perspectives on virtue: The hierarchical structure of character strengths. *Journal of Positive Psychology, 10*(5), 407–424, http://doi.org/10.10 80/17439760.2014.994222

McGrath, R. E. (2017). *Technical report – the VIA test suite for adults: Development and preliminary evaluation.* Cincinnati, OH: VIA Institute on Character. Available at www.viacharacter.org

McGrath, R. E., Rashid, T., Park, N., & Peterson, C. (2010). Is optimal functioning a distinct state? *The Humanistic Psychologist, 38*, 159–169. http://doi.org/10.1080/08873261003635781

McGrath, R. E., & Walker, D. I. (2016). Factor structure of character strengths in youth: Consistency across ages and measures. *Journal of Moral Education, 45*, 400–418.

McGovern, T. V., & Miller, S. L. (2008). Integrating teacher behaviors with character strengths and virtues for faculty development. *Teaching of Psychology, 35*(4), 278–285. http://doi.org/10.1080/00986280802374609

McNulty, J., & Russell, V. M. (2010). When "negative" behaviors are positive: A contextual analysis of the long-term effects of problem-solving behaviors on changes in relationship satisfaction. *Journal of Personality and Social Psychology, 98*, 587–604. http://doi.org/10.1037/a0017479

McQuaid, M., & Lawn, E. (2014). *Your strengths blueprint: How to be engaged, energized, and happy at work.* Albert Park, Australia: McQuaid Pty. Ltd.

McQuaid, M., Niemiec, R. M., & Doman, F. (in press). Character strengths-based approaches in positive psychology coaching. In S. Green, & S. Palmer (Eds.), *Positive psychology coaching in practice.* London, UK: Routledge.

McQuaid, M., & VIA Institute on Character (2015). *VIA character strengths at work* [Web log post]. Retrieved from https://www.viacharacter.org/blog/category/via-character-strengths-in-use/

Meevissen, Y. M. C., Peters, M. L., & Alberts, H. J. E. M. (2011). Become more optimistic by imagining a best possible self: Effects of a two-week intervention. *Journal of Behavior Therapy and Experimental Psychiatry, 42*, 371–378. http://doi.org/10.1016/j.jbtep.2011.02.012

Meyers, M. C., & van Woerkom, M. (2016). Effects of a strengths intervention on general and work-related well-being: The mediating role of positive affect. *Journal of Happiness Studies.* Advance online publication.

Meyers, M. C., van Woerkom, M., de Reuver, R., Bakk, Z., & Oberski, D. L. (2015). Enhancing psychological capital and personal growth initiative: Working on strengths or deficiencies? *Journal of Counseling Psychology, 62*(1), 50–62. http://doi.org/10.1037/cou0000050

Miller, C. A., & Frisch, M. B. (2009). *Creating your best life: The ultimate life list guide.* New York, NY: Sterling.

Miller, C. B. (2013). *Moral character: An empirical theory.* Oxford, UK: Oxford University Press. http://doi.org/10.1093/acprof:oso/9780199674350.001.0001

Miller, W. R., & Rollnick, S. (2002). *Motivational interviewing: Preparing people for change* (2nd ed.). New York, NY: Guilford.

Minhas, G. (2010). Developing realised and unrealised strengths: Implications for engagement, self-esteem, life satisfaction and well-being. *Assessment and Development Matters, 2*, 12–16.

Mitchell, J., Stanimirovic, R., Klein, B., & Vella-Brodrick, D. (2009). A randomised controlled trial of a self-guided Internet intervention promoting well-being. *Computers in Human Behavior, 25*, 749–760. http://doi.org/10.1016/j.chb.2009.02.003

Moberg, D. J. (2008). Mentoring for protégé character development. *Mentoring & Tutoring: Partnership in Learning, 16*(1), 91–103. http://doi.org/10.1080/13611260701801056

Money, K., Hillenbrand, C., & Camara, N. D. (2008). Putting positive psychology to work in organizations. *Journal of General Management, 34*(2), 21–26.

Mongrain, M., & Anselmo-Matthews, T. (2012). Do positive psychology exercises work? A replication of Seligman et al. (2005). *Journal of Clinical Psychology, 68*, 382–389. http://doi.org/10.1002/jclp.21839

Moore, W. (2011). An investigation of character strengths among college attendees with and without a history of child abuse. *Dissertation Abstracts International: Section B: The Sciences and Engineering, 71*(8-B), 5137.

Moradi, S., Nima, A. A., Ricciardi, M. R., Archer, T., & Garcia, D. (2014). Exercise, character strengths, well-being, and learning climate in the prediction of performance over a 6-month period at a call center. *Frontiers in Psychology, 5*, Article 497.

Muller, L., & Ruch, W. (2011). Humor and strengths of character. *Journal of Positive Psychology, 6*(5), 368–376.

Murray, S.L., Rose, P., Holmes, J.G., Derrick, J., Podchaski, E.J., Bellavia, G., & Griffin, D.W. (2005). Putting the partner within reach: A dyadic perspective on felt security in close relationships. *Journal of Personality and Social Psychology, 88*(2), 327–347. http://doi.org/10.1037/0022-3514.88.2.327

Neff, K.D. (2003). The development and validation of a scale to measure self-compassion. *Self and Identity, 2*, 223–250. http://doi.org/10.1080/15298860309027

Neff, K.D. (2011). *Self-compassion: The proven power of being kind to yourself.* New York, NY: HarperCollins Publishers.

Neff, K.D., & Germer, C.K. (2013). A pilot study and randomized controlled trial of the mindful self-compassion program. *Journal of Clinical Psychology, 69*(1), 28–44. http://doi.org/10.1002/jclp.21923

Neff, K.D., Rude, S.S., & Kirkpatrick, K.L. (2007). An examination of self-compassion in relation to positive psychological functioning and personality traits. *Journal of Research in Personality, 41*, 908–916. http://doi.org/10.1016/j.jrp.2006.08.002

Neff, K.D., & Vonk, R. (2009). Self-compassion versus global self-esteem: Two different ways of relating to oneself. *Journal of Personality, 77*(1), 23–50. http://doi.org/10.1111/j.1467-6494.2008.00537.x

Nelis, D., Quoidbach, J., Mikolajczak, M., & Hansenne, M. (2009). Increasing emotional intelligence: (How) is it possible? *Personality and Individual Differences, 47*, 36–41. http://doi.org/10.1016/j.paid.2009.01.046

Ng, V., Cao, M., Marsh, H.W., Tay, L., & Seligman, M.E.P. (2016). The factor structure of the values in action inventory of strengths (VIA-IS): An item-level exploratory structural equation modeling (ESEM) bifactor analysis. *Psychological Assessment.* Advance online publication.

Nhat Hanh, T. (1979). *The miracle of mindfulness: An introduction to the practice of meditation.* Boston, MA: Beacon.

Nhat Hanh, T. (1993). *For a future to be possible: Commentaries on the five mindfulness trainings.* Berkeley, CA: Parallax Press.

Nhat Hanh, T. (2001). *Anger: Wisdom for cooling the flames.* New York, NY: Riverhead Books.

Nhat Hanh, T. (2009). *Happiness.* Berkeley, CA: Parallax Press.

Niemiec, R.M. (2005). Friendship: A spiritual antidote to loneliness [Review of the motion picture The station agent]. *PsycCRITIQUES, 50* (24). http://doi.org/10.1037/041054

Niemiec, R.M. (2007). What is a positive psychology film? [Review of the motion picture The pursuit of happyness]. *PsycCRITIQUES, 52*(38). http://doi.org/10.1037/a0008960

Niemiec, R.M. (2008). A call to the sacred. [Review of the motion picture The flight of the red balloon]. *PsycCRITIQUES, 53*(48).

Niemiec, R.M. (2009). *VIA intensive manual: Character strengths and virtues in practice.* Cincinnati, OH: VIA Institute on Character.

Niemiec, R.M. (2010a). Character strengths and positive psychology: On the horizon in family therapy. *The Family Psychologist, 26*(1), 16–17.

Niemiec, R.M. (2010b). A wonderland journey through positive psychology interventions. [Review of the motion picture Alice in wonderland]. *PsycCRITIQUES, 55*(31). http://doi.org/10.1037/a0020690

Niemiec, R.M. (2010c). The true meaning of character. [Review of the motion picture Invictus]. *PsycCRITIQUES, 55*(19). http://doi.org/10.1037/a0019539

Niemiec, R.M. (2012). Mindful living: Character strengths interventions as pathways for the five mindfulness trainings. *International Journal of Wellbeing, 2*(1), 22–33. http://doi.org/10.5502/ijw.v2i1.2

Niemiec, R.M. (2013). VIA character strengths: Research and practice (The first 10 years). In H.H. Knoop & A. Delle Fave (Eds.), *Well-being and cultures: Perspectives on positive psychology* (pp. 11–30). New York, NY: Springer Science + Business Media.

Niemiec, R.M. (2014a). *Mindfulness and character strengths: A practical guide to flourishing.* Boston, MA: Hogrefe.

Niemiec, R.M. (2014b). The overuse of strengths: 10 principles. [Review of the motion picture Divergent]. *PsycCRITIQUES, 59*(33).

Niemiec, R.M. (2016). The best mindfulness exercise most people don't know. *Psychology Today.* Retrieved from https://www.psychologytoday.com/blog/what-matters-most/201604/the-best-mindfulness-exercise-most-people-don-t-know

Niemiec, R.M. (2017). The positive psychology of zombies. [A review of the motion picture Train to Busan]. *PsycCRITIQUES, 62*(10), Article 10. http://dx.doi.org/10.1037/a0040769

Niemiec, R.M., & Bretherton, R. (2015). The character-driven person: How Frozen's Anna, not Elsa, is an exemplar. *PsycCRITIQUES, 60*(26). http://doi.org/10.1037/a0039283

Niemiec, R. M., & Clyman, J. (2009). Temperance: The quiet virtue finds a home. [Review of the motion picture Twilight]. *PsycCRITIQUES, 54*(46). http://doi.org/10.1037/a0017924

Niemiec, R. M., & Ferland, D. (2006). The layers of transformation [Review of the motion picture Batman begins]. *PsycCRITIQUES, 51*(2).

Niemiec, R. M., & Lissing, J. (2016). Mindfulness-based strengths practice (MBSP) for enhancing well-being, life purpose, and positive relationships. In I. Ivtzan & T. Lomas (Eds.), *Mindfulness in positive psychology: The science of meditation and wellbeing* (pp. 15–36). New York, NY: Routledge.

Niemiec, R. M., Rashid, T., Linkins, M., Green, S., & Mayerson, N. H. (2013). Character strengths in practice. *IPPA Newsletter, 5*(4).

Niemiec, R. M., Rashid, T., & Spinella, M. (2012). Strong mindfulness: Integrating mindfulness and character strengths. *Journal of Mental Health Counseling, 34*(3), 240–253. http://doi.org/10.17744/mehc.34.3.34p6328x2v204v21

Niemiec, R. M., Shogren, K. A., & Wehmeyer, M. L. (2017). Character strengths and intellectual and developmental disability: A strengths-based approach from positive psychology. *Education and Training in Autism and Developmental Disabilities, 52*(1).

Niemiec, R. M., & Wedding, D. (2014). *Positive psychology at the movies: Using films to build character strengths and well-being* (2nd ed.). Boston, MA: Hogrefe Publishing.

Noftle, E. E. (2014, February). *Are you a moral person? Examining the substance, stability, and outcomes of explicit moral self-views to gain insight into character.* Conference presentation at the 15th Annual Meeting of the Society for Personality and Social Psychology, Austin, Texas.

Norcross, J. C., & Goldfried, M. R. (Eds.). (2005). *Handbook of psychotherapy integration.* New York, NY: Oxford University Press. http://doi.org/10.1093/med:psych/9780195165791.001.0001

Norrish, J. M. (2015). *Positive education: The Geelong Grammar School journey.* New York, NY: Oxford University Press. http://doi.org/10.1093/acprof:oso/9780198702580.001.0001

Nusbaum, E. C., Silvia, P. J., & Beaty, R. E. (2014). Ready, set, create: What instructing people to "be creative" reveals about the meaning and mechanisms of divergent thinking. *Psychology of Aesthetics, Creativity, and the Arts, 8*(4), 423–432. http://doi.org/10.1037/a0036549

Oettingen, G., Kappes, H. B., Guttenberg, K. B., & Gollwitzer, P. M. (2015). Self-regulation of time management: Mental contrasting with implementation intentions. *European Journal of Social Psychology, 45*, 218–229. http://doi.org/10.1002/ejsp.2090

Oettingen, G., Marquardt, M. K., & Gollwitzer, P. M. (2012). Mental contrasting turns positive feedback on creative potential into successful performance. *Journal of Experimental Social Psychology, 48*, 990–996. http://doi.org/10.1016/j.jesp.2012.03.008

Oliver, M. B., & Bartch, A. (2010). Appreciation as audience response: Exploring entertainment gratifications beyond hedonism. *Human Communication Research, 36*, 53–81. http://doi.org/10.1111/j.1468-2958.2009.01368.x

Oman, D., Shapiro, S. L., Thoresen, C. E., Flinders, T., Driskill, J. D., & Plante, T. G. (2007). Learning from spiritual models and meditation: A randomized evaluation of a college course. *Pastoral Psychology, 55*(4), 473–493. http://doi.org/10.1007/s11089-006-0062-x

Oman, D., & Thoresen, C. E. (2007). How does one learn to be spiritual? The neglected role of spiritual modeling in health. In T. G. Plante & C. E. Thoresen (Eds.), *Spirit, science and health: How the spiritual mind fuels physical wellness* (pp. 39–54). Westport, CT: Praeger.

Oman, D., Thoresen, C. E., Park, C. L., Shaver, P. R., Hood, R. W., & Plante, T. G. (2009). How does one become spiritual? The Spiritual Modeling Inventory of Life Environments (SMILE). *Mental Health, Religion & Culture, 12*(5), 427–456. http://doi.org/10.1080/13674670902758257

Oppenheimer, M. F., Fialkov, C., Ecker, B., & Portnoy, S. (2014). Teaching to strengths: Character education for urban middle school students. *Journal of Character Education, 10*(2), 91–105.

Otake, K., Shimai, S., Tanaka-Matsumi, J., Otsui, K., & Fredrickson, B. (2006). Happy people become happier through kindness: A counting kindness intervention. *Journal of Happiness Studies, 7*(3), 361–375. http://doi.org/10.1007/s10902-005-3650-z

Padesky, C. A., & Mooney, K. A. (2012). Strengths-based cognitive-behavioural therapy: A four-step model to build resilience. *Clinical Psychology & Psychotherapy, 19*(4), 283–290. http://doi.org/10.1002/cpp.1795

Palmer, S. (2008). The PRACTICE model of coaching: Towards a solution-focused approach. *Coaching Psychology International, 1*(1), 4–6.

Pargament, K. I., Lomax, J. W., McGee, J. S., & Fang, Q. (2014). Sacred moments in psychotherapy from the perspectives of mental health providers and clients: Prevalence, predictors, and consequences. *Spirituality in Clinical Practice, 1*(4), 248–262. http://doi.org/10.1037/scp0000043

Pargament, K., & Mahoney, A. (2002). Spirituality: Discovering and conserving the sacred. In C. R. Snyder & S. J. Lopez (Eds.), *Handbook of positive psychology* (pp. 646– 659). New York, NY: Oxford University Press.

Park, N., & Peterson, C. (2006a). Methodological issues in positive psychology and the assessment of character strengths. In A. D. Ong & M. van Dulmen (Eds.), *Handbook of methods in positive psychology* (pp. 292–305). New York, NY: Oxford University Press.

Park, N., & Peterson, C. (2006b). Moral competence and character strengths among adolescents: The development and validation of the Values in Action Inventory of Strengths for Youth. *Journal of Adolescence, 29,* 891–905.

Park, N., & Peterson, C. (2006c). Character strengths and happiness among young children: Content analysis of parental descriptions. *Journal of Happiness Studies, 7*, 323–341. http://doi.org/10.1007/s10902-005-3648-6

Park, N., Peterson, C., & Seligman, M. E. P. (2004). Strengths of character and well-being. *Journal of Social & Clinical Psychology, 23*, 603–619. http://doi.org/10.1521/jscp.23.5.628.50749

Park, N., Peterson, C., & Seligman, M. E. P. (2006). Character strengths in fifty-four nations and the fifty US states. *Journal of Positive Psychology, 1*(3), 118–129. http://doi.org/10.1080/17439760600619567

Park, N., & Peterson, C. (2009). Character strengths: Research and practice. *Journal of College and Character, 10*(4), np. http://doi.org/10.2202/1940-1639.1042

Park, N., & Peterson, C. (2010). Does it matter where we live? The urban psychology of character strengths. *American Psychologist, 65*(6), 535–547. http://doi.org/10.1037/a0019621

Parks, A. C., & Schueller, S. (Eds.) (2014). *The Wiley-Blackwell handbook of positive psychological interventions*. Hoboken, NJ: Wiley-Blackwell. http://doi.org/10.1002/9781118315927

Passmore, J., & Marianetti, O. (2007). The role of mindfulness in coaching. *The Coaching Psychologist, 3*(3), 130–136.

Pearsall, P. (2007). *Awe: The delights and dangers of our eleventh emotion.* Deerfield Beach, FL: Health Communications.

Peters, M. L., Flink, I. K., Boersma, K., & Linton, S. J. (2010). Manipulating optimism: Can imagining a best possible self be used to increase positive future expectancies? *Journal of Positive Psychology, 5*(3), 204–211. http://doi.org/10.1080/17439761003790963

Peterson, C. (2006a). *A primer in positive psychology.* New York, NY: Oxford University Press.

Peterson, C. (2006b). The values in action (VIA) classification of strengths. In M. Csikszentmihalyi & I. Csikszentmihalyi (Eds.), *A life worth living: Contributions to positive psychology* (pp. 29–48). New York, NY: Oxford University Press.

Peterson, C. (2014). Foreword to the second edition. In R. M. Niemiec & D. Wedding, *Positive psychology at the movies* (2nd ed.). Boston, MA: Hogrefe Publishing.

Peterson, C., & Park, N. (2009). Classifying and measuring strengths of character. In S. J. Lopez & C. R. Snyder (Eds.), *Oxford handbook of positive psychology* (2nd ed., pp. 25–33). New York, NY: Oxford University Press.

Peterson, C., Park, N., & Castro, C. A. (2011). Assessment for the US Army comprehensive soldier fitness program: The global assessment tool. *American Psychologist, 66*(1), 10–18. http://doi.org/10.1037/a0021658

Peterson, C., Park, N., Hall, N., & Seligman, M. E. P. (2009). Zest and work. *Journal of Organizational Behavior, 30*, 161–172. http://doi.org/10.1002/job.584

Peterson, C., Park, N., Pole, N., D'Andrea, W., & Seligman, M. E. P. (2008). Strengths of character and posttraumatic growth. *Journal of Traumatic Stress, 21*, 214–217. http://doi.org/10.1002/jts.20332

Peterson, C., Park, N., & Seligman, M. E. P. (2005). Orientations to happiness and life satisfaction: The full life versus the empty life. *Journal of Happiness Studies, 6*, 25–41. http://doi.org/10.1007/s10902-004-1278-z

Peterson, C., Ruch, W., Beermann, U., Park, N., & Seligman, M. E. P. (2007). Strengths of character, orientations to happiness, and life satisfaction. *Journal of Positive Psychology, 2*, 149–156. http://doi.org/10.1080/17439760701228938

Peterson, C., & Seligman, M. E. P. (2001). *Complementarity of VIA classification and Gallup Strengths-Finder.* Unpublished manuscript.

Peterson, C., & Seligman, M. E. P. (2003). Character strengths before and after September 11. *Psychological Science, 14*, 381–384. http://doi.org/10.1111/1467-9280.24482

Peterson, C., & Seligman, M. E. P. (2004). *Character strengths and virtues: A handbook and classification*. New York, NY: Oxford University Press/ Washington, DC: American Psychological Association.

Peterson, T. D., & Peterson, E. W. (2008). Stemming the tide of law student depression: What law schools need to learn from the science of positive psychology. *Yale Journal of Health Policy, Law, and Ethics, 9*(2), 358–359.

Pinquart, M., & Forstmeier, S. (2012). Effects of reminiscence interventions on psychosocial outcomes: A meta-analysis. *Aging & Mental Health, 16*, 541–558. http://doi.org/10.1080/13607863.2011.651434

Plante, T. G. (2008). What do the spiritual and religious traditions offer the practicing psychologist? *Pastoral Psychology, 56*, 429–444. http://doi.org/10.1007/s11089-008-0119-0

Pocono Record. (2012). *Obituary for Mary E. Craig*. Retrieved from www.poconorecord.com/article/20110102/NEWS07/101020334

Pollak, S. M., Pedulla, T., & Siegel, R. D. (2014). *Sitting together: Essential skills for mindfulness-based psychotherapy*. New York, NY: Guilford Press.

Polly, S., & Britton, K. (2015). *Character strengths matter: How to live a full life*. Washington, DC: Positive Psychology News.

Pressman, S. D., Kraft, T. L., & Cross, M. P. (2015). It's good to do good and receive good: The impact of a "pay it forward" style kindness intervention on giver and receiver well-being. *Journal of Positive Psychology, 10*(4), 293–302. http://doi.org/10.1080/17439760.2014.965269

Prochaska, J. O., & DiClemente, C. C. (1982). Transtheoretical therapy: Toward a more integrative model of change. *Psychotherapy: Theory, Research, and Practice, 19*, 276–288. http://doi.org/10.1037/h0088437

Proctor, C., & Fox Eades, J. (2011). *Strengths gym: Build and exercise your strengths!* St. Peter Port, UK: Positive Psychology Research Centre.

Proctor, C., Maltby, J., & Linley, P. A. (2009). Strengths use as a predictor of well-being and health-related quality of life. *Journal of Happiness Studies, 10*, 583–630.

Proctor, C., Tsukayama, E., Wood, A. M., Maltby, J., Eades, F., & Linley, P. A. (2011). Strengths gym: The impact of a character strengths-based intervention on the life satisfaction and well-being of adolescent students. *Journal of Positive Psychology, 6*, 377–388. http://doi.org/10.1080/17439760.2011.594079

Proctor, C., Tweed, R., & Morris, D. (2016). The Rogerian fully functioning person: A positive psychology perspective. *Journal of Humanistic Psychology, 56*(5), 503–529.

Proyer, R. T., Gander, F., Wellenzohn, S., & Ruch, W. (2013). What good are character strengths beyond subjective well-being? The contribution of the good character on self-reported health-oriented behavior, physical fitness, and the subjective health status. *Journal of Positive Psychology, 8*(3), 222–232. http://doi.org/10.1080/17439760.2013.777767

Proyer, R. T., Gander, F., Wellenzohn, S., & Ruch, W. (2014a). Positive psychology interventions in people aged 50–79 years: Long-term effects of placebo-controlled online interventions on well-being and depression. *Aging & Mental Health, 18*, 997–1005. http://doi.org/10.1080/13607863.2014.899978

Proyer, R. T., Gander, F., Wellenzohn, S., & Ruch, W. (2014b). The European football championship as a positive festivity: Changes in strengths of character before, during, and after the Euro 2008 in Switzerland. In H. A. Marujo & L. M. Neto (Eds.), *Positive nations and communities: Collective, qualitative and cultural-sensitive processes in positive psychology* (pp. 119–134). New York, NY: Springer.

Proyer, R. T., Gander, F., Wellenzohn, S., & Ruch, W. (2015). Strengths-based positive psychology interventions: A randomized placebo-controlled online trial on long-term effects for a signature strengths vs. a lesser strengths-intervention. *Frontiers in Psychology, 6*. http://doi.org/10.3389/fpsyg.2015.00456

Proyer, R. T., Gander, F., Wyss, T., & Ruch, W. (2011). The relation of character strengths to past, present, and future life satisfaction among German-speaking women. *Applied Psychology: Health and Well-Being, 3*(3), 370–384. http://doi.org/10.1111/j.1758-0854.2011.01060.x

Proyer, R. T., & Ruch, W. (2011). The virtuousness of adult playfulness: The relation of playfulness with strengths of character. *Psychology of Well-Being: Theory, Research and Practice, 1*(4).

Proyer, R. T., Ruch, W., & Buschor, C. (2013). Testing strengths-based interventions: A preliminary study on the effectiveness of a program targeting curiosity, gratitude, hope, humor, and zest for enhancing life satisfaction. *Journal of Happiness Studies, 14*(1), 275–292. http://doi.org/10.1007/s10902-012-9331-9

Proyer, R. T., Sidler, N., Weber, M., & Ruch, W. (2012). A multimethod approach to studying the relationship between character strengths and vocational interests in adolescents. *International Journal for Educational and Vocational Guidance, 12*(2), 141–157. http://doi.org/10.1007/s10775-012-9223-x

Proyer, R. T., Wellenzohn, S., Gander, F., Ruch, W. (2014). Toward a better understanding of what makes positive psychology interventions work: Predicting happiness and depression from the person × intervention fit in a follow-up after 3.5 years. *Applied Psychology: Health and Well-Being, 7*(1), 108–128. http://doi.org/10.1111/aphw.12039

Pury, C. L. S. (2008). Can courage be learned? In S. J. Lopez (Ed.), *Positive psychology: Exploring the best in people, Vol 1: Discovering human strengths* (pp. 109–130). Westport, CT: Praeger.

Pury, C. L. S., & Kowalski, R. M. (2007). Human strengths, courageous actions, and general and personal courage. *Journal of Positive Psychology, 2*(2), 120–128.

Pury, C. L. S., Starkey, C. B., Kulik, R. E., Skjerning, K. L., & Sullivan, E. A. (2015). Is courage always a virtue? Suicide, killing, and bad courage. *Journal of Positive Psychology*, 10(5), 383–388.

Putnam, D. (1997). Psychological courage. *Philosophy, Psychiatry, and Psychology, 4*, 1–11. http://doi.org/10.1353/ppp.1997.0008

Quinlan, D., Swain, N., & Vella-Brodrick, D. A. (2011). Character strengths interventions: Building on what we know for improved outcomes. *Journal of Happiness Studies, 13*, 1145–1163. http://doi.org/10.1007/s10902-011-9311-5

Quinlan, D. M., Swain, N., Cameron, C., & Vella-Brodrick, D. A. (2014). How "other people matter" in a classroom-based strengths intervention: Exploring interpersonal strategies and classroom outcomes. *Journal of Positive Psychology, 10*(1), 77–89. http://doi.org/10.1080/17439760.2014.920407

Quinn, J., Pascoe, A., Wood, W., & Neal, D. (2010). Can't control yourself? Monitor those bad habits. *Personality and Social Psychology Bulletin, 36*, 499–511. http://doi.org/10.1177/0146167209360665

Quoidbach, J., Berry, E. V., Hansenne, M., & Mikolajczak, M. (2010). Positive emotion regulation and well-being: Comparing the impact of eight savoring and dampening strategies. *Personality and Individual Differences, 49*, 368–373. http://doi.org/10.1016/j.paid.2010.03.048

Quoidbach, J., Mikolajczak, M., & Gross, J. J. (2015). Positive interventions: An emotion regulation perspective. *Psychological Bulletin, 141*(3), 655–693. http://doi.org/10.1037/a0038648

Quoidbach, J., Wood, A. M., & Hansenne, M. (2009). Back to the future: The effect of daily practice of mental time travel into the future on happiness and anxiety. *Journal of Positive Psychology, 4*(5), 349–355. http://doi.org/10.1080/17439760902992365

Rashid, T. (2004). Enhancing strengths through the teaching of positive psychology. *Dissertation Abstracts International, 64*, 6339.

Rashid, T. (2009). Positive interventions in clinical practice. *Journal of Clinical Psychology: In Session, 65*(5), 461–466. http://doi.org/10.1002/jclp.20588

Rashid, T. (2012, May). *The role of positive psychology in maximizing human potential*. Presentation at the Diversity Roundtable, Toronto, Ontario, Canada.

Rashid, T. (2015). Positive psychotherapy: A strength-based approach. *Journal of Positive Psychology, 10*(1), 25–40. http://doi.org/10.1080/17439760.2014.920411

Rashid, T., & Anjum, A. (2008). Positive psychotherapy for young children and adults. In J. R. Z. Abela & B. L. Hankin (Eds.), *Handbook of depression in children and adolescents* (pp. 250–287). New York, NY: Guilford Press.

Rashid, T., & Niemiec, R. M. (2013). Character strengths. In A. Michalos (Ed.), *Encyclopedia of quality of life and well-being research*. New York, NY: Springer Science & Business Media.

Rashid, T., & Ostermann, R. F. (2009). Strength-based assessment in clinical practice. *Journal of Clinical Psychology, 65*(5), 488–498. http://doi.org/10.1002/jclp.20595

Rashid, T., & Seligman, M. E. P. (2013). Positive psychotherapy. In D. Wedding & R. J. Corsini (Eds.), *Current Psychotherapies* (pp. 461–498). Belmont, CA: Cengage.

Rath, T. (2007). *StrengthsFinder 2.0*. New York, NY: Gallup Press.

Reis, H., Smith, S., Carmichael, C., Caprariello, P., Tsai, F., Rodrigues, A., & Maniaci, M. R. (2010). Are you happy for me? How sharing positive events with others provides personal and interpersonal benefits. *Journal of Personality and Social Psychology, 99*(2), 311–329. http://doi.org/10.1037/a0018344

Reivich, K. J., Seligman, M. E. P., & McBride, S. (2011). Master resilience training in the U. S. Army. *American Psychologist, 66*(1), 25–34. http://doi.org/10.1037/a0021897

Reivich, K. J., & Shatté, A. J. (2003). *The resilience factor*. New York, NY: Broadway Books.

Rempel, G. R., Neufeld, A., & Kushner, K. E. (2007). Interactive use of genograms and ecomaps in family caregiving research. *Journal of Family Nursing, 13*(4), 403–419. http://doi.org/10.1177/1074840707307917

Resnick, S. G., & Rosenheck, R. A. (2006). Recovery and positive psychology: Parallel themes and potential synergies. *Psychiatric Services, 57*(1), 120–122. http://doi.org/10.1176/appi.ps.57.1.120

Riches, S., Schrank, B., Rashid, T., & Slade, M. (2016). WELLFOCUS PPT: Modifying positive psychotherapy for psychosis. *Psychotherapy, 53*(1), 68–77. http://doi.org/10.1037/pst0000013

Roberts, L. M., Dutton, J. E., Spreitzer, G., Heaphy, E., & Quinn, R. (2005). Composing the reflected best-self portrait: Building pathways to becoming extraordinary in work organizations. *Academy of Management Review, 30*, 712–736. http://doi.org/10.5465/AMR.2005.18378874

Roberts, B. W., Luo, J., Briley, D. A., Chow, P. I., Su, R., & Hill, P. L. (2017). A systematic review of personality trait change through intervention. *Psychological Bulletin, 143*(2), 117–141.

Rock, D., & Page, L. J. (2009). *Coaching with the brain in mind: Foundations for practice*. Hoboken, NJ: Wiley.

Rogers, C. (1961). *On becoming a person*. Boston, MA: Houghton Mifflin.

Rubin, R. S. (2002). Will the real SMART goals please stand up? *The Industrial-Organizational Psychologist, 39*(4), 26–27.

Ruch, W., Bruntsch, R., & Wagner, L. (2017). The role of character traits in economic games. *Personality and Individual Differences, 108*, 186–190.

Ruch, W., Gander, F., Platt, T., & Hofmann, J. (2016). Team roles: Their relationships to character strengths and job satisfaction. *Journal of Positive Psychology*. Advanced online publication.

Ruch, W., & Proyer, R. T. (2015). Mapping strengths into virtues: The relation of the 24 VIA-strengths to six ubiquitous virtues. *Frontiers in Psychology, 6*. http://doi.org/10.3389/fpsyg.2015.00460

Ruch, W., Proyer, R. T., Harzer, C., Park, N., Peterson, C., & Seligman, M. E. P. (2010). Values in action inventory of strengths (VIA-IS): Adaptation and validation of the German version and the development of a peer-rating form. *Journal of Individual Differences, 31*(3), 138–149.

Rusbult, C. E., Kumashiro, M., Kubacka, K. E., & Finkel, E. J. (2009). "The part of me that you bring out": Ideal similarity and the Michelangelo phenomenon. *Journal of Personality and Social Psychology, 96*(1), 61–82. http://doi.org/10.1037/a0014016

Rust, T., Diessner, R., & Reade, L. (2009). Strengths only or strengths and relative weaknesses?: A preliminary study. *Journal of Psychology, 143*(5), 465–476. http://doi.org/10.3200/JRL.143.5.465-476

Ryan, R. M., & Deci, E. L. (2008). From ego-depletion to vitality: Theory and findings concerning the facilitation of energy available to the self. *Social and Personality Psychology Compass, 2*, 702–717. http://doi.org/10.1111/j.1751-9004.2008.00098.x

Ryan, R. M., Weinstein, N., Bernstein, J., Brown, K. W., Mistretta, L., & Gagné, M. (2010). Vitalizing effects of being outdoors and in nature. *Journal of Environmental Psychology, 30*, 159–168. http://doi.org/10.1016/j.jenvp.2009.10.009

Saleebey, D. (1996). The strengths perspective in social work practice: Extensions and cautions. *Social Work, 41*(3), 296–306.

Salzberg, S. (1995). *Lovingkindness: The revolutionary art of happiness*. Boston, MA: Shambhala.

Samson, A. C., & Antonelli, Y. (2013). Humor as character strength and its relation to life satisfaction and happiness in autism spectrum disorders. *Humor: International Journal of Humor Research, 26*(3), 477–491.

Sansom, L., Bretherton, R., & Niemiec, R. M. (2016). Doing the right thing: Character, moral goodness and Star Wars [A review of Star Wars: Episode VII – The Force Awakens] *PsycCRITIQUES, 61*(25). http://doi.org/10.1037/a0040387

Schnall, S., Roper, J., & Fessler, D. M. T. (2010). Elevation leads to altruistic behavior. *Psychological Science, 21*, 315–320. http://doi.org/10.1177/0956797609359882

Schnall, S., & Roper, J. (2011). Elevation puts moral values into action. *Social Psychological and Personality Science, 3*, 373–378. http://doi.org/10.1177/1948550611423595

Schnitker, S. A., & Emmons, R. A. (2007). Patience as a virtue: Religious and psychological perspectives. *Research in the Social Scientific Study of Religion, 18*, 177–207. http://doi.org/10.1163/ej.9789004158511.i-301.69

Schramm, D. G., Marshall, J. P., Harris, V. W., & Lee, T. R. (2005). After "I do": The newlywed transition. *Marriage and Family Review, 38*, 45–67. http://doi.org/10.1300/J002v38n01_05

Schueller, S. M. (2010). Preferences for positive psychology exercises. *Journal of Positive Psychology, 5*(3), 192–203. http://doi.org/10.1080/17439761003790948

Schueller, S. M. (2011). To each his own well-being boosting intervention: Using preference to guide selection. *Journal of Positive Psychology, 6*(4), 300–313. http://doi.org/10.1080/17439760.2011.577092

Schueller, S. M., & Parks, A. C. (2012). Disseminating self-help: Positive psychology exercises in an online trial. *Journal of Medical Internet Research, 14*(3), e63. http://doi.org/10.2196/jmir.1850

Schutte, N. S., & Malouff, J. M. (2011). Emotional intelligence mediates the relationship between mindfulness and subjective well-being. *Personality and Individual Differences, 50*(7), 1116–1119. http://doi.org/10.1016/j.paid.2011.01.037

Schwartz, B., & Sharpe, K. E. (2006). Practical wisdom: Aristotle meets positive psychology. *Journal of Happiness Studies, 7*, 377–395. http://doi.org/10.1007/s10902-005-3651-y

Schwartz, B., & Sharpe, K. E. (2011). *Practical wisdom: The right way to do the right thing*. New York, NY: Riverhead Books.

Scott, G., Leritz, L. E., & Mumford, M. D. (2004). The effectiveness of creativity training: A quantitative review. *Creativity Research Journal, 16*(4), 361–388. http://doi.org/10.1080/10400410409534549

Segal, Z. V., Williams, J. M. G., & Teasdale, J. D. (2013). *Mindfulness-based cognitive therapy for depression: A new approach to preventing relapse* (2nd ed.). New York, NY: Guilford.

Seligman, M. E. P. (1991). *Learned optimism*. New York, NY: Knopf.

Seligman, M. E. P. (2000). *The VIA taxonomy meeting minutes*. Retrieved from https://www.sas.upenn.edu/psych/seligman/glasbernsummary1.htm

Seligman, M. E. P. (2002). *Authentic happiness*. New York, NY: Free Press.

Seligman, M. E. P. (2011). *Flourish*. New York, NY: Free Press.

Seligman, M. E. P., Ernst, R. M., Gillham, J., Reivich, K., & Linkins, M. (2009). Positive education: Positive psychology and classroom interventions. *Oxford Review of Education, 35*(3), 293–311. http://doi.org/10.1080/03054980902934563

Seligman, M. E. P., Rashid, T., & Parks, A. C. (2006). Positive psychotherapy. *American Psychologist, 61*, 774–788. http://doi.org/10.1037/0003-066X.61.8.774

Seligman, M. E. P., Steen, T. A., Park, N., & Peterson, C. (2005). Positive psychology progress: Empirical validation of interventions. *American Psychologist, 60*, 410–421. http://doi.org/10.1037/0003-066X.60.5.410

Shapira, L. B., & Mongrain, M. (2010). The benefits of self-compassion and optimism exercises for individuals vulnerable to depression. *Journal of Positive Psychology, 5*(5), 377–389. http://doi.org/10.1080/17439760.2010.516763

Sharp, J. E., Niemiec, R. M., & Lawrence, C. (2016). Using mindfulness-based strengths practices with gifted populations. *Gifted Education International*. Advance online publication. http://doi.org/10.1177/0261429416641009

Sheeran, P., Harris, P., Vaughan, J., Oettingen, G., & Gollwitzer, P. M. (2013). Gone exercising: Mental contrasting promotes physical activity among overweight, middle-aged, low-SES fishermen. *Health Psychology, 32*, 802–809. http://doi.org/10.1037/a0029293

Shek, D. T. L., & Yu, L. (2015). Character strengths and service leadership. *International Journal on Disability and Human Development, 14*(4), 299–307.

Sheldon, K. M., & Elliot, A. J. (1999). Goal striving, need satisfaction, and longitudinal well-being: The self-concordance model. *Journal of Personality and Social Psychology, 76*, 482–497. http://doi.org/10.1037/0022-3514.76.3.482

Sheldon, K. M., & Houser-Marko, L. (2001). Self-concordance, goal attainment, and the pursuit of happiness: Can there be an upward spiral? *Journal of Personality and Social Psychology, 80*, 152–165. http://doi.org/10.1037/0022-3514.80.1.152

Sheldon, K. M., & Kasser, T. (1998). Pursuing personal goals: Skills enable progress but not all progress is beneficial. *Personality and Social Psychology Bulletin, 24*, 546–557. http://doi.org/10.1177/01461672982412006

Sheldon, K. M., & Lyubomirsky, S. (2012). The challenge of staying happier: Testing the hedonic adaptation prevention (HAP) model. *Personality and Social Psychology Bulletin, 38*, 670–680. http://doi.org/10.1177/0146167212436400

Sheldon, K. M., Ryan, R. M., Rawsthorne, L. J., & Ilardi, B. (1997). Trait self and true self: Cross-role variation in the big-five personality traits and its relations with psychological authenticity and subjective well-being. *Journal of Personality and Social Psychology, 73*(6), 1380–1393. http://doi.org/10.1037/0022-3514.73.6.1380

Sheridan, S. M., & Burt, J. D. (2009). Family-centered positive psychology. In S. J. Lopez & C. R. Snyder (Eds.), *Oxford handbook of positive psychology* (pp. 551–559). New York, NY: Oxford University Press.

Sherman, D., Nelson, L., & Steele, C. (2000). Do messages about health risks threaten the self? Increasing the acceptance of threatening health messages via self-affirmation. *Personality and Social Psychology Bulletin, 26*, 1046–1058. http://doi.org/10.1177/01461672002611003

Shermer, M. (2015). *The moral arc: How science and reason lead humanity toward truth, justice, and freedom.* New York, NY: Henry Holt & Co.

Shimai, S., Otake, K., Park, N., Peterson, C., & Seligman, M. E. P. (2006). Convergence of character strengths in American and Japanese young adults. *Journal of Happiness Studies, 7*, 311–322. http://doi.org/10.1007/s10902-005-3647-7

Shogren, K. A., Shaw, L. A., Khamsi, S., Wehmeyer, M. L., Niemiec, R., & Adkins, M. (in press). Assessing character strengths in youth with intellectual disability: Reliability and factorial validity of the VIA-Youth. *Intellectual and Developmental Disabilities.*

Shogren, K. A., Wehmeyer, M. L., Lang, K., & Niemiec, R. M. (2017). *The application of the VIA classification of strengths to youth with and without disabilities.* Manuscript submitted for publication.

Shoshani, A., & Ilanit Aviv, I. (2012). The pillars of strength for first-grade adjustment: Parental and children's character strengths and the transition to elementary school. *Journal of Positive Psychology, 7*(4), 315–326. http://doi.org/10.1080/17439760.2012.691981

Shoshani, A., & Slone, M. (2012). Middle school transition from the strengths perspective: Young adolescents' character strengths, subjective well-being, and school adjustment. *Journal of Happiness Studies, 14*(4), 1163–1181. http://doi.org/10.1007/s10902-012-9374-y

Shoshani, A., & Slone, M. (2016). The resilience function of character strengths in the face of war and protracted conflict. *Frontiers in Psychology, 6.* http://doi.org/10.3389/fpsyg.2015.02006

Shryack, J., Steger, M. F., Krueger, R. F., & Kallie, C. S. (2010). The structure of virtue: An empirical investigation of the dimensionality of the virtues in action inventory of strengths. *Personality and Individual Differences, 48*, 714–719. http://doi.org/10.1016/j.paid.2010.01.007

Siegel, J. T., Thomson, A. L., & Navarro, M. A. (2014). Experimentally distinguishing elevation from gratitude: Oh, the morality. *Journal of Positive Psychology, 9*, 414–427. http://doi.org/10.1080/17439760.2014.910825

Silvia, P. J., Wigert, B., Reiter-Palmon, R., & Kaufman, J. C. (2012). Assessing creativity with self-report scales: A review and empirical evaluation. *Psychology of Aesthetics, Creativity, and the Arts, 6*(1), 19–34. http://doi.org/10.1037/a0024071

Simonton, D. K. (2000). Creative development as acquired expertise: Theoretical issues and an empirical test. *Developmental Review, 20*, 283–318. http://doi.org/10.1006/drev.1999.0504

Sims, A., Barker, C., Price, C., & Fornells-Ambrojo, M. (2015). Psychological impact of identifying character strengths in people with psychosis. *Psychosis: Psychological, Social and Integrative Approaches, 7*(2), 179–182.

Sin, N. L., & Lyubomirsky, S. (2009). Enhancing well-being and alleviating depressive symptoms with positive psychology interventions: A practice-friendly meta-analysis. *Journal of Clinical Psychology: In Session, 65*(5), 467–487. http://doi.org/10.1002/jclp.20593

Singh, K., & Choubisa, R. (2010). Empirical validation of values in action-inventory of strengths (VIA-IS) in Indian context. *National Academy of Psychology India Psychological Studies, 55*(2), 151–158.

Smith, B. W. (2014). *Positive psychology movies and pre-post changes.* Unpublished data.

Smith, E. N., & Barros-Gomes, P. (2015). Soliciting strengths systemically: The use of character strengths in couple and family therapy. *Journal of Family Psychotherapy, 26*(1), 42–46.

Smith, J. L., Harrison, P. R., Kurtz, J. L., & Bryant, F. B. (2014). Nurturing the capacity to savor: Interventions to enhance the enjoyment of positive experiences. In A. C. Parks & S. Schueller (Eds.), *The Wiley-Blackwell handbook of positive psychological interventions* (pp. 42–65). Oxford, UK: Wiley-Blackwell.

Smithikrai, C. (2016). Effectiveness of teaching with movies to promote positive characteristics and behaviors. *Procedia – Social and Behavioral Sciences, 217*, 522–530. http://doi.org/10.1016/j.sbspro.2016.02.033

Snow, N. (2016). Virtue acquisition: The paradox of striving. *Journal of Moral Education, 45*(2), 179–191.

Snyder, C. R. (2000). *Handbook of hope: Theory, measures, and applications.* San Diego, CA: Academic Press.

Snyder, C. R., & Lopez, S. J. (Eds.) (2002). *Handbook of positive psychology*. New York, NY: Oxford University Press.

Snyder, C. R., Rand, K. L., & Sigmon, D. R. (2002). Hope theory: A member of the positive psychology family. In C. R. Snyder & S. J. Lopez (Eds.), *Handbook of positive psychology* (pp. 257–276). New York, NY: Oxford University Press.

Son, V., Jackson, B., Grove, J. R., & Feltz, D. L. (2011). "I am" versus "we are": Effects of distinctive variants of self-talk on efficacy beliefs and motor performance. *Journal of Sports Sciences, 29*, 1417–1424. http://doi.org/10.1080/02640414.2011.593186

Sorenson, S. (2014, February). How employees' strengths make your company stronger. *Gallup Business Journal*. Retrieved from https://www.gallup.com/businessjournal/167462/employees-strengths-company-stronger.aspx

Spreitzer, G. (2006). Leadership development lessons from positive organizational studies. *Organizational Dynamics, 35*, 305–315.

Spreitzer, G., Stephens, J. P., & Sweetman, D. (2009). The reflected best self field experiment with adolescent leaders: Exploring the psychological resources associated with feedback source and valence. *Journal of Positive Psychology, 4*, 331–348. http://doi.org/10.1080/17439760902992340

Stadler, G., Oettingen, G., & Gollwitzer, P. M. (2010). Intervention effects of information and self-regulation on eating fruits and vegetables over two years. *Health Psychology, 29*(3), 274–283. http://doi.org/10.1037/a0018644

Stapel, D. A., & van der Linde, L. A. (2011). What drives self-affirmation effects?: On the importance of differentiating value affirmation and attribute affirmation. *Journal of Personality and Social Psychology, 101*(1), 34–45. http://doi.org/10.1037/a0023172

Steele, C. M. (1999). The psychology of self-affirmation: Sustaining the integrity of the self. In R. F. Baumeister (Ed.), *The self in social psychology* (pp. 372–390). New York, NY: Psychology Press.

Steen, T. A., Kachorek, L. V., & Peterson, C. (2003). Character strength among youth. *Journal of Youth & Adolescence, 32*(1), 5–16. http://doi.org/10.1023/A:1021024205483

Steger, M. F., Hicks, B., Kashdan, T. B., Krueger, R. F., & Bouchard, T. J., Jr. (2007). Genetic and environmental influences on the positive traits of the values in action classification, and biometric covariance with normal personality. *Journal of Research in Personality, 41*, 524–539. http://doi.org/10.1016/j.jrp.2006.06.002

Steger, M. F., Kashdan, T. B., & Oishi, S. (2008). Being good by doing good: Daily eudaimonic activity and wellbeing. *Journal of Research in Personality, 42*(1), 22–42. http://doi.org/10.1016/j.jrp.2007.03.004

Steimer, A., & Mata, A. (2016). Motivated implicit theories of personality: My weaknesses will go away, but my strengths are here to stay. *Personality and Social Psychology Bulletin, 42*(4), 415–429. http://doi.org/10.1177/0146167216629437

Stichter, M. (2007). Ethical expertise: the skill model of virtue. *Ethical Theory and Moral Practice, 10*(2), 183–194. http://doi.org/10.1007/s10677-006-9054-2

Stichter, M. (2015). Practical skills and practical wisdom in virtue. *Australasian Journal of Philosophy, 94*, 435–448. http://doi.org/10.1080/00048402.2015.1074257

Stoltzfus, T. (2008). *Coaching questions: A coach's guide to powerful asking skills*. Virginia Beach, VA: Coach22.

Summers, R. F., & Lord, J. A. (2015). Positivity in supportive and psychodynamic therapy. In D. V. Jeste & B. W. Palmer (Eds.), *Positive psychiatry: A clinical handbook* (pp. 167–192). Arlington, VA: American Psychiatric Press.

Sumner-Armstrong, C., Newcombe, P., & Martin, R. (2008). A qualitative investigation into leader behavioural flexibility. *Journal of Management Development, 27*(8), 843–857. http://doi.org/10.1108/02621710810895668

Sun, L. (2013). *The fairness instinct: Robin Hood mentality and our biological nature*. New York, NY: Prometheus Books.

Tangney, J. P. (2005). Humility. In C. R. Snyder & S. J. Lopez (Eds.), *Handbook of positive psychology* (pp. 411–419). New York, NY: Oxford University Press.

Thomson, A. L., Nakamura, J., Siegel, J. T., & Csikszentmihalyi, M. (2014). Elevation and mentoring: An experimental assessment of causal relations. *Journal of Positive Psychology, 9*, 402–413. http://doi.org/10.1080/17439760.2014.910824

Tomasulo, D. (2014). Positive group psychotherapy modified for adults with intellectual disabilities. *Journal of Intellectual Disabilities, 18*(4), 337–350. http://doi.org/10.1177/1744629514552153

Tomich, P. L., & Helgeson, V. S. (2004). Is finding something good in the bad always good? Benefit finding among women with breast cancer. *Health Psychology, 23*, 16–23. http://doi.org/10.1037/0278-6133.23.1.16

Tweed, R. G., Biswas-Diener, R., & Lehman, D. R. (2012). Self-perceived strengths among people who are homeless. *Journal of Positive Psychology, 7*(6), 481–492. http://doi.org/10.1080/17439760.2012.719923

Vaillant, G. E. (2008). *Spiritual evolution: A scientific defense of faith.* New York, NY: Broadway Books.

van Woerkom, M., Bakker, A. B., & Nishii, L. H. (2016). Accumulative job demands and support for strengths use: Fine-tuning the job demands-resources model using conservation of resources theory. *Journal of Applied Psychology, 101*(1), 141–150. http://doi.org/10.1037/apl0000033

van Woerkom, M., & Meyers, M. C. (2014). My strengths count! Effects of a strengths-based psychological climate on positive affect and job performance. *Human Resource Management, 54*(1), 81–*103*. http://doi.org/10.1002/hrm.21623

van Woerkom, M., Mostert, K., Els, C., Bakker, A. B., de Beer, L., & Rothmann, S. (2016). Strengths use and deficit correction in organizations: Development and validation of a questionnaire. *European Journal of Work and Organizational Psychology, 25*, 960–975. http://doi.org/10.1080/1359432X.2016.1193010

van Woerkom, M., Oerlemans, W., & Bakker, A. B. (2016). Strengths use and work engagement: A weekly diary study. *European Journal of Work and Organizational Psychology, 25*, 384–397. http://doi.org/10.1080/1359432X.2015.1089862

Veldorale-Brogan, A., Bradford, K., & Vail, A. (2010). Marital virtues and their relationship to individual functioning, communication, and relationship adjustment. *Journal of Positive Psychology, 5*(4), 281–293. http://doi.org/10.1080/17439760.2010.498617

Vella-Brodrick, D. A., Park, N., & Peterson, C. (2009). Three ways to be happy: Pleasure, engagement, and meaning: Findings from Australian and US samples. *Social Indicators Research, 90*, 165–179. http://doi.org/10.1007/s11205-008-9251-6

VIA Institute on Character (2014). *VIA Pro: Character strengths profile (a personalized report).* Available at http://www.viacharacter.org

Vie, L. L., Scheier, L. M., Lester, P. B., & Seligman, M. E. P. (2016). Initial validation of the US Army global assessment tool. *Military Psychology, 28*(6), 468–487. http://doi.org/10.1037/mil0000141

Wachholtz, A., & Pargament, K. (2005). Is spirituality a critical ingredient of meditation? Comparing the effects of spiritual meditation, secular meditation, and relaxation on spiritual, psychological, cardiac, and pain outcomes. *Journal of Behavioral Medicine, 28*, 369–384. http://doi.org/10.1007/s10865-005-9008-5

Wagner, L., & Ruch, W. (2015). Good character at school: Positive classroom behavior mediates the link between character strengths and school achievement. *Frontiers in Psychology, 6.* http://doi.org/10.3389/fpsyg.2015.00610

Walker, L. J., & Frimer, J. A. (2007). Moral personality of brave and caring exemplars. *Journal of Personality and Social Psychology, 93*, 845–860. http://doi.org/10.1037/0022-3514.93.5.845

Walker, L. J., & Hennig, K. H. (2004). Differing conceptions of moral exemplarity: Just, brave, and caring. *Journal of Personality and Social Psychology, 86*, 629–647. http://doi.org/10.1037/0022-3514.86.4.629

Wallin, L. (2013). *Styrkebaserat arbete* [Strengths-based work]. Stockholm, Sweden: In focus & wb AB.

Walton, G. M. (2014). The new science of wise psychological interventions. *Current Directions in Psychological Science, 23*, 73–82. http://doi.org/10.1177/0963721413512856

Waterman, A. S. (2012). In support of labeling psychological traits and processes as positive and negative. *American Psychologist, 67*(7), 575–576. http://doi.org/10.1037/a0029735

Watts, R. E. (2013, April). Reflecting "as if." *Counseling Today: A Publication of the American Counseling Association.* Retrieved from http://ct.counseling.org/2013/04/reflecting-as-if/

Webb, J. R., Phillips, T. D., Bumgarner, D., & Conway-Williams, E. (2012). Forgiveness, mindfulness, and health. *Mindfulness, 4*(3), 235–245. http://doi.org/10.1007/s12671-012-0119-0

Weber, M., & Ruch, W. (2012a). The role of character strengths in adolescent romantic relationships: An initial study on partner selection and mates' life satisfaction. *Journal of Adolescence, 35*, 1527–1546.

Weber, M., & Ruch, W. (2012b). The role of a good character in 12-year-old school children: Do character strengths matter in the classroom? *Child Indicators Research, 5*(2), 317–334. http://doi.org/10.1007/s12187-011-9128-0

Weber, M., Wagner, L., & Ruch, W. (2016). Positive feelings at school: On the relationships between students' character strengths, school-related affect, and school functioning. *Journal of Happiness Studies, 17*, 341–355. http://doi.org/10.1007/s10902-014-9597-1

Wedding, D., & Corsini, R.J. (2013). *Current psychotherapies* (10th ed.). Belmont, CA: Cengage Learning.

Wedding, D., & Niemiec, R.M. (2003). The clinical use of films in psychotherapy. *Journal of Clinical Psychology, 59*, 207–215. http://doi.org/10.1002/jclp.10142

Wedding, D., & Niemiec, R.M. (2014). *Movies and mental illness: Using films to understand psychopathology* (4th ed.). Boston, MA: Hogrefe Publishing.

Weick, M., & Guinote, A. (2010). How long will it take? Power biases time predictions. *Journal of Experimental Social Psychology, 46*(4), 595–604. http://doi.org/10.1016/j.jesp.2010.03.005

Wellenzohn, S., Proyer, R.T., & Ruch, W. (2016a). Humor-based online positive psychology interventions: A randomized placebo-controlled long-term trial. *The Journal of Positive Psychology, 11*(6), 584–594. http://doi.org/10.1080/17439760.2015.1137624

Wellenzohn, S., Proyer, R.T., & Ruch, W. (2016b). How do positive psychology interventions work? A short-term placebo-controlled humor-based study on the role of the time focus. *Personality and Individual Differences, 96*, 1–6. http://doi.org/10.1016/j.paid.2016.02.056

West, B.J., Patera, J.L., & Carsten, M.K. (2009). Team level positivity: Investigating positive psychological capacities and team level outcomes. *Journal of Organizational Behavior, 30*, 249–267. http://doi.org/10.1002/job.593

West, M.A. (2012). *Effective teamwork: Practical lessons from organizational research* (3rd ed.). Oxford, UK: Blackwell Publishing.

Wethington, E. (2003). Turning points as opportunities for psychological growth. In C.L.M. Keyes & J. Haidt (Eds.), *Flourishing: Positive psychology and the life well-lived* (pp. 37–53). Washington, DC: American Psychological Association.

White, M.A., & Murray, A.S. (Eds.) (2015). *Evidence-based approaches in positive education: Implementing a strategic framework for well-being in schools*. New York, NY: Springer. http://doi.org/10.1007/978-94-017-9667-5

White, M.A., & Waters, L.E. (2014). A case study of "The Good School:" Examples of use of Peterson's strengths-based approach with students. *Journal of Positive Psychology, 10*(1), 69–76. http://doi.org/10.1080/17439760.2014.920408

Whitmore, J. (1996). *Coaching for performance*. London, UK: Nicholas Brealey Publishing.

Witvliet, C.V.O., DeYoung, N.J., Hofelich, A.J., & DeYoung, P.A. (2011). Compassionate reappraisal and emotional suppression as alternatives to offense-focused rumination: Implications for forgiveness and psychophysiological well-being. *Journal of Positive Psychology, 6*(4), 286–299. http://doi.org/10.1080/17439760.2011.577091

Witvliet, C.V.O., Knoll, R.W., Hinman, N.G., & DeYoung, P.A. (2010). Compassion-focused reappraisal, benefit-focused reappraisal, and rumination after an interpersonal offense: Emotion-regulation implications for subjective emotion, linguistic responses, and physiology. *Journal of Positive Psychology, 5*(3), 226–242. http://doi.org/10.1080/17439761003790997

Wolf, S. (2007). Moral psychology and the unity of the virtues. *Ratio, 20*, 145–167. http://doi.org/10.1111/j.1467-9329.2007.00354.x

Wong, P.T.P. (2010). Meaning therapy: An integrative and positive existential psychology. *Journal of Contemporary Psychotherapy, 40*(2), 85–99. http://doi.org/10.1007/s10879-009-9132-6

Wong, P.T.P. (2015). Meaning therapy: Assessments and interventions. *Existential Analysis, 26*(1), 154–167.

Wong, Y.J. (2006). A strength-centered therapy: A social constructionist, virtues-based psychotherapy. *Psychotherapy: Theory, Research, Practice, Training, 43*, 133–146. http://doi.org/10.1037/0033-3204.43.2.133

Wood, A.M., Linley, P.A., Matlby, J., Kashdan, T.B., & Hurling, R. (2011). Using personal and psychological strengths leads to increases in well-being over time: A longitudinal study and the development of the strengths use questionnaire. *Personality and Individual Differences, 50*, 15–19. http://doi.org/10.1016/j.paid.2010.08.004

Wood, A. M., & Tarrier, N. (2010). Positive clinical psychology: A new vision and strategy for integrated research and practice. *Clinical Psychology Review, 30*, 819–829. http://doi.org/10.1016/j. cpr.2010.06.003

Woodard, C. (2009). Psychometric properties of the ASPeCT-DD: Measuring positive traits in persons with developmental disabilities. *Journal of Applied Research in Intellectual Disabilities, 27*, 433–444. http://doi.org/10.1111/j.1468-3148.2009.00494.x

Woodworth, R. J., O'Brien-Malone, A., Diamond, M. R., & Schüz, B. (2017). Web-based positive psychology interventions: A reexamination of effectiveness. *Journal of Clinical Psychology, 73*(3), 218–232.

World Health Organization. (1992). *ICD-10 classification of mental and behavioural disorder: Clinical descriptions and diagnostic guidelines*. Geneva, Switzerland: The author.

Worthington, E. L. (2007). *Humility: The quiet virtue*. Philadelphia, PA: Templeton Foundation Press.

Wrzesniewski, A., LoBuglio, N., Dutton, J. E., & Berg, J. M. (2013). Job crafting and cultivating positive meaning and identity in work. *Advances in Positive Organizational Psychology, 1*, 281–302. http:// doi.org/10.1108/S2046-410X(2013)0000001015

Yapko, M. D. (2011). *Mindfulness and hypnosis: The power of suggestion to transform experience*. New York, NY: W. W. Norton & Co.

Yeager, D. S., Henderson, M. D., Paunesku, D., Walton, G. M., D'Mello, S., Spitzer, B. J., & Duckworth, A. L. (2014). Boring but important: A self-transcendent purpose for learning fosters academic self-regulation. *Journal of Personality and Social Psychology, 107*(4), 559–580. http://doi.org/10.1037/ a0037637

Yeager, D. S., Johnson, R., Spitzer, B. J., Trzesniewski, K. H., Powers, J., & Dweck, C. S. (2014). The far-reaching effects of believing people can change: Implicit theories of personality shape stress, health, and achievement during adolescence. *Journal of Personality and Social Psychology, 106*(6), 867–884. http://doi.org/10.1037/a0036335

Yeager, J. M., Fisher, S. W., & Shearon, D. N. (2011). *Smart strengths: Building character, resilience and relationships in youth*. Putnam Valley, NY: Kravis Publishing.

Yearley, L. H. (1990). *Mencius and Aquinas: Theories of virtue and conceptions of courage*. Albany, NY: State University of New York Press.

Young, K. C., Kashdan, T. B., & Macatee, R. (2014). Strength balance and implicit strength measurement: New considerations for research on strengths of character. *Journal of Positive Psychology, 10*, 17–24. http://doi.org/10.1080/17439760.2014.920406

Appendices

Appendix A

Background on the VIA Classification of Character Strengths and the VIA Survey

VIA Classification: Background

Positive Psychology

While president of the American Psychological Association in 1998, Martin Seligman called for the field of psychology to balance itself out and give equal scientific attention to what is positive about human experiences. Up to that point, psychologists had studied positive experiences, however, there had been far more weight and attention given to disorders, disease, conflict, and other problems. Seligman outlined the focus of positive psychology as the study of positive subjective experiences, positive traits, and positive institutions. This created a two-fold opportunity:

1. To highlight and bring to the forefront the best research and practices that had been done prior to the late 1990s (e.g., Ed Diener's many decades of work on subjective well-being, Csikszentmihalyi's work on flow theory, Jon Kabat-Zinn's work on mindfulness meditation, and Daniel Batson's work on empathy, to name a few). Indeed, several texts on positive psychology soon emerged and served to help integrate the many areas of well-being, where researchers and practitioners could find many concepts under one umbrella. For example, in one of these early texts, the *Handbook of Positive Psychology*, there were 55 chapters denoting a rich array of scholarly work that had already been conducted on the positive side of life, many of these previously unknown to most practitioners (Snyder & Lopez, 2002).

2. To promote new research along several avenues of well-being (and stimulate funding for this research). There has been an explosion of research in positive psychology since 2000. Scholarly articles on happiness, resilience, mindfulness, positive emotions, character strengths, well-being, and many other areas abound. The field has rapidly spread to professions outside of psychology, particularly evident in the domains of coaching, business, and education.

Seligman described character strengths as the backbone of the field of positive psychology and of creating authentic happiness (Seligman, 2002), and later argued that the focus on the 24 character strengths is the central pathway to five core areas of well-being (i.e., PERMA; Seligman, 2011).

Early Scientific Meetings

Neal Mayerson, a psychologist and philanthropist in Cincinnati, Ohio, became interested in Seligman's writings on positive psychology and decided to contact him to explore collaborating in advancing positive psychology. Mayerson was interested in the study of positive youth development and whether a paradigm shift could be made from problem-focused approaches to strength-based approaches. In February 2000, the two organized a minisummit of leading evidenced-based programs – titled the "Power of Positive Psychology Conference" – to potentially choose which program might be best to study more deeply and roll out nationally in the US. Several teams presented to a "panel of listeners" who represented thought leaders in positive youth development, product development, and government funding programs. After hearing from each group, an insight arose and reverberated among the panel of listeners. They recognized that instead of bringing forward one or more specific programs, it was more important to legitimize future programs by establishing an intellectual and scientific framework from which many future programs could grow. At that point Seligman and Mayerson switched gears to respond to this insight by focusing their collaborative effort on developing basic tools needed to advance the science of character – namely a nomenclature that would describe the elements of character needing investigation as well as tools for measuring these characteristics.

Mayerson then asked Seligman: "Who is the best person to lead a large-scale project on the creation of a classification of character strengths?" Seligman responded without hesitation: "Chris Peterson, an accomplished research psychologist and professor at the University of Michigan, would be the best in the country. I don't know if he's available. But I will call him." In that phone call, Peterson (2014) reports that Seligman asked him: "What do you want to do with the rest of your life?" and Peterson jokingly thought he was going to finally hear a marriage proposal. As the question got clarified, Peterson decided to take the position during the conversation (p. ix). Mayerson negotiated with the University of Michigan for Peterson to take a 3-year hiatus from his position at the university, and Peterson temporarily moved his office to the University of Pennsylvania. Next, they gathered a diverse group of scientists and practitioners for a weekend retreat at the Glasbern Inn. Among the participants were top scholars from the field of psychology, philosophy, and biology, as well as top youth development practitioners and key people involved with developing the *Diagnostic and Statistical Manual,* the diagnostic system used in the field of mental illness. The group's charge was to help Peterson and Seligman figure out how to tackle the challenge of creating a science to understand what's best about human beings and how those characteristics are used to create good lives for individuals and society at large. Seligman (2000) summed up the conference with the following:

> I learned today that learning theory made a huge mistake. It regarded negative and positive emotion as reinforcers. And that surely is true, but it's minor. The theory that I see emerging is that negative emotion is a signal that tells you that you are in a zero-sum game. It activates a set of narrowing responses. But positive emotion is a signal that says you are in a nonzero-sum game. It's a broadening, building system. I think we have the beginnings of a categorization ...we don't have a taxonomy, we have a categorization...the VIA Categorization of Strengths and Virtues. I actually think that we have a new theory of human motivation.

Peterson and Seligman then led an effort that included input from an impressive group of 55 scientists in this inquiry, among them being Barbara Fredrickson, Mihaly Csikszentmihalyi, Ed Diener, Donald Clifton, Howard Gardner, Robert Sternberg, and George Vaillant. The entire project was conducted under the auspices of a new nonprofit organization named Values in Action Institute, which was founded and funded by the Manuel D. & Rhoda Mayerson Foundation in Cincinnati, Ohio under the leadership of Dr. Mayerson as its President. (see Appendix H for more on the VIA Institute).

VIA Classification: Development

There exist classification systems for studying what is wrong with people – the *DSM-5* (American Psychiatric Association, 2013) and the *ICD-10* (World Health Organization, 1992) – but prior to the VIA classification, there was nothing comparable for human strengths. Positive psychology needed a consensual nomenclature for classifying positive traits to serve as a backbone for research, diagnosis, and intervention.

Virtues

Peterson led a substantial historic analysis reviewing the best thinking on virtue, strength, and human goodness, spanning over 2,600 years. This was a daunting task that was fraught with challenges, as many previous attempts fell short for not including universal virtues or the system was culturally bound or overrepresentative of the investigator's or the organization's (political, religious, or otherwise) personal values (Dahlsgaard et al., 2005). These scientists took a systematic, two-fold approach: a literature review of previous attempts to classify virtue and an empirical approach driven by two questions: Would the virtue catalogs of early thinkers converge? Would certain virtues, regardless of tradition or culture, be widely valued? (Dahlsgaard et al., 2005; Peterson & Seligman, 2004). The researchers looked for "coherent resemblance," reflecting that "the higher order meaning behind a particular core virtue lined up better with its cross-cultural counterparts than with any other core virtue" (Dahlsgaard et al., 2005, p. 204). What emerged were six similar themes (virtues) emerging across the traditions of Athenian philosophy, Confucianism, Taoism, Buddhism, Hinduism, Christianity, Judaism, and Islam. These paralleling themes were wisdom, courage, humanity, justice, temperance, and transcendence.

Character Strengths

The next challenge was to devise a scholarly process for making choices about which character strengths would be included. Initial brainstorming involved several elite scholars including Donald Clifton and Marcus Buckingham of the Gallup Organization, flow founder Mihaly Csikszentmihalyi, happiness researcher Ed Diener, scholars Kathleen Hall Jamieson and George Vaillant, positive psychology founder Martin Seligman, and project director Chris Peterson, among others. Peterson and his team expanded the scope beyond the major world religions and philosophers throughout modern time to review any text, cultural artifact, or product they could find that in some way outlined the best qualities in human beings and/or spoke about virtue, strength, and human goodness: This included works such those of Benjamin Franklin, Thomas Aquinas, Aristotle, King Charlemagne, as well as the work of well-known psychologists such as Abraham Maslow, who studied the characteristics of self-actualized individuals (Maslow, 1970), and lesser known figures such as Marie Jahoda, who wrote one of the first positive-oriented psychology books in 1958 (Jahoda, 1958). They also reviewed the core tenets of the Boy Scouts of America, fictional depictions (e.g., Star Trek's Klingon Code), the wisdom found in greeting cards, eulogies, popular songs, testimonials, tombstones, and other places where virtue and positive sentiments are commonly expressed. They studied related research literatures revolving around character from a variety of sciences including psychiatry, youth development, philosophy, and psychology. The literature from character education programs (Berkowitz, 2000) and strengths-oriented social work (Saleebey, 1996) were also reviewed. The pioneering work with talents by Gallup was reviewed, and various discussions were held with senior scientists at Gallup (Peterson & Seligman, 2001). The basic premise was to leave no stone unturned (Peterson & Seligman, 2004; Peterson, 2006a).

The character strengths were then determined based on how well they met 10 specific strengths criteria (Peterson & Seligman, 2004), such as whether the qualities were trait-like in that they manifest across situations, are stable over time, and emerge in thoughts, feelings, and behavior. Other criteria included whether the quality was fulfilling in and of itself, whether or not it diminishes others when it's expressed, and whether there exist paragons or exemplary portrayals of the strength. Each of the 24 character strengths met at least 9 or 10 of these 10 criteria; the only exceptions were zest and love of learning, which met 8 of the 10 criteria. For example, the strength of curiosity meets all 10 criteria since it is fulfilling, morally valued, does not diminish others, has a nonfelicitous opposite, is traitlike, distinct from other character strengths, can be absent in some people in some situations, and there exist curiosity paragons, prodigies, and institutions to support its development.

Other strengths did not sufficiently meet the strengths criteria thus were not included in the VIA classification: Reasons include that the strength was not universally valued (e.g., consider the dominant, Western-valued strengths of ambition and autonomy), was a prerequisite to other strengths (e.g., politeness, gentleness), or was a blend of several of the basic character strengths (Peterson, 2006; Peterson & Seligman, 2004). For example, the positive psychology construct of grit, which involves maintaining effort and interest in a task or project over the long run (Duckworth, Peterson, Matthews, & Kelly, 2007) seems to be largely explained as a blend of the character strengths of perseverance and curiosity. Similar character strengths "compounds" have been argued for: patience, tolerance, responsibility, mindfulness, and other positive psychology constructs.

Universality

In the early 2000s, data from over 30 nations supported the ubiquitous nature of character strengths (Peterson & Seligman, 2004), and a couple years later data was published on the ubiquity of character strengths in over 50 countries (Park et al., 2006), and again 9 years later, studying 75 countries (McGrath, 2015b). In addition, Robert Biswas-Diener (2006) conducted some of the pioneering cross-cultural research with the VIA classification, offering support for the universality of the VIA strengths showing that these characteristics are more than a Western cultural phenomenon. He traveled to some of the most remote areas on the planet to inquire about the existence of these 24 strengths and whether these criteria were expressed. In his article, he focused his attention on three cultures in particular – Maasai tribal people in Kenya, Inuit people in Northern Greenland, and university students in the US. These groups were selected as they represent far-ranging differences from one another as evidenced in language, technological development, cultural and spiritual practices, geography, and history. Biswas-Diener and his team found high rates of agreement on the existence, importance, and desirability of all 24 character strengths in these cultures. The cultures also acknowledged the possibility that people of any age and gender could develop the strengths and that there are cultural institutions to foster them. Some cultural differences were found: the Inuit women were rated higher in kindness and men were rated higher in self-regulation, whereas women were rated higher in self-regulation among the Maasai people.

Measurability

Some strengths are more easily measured than others, for example, creativity can accurately be measured by self-report questions (Silvia, Wigert, Reiter-Palmon, & Kaufman, 2012); similarly, curiosity can also be validly measured by querying the individual's motivation to seek out new experiences and their willingness to embrace novelty and uncertainty (Kashdan et al., 2009). The strength of humility, on the other hand, is less easily measured because if a person responds positively to the statement, "I am a humble person," then it is questionable whether they are reporting accurately or do they actually lack humility. Indeed, the use of self-report in measuring humility has been critiqued strongly, noting the use of informant reports as a superior approach (Davis, Worthington, & Hook, 2010).

VIA Survey

An important necessity of scientific domains in which a classification has been devised is to have a measurement tool to study the classification. Therefore, part of the focus of the VIA project from the outset was the creation of a scientifically valid assessment tool to measure the 24 character strengths. This was done successfully by VIA project director Christopher Peterson. Following several revisions, the VIA Inventory of Strengths (VIA-IS; nicknamed VIA Survey) was completed, good psychometrics achieved (good reliability and validity), and released to the public for free use (Park & Peterson, 2006a; Peterson & Seligman, 2004).

The VIA Survey is a self-report questionnaire that identifies 24 elements of positive personality characteristics ("character") that are expressed alone and in combinations in characteristic ways by each individual. The original questionnaire consisted of 240 questions, 10 questions for each strength, and now the default survey is 120 questions, 5 questions for each strength. Additional versions, being held to further rigorous, scientific standards are being released on the VIA site (McGrath, 2017). There is also a VIA Youth Survey for youth between the ages of 10 and 17. Good psychometrics were established in developing this measure (see Park & Peterson, 2006b), and a large study found the data best fit a four-factor model involving two interpersonal factors, a general engagement factor, and an other-oriented factor (McGrath & Walker, 2016). Due to the shorter attention span of youth, the 198 questions of this measure posed a logistic problem for many schools and children, therefore it was substantially shortened, but it retained acceptable psychometric levels. The psychometrics on these surveys, a shorter version of the VIA Survey for adults used by researchers consisting of 72 items and additional measures, can be found on the VIA Institute website. The VIA Survey has been translated into more than 35 languages; McGrath (2015a) published analyses and validity information on several of these translations, including Danish, Dutch, French, German, Hebrew, Italian, Japanese, Korean, Portuguese, Brazilian Portuguese, Spanish, Swedish, Turkish, simplified Chinese (mainland China), and traditional Chinese (Hong Kong).

The VIA Survey offers a comprehensive look at one's strengths of character. The user receives rank-ordered results to allow one to view one's highest strengths and one's middle and lower strengths. This enables the user to make relative comparisons between strengths; the test was not designed to allow the user to make comparisons between different users. It is important to note that the results one receives do not trump the life that one lives. Thus, if an individual lives a life of kindness but kindness comes in toward one's Bottom 5, one should prioritize the finding in one's own life rather than the finding of the test, especially if one's family and friends would support that kindness is a core part of that individual.

Appendix B

Checklist for Strengths-Based Practitioners

Are you really strengths-based? Examine several of your therapy or coaching sessions or your business or school meetings through the lens of these questions. If you believe you are struggling in a particular area, review the concepts and the related practices in this book to help you move forward. This is not meant to be an exhaustive list of all possible strengths-based actions, rather a substantive jumping-off point for practitioners to review their work and make progress.

☐ Do you use the VIA Survey prior to or early on when you meet with a client?

☐ Do you ask several questions to assess and explore what is best in each client?

☐ Do you offer an equal amount of exploratory questions that target strengths/competencies compared with weaknesses/deficits?

☐ Do you address the various categories of human strengths, such as abilities/talents, skills, interests, and resources?

☐ Do you deliberately use character strengths to offer an insight or a reframe on problems, relationship conflicts, and stressors?

☐ Do you label character strengths in the moment during sessions and offer an explanation for the strength you spotted?

☐ Do you offer summary feedback on your client's character strengths in every meeting?

☐ Do you consciously use your own character strengths, especially your signature strengths, in your meetings with clients?

☐ Do you prepare for meetings by reviewing your client's signature strengths before you meet with them?

☐ Do you adhere to a structured model/approach when helping a client to develop their character strengths?

☐ Do you collaboratively discuss and draw direct links between client goals and their character strengths?

☐ Do you "see" your clients? Do you really understand who they are, using their signature strengths as a lens?

☐ Do you coherently link, at least in your mind, various character strengths concepts and applications throughout your theoretical orientation/approach (e.g., solution-focused, CBT, dynamic, performance-oriented, etc.)?

☐ Do you know at least a handful of character strengths interventions and how to tailor them to your client?

Appendix C

A Sampling of Strengths-Based Models

Several of these strengths-based models are discussed in this book. Models are distinguished from strengths-based programs like mindfulness-based strengths practice (MBSP) and from solely strengths-based theories such as that of Saleeby (1996).

- *Aware-explore-apply* (Niemiec, 2013, 2014a). The character strengths process model that describes the steps clients go through as they work on character strengths. Aware: break through strengths blindness and bring character strengths to the surface. Explore: dig into past use, future potential use, how character strengths have been used during good and bad times. Apply: take action and set goals to develop character strengths (see Chapter 3).
- *Aware-align-appreciate (AAA).* Developed by Neal Mayerson, VIA Chairman, for the business sector. Aware: cultivate an awareness of character strengths. Align: connect character strengths with work relationships, tasks, organizational mission/values. Appreciate: not only acknowledge but express value for the strengths of those you work with.
- *Appreciative inquiry (AI) model* (Cooperrider & Whitney, 2005). Popular among positive psychology enthusiasts who work in the organizational sector. The AI-4D framework helps people to create positive, systemic change: Discover what is the best (the strengths of the individual and organization) from the past, dream what is possible for the future, design pathways forward, and deliver on the changes most desired (Cooperrider & Whitney, 2005).
- *Strengths-based CBT* (Padesky & Mooney, 2012). Four steps that were created as a model for building resilience in the therapy context. Clients are invited to search for strengths, construct a personal model of resilience, apply the model, and then practice resilience through behavioral experiments.
- *The 4 E's model* (Wong, 2006). Joel Wong articulates strengths-centered therapy which is a social-constructionist approach to psychotherapy. Explicitizing phase: identifying strengths using techniques such as reframing and polyvocality. Envisioning phase: naming the character strengths the client would like to develop in order to advance therapeutic goals. Empowering phase: developing strengths habits and experiences to feel more empowered. Evolving phase: review and celebrate gains, especially the growth in character strengths.
- *GROW model*: Developed by Sir John Whitmore (1996), used by various types of coaches. The four steps are goal, reality, options, and will/way forward.
- *ACHIEVE model*: Developed by Sabine Dembkowski and Fiona Eldridge (2003), and used by executive coaches. The seven steps are: assess current situation, creative brainstorming of alternatives, hone goals, initiate options, evaluate options, valid action program design, encourage momentum.
- *PRACTICE model*: Developed by Steven Palmer (2008), and used by coaches. The steps are: problem identification; development of realistic, relevant goals; generation of alternative solutions; consideration of consequences; targeting most feasible solutions; implementation; chosen solution(s); evaluation.

Appendix D
Frequently Asked Questions About Character Strengths

These are common questions asked by both practitioners and their clients. While most have been answered in the preceding text, these offer perhaps another angle for learning about character strengths.

What is the difference between a signature strength and a character strength?

A character strength refers to any of the 24 positive, universal traits in the VIA classification, while a signature strength is a subset of these character strengths. Signature strengths are those strengths highest in one's profile and are viewed as most essential to the person as well as being qualities that are especially energizing and natural to use.

Is it better to work on signature strengths or lesser strengths?

It is generally best not to view this as an either/or issue. Each will be important for different clients in different situations. Research has found benefit for both approaches. That said, it is likely that participants will enjoy and be more energized by working on their signature strengths. Often they might not realize this and request to focus on building up a lower strength. Practitioners need to be aware of the many factors working in their favor when focusing on signature strengths, such as positive reinforcement, a greater chance of boosting self-efficacy as it's easier to focus on a strength that comes naturally, and potentially higher retention rates and adherence to interventions as signature strengths are energizing. These may collectively lead to a wider range of benefits for the client. Further research is needed to confirm these hypotheses.

Practically speaking, the client's signature strengths are a great starting place for understanding who they are. It is important for the client to confirm or disconfirm which strengths are actually signature. Many clients will spot other strengths in their Top 10 that they believe are signature and, at the same time, clients will sometimes note one or two strengths in their Top 5 that do not resonate with them, even after considerable reflection and discussion. This is where the practitioner–client dialogue/relationship is important for fleshing out signature strengths.

Are the results of the VIA Survey affected by mood?

Mood is similar to the concept of state (like the transient states of positive emotions or upsetting emotions) but character is more synonymous with our traits (enduring, stable characteristics that stand the test of time and circumstance). It may feel as though a bad mood or a stressful day is having a significant impact and that it will influence our test responses. Indeed, a mood may influence a trait/strength in a given situation one way or the other. However, the overarching idea is that our character ultimately transcends mood/values. Character is who we are and we take that with us from situation to situation and it's there through the good days and bad days. So, one day I might take the VIA when I'm upset and then a few weeks later take it when I'm happy, but my signature strengths of hope and curiosity are right there with me in both scenarios so the results are likely to be similar. This is supported by the finding that the VIA Survey has good test-retest reliability. In addition, it is unlikely that my core character is going to substantively change in such a short period of time.

My lowest strengths are weaknesses, right?

The belief that our lower strengths are weaknesses is an extraordinarily common sentiment, especially given our weakness-driven, problem-focused world. It's important to remember that the VIA Survey does not measure weaknesses so we cannot determine that as a result of the VIA Survey we are seeing our weaknesses come in at the bottom. Since the VIA Survey only measures and ranks our strengths, the best we can articulate is that we have higher, middle, and lower strengths. We can give them additional names like "signature," "phasic" strengths, "focus" strengths," "balance" strengths, or of course "lesser" or "lower" strengths. There is no doubt whatever you are lowest in, you have still used this strength (probably even today to some degree). Did you not express some self-regulation when you got out of bed and brushed your teeth and ate breakfast? Did you not express some prudence in how you spoke with your client? Did you not express some humility in how you interacted with your colleagues at work?

This is quite important for practitioners to understand because what you believe/understand will be passed down to your clients/students/etc., and we don't want to pass down incorrect messages or messages that don't serve the highest good and the best potential of our clients. I had a poignant back-and-forth conversation on this issue with one client who hated using the word "strength" in the same sentence as those qualities coming up lower for her. After a long discussion, what she came to realize is that some strengths she uses "broadly" (for her it was her creativity and curiosity, which she realized she used in all domains of her life and every situation she encountered) and some strengths she used "narrowly" (just at certain times and in certain situations).

At the same time, it is good to normalize this topic for clients who look to the bottom and talk about weakness. You might say something like this to them:

> Yes, Maria, that is a common thought to see your bottom qualities as weaknesses. However, Maria, I want you to understand that this test only measures strengths, so all of these are strength *capacities* within you. It is likely that you simply do not use these lower strengths as often, you are not as familiar with them, or you are actually wanting to do more with them but feel you can't. Maria, if you view these as less-used strengths then you and I can talk about ways to use them more or to boost them up; however, if you continue to see them as weaknesses, you may simply feel worse about yourself and feel that they are incapacities in you that cannot be changed. Now, it might be, Maria, that these lesser strengths are ones that you will need to give extra attention to in order to boost or you will have to use your signature strengths to support you to counterbalance them. They may or may not become as strong as your signature strengths, but I have seen people who have made substantial changes with their lower strengths. So, it will be interesting to see what you discover as we discuss them further and you begin to focus on them more.

Recently, I was collaborating with a positive psychology leader who was throwing the word "weakness" around in relation to his lowest strength of prudence. He believed he had the strengths tests (multiple ones) to prove his prudence was weak and that it being 24 in his

VIA results was somehow confirming that. Because he viewed it as a weakness, his optimistic perception of himself in regard to prudence shifted … he became disempowered around this strength, as if there was something wrong in him that couldn't be changed. He was not viewing prudence as a lower strength – a true capacity to be improved. It was as if he had constructed his own made-up world around this word and that world became his reality. The ironic thing about this is that he couldn't have been more incorrect about this strength – prudence – in relation to his behavior. This was a man who was enormously planful and practical, very respectful, always on time, conscientious to a fault, terrific at setting and reaching personal goals, and, from my view of collaborating with him on papers, presentations, and focus group meetings, quite "practically wise." These are exemplary prudence behaviors! If I had been asked about his strengths I might have labeled prudence as his #1 strength. The problem here is that seeing his lower strength as a "weakness" shifted and narrowed his perception of himself – it limited him. He had concluded that the test showed this, and when he reflected on it, he agreed that prudence indeed did not make him all that happy or energized, so then that must be the conclusion of the story. And, in this case, it was only the beginning of the story, as strengths-spotting, along with multiple clear examples across two conversations, helped him to make a shift in how he viewed not only his prudence and his lower strengths, but his entire strengths profile.

Early research on other strength categories is beginning to show that a focus on building strengths is superior to approaches that focus on remediating weaknesses. Research on character strengths so far is finding benefit in working on any of the character strengths in our profile. The reason for this, it seems, is that in the short-run, it is energizing to try to improve oneself and to turn to any of our natural capacities. But, it's likely that most people will run low on energy and motivation as they try – day after day – to build up lower strengths. It's interesting for a short while, but in the long run, we at the VIA Institute hypothesize that it is the expanding, sharing, promoting, and expressing of our signature strengths that is likely to lead to *long-term* benefit. We suggest that this is likely the case because signature strengths help us to be ourselves, to act authentically in accordance with our inner, core self, and this will probably lead us to discover unique benefits relating to happiness, energy, intimacy, connections, and success.

What I find for myself and others is that if you target a higher strength – and creatively expand upon it, mindfully work with it throughout the day, stretch it beyond what you ever thought possible – that the middle and lower strengths will often "come along for the ride." In other words, the expansion of signature strengths lifts all the others (perhaps the metaphor "the rising tide lifts all boats" applies here). That's the signature strengths expansion approach, also referred to as the "towing effect."

When you boil this down, it may simply be an experience in semantics. Because we all have weaknesses and blind spots for sure and context plays an important role in what we bring forth strongly. But, as all good practitioners know, language and how we communicate is a huge part of the process. So not only is the language of VIA highly important for clients, but also the language in how we introduce it, explain strength principles, explain the importance of context, and the issues therein.

How does the VIA Survey differ from Gallup's Strengths-Finder 2.0?

The strengths assessment tool most often compared to the VIA Survey is the Gallup Strengths-Finder. It is clear why people frequently compare these two measures as the latter has been around for a couple decades due to the pioneering work in the 1990s of Donald Clifton, who was interested in creating an objective measure of personal talent. Clifton viewed strengths as an extension of talent and that when talents are consistently combined with knowledge and skill the individual expresses near-perfect performance (i.e., strength). Clifton and many other scientists at Gallup have continued their pioneering work with strengths for decades and have helped bring strengths to the forefront of the minds of countless individuals and organizations.

While the VIA Survey and StrengthsFinder are similar in that both measure positive qualities with a self-report scale, there are a number of important distinctions (see Appendix E). The VIA Survey focuses on universal strengths of character, whereas StrengthsFinder focuses on talents and skills in the workplace setting. The StrengthsFinder, like most strengths measures, is not open to the scientific scrutiny of peer review. A unique quality about the VIA Survey and the VIA Institute's other measurements is that it encourages peer review! Indeed, each year, hundreds of scientists, students, and others conduct research using one of the VIA (free) measures.

Do the results on the VIA Survey change over time?

It is possible that the results can change, however, in a different manner to what people typically imagine when asking this question. The VIA Survey has good reliability which means it is repeatable over time – individuals are likely to receive similar results. The general idea is that people will receive consistent results over time because our personality is stable over time and we are who we are – whether we are stressed, in the midst of turmoil, at our best, 2 years older, feeling down, etc. Now, that's not to say that if someone grows into a deeper self-understanding, experiences a traumatic event, gets married, has a child, or joins the military that their strengths will not change. Still, it won't be changes such as one's Top 5 becoming one's Bottom 5 and vice versa. It is particularly common and expected for one's top strengths to shuffle around in the Top 10 or so and the same for one's bottom strengths.

The first step in assessing whether one's VIA Survey results have changed is to look at the summaries of the raw scores (offered in detailed VIA interpretive reports). This is because there might actually be ties or meaningless differences (e.g., differences of raw scores of .1 or .2) between top strengths. After taking this into consideration, the individual can then properly make relative comparisons between their tests.

In addition, if a practitioner discovers a substantive change in a client's raw score, then it is important to query the client about this. For example: What do you make of gratitude popping into your Top 5? Have you been focusing more on being curious these days? What has been going on in your life that might account for your high strength of teamwork this year?

Are character strengths more nature-based or nurture-based?

When it comes to our personality, the answer is almost always – "both are important." And, some scientists believe that with advancements in epigenetics and the study of the interaction of our genes and environment, the nature/nurture question becomes rhetorical and fruitless, similar to the question: What contributes more to the area of a rectangle – the height or the width? Instead of viewing which has more of an effect, we can attempt to learn from both sides and hence make this immediately practical. Both nature and nurture have played an important role in our lives. I can think of how I genetically share similar strengths to my biological mother as both of us are high in love and I share similar strengths with my adoptive father (who raised me from age 3) as both of us are high in fairness.

Character strengths researchers examined the genetics of the 24 character strengths by studying 336 twins and found significant genetic effects for most of the 24 (Steger, Hicks, Kashdan, Krueger, & Bouchard, 2007). They were able to determine this by looking at monozygotic (identical) twins and dizygotic (fraternal) twins, and they found very strong correlations for the former twins but not the latter. It is clear that genes play a strong role, but they also found that there is an important role the environment plays in accounting for our character strengths.

The phenotype, the expression of our genes (genotype), is seemingly infinite. Let's say there are 10 people in a room who are high in creativity. The expression of that creativity is likely to vary widely. One person expresses creativity through writing poems and short stories, another person is great at coming up with numerous creative ideas during team brainstorming meetings, another is an artist who paints brilliant watercolors, and yet another person is great at finding unique ways to solve problems. To offer a metaphor from Neal Mayerson, there are a finite number of universal facial expressions, such as the display of joy and sadness, but the expression of those facial gestures varies widely and is unique to the given individual. Similarly, each person express their character strengths in a unique way, no doubt a result of an interaction of our genes and environment, both of which have already played an important role in our life.

How well does research support the mapping of the six virtues and the 24 character strengths nesting underneath them?

The first point to remember is that the VIA classification was developed as a conceptual rather than correlational model. In the VIA classification, the six virtues are the broader category that capture the complexity of human goodness and the character strengths are the more specific components as they are the positive qualities that make up the virtues. There have been many analyses conducted and published. Factor analysis is a research procedure designed to examine how constructs cluster. Factor analyses of the VIA Survey have found a number of factors (clusters) emerge, usually finding four or five factors (see Azañedoa, Fernández-Abascalb, & Barracac, 2014; Brdar & Kashdan, 2010; Choubisa & Singh (2011); Khumalo, Wissing, & Temane, 2008; Littman-Ovadia & Lavy, 2012; MacDonald, Bore, & Munro, 2008; McGrath, 2014; Peterson, Park, Pole, D'Andrea, & Seligman, 2008; Ruch et al., 2010; Shryack, Steger, Krueger, & Kallie, 2010; Singh & Choubisa, 2010) and in one case six factors, which were described as the six virtues of the VIA classification (Ng, Cao, Marsh, Tay, & Seligman, 2016). The largest of these studies, using over 650,000 subjects, was by McGrath (2014), who found four factors. While these studies do not reveal an identical layout to the VIA classification, good integrity is maintained, and the framework holds up conceptually. This is further supported by Ruch and Proyer (2015), who conducted an analysis of the strengths and virtues concepts, synonyms, short and long definitions, and item content, involving ratings from 70 experts and 41 laypersons, and followed by a factor analysis. There was substantial convergence from the ratings and six factors emerged. Many, but not all, strengths aligned with their original virtue. In their publication, Peterson & Seligman (2004) note that while the justice and humanity strengths could be merged as one set of interpersonal strengths, the virtue distinction is conceptually useful.

Other studies have found that some strengths may fit better under different virtue categories, for example, one study has found that hope loads up strongly under courage whereas zest does not (Pury & Kowalski, 2007), and another study found that humor aligns strongly under several virtue categories especially the virtues of wisdom and humanity (Muller & Ruch, 2011).

Another strong study identified a three-virtue model across multiple measures of character strengths and used four samples consisting of over one million cases (McGrath, 2015c). The pattern revealed a reliable structure consisting of "inquisitiveness," "caring," and "self-control" strengths. In practical terms, this might be viewed as using strengths of the "head, heart, and hands."

As researchers look to the future in writing a revision of the Peterson and Seligman (2004) text, it is assumed that any changes to the VIA classification will be the result of extensive analyses, replication studies, and converging cross-cultural data – quantitative and qualitative – from a wide array of sources, rather than the results of a single study.

Is the VIA Survey recommended as a tool for helping people select their optimal career or for employee selection purposes?

The short answer is "no." Here are the details, starting with how the VIA Survey can be helpful for career decision-making and career counseling. It is pivotal for self-awareness in that knowledge about one's signature strengths, middle strengths, and lesser strengths can offer deep awareness and personal insights that can lead to change. This can then lead to individuals becoming more informed on the interplay between their unique character strengths profile and potential career paths and optimal work settings they might be interested in. The character strengths work also promotes positivity for those on the career path, catalyzing pleasure, engagement, and meaning through awareness of strengths, which can then be used with greater frequency, intensity, or duration, and with greater balance, fluency, and savvy to support their aspirations.

The VIA Survey is generally not recommended for making automated career matching decisions (e.g., "You are high in curiosity so therefore you should go to graduate school to become a psychologist," or you should not go into law because you are not high in judgment/critical thinking). The rationale here is that there are many different kinds of jobs and roles in any particular career. For example, an accountant might have a nonsocial, isolated bookkeeping job or a creative and social job as a chief financial officer. Career selection is complex, nuanced, and a highly individualized, personal decision.

The VIA Survey is generally not recommended for employee hiring, firing, promoting, and other selection decisions because this instrument was not designed for this purpose (other instruments were designed for those intentions). In addition, employees can fake the test by giving the answer they believe their employer wants to see. This, of course, invalidates the results. Also, the VIA Survey was not designed to make comparisons between people, so comparing one applicant's results and raw scores with another applicant's would not be an optimal procedure.

Appendix E

Comparison of VIA Survey with StrengthsFinder (Gallup) and Myers-Briggs Type Indicator (MBTI)

	VIA Institute/VIA Survey	Gallup/StrengthsFinder 2.0
Key offering:	Common language	Talent themes
Intended domains:	All of life (home, work, school, social)	Work
Link to personality:	Identity	N/A
Core phenomena:	Being and doing	Doing
Strengths identified:	Core character	Talents/skills
Basis for validity:	Historical analyses, criteria, psycho-metrics	Polling
Focus:	Signature strengths, but all 24 matter	Top 5
Organization:	Nonprofit	For profit
Involvement of science:	Open to all scientists	Proprietary
Scrutiny of science:	Peer-reviewed	Not peer-reviewed

	VIA Survey	Myers-Briggs Type Indicator (MBTI)
Key offering:	Common language	Types/themes
Intended domains:	All of life (home, work, school, social)	All of life (home, work, school, social)
Approach:	Dimensional (you have more or less of each strength)	Categorical (you have a particular type)
Strengths identified:	Core character	Preferences
Basis for validity:	Historical analyses, criteria, psycho-metrics	Theory rooted in C. G. Jung
Focus:	Who you are and what you do in the world	Orientation for viewing the world
Interventions:	Very important	Not relevant
Personality (Big 5):	Incremental validity (unique)	Subsumed under Big 5 (not unique)
Cost:	Free	Charge per use
Organization:	Nonprofit	For profit
Involvement of science:	Open to all scientists	Proprietary; not open
Scrutiny of science:	Peer-reviewed	Not peer-reviewed

Appendix F

Flagship Papers on Character Strengths

There are several elements to consider with the unofficial label of a published article being a flagship or seminal paper in the field of character strengths. The list here focuses on flagship papers that have direct ramification for *practice*. If this were focused on character strengths flagship papers in basic research or measurement then there would be an abundance of papers by Willibald Ruch and Robert McGrath. Here are the elements considered:

- **Domain specific:** The paper offers a seminal, authoritative, thorough discussion laying the conceptual groundwork or research basis for character strengths integration in a specific domain (e.g., education), with a particular population (e.g., people with addictions), or application approach (e.g., interventions). It reviews what is known at the present time and reflects an openness to new insights and research/practice developments. This will typically involve a review of theory, research, and/or practice for that area. It may or may not include an empirical study.
- **Practical:** The paper offers immediate ways practitioners can take action using character strengths in the area focused on. It might also offer suggestions for future research.
- **Character strengths:** The focus of the paper is on strengths of character, *not* positive psychology at large, *not* other categories of strengths such as talents/abilities, skills, or resources, and *not* generic strengths.
- **Peer-review journal:** The paper is published in a peer-reviewed journal, *not* a book, chapter, newsletter, or blog publication.

Business/Organizations

Mayerson, N. M. (2016). Creating sustained organizational success: An application of character science. *Positive Work and Organizations: Research and Practice, 2*. An expanded version was originally published in Danish in the journal, *Kognition & Paedagogik* in 2015 under the editorship of Mads Bab.

Education

Linkins, M., Niemiec, R. M., Gillham, J., & Mayerson, D. (2015). Through the strengths lens: A framework for educating the heart. *Journal of Positive Psychology, 10*(1), 64–68.

Disability (Intellectual/Developmental)

Niemiec, R. M., Shogren, K. A., & Wehmeyer, M. L. (2017). Character strengths and intellectual and developmental disability: A strengths-based approach from positive psychology. *Education and Training in Autism and Developmental Disabilities, 52*(1).

Psychotherapy

Seligman, M. E. P., Rashid, T., & Parks, A. C. (2006). Positive psychotherapy. *American Psychologist*, *61*, 774–788.

Career Counseling

Littman-Ovadia, H., Lazar-Butbul, V., & Benjamin, B. A. (2014). Strengths-based career counseling: Overview and initial evaluation. *Journal of Career Assessment, 22*(3), 403–419.

Mindfulness

Niemiec, R. M., Rashid, T., & Spinella, M. (2012). Strong mindfulness: Integrating mindfulness and character strengths. *Journal of Mental Health Counseling, 34*(3), 240–253.

Interventions

Seligman, M. E. P., Steen, T. A., Park, N., & Peterson, C. (2005). Positive psychology progress: Empirical validation of interventions. *American Psychologist, 60*, 410–421.

What's Missing?

Plenty. In addition to advancing those mentioned here, flagship papers for character strengths would be welcomed in higher education; close/positive relationships, parenting, health/medicine (prevention, lifestyle, chronic disease management), mental illness/clinical psychology, addictions, sport (performance enhancement), and humanities (art, music, literature, etc.), to name a few.

Appendix G

10 Character Strengths Concepts and Applications in Specific Movies

Moral Goodness

Star Wars: Episode VII – The Force Awakens (2015)
Article: Sansom, Bretherton, & Niemiec (2016)

Overuse of Character Strengths

Divergent (2014)
Article: Niemiec (2014b)

Signature Strengths Exemplar and Strengths Underuse: A Contrast

Frozen (2013)
Article: Niemiec and Bretherton (2015)

Positive Interventions

Alice in Wonderland (2010)
Article: Niemiec (2010b)

The True Meaning of the Concept "Character"

Invictus (2009)
Article: Niemiec (2010c)

Understanding Humility

Twilight (2008)
Article: Niemiec and Clyman (2009)

Understanding Spirituality

Flight of the Red Balloon (2007)
Article: Niemiec (2008)

Criteria for a Positive Psychology Movie

The Pursuit of Happyness (2006)
Article: Niemiec (2007)

Overcoming Fear With Strengths

Batman Begins (2005)
Article: Niemiec and Ferland (2006)

Overcoming Loneliness With Strengths

The Station Agent (2003)
Article: Niemiec (2005)

Appendix H

About the VIA Institute on Character

Present Day

- **Organization:** The VIA Institute on Character is a nonprofit organization headquartered in Cincinnati, Ohio. Website: https://www.viacharacter.org
- **Mission:** Advance the science and practice of character strengths.
- **Team:** Core team of five, along with two senior scientists, several consultants, and numerous enthusiasts around the globe.
- **Action:** Creates and validates surveys of character, develops practical tools for individuals and practitioners, educates people on character strengths.
    - Gives out research codes to hundreds of new and established researchers every year to use character strengths surveys in basic and applied science.
    - Gives presentations on character strengths to hundreds of practitioners each year.
    - Offers practical tools and resources on its website, which is visited by over a million people a year.
    - Partners with global leaders to help advance VIA's mission.
- Receives grants, but also uses the money from VIA reports and courses to give grants to support new research in the science of character.

History

Originally the Values in Action Institute, VIA was created in 2000 by Dr. Neal Mayerson, following extensive discussion and collaboration with Dr. Martin Seligman, the founder of positive psychology, and a number of top scientists in the social sciences.

Published *Character Strengths and Virtues: A Handbook and Classification* (Peterson & Seligman, 2004), with Oxford University Press and the American Psychological Association.

The nonprofit's name was formally changed in 2006 to VIA Institute on Character (and VIA classification, VIA Survey/VIA Inventory of Strengths, VIA Youth Survey) in order to place emphasis on the core of this work – character. The word "VIA" stands on its own, in Latin meaning "path" or "road," which serves as a good metaphor.

The VIA Institute has been supported generously by the Manuel D. and Rhoda Mayerson Foundation, a private family philanthropy in Cincinnati, Ohio.

Index

The 24 character strengths are highlighted in bold.

360° – Character Strengths 360° (CSI 7) 150, 153, 154, 165

A
accomplishment/achievement 2, 14, 54, 77, 92, 138, 166, 188, 193, 199, 226
ACHIEVE model [executive coaching] 280
Acting "As If" (CSI 12) 150, 154, 173
Activate Your Zest! (CSI 29) 151, 153, 155, 190, 193
admiration 141, 180, 189, 200, 206
aerobic laughter 241
Alice in Wonderland [movie] 290
alignment of strengths 17, 29, 48, 55–57, 149, 150, 183
 – with family activities 57
ambition 8, 277
American Psychological Association XI, 274, 292
anchoring 40, 43, 45
applied morals 109
appreciation of beauty and excellence 12, 13, 42, 44, 55, 97, 110, 111, 141, 166, 179, 234, 242
appreciation of strengths 23, 36, 42, 44, 51, 52, 60, 68, 74, 115, 150, 151, 153, 154, 163, 206, 208, 211, 213
appreciative inquiry 280
authenticity 21, 24, 112, 242
autism 31
avoidance 91, 92, 113
aware-align-appreciate model 280
aware-explore-apply model 40, 58–60, 81, 104, 153, 280
awe 116, 141, 166, 200, 204

B
Batman Begins [movie] 291
Beck Depression Inventory 32
behavioral activation 70, 81, 193
Believing Change Is Possible (CSI 51) 151, 154, 216, 217
Benefit-Finding With Strengths (CSI 53) 151, 216, 219

Best Possible Self (CSI 64) 61, 143, 149, 152, 153, 186, 226, 231, 241
Big 5 196, 287
boosting curiosity 151, 153, 154, 190, 191
boosting humility 151, 153, 190, 199
Boost Your Motivation (CSI 4) 150, 156, 161
bravery 8, 9, 11, 13, 17, 25, 41, 44, 47, 49, 54, 57, 59, 62, 66, 67, 73, 95, 96, 101, 102, 106, 110, 112, 113, 118, 122, 126–129, 133, 139, 166, 173, 174, 179, 185, 202, 210, 222, 227, 242
broaden-and-build theory 35
business 6, 28, 29, 32, 45, 81, 85, 101, 274, 279, 280, 288

C
calling/work-as-a-calling XIII, 23, 29, 35, 56, 74, 130, 142, 183, 193
capitalization model 33, 218
career counseling 28, 286, 289
Character Strengths and Virtues [book] XI, XV, XIX, 3, 4, 5, 22, 23, 111, 292
Character Strengths Genogram (CSI 6) 150, 156, 164
circumplex (2-factor balance graph) 43, 119, 120, 177
cognitive-behavior therapy (CBT) 33, 66, 68, 222, 279
collisions XVI, 94, 99–101, 105, 106, 118, 225
 – interpersonal 99, 103, 104
 – intrapersonal 43, 44, 99–101, 177
common language XIII, 1–3, 21, 60, 90, 159, 287
compassion-focused reappraisal 108, 137, 221
compensation model 218
Compliment Review (CSI 48) 151, 205, 213
compound strengths/strength combinations 8, 277
confidence 51–53, 74, 148, 161, 162, 187, 213

congruence 65
conscientiousness 11, 12, 173
context 1, 3–8, 10, 19, 21, 24, 28, 30, 37,
    45, 59, 69, 71, 93–95, 98, 99, 114, 120,
    126, 133, 144, 148, 149, 152, 165, 169,
    172, 176, 192, 208, 212, 217, 219, 224,
    233, 283
context-mapping 40, 43, 45
corrective virtue 124
couples 23, 32, 77, 100, 107, 177, 206–208,
    210, 212, 213
courage 3, 5, 10, 31, 51, 52, 95, 97, 101,
    113, 127–130, 173, 174, 178, 188, 276,
    285
    – civil courage 225
    – general courage 127
    – personal courage 127
creativity 6, 7, 9, 11–13, 15, 17, 24, 25,
    30, 41, 44, 54, 57, 67, 68, 70, 73, 83,
    84, 86, 96, 98, 103, 105, 108, 110, 113,
    117, 122, 123, 125, 127, 141, 160, 166,
    173, 179, 183, 214, 230, 242, 277, 282,
    285
Cultivate Inner Self-Worth (CSI 24) 150,
    154, 182, 187
Cultivating Sacred Moments (CSI 40) 151,
    154, 190, 204
culture 2, 3, 6, 8, 9, 18, 27, 41, 51, 76, 88,
    91, 92, 126, 159, 172, 178, 184, 192,
    206, 276, 277
curiosity 4, 7–16, 18, 24, 25, 30, 37, 38, 41,
    44, 46, 47, 54, 56, 59, 62, 65, 66, 71–
    74, 82–84, 89, 94–96, 100, 103, 104,
    106, 108, 110, 114, 117, 122, 123, 125,
    130, 141, 163, 164, 166, 173, 177–179,
    181, 191, 194, 208, 214, 225, 227, 230,
    236, 242, 243, 277, 278, 282, 286

D

Deathbed Test, The (CSI 21) 150, 182, 184
Defining Moments Exercise (CSI 25) 151,
    153, 154, 182, 188
depression 11, 12, 17, 26–28, 33–35, 45, 51,
    58, 64, 84, 97, 134, 136, 137, 147, 164,
    172, 176–178, 185, 186, 193–196, 201,
    203, 215, 220, 223, 224, 228
Diagnostic and Statistical Manual (DSM)
    [book] 275
dimensionality 1, 6, 10, 76

disability (intellectual/developmental) 31,
    52, 88, 93
disengagement 22, 23, 157
Divergent [movie] 290
divergent thinking 122

E

elevation 27, 110, 111, 141, 172, 189, 200,
    204
engagement XI, XII, 2, 11, 14, 20, 22, 23,
    27–30, 32, 35, 63, 71, 72, 91, 108, 111,
    123, 126, 128, 130, 143, 146, 154, 175,
    182–189, 193, 200, 286
Engaging With Beauty (CSI 36) 151, 153,
    190, 200
entity theory 217

F

factor analysis 4, 285
fairness 6, 8, 11, 13, 15, 16, 42–44, 53,
    55, 66, 86, 90, 91, 94–96, 101, 104,
    106–108, 110, 112, 124, 129, 132,
    134–139, 166, 174, 179, 190, 208, 225,
    233, 237, 242, 284
family 7, 8, 11, 13, 16, 23, 30, 41, 43, 44,
    47, 54, 55, 57, 65, 106, 108, 109, 134,
    158, 160, 164, 165, 173, 176, 227, 236
family strengths culture 68
family therapy 68
family tree of strengths 28, 69
fixed mindset 1, 37, 217
Flight of the Red Balloon [movie] 290
flourishing XI, 2, 10, 12, 14, 17, 20, 22, 32,
    39, 40, 42, 52, 64, 84, 97, 148, 155,
    157, 175, 183, 187, 224
flow XVI, 8, 23, 59, 63, 79, 94, 108, 113,
    117, 118, 274, 276
forgiveness 8, 11–13, 16, 28, 42, 44, 49, 55,
    65, 74, 96, 98, 107, 108, 110, 131, 135,
    137, 152, 166, 174, 178, 179, 190, 199,
    208, 210, 221, 231, 237, 239, 242
Frozen [movie] 189, 290

G

Gallup/StrengthsFinder 2.0 15, 284, 287
gentleness 74, 80, 277
Gift Of Time (CSI 31) 28, 151, 152, 190,
    195
goal-setting 35, 63, 71, 146, 151, 153, 170,
    185, 226–231

– Hope for Your Goals (CSI 61) 151,
    226, 228
– self-concordance 34, 129
– self-concordant goals 227
– SMART goals 227
golden mean 94, 95, 118, 121
goodness XIII, 3, 21, 65, 109–113, 113,
    127, 141, 178, 179, 189, 200, 233, 276,
    285, 290
gratitude 7, 11–14, 16, 18, 19, 26–28, 32,
    42–44, 49, 55, 64–66, 74, 95, 97, 98,
    105–107, 110, 116, 130–132, 136,
    141–143, 145, 146, 163, 166, 173, 177,
    179, 184, 185, 190, 196, 201, 204, 206,
    211, 214, 215, 220, 221, 233, 234,
    237–240, 242, 284
Gratitude Letter/Visit (CSI 38) 26, 142, 151,
    153, 190, 202, 211
GROW model [coaching] 71, 280
growth mindset 37, 60, 88, 99, 187, 217,
    221

H

habit theory/strengths habit 20, 150, 155,
    171, 175
happiness strengths 18, 21, 29
harmonious passion 16, 34, 59
Healthy, Fair Fighting (CSI 45) 151, 154,
    205, 210
heart strength 124
Helping or Harming? (CSI 56) 151, 216,
    222
holistic mapping 40, 43–45
honesty 6, 11, 13, 17, 41, 44, 54, 65, 66, 74,
    86, 90, 95, 96, 100, 101, 107, 110, 111,
    124, 126–129, 134, 135, 138–140, 166,
    179, 240, 242
hope 9, 10, 12–19, 27, 28, 42, 44, 47, 48,
    51, 55, 57, 63, 71, 82, 94–97, 100, 104,
    105, 110, 116, 123, 126–128, 130, 131,
    140, 142–145, 153, 166, 173, 178, 179,
    183, 200, 220, 227, 228, 231, 241, 242,
    282, 285
hospitality 8
hot buttons 94, 105, 106, 118, 149, 225
– definition 105, 106
– examples 106
– Managing Your Strength Hot Buttons
    (CSI 59) 150, 151, 154, 155, 216, 225

humanistic approaches 65, 66
humility 9–11, 13, 37, 38, 40, 42, 44, 53,
    55, 66, 82, 84, 91, 92, 94, 97, 98, 102,
    103, 108, 110, 111, 120, 121, 138, 139,
    152, 166, 173, 179, 181, 199, 202, 234,
    240, 242, 278, 282, 290
humility card 49, 91, 92
humor 7, 12–16, 34, 42, 44, 54, 55, 97, 98,
    103, 110, 111, 130, 133, 144, 149, 152,
    155, 160, 166, 173, 175, 178, 179, 195,
    203, 216, 223, 237, 241–243, 285
hypnosis trances 94, 113, 117, 118, 192,
    235, 237

I

ICD-10 (World Health Organization) 276
ideal self 65, 206
Imagined Conversation (CSI 28) 151, 153,
    190, 192
Implementation Intentions (CSI 63) 152,
    155, 226, 229, 230
incremental theory 217
inner advisor 117, 192
intelligence 11, 12, 89, 123
intentional activities 146
intercorrelation 10, 89, 240
interests [type of strength] 15–17, 21, 34,
    56, 89, 100, 129, 227, 279
International Coach Federation (ICF) 70
interpersonal strengths 285
interventions packages 152–155
intrapersonal strengths 177
Invictus [movie] 189, 290

J

jack of all strengths 94
judgment/critical thinking 8, 9, 11, 13, 16,
    17, 41, 44, 54, 65, 66, 72, 74, 96, 100,
    103, 108, 110, 111, 120, 122, 124–126,
    139, 149, 166, 177, 179, 237, 242, 286

K

kindness 6–13, 16, 19, 25–28, 40, 41, 43,
    44, 49, 52, 53, 55, 56, 64–66, 70, 72,
    74, 80, 86, 89–91, 95–98, 101, 104,
    106, 108, 110–112, 119, 129, 131, 132,
    134–138, 141, 142, 144, 145, 152, 160,
    162, 166, 174, 179, 185, 188, 190,
    194–197, 209, 222, 223, 225, 229, 241,
    242, 277, 278

King's Speech, The [movie] 25

L

languishing 154

Law of Jante 92, 93

leadership 7, 9, 11, 13, 19, 21, 31, 37, 39, 42, 44, 55, 57, 66, 68, 72, 86, 96, 102, 110, 111, 117, 132–137, 166, 179, 240, 242

Letter From the Future 241

Life Summary (CSI 22) 150, 182

little character strengths use 13

lost strengths 18

love 11, 13, 14, 16, 18, 19, 21, 28, 32, 41, 44, 54, 55, 65, 73, 82, 89, 95, 96, 100, 106, 108, 110, 116, 131, 132, 134, 137, 142–146, 160, 162, 166, 176, 177, 179, 185, 194, 202, 220, 225, 227, 233, 237, 240, 241–243, 284

Love Letter (CSI 42) 151, 205, 207

love of learning 10, 11, 13, 16, 30, 41, 44, 54, 57, 59, 82, 86, 89, 96, 100, 110, 117, 123–125, 141, 166, 169, 179, 222, 231, 242, 277

Loving-Kindness Meditation (CSI 30) 131, 151, 153, 190, 194, 237

lower/lesser strengths 9, 15, 18, 29, 30, 33, 69, 77–79, 89, 93, 95, 181, 278, 281–283, 286

M

malevolent creativity 113

master strength 6, 240

meaning XI, XIV, 2, 10, 12–14, 17, 22, 28, 35–38, 42, 50, 51, 63, 71, 74–76, 85, 95, 110, 123, 125, 130, 143, 145, 146, 182–189, 195, 201, 213, 228, 234, 237, 276, 286, 290

Mental Contrasting (CSI 62) 151, 154, 155, 226, 229

mental subtraction 24, 163, 211

Mentors/Role Models (CSI 10) 150, 154, 156, 170

Michelangelo phenomenon, the 206

middle strengths 9, 18, 95, 286

military 14, 19, 28, 31, 45, 89, 185, 284

mindfulness XVI, 13, 16, 20, 33, 37, 38, 45, 58, 59, 63, 64, 73, 94, 113–118, 133, 141, 146, 189, 194, 204, 207, 209, 232–240, 242, 274, 277, 289

– autopilot 52, 63, 78, 97, 163, 167, 175, 191, 233, 236, 240

– being and doing 1, 20, 287

– Fresh Look Meditation (CSI 67) 152, 154, 232, 235

– From Mindless to Mindful (CSI 68) 152, 155, 232, 236

– Meditation Targeting a Character Strength (CSI 69) 152, 232, 237

– Mindful Listening and Speaking (CSI 44) 151, 153, 154, 205, 209

– mindfulness-based strengths practice (MBSP) II, XII, 37, 48, 64, 82, 111, 114, 152, 165, 188, 191, 194, 204, 209, 224, 232, 235, 236, 238, 242, 280

– Mindful Pause, The (CSI 65) 75, 114, 152, 155, 232, 233

– mindful strengths use 124

– momentarily strengths-based 58

– scientific definition 114

– Strengths Gatha (CSI 70) 150, 152, 155, 232, 238

– strong mindfulness 37, 114, 152, 153, 232, 234

mindlessness 52, 78, 152, 155, 191, 232, 236, 240

miracle question 69, 70

misuse of strengths 113

morality XVI, 94, 109, 111, 113, 118

– behavioral acts of goodness 110

– moral dilemmas 135

– moral exemplars 112

– moral reasoning 135

– virtuous character 111, 112

motivational interviewing 162

multidimensionality 7, 93

multiple intelligence XIII, 15

Myers-Briggs Type Indicator (MBTI) 15, 287

N

narrative XII, 30, 48, 188, 217

negative mindset 88

O

observational learning 112, 189

optimal strengths use 95–97, 105, 224

overuse of strengths XII, XVI, 37, 61, 66, 68, 77, 84, 85, 92, 94–99, 101, 105,

106, 114, 118, 119, 121, 136, 206, 235, 238, 290
- Managing Character Strengths Overuse (CSI 58) 151, 154, 216
- principles 94–97
- types 98

P

parenting 104, 134, 145, 289
patience 8, 82, 199, 277
Pay It Forward (CSI 32) 151, 190, 196
PERMA 2, 14, 146, 189, 274
perseverance 8, 10, 11, 13–16, 25, 26, 28, 34, 37, 41, 44, 54, 62, 63, 71, 80, 82–84, 86, 89, 96–98, 102, 104–106, 110, 115–117, 128–130, 140, 143, 166, 170, 179, 183, 185, 227, 231, 241, 242, 277
person-activity fit 35
perspective 9, 11, 13–16, 25, 41, 44, 49, 50, 54, 57, 61, 66, 72, 83, 86, 96, 100, 102, 104, 108, 110, 117, 122–124, 126, 127, 129, 133, 135, 142, 143, 153, 166, 173, 174, 179, 184–187, 192, 202, 210, 211, 219, 220, 225, 231, 240–242
perspective-taking 135, 151, 205, 212, 216, 221
phasic strengths XII, 15, 18, 21, 282
playfulness [see humor]
plurality 1, 9, 10, 21, 88, 90, 93
Pollyannaism 87, 93, 96, 97, 143
polyvocality 239, 280
Positive Action Through Movies (CSI 26) 151, 153, 182, 189
positive contagion 80, 114
positive education 29, 30
positive emotions XI, 2, 11, 14, 22, 27–29, 32, 34, 35, 45, 51, 67, 87, 147, 169, 194–196, 214, 231, 241, 281
Positive Mental Time Travel 115, 241
positive psychology XI, 274–277, 280, 282, 288, 291, 292
positive psychotherapy 28, 64, 152, 164, 195, 220
Positive Reappraisal With Strengths (CSI 55) 58, 84, 93, 95, 105, 114, 128, 151, 152, 198, 216, 220, 221, 235, 280
positive reminiscence 75, 115, 116, 154
Positive Reminiscence With Strengths (CSI 49) 151, 205, 214

power zone 17
PRACTICE model [coaching] 280
preconscious 39, 74
Prosocial Spending (CSI 33) 151, 190, 197
prudence 12, 13, 15, 25, 37, 40, 42, 44, 48, 49, 55, 57, 63, 71, 73, 85, 97, 98, 100, 101, 104, 108, 110, 118, 121, 124, 138–140, 166, 169, 173, 176, 179, 183, 227, 231, 241, 282, 283
psychodynamic approaches 64, 65
psychojudo 79
psychological mindedness 36
Pursuit of Happyness, The [movie] 291

R

reflected best self portrait 165
refractions 2, 109
reframing 198, 216, 220, 235
relationships 2, 11, 22, 146, 155, 195, 205–215, 289
religiousness 11, 145
resilience XV, 28, 31, 65, 66, 72, 87, 127, 134, 146, 155, 160, 189, 190, 216–225, 274, 280
Resource Priming (CSI 52) 151, 154, 155, 216, 218
resource priming general 75, 77, 93
resources [type of strength] 75, 77, 93
ROAD-MAP [for interventions] 149, 153

S

Satisfaction With Life Scale 32
savoring XVI, 16, 34, 38, 58, 94, 113, 115, 116, 118, 188, 206, 214, 233, 241
- savored strength 115
- strategy 116
- strength that rises, the 116
- strong savoring 115
self-actualization 11, 66
self-assessment 47, 129, 138
self-bravery 174
self-compassion/self-kindness 75, 174, 177, 194
self-determination 34
self-efficacy 11, 29, 74, 117, 147, 188, 281
self-esteem 11, 12, 27, 28, 34, 92, 97, 147, 213, 228, 239
self-fairness 75, 174
self-forgiveness 75, 174
self-honesty 174

self-leadership 174
self-monitoring 48, 150, 153, 167
Self-Monitor Your Strengths (CSI 8) 156
self-perspective 174
self-regulation 7, 8, 10–13, 15, 18, 37, 40,
    42, 44, 55, 71, 73, 79, 80, 82, 86, 89,
    94, 97–103, 108, 110, 114, 117, 118,
    128, 139, 140, 164, 166, 175, 179, 230,
    234, 239–242, 277, 282
signature strengths XII, XVI, 5, 15, 16,
    22, 23, 26, 34–37, 40, 48, 50, 56–58,
    60–62, 64–66, 69, 72–75, 77–80, 83,
    85, 87, 89, 95, 98, 99, 108, 112, 114,
    117, 149, 157, 162, 165, 181, 183, 186,
    195, 198, 206, 208, 224, 225, 227, 233,
    234, 237, 240, 279, 283, 286, 287, 290
  – behaviors 34, 35
  – definition 18, 23, 24, 26, 281
  – identity 21, 24, 26, 55
  – in the movies 25, 26, 69, 112, 153,
    170, 189, 290
  – mechanisms 34, 35
  – practices 22, 27–29, 31–33, 36, 39–41,
    43, 76, 93, 163, 164, 172, 177, 281
  – research 22, 26, 27
Signature Strengths Across Domains
    (CSI 15) 150, 153, 171, 176
Signature Strengths Survey 4
simple behaviors 40, 45
sisu 8
skills [type of strength] 15–17, 70, 117, 118,
    125, 166, 180, 208, 279, 284, 287, 288
social anxiety 96
social intelligence 11, 13–17, 25, 41, 44,
    53, 55, 65, 70, 72, 82, 91, 95–97, 101,
    102, 108, 110, 126, 127, 131, 133, 136,
    144, 166, 179, 195, 202, 208, 210, 223,
    225, 231, 239, 242
solution-focused approaches 69
spirituality 12–14, 16, 19, 42, 44, 55, 66,
    74, 86, 97, 102, 110, 142, 145, 146,
    160, 162, 166, 179, 187, 204, 237, 240,
    242, 290
  – sacred, the 97, 145, 187, 204
stages of change model 161, 230
*Star Wars: Episode VII – The Force
    Awakens* [movie] 112, 189, 290
Station Agent, The [movie] 291
strength combinations 90

strengths-based
  – CBT 280
  – checklist for practitioners 24, 46, 58,
    279
  – functional analysis 66, 67
  – goal-setting 68
  – models 58, 280
  – practitioner tips 1, 3, 7, 10, 13, 17, 20,
    23, 46, 47, 49, 53, 54, 73, 91, 99, 112,
    121
strengths blindness/blind spots 36–39, 45,
    90, 93, 97, 157, 165, 280, 283
strengths fluency 46, 51, 53, 169
Strengths Gym 30
strengths paradox 38, 39
strengths-spotting 51, 53, 60, 61, 68–71, 78,
    80, 83, 157, 185, 189, 206, 283
  – in oneself 46, 47, 49, 50
  – in others 31, 46, 50, 75, 169
  – secret 239
  – steps (labeling, explaining, appreciat-
    ing) 51
  – Stories and Character Strengths (De-
    velop Strengths-Spotting) (CSI 9) 150,
    153, 154, 156, 169
stress management 27, 29, 50, 55, 58, 65,
    126, 132, 133, 155, 160, 217, 218, 220,
    233, 235
  – intervention package 152
  – Overcome Stress With Humor (CSI 57)
    151, 223
synergies 94, 99, 100, 118, 212
  – interpersonal 100
  – intrapersonal 100

T
talents [type of strength] 15, 17, 21, 89, 276,
    279, 284, 287, 288
tall poppy syndrome 92
team roles 198
teamwork 7, 8, 11, 13, 16, 19, 37, 39, 42,
    44, 54, 55, 65, 67, 72, 73, 80, 91, 96,
    102, 106, 110, 111, 132, 134–138, 166,
    177, 179, 185, 208, 220, 227, 233, 242,
    284
  – Enhance Teamwork Through Role
    Matching (CSI 34) 151, 190, 198
Three Funny Things (CSI 39) 27, 151, 154,
    190, 203

Three Good Things (CSI 37) 26, 27, 35, 151, 190, 201
thriving learning communities 30
tolerance 8, 11, 131, 135, 277
towing effect 181, 283
transactional vs. transormational leadership 136
Twilight [movie] 290

U

underuse (of strengths) XII, 37, 84, 94–99, 101, 105, 106, 114, 118, 119, 121, 136, 206, 224, 235, 290
 – types 96, 97

V

value-added strength 28, 111
values affirmation 160, 218
values [type of strength] 15, 16, 20, 50, 85, 89, 109, 129, 160, 161, 165, 189, 192, 227, 276, 282
veterans 28, 159
VIA classification XIII, XV, 1–3, 5, 6, 8, 9, 16, 19, 22, 23, 25, 43, 47, 51, 58, 109, 112, 119, 157, 159, 169, 173, 178, 190, 199, 213, 274, 276, 281, 285, 286, 292
VIA Institute XI–XIII, 1, 2, 4, 9, 16, 19, 24, 30, 83, 96, 119–121, 159, 177, 198, 242, 278, 283, 284, 287, 292
VIA interpretive reports 284
VIA Survey (VIA Inventory of Strengths) XI, XII, 3, 4, 6, 10, 15, 16, 18, 19, 24, 26–29, 31, 37, 39, 40, 47, 60, 68, 73, 74, 77, 79, 81, 83, 119, 120, 157, 159, 160, 164, 165, 172, 181, 183, 198, 274, 278, 279, 281–287, 292
VIA Youth Survey 3, 60, 68, 159, 172, 181, 278, 292
vices 95, 97, 140, 178, 236
virtues XVI, 2–5, 10, 19, 20, 40, 94, 95, 97, 109, 111, 112, 121, 178, 179, 184, 188, 208, 224, 237, 276, 285
virtuous circle XIV, 29, 59, 114

W

Weaknesses 18, 33, 56, 63, 65, 77–79, 93, 159, 181, 218, 279, 282, 283
What Matters Most? (CSI 23) 150, 154, 182, 186
wise interventions 148, 212
wonder 141, 166

Y

you at your best 26, 61, 169

Z

zest 6, 7, 9–11, 13–18, 24, 41, 44, 49, 50, 55, 57, 66, 67, 89, 94, 96–98, 100, 102, 105, 106, 110, 122, 123, 125, 128, 130, 131, 133, 140, 142–145, 149, 164, 166, 173, 177, 179, 185, 202, 239, 242, 277, 285